PENGUIN BOOKS

ALL THAT GLITTERS: THE FALL OF BARINGS

John Gapper has been banking editor of the *Financial Times* for three years. He graduated from Exeter College, Oxford, in 1981 and went to work for several newspapers, including the *Daily Mail* and the *Daily Telegraph*. He joined the *Financial Times* in 1987 and is currently in charge of a team of eight reporters covering banking and financial services in London.

Nicholas Denton writes about investment banking for the *Financial Times*. He graduated from University College, Oxford, in 1988, where he edited and designed *Isis*, the award-winning university magazine. He covered the Romanian revolution of 1989 as a freelance journalist, before becoming Budapest correspondent of the *Financial Times* in 1990.

D1427567

ALL THAT GLITTERS

The Fall of Barings

John Gapper and Nicholas Denton

PENGUIN BOOKS

PENGUIN BOOKS

Published by the Penguin Group
Penguin Books Ltd, 27 Wrights Lane, London W8 5TZ, England
Penguin Putnam Inc., 375 Hudson Street, New York, New York 10014, USA
Penguin Books Australia Ltd, Ringwood, Victoria, Australia
Penguin Books Canada Ltd, 10 Alcorn Avenue, Toronto, Ontario, Canada M4V 3B2
Penguin Books (NZ) Ltd, Private Bag 102902, NSMC, Auckland, New Zealand

Penguin Books Ltd, Registered Offices: Harmondsworth, Middlesex, England

First published by Hamish Hamilton 1996
Published in Penguin Books 1997
5 7 9 10 8 6 4

Copyright © John Gapper and Nicholas Denton, 1996
All rights reserved

The moral right of the authors has been asserted

Photographic credits: *Financial Times*: 5, 6, 9, 11, 18, 24;
Popperfoto: 17; Press Association: 23; Rex Features: 21, 22;
Sygma: 2, 3, 12, 19, 20; Times Syndication: 4, 7, 13, 14, 25;
Topham Picturepoint: 16; Universe Pictorial Press & Agency: 8

Printed in England by Clays Ltd, St Ives plc

Except in the United States of America, this book is sold subject
to the condition that it shall not, by way of trade or otherwise, be lent,
re-sold, hired out, or otherwise circulated without the publisher's
prior consent in any form of binding or cover other than that in
which it is published and without a similar condition including this
condition being imposed on the subsequent purchaser

In memory of
Mark Gapper
1928–87

CONTENTS

PREFACE

The roots of this book lie in the *Financial Times'* coverage of the
Barings collapse, in which both authors participated. Working for
the *FT* provided us with an unparalleled opportunity to write about
the immediate aftermath in detail, and to build some of the contacts
with those involved that have been vital in researching and writing
this work. Our thanks are therefore due to Richard Lambert, the *FT*'s
editor, both for backing us in our work for the newspaper and allowing
us leave to finish the book. In addition we would like to thank all
our colleagues on the *FT* with whom we worked at the time. While
we were researching and writing this book a particular burden fell on
other members of the financial services team. We would like to thank
Ralph Atkins, Norma Cohen, George Graham, Jim Kelly, Simon
London, Alison Smith, Andrew Taylor and Paru Pandya for their help
and understanding.

In researching and writing this book we have gained much cooperation from many of those who used to work at Barings, and others
who are still employed by ING Barings. Only a handful of those
most closely involved declined to talk to us, and many who talked to
us took great pains to help. The list is too long to single out everyone,
and many have asked not to be mentioned. However, we would like
to thank Danny Argyropoulous, Lord Ashburton, Ron Baker, Francis
Baring, Michael Baring, Geoffrey Barnett, Andrew Baylis, Win
Bischoff, John Bolsover, Geoff Broadhurst, Terry Burns, John Dare,
Andrew Fraser, Tony Gamby, Eddie George, Vanessa Gibson, Chris
Goekjian, Richard Greer, Fernando Gueler, Tony Hawes, Christopher
Heath, Maggie Heath, Ben Hoffman, Ian Hopkins, Roy Johnson,
Richard Johnston, Richard Katz, Diarmaid Kelly, Su Khoo, Mike
Killian, Rob Leaning, Hessel Lindenbergh, George Maclean, John

Manser, Ian Martin, Sundaresh Menon, Ming San Lee, Alex Murray, James Nelson, Peter Norris, John Orbell, Jim Peers, Rupert Pennant-Rea, William Phillips, Stephen Pollard, Warren Primhak, Jim Reed, David Roberts, Miles Rivett-Carnac, Sajeed Sacranie, David Scholey, Trevor Sliwerski, Andrew Tuckey and Mary Walz.

We have received no help from Nick Leeson, although we have had access to his book *Rogue Trader* and unbroadcast sections of an interview given by him to Adam Curtis of the BBC. Early on he took the view that he did not want to talk to us. However, many of those who worked alongside him in the UK and Singapore have helped us to reconstruct what we believe to be the first complete account of what he did. The problem we have faced in writing this book is how to treat his version of events. We have been very wary about taking anything on face value, without some other corroborating evidence. It will be clear from the text that we reach a fundamentally different view of what he did, and how he came to be drawn into his deception, from his own version of events.

Leeson's book, for example, says that an error by a female assistant on 17 July 1992 was the start of his hidden trading. He says that on that day the Nikkei 225 index 'soared by 400 points', creating a £20,000 loss that he had to hide in Account 88888. In fact, the Nikkei cash index fell by 440 points on that day, which would have brought a profit of £20,000 on the error he describes, so this version of events cannot be accurate. We believe he picked this date because it was identified in the Singapore inspectors' report into the collapse as the first one on which a large volume of futures passed through Account 88888. With the help of others who were there that night we have identified the true date of the incident as being over a month later. This, of course, leaves unexplained what he was doing in July. We provide our own explanation in Chapter 8. Generally we regard his version that he simply fell into trouble by good-naturedly hiding a number of 'errors' by other traders in the account to be only a small part of the truth. In our view he has fashioned a similar mix of truth, half-truth, obfuscation and fantasy to that with which he fooled many of those in charge of him in the first place.

There are two technical points. Some readers will notice that the rates at which currencies are translated are inconsistent. This is because the yen–sterling exchange rate changed substantially during the period that Nick Leeson was in Singapore. We have translated yen into sterling at the year-end exchange rate in each case, which gives a slightly confusing impression but is the most accurate. The second point is that there are three relevant Nikkei 225 indices: the cash index on the Tokyo Stock Exchange, and the futures indices on the Singapore International Monetary Exchange and the Osaka Securities Exchange. They are slightly out of line for reasons explored in the book, which contributed to the deception that lay at the heart of Barings' downfall. For the sake of simplicity, we use the relevant Tokyo Stock Exchange cash index level in all cases.

The material on the eighteenth-, nineteenth- and early twentieth-century history of Baring Brothers & Co. in Chapter 3 is largely drawn from two books, which both deserve mention. These are *The Sixth Great Power: Baring Brothers 1762–1929* by Philip Ziegler and *Baring Brothers & Co., Limited. A History to 1939* by John Orbell. John Orbell, who is Barings' official archivist, also gave us access to some of the more recent published material about the bank, for which we are grateful. No doubt in time historians will have access to fascinating material on these events from the archives. Since ING Barings decided that we should not be given such access, all private papers quoted were obtained from elsewhere.

Nick Fraser suggested that we write this book, and Gill Coleridge helped and guided us in doing so. John Gapper also gives heartfelt thanks to Rosie Dastgir, who contributed so much to it as well as enduring the disruption of the first year of their marriage.

JOHN GAPPER
NICHOLAS DENTON
June 1996

THE PLAYERS

Baring Securities

Christopher Heath *Chairman*

Neil Andrews *Manager of Settlements*

James Baker *Internal Auditor*

Andrew Baylis *Managing Director* John Bonfield *Director*

Gordon Bowser *Head of Futures and Options Settlement*

Andrew Fraser *Managing Director*

Tony Gamby *Head of Settlements, Baring Investment Bank*

Vanessa Gibson *Manager of Derivatives*

Brenda Granger *Manager of Futures and Options Settlement*

John Guy *Head of Settlements*

Richard Katz *Head of Equity Trading*

Diarmaid Kelly *Managing Director*

Ian Martin *Finance Director*

Kevin Peat *Manager of Futures and Options Settlement*

Tony Railton *Futures and Options Settlement Clerk*

Trevor Sliwerski *Head of Japanese Equity Warrant Trading*

Baring Asset Management

John Bolsover *Chief Executive*

David Band (1942–96) *Chief Executive of Barclays de Zoete Wedd*
Win Bischoff *Chief Executive of Schroders*
Andrew Buxton *Chairman of Barclays*
Sir Terry Burns *Permanent Secretary to the Treasury*
Michael Foot *Deputy Director of Banking Supervision, Bank of England*
Eddie George *Governor of the Bank of England*
Chris Goekjian *Chief Executive, Credit Suisse Financial Products*
Sir Chippendale Keswick *Deputy Chairman of Hambros*
George Mallinckrodt *Chairman of Schroders*
John Manser *Chief Executive of Flemings*
Rupert Pennant-Rea *Deputy Governor of the Bank of England*
Brian Quinn *Executive Director of the Bank of England*
Sir Evelyn de Rothschild *Chairman of N. M. Rothschild & Sons*
Sir David Scholey *Chairman of S. G. Warburg Group*
Christopher Thompson *Senior Manager, Bank of England*
David Verey *Chariman of Lazard Brothers*

NEW YORK

Jim Reed *Managing Director, Baring Securities*
Heather Nicol *Head of Derivatives Trading*
Wolfgang Flottl *Founder of Ross Capital*
George Soros *Head of the Quantum Fund*

SINGAPORE

Nick Leeson *Manager, Baring Futures*
Lisa Leeson *Nick Leeson's wife*
James Bax *Head of South Asia*
Ang Swee Tien *President of Singapore International Monetary Exchange*
Danny Argyropoulous *First Continental Trading Trader*
Eric Chang *Baring Futures Floor Trader*
Pamela Chiu *Baring Futures Phone Broker*
Norhaslinda Hassan *Baring Futures Senior Settlements Clerk*
Simon Jones *Operations Manager for South Asia*
Rob Leaning *Baring Futures Floor Trader*
George Seow *Baring Futures Floor Trader*
Riselle Sng *Settlements Clerk*
Teo Fai *Baring Futures Floor Trader*
Teo Kok Eng *Local Trader, Simex*
Rachel Yong *Financial Controller*

TOKYO AND OSAKA

Su Khoo *Futures and Options Trader*
Bruce Benson *Futures and Options Salesman*
Adrian Brindle *Futures and Options Trader*
Robin Cohen *Futures and Options Salesman*
Benjamin Fuchs *Futures and Options Trader*
Richard Greer *Head of Tokyo Office*
Fernando Gueler *Head of Futures and Options Trading*
Richard Johnston *Manager of Futures and Options Trading*
Mike Killian *Head of Futures and Options Sales*
Warren Primhak *Equity Salesman*

HONG KONG

Richard Magides *Futures and Options Trader*
Willie Phillips *Head of Baring Securities*

NASSAU

Philippe Bonnefoy *Trader at European Bank and Trust*

BRUNEI

The Sultan of Brunei
Prince Jefri Bolkiah *Finance Minister*

Chart 1: Nikkei 225 index 1974–95

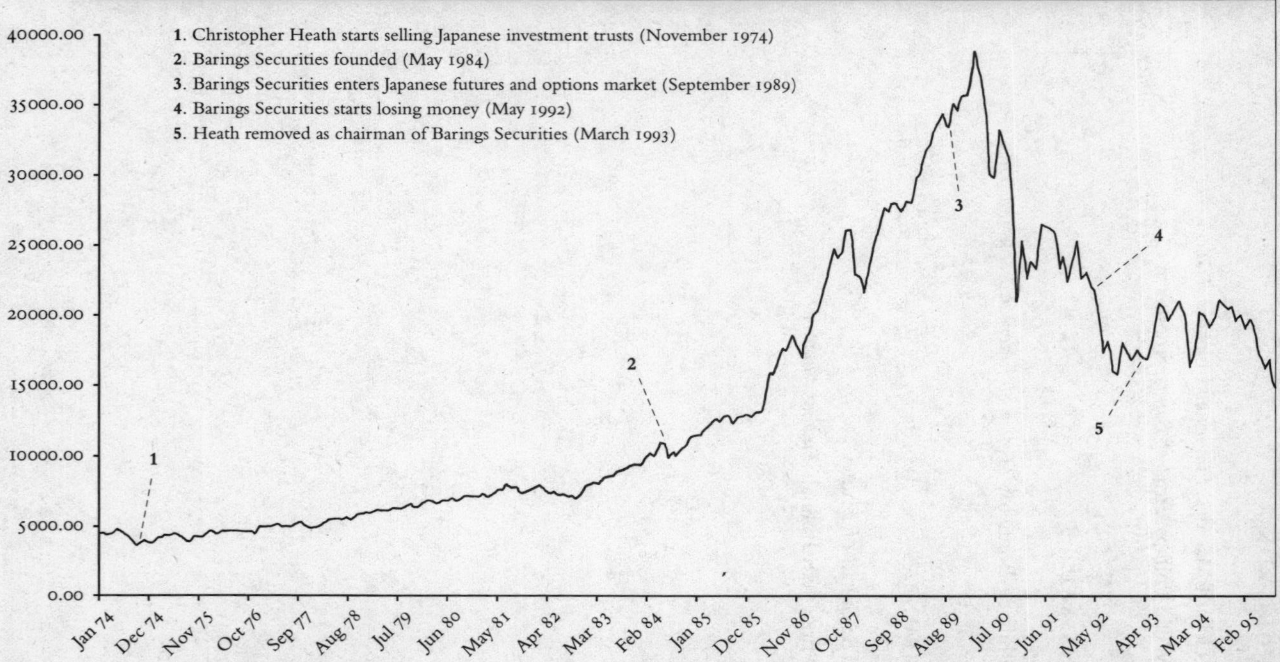

1. Christopher Heath starts selling Japanese investment trusts (November 1974)
2. Barings Securities founded (May 1984)
3. Barings Securities enters Japanese futures and options market (September 1989)
4. Barings Securities starts losing money (May 1992)
5. Heath removed as chairman of Barings Securities (March 1993)
40000.00
35000.00
30000.00
25000.00
20000.00
15000.00
10000.00
5000.00
0.00
1
2
3
4
5
Jan 74
Dec 74
Nov 75
Oct 76
Sep 77
Aug 78
Jul 79
Jun 80
May 81
Apr 82
Mar 83
Feb 84
Jan 85
Dec 85
Nov 86
Oct 87
Sep 88
Aug 89
Jul 90
Jun 91
May 92
Apr 93
Mar 94
Feb 95

Chart 2: Nikkei 225 index July 1992 – June 1995

1. Nick Leeson starts work at Simex (July 1992)
2. First significant loss hidden in Account 88888 (August 1992)
3. Account 88888 goes back into profit (June 1993)
4. Nikkei falls sharply, and Leeson loses £22 million (November 1993)
5. Leeson given official authorization from London to trade (March 1994)
6. Leeson loses £71 million in failed attempt to support the market (September 1994)
7. Kobe earthquake (17 January 1995)
8. Leeson flees Singapore and Barings collapses (23 February 1995)

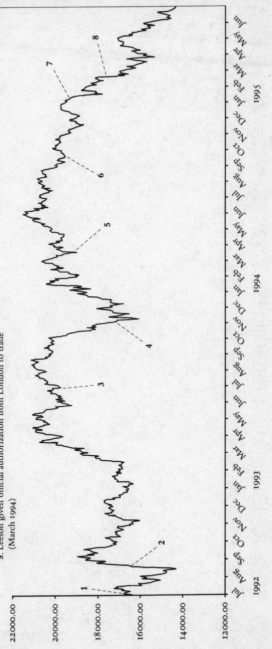

PROLOGUE

In February 1995 the sound of drilling and hammering could be heard each day along Bishopsgate. Slowly, the damage caused by the Irish Republican Army bomb that had devastated the City of London two years before was being repaired. Scaffolding still covered some of the tallest buildings along the wide City thoroughfare. The banks at the southern end of Bishopsgate, near the Bank of England, had escaped serious damage. The most imposing of these was a sleek twenty-storey modernist block at Number 8 Bishopsgate. There was no name plate by the revolving door at the entrance to tell passers-by who occupied it. The bank's directors felt no need to advertise its presence, for it had stood on the same site since 1805, occupying a series of buildings starting with a Georgian house, with gardens at the back and stables to one side.[1] This was Baring Brothers & Co., the oldest merchant bank in the City of London, founded by the son of a German immigrant in 1763. Those invited to talk to its directors in the offices and dining-rooms on the top three floors of 8 Bishopsgate were often over-whelmed by a sense of history. Portraits of the Barings who had owned and run the bank since the eighteenth century gazed down from the walls, and the wooden display cases on the top floor contained memorabilia of its most powerful days in the nineteenth century, when it had financed the Louisiana Purchase for the US government, and raised funds for the British to fight the Napoleonic wars. A century later the name Barings still held its mystique in Latin America and Asia, where it had symbolized the ultimate in financial sophistication and probity.

Inside the top floors of Barings the sounds of reconstruction were muffled and distant, as if the stresses of the City could not penetrate the lofty height. The chairmen or chief executives of companies seeking advice on a merger or acquisition would step from the lift on the eighteenth floor to see a bronze bust of John Baring, the second Lord Revelstoke, who had died in 1929. The bust was set in white marble, with a dedication from the staff 'to a loved and trusted leader'. 'Loved' was an exaggeration, for Revelstoke had been a thin, autocratic man, with the Baring family's characteristic coldness and reserve. But he had earned trust, for he had led Barings out of a crisis that almost overwhelmed it in 1890. Under his father, Baring Brothers had lent recklessly to finance railways, power and water in Argentina, and come to the edge of bankruptcy. After Barings had been rescued by the Bank of England, it was Revelstoke who had restored its fortunes and coined what became an unwritten motto: 'I am going to take no risks.'[2] For a century, that attitude permeated everything done by the merchant bankers of Bishopsgate. Barings might pass up exciting ventures, and be scorned for its caution, but it would never again put its capital at risk. It would never again be forced to go cap in hand to the rest of the City. As long as it stayed cautious, it would remain independent. For it was not a public company, at risk of being taken over by a larger bank; it was owned by a charitable foundation set up by the Baring family and its directors controlled all the voting shares in the holding company Barings plc, giving them power over their destiny.

This proud independence allowed Barings to continue the tradition of family members leading the bank, although they no longer owned it. The latest one to do so was Peter Baring, the fifty-nine-year-old chairman, who had worked there for thirty-five years. Like the second Lord Revelstoke, from whose branch of the family he was descended, Baring was an aloof man. He was quietly-spoken and deliberate and his normally stony features lit up with a smile only occasionally when he relaxed. He lived an austere life, with merely a few trappings of the wealth he had acquired from Barings' success in the previous decade. Rather than being driven to work, he took an underground train from his home in Notting Hill, west London, and read the *Financial Times* like any City commuter. He was almost teetotal and strenuously fit. His biggest extravagance was a partiality for skiing on powder snow in mountain resorts. Although Baring seemed forbidding to outsiders, those with whom he worked closely were fond of him. His air of remoteness stemmed more from shyness than arrogance.

Sometimes he even gave the impression of being a little embarrassed to be chairman, when others lacking the family name deserved it on merit. He had joined straight from Cambridge, following his elder brother Nicholas. As a merchant banker, he was noted more for diligence than inspiration. His most striking trait was decisiveness. He never hesitated long before deciding what should be done. His desk in his bare office was always kept clean of paper, and his mind seemed equally free of doubts and second thoughts.

Peter Baring's diffidence was partly due to a general recognition in the City that the head of the bank in all but name was Andrew Tuckey, the fifty-two-year-old deputy chairman. When Peter Baring succeeded his cousin Sir John Baring (who later became Lord Ashburton) in 1989 as chairman of the Barings group, Tuckey was made chairman of Baring Brothers & Co., which was its merchant banking arm. This was an acknowledgement of his pivotal role at Barings. Tuckey was an outsider to the City, the son of a tobacco farmer in the former British colony of Rhodesia, who had worked at British American Tobacco before joining the bank. He was a self-confident, ambitious man who had assimilated seamlessly into the British establishment. He was a director of the Royal Opera House, and owned a country house in Wiltshire. It was Tuckey who had pioneered Baring Brothers' push into Asia in the 1970s; Tuckey who had won the £100 million bond issue for the World Bank in 1981 that re-established Barings' historic role as financier to governments; Tuckey who had revived a lacklustre corporate finance department in the mid-1980s. He had a rare talent for gaining the confidence of the chairmen of companies that were customers of Barings with an anecdote or a piece of adroit flattery. He also had the energy and persistence to bring off large mergers and take-overs. Tuckey and Baring worked amiably alongside each other in adjoining offices, and in October 1995 he was to cap his career at Barings with the ultimate honour. He would become only the second non-family chairman of the Barings group, when Peter Baring retired from the post.

That winter on the upper floors of 8 Bishopsgate the usual calm seemed to prevail. But it was deceptive. For in the previous two years Barings had been going through one of the most intense upheavals in its history. It had started when Baring and Tuckey ousted a group of executives who had led Baring Securities, its stockbroking subsidiary.

The group included Christopher Heath, a charismatic leader who had turned his firm in seven years from a tiny operation into one of the most profitable of British stockbrokers. Heath was an army general's son who established a niche selling Japanese shares to British investors in the late 1970s. He worked for a crusty City broker called Henderson Crosthwaite, but had persuaded its partners to let him sell the operation to Barings in 1984. Even more than Tuckey within Baring Brothers, Heath inspired loyalty in his staff, using a mixture of charm and intimidation to galvanize them. He was a portly man with prominent front teeth, who peered through big spectacles, and his hesitant manner, together with his boyish enthusiasm for whatever was his latest money-spinning idea, gave him the air of an overgrown schoolboy. He loved making money and he loved spending it. His share of the profits of Baring Securities had earned him £33 million over six years and turned him into Britain's highest-paid businessman. He had spent most of it, buying a country house, a yacht, fine paintings and, above all, his stable of twenty-five horses. He had exerted an almost spiritual grip on Baring Securities, surrounded by a group of loyal managers. It might be called after the Barings, but everyone knew it was his.

When they ousted Heath from the helm of his business eight years later, Baring and Tuckey's ruthlessness provoked recrimination and outrage. Some Heath loyalists talked of it as an act of theft. They had stolen Christopher Heath's creation, to which they had no moral right. The upheaval had not stopped there. For two centuries, Baring Brothers had stuck to merchant banking. Baring Securities had been intended only as a dabble in broking, a more volatile activity where large profits could be made, but risks were higher. But Baring Securities had made far more money than anybody had expected, and Tuckey had gradually decided that it should be merged with Baring Brothers to create an investment bank similar to the large US firms, such as Morgan Stanley and Goldman Sachs, that had overtaken the British merchant banks in the twentieth century, and which operated like financial supermarkets, selling a huge range of services to their customers. Heath had never wanted anything to do with 'The Brothers' of Bishopsgate apart from the use of its name and capital. 'Banks bugger up brokers' he would retort at any suggestion that Baring Securities should come under the wing of Bishopsgate. With Heath gone, there was nothing to stand in Tuckey's way. But merging the two was easier said than done. Baring Brothers was deliberate and cautious, priding itself on waiting patiently until the moment a company needed its advice. Baring Securities was utterly different. Brokers lived by the second, buying and selling shares as prices rose and fell. They were laid-back extroverts who regarded the Brothers as self-important stuffed shirts.

How could two opposites be merged into one? To solve the conundrum Tuckey had turned to the one Baring Brothers man who could bridge this gap. Peter Norris was then a thirty-seven-year-old who had been recruited as a graduate trainee in 1976. Barings tended to mark out its leaders early on. When Peter Baring came across Tuckey in 1968 he felt this was somebody who could climb to the very top of the bank. Tuckey felt the same about Norris when he arrived at Barings at twenty-one armed with a first-class degree from Magdalen College, Oxford. Norris was intelligent and, as importantly for a merchant banker who would have to persuade the chairman and chief executives of companies to take his advice, he was suave and self-assured. He was the son of an army major, and had attended Charterhouse, the public school in Surrey. He was athletic, playing rugby, tennis and Fives, a game played at British public schools. It was similar to squash, but instead of using racquets, the players hit the ball with their gloved hands. Norris was so good at it that he went on to play for Oxford against Cambridge. At Oxford, Norris had tipped horses for the student newspaper *Cherwell*, under the pseudonym Brigadier Gerard. It was the kind of pedigree that merchant banks loved: studious without being too bookish, someone who worked hard and played hard. Norris was good-looking, with a mane of thick brown hair and handsome, wolfish features. As a young trainee at Baring Brothers, he had smoked cigarettes from the side of his mouth, like the raffish City man he aspired to be. He was going far and he gave every impression of knowing it.

When Heath left, Norris became chief executive of Baring Securities. Tuckey wanted him to get Heath's firm under control. It was not an easy task, for Baring Securities was an anarchic institution and many of its traders were rich, temperamental, and unwilling to take orders. The difference from Baring Brothers was apparent even in the two offices. Baring Securities operated from a building on the fringes of the City in America Square, near Tower Bridge. It was a shiny Art

Deco-style edifice with chrome fittings that had been built in the 1980s but was showing signs of age, in which the lift indicators were styled like clocks, but the pointer was always one floor behind the lift. The firm's heart was a huge trading floor 100 yards long and fifty yards wide filled with rows of trading screens. In each corner were banks of clocks showing the time not only in the big financial centres of London, New York, Tokyo and continental Europe, but also in the small markets in which Baring Securities specialized: Bombay, Mexico and Sydney. A glass-panelled spiral staircase rose from the centre of the trading floor to the offices of the senior managers on the floor above. Even in these, furniture was tattier than at Baring Brothers. Norris shared an office with his assistant Sajeed Sacranie and another manager. It was ten yards square with two big windows facing eastwards over the roofs of City buildings. Norris's ebullience was evident in the painting that he hung over his desk. In contrast to the oil paintings of Barings that adorned the walls of Bishopsgate, it was a print of the Lichtenstein pop art painting *Wham!* showing a fighter plane exploding.

Norris had been horrified at Baring Securities when he first took over. It had become a victim of its own success. Heath's early niche in Japanese shares had turned into a money-spinner as the Japanese economy expanded rapidly in the 1980s. Baring Securities grew from employing twenty people to 1,400 in seven years, opening offices across Asia and Latin America, but Heath still ran it like a small firm. He would fly around the world to Bogotá or Kuala Lumpur, acting as though he was the only manager. 'What do you want?' he would demand of the local office manager, peering at him intensely through his glasses and scribbling answers on a sheet of paper. More money, less interference from London, would come the reply. 'Yes, yes,' he would say, before boarding the next plane. The firm became a federation of regional fiefdoms. All the managers thought they had a direct line to Heath and could ignore everyone else. Heath hated the idea of management committees and bureaucratic controls. As far as he was concerned the important thing was to recruit good people and let them get on with it. 'Are you hungry?' he would ask everybody he interviewed. It was code for: 'Are you like me? Do you want to be rich, and will you sacrifice anything else to achieve that?' Once somebody was recruited, he or she was there for good. Heath would shout at the culprit when something went wrong, but never sack him. He hated to lose any member of staff, preferring familiar faces around. Baring Securities was a family. There were old jokes lovingly retold, rows and reconciliations, strange ways of doing things that somehow worked.

Norris could not stand this approach. He wanted a clear structure above all. He set about imposing a management 'matrix' with each manager having to report both to a boss in their local office and to the head of the operation in London. On paper this would create two lines of control over everyone. He drew a chart of a Greek temple with columns and floors. The floors represented countries and the columns represented divisions. It was a fine structure for a global investment bank, but it had been hard to make it work in practice. There were still many people who were used to the Heath way of doing things, and did not relish fitting into a matrix. Singapore was a thorny problem. Baring Securities' Asian arm was run from there by James Bax, the regional manager, and Simon Jones, the local head of operations. Jones was a staunch defender of his empire who for some months had refused to talk to Geoffrey Broadhurst, the finance director in London. The other problem was that Tuckey had insisted on putting old stalwarts of Baring Brothers in key posts under Norris. Several of them were older and harboured ill-feelings about his promotion. Norris was impatient with some, in particular Ian Hopkins, the director who was in charge of risk control. Hopkins had also fallen out with Broadhurst over the division of their responsibilities, and Norris regarded him as incapable of working effectively with others. He distrusted Hopkins's motives, and largely ignored what he said. His frustration with Hopkins was so great that Tuckey had just removed Hopkins from the management committee in charge of the investment bank.

Despite these tribulations Norris had plenty of reason for satisfaction. On Wednesday 22 February the directors of Barings met to consider the results for 1994. Nearly all banks had made big profits in 1993 because markets were rising, but in 1994 they had suffered from volatile markets that damaged many of them. Yet Barings seemed to have emerged unscathed. It would shortly declare that pre-tax profits had actually risen slightly, from £100 million in 1993 to £102 million. It was a remarkable feat, and it was largely due to the man who could join the management committee now that Hopkins had left: Ron Baker. Baker was among a new generation of managers that Norris had promoted. He was an intense, hard-working Australian, who was utterly unlike the Baring Brothers stalwarts. He was bearded and stocky, and had no time for formality and ritual. Baker had endeared himself to Norris with his enthusiasm and drive. Baker was constantly on a plane, regularly gathering his traders at weekend meetings in New York or Hong Kong, urging them on to greater efforts. He knew how to manage his people and squeeze the most out of them. It was not only Baker's energy that Norris liked. It was also the amount of money his division was making. For the past year Baker had been in charge of derivatives trading, an arcane area of finance that many traditional brokers and bankers found almost impossible to understand. Yet many banks had poured money into the activity during the early 1990s. Those that made a success of derivatives trading could make better returns that way than through any other operation.

Derivatives were financial contracts like shares and bonds but were a stage more complex. They had no value in themselves but derived it from something else. That could be anything from the price of orange juice to a share index such as the Financial Times-Stock Exchange 100 in London. The commonest and easiest to understand derivatives were called 'futures'. They were a type of contract that first developed as a means for farmers to protect themselves against the risks of commodities fluctuating in value. There was an early example of a rice futures market at Dojima, near Osaka, in the late seventeenth century, but modern futures markets developed in the 1850s with the opening of the Chicago Board of Trade. A farmer who grew wheat wanted to ensure that he could gain a certain price for his crop when he harvested and sold it. There was a risk that the price would have fallen by then, but he could fix it by reaching a deal with a trader, who would promise to buy wheat at a set price in three months' time. If the actual price of wheat was lower by then, he would absorb the loss; if it was higher, he would take the profit. This was what became known as a futures contract, or future, and it enabled a farmer to pass on his financial risk. The participants soon realized that this effect could be achieved without actually transferring the wheat. The farmer could sell the wheat himself, but make a separate deal with a futures trader to offset his risk. Farmers used futures to

8

neutralize, or 'hedge', the financial risk they were running, while professional traders took on risk, earning a living by guessing correctly the future price of commodities.

In the 1980s financial futures markets developed which dealt with financial contracts, such as shares or bonds, rather than commodities, but the same logic applied. An investor might hold a portfolio of shares and want to ensure that he could sell it for its current price in three months' time. Financial futures gave him exactly the same comfort as the farmer holding wheat. By selling a future on the FT-SE 100 an investor could lock in today's price. At first, financial futures markets were only used to hedge risks or speculate. Then banks came across a third reason for buying and selling futures that stemmed from the link between the value of futures and the underlying assets. In the case of financial futures, these were share or bond markets and were known by futures traders as 'cash markets'. As the FT-SE 100 index rose or fell, it was followed by the price of FT-SE 100 futures. The two would be slightly out of line to reflect the cost of investing in a cash market rather than futures, and this relationship was known as the 'fair value' of the future. Then banks discovered that futures prices did not always reflect that value. Prices in futures markets sometimes moved out of line with those of stock markets for seconds or minutes at a time. This implied that either the futures market or the cash market was relatively cheap. When it happened, those traders who had computers capable of tracking fair value could buy in the cheap market and sell in the expensive one. This would enable them to make a profit on the gap between the two markets. It was a bewilderingly complicated strategy to outsiders, which became known as 'arbitrage'.

It was as if a man promised to buy an orange from you for 10p in a week's time, when you could buy the orange today for 9p at a local market. If he only offered to buy one orange, it would not be worth taking the trouble, but if the man promised to buy 1,000 oranges for 10p each – a standard futures contract – it would be worthwhile. You could spend £90 on buying 1,000 oranges at 9p each, and make a £10 profit by selling them to the man for £100 in a week's time. There would be no financial risk involved. Rather than betting on the way that orange prices would move in the coming week, you would exploit the difference between the future value he attached to oranges and their current price. In effect, the futures market would have risen above the cash market. Apart from having to store and carry the oranges, the only drawback would be that you would have to pay £90 today to buy them, and wait for a week to get your £100 from the man. This was what arbitrage traders did. When their computers showed them that futures contracts were worth more than shares or bonds, they sold futures and bought the assets in the cash market. If the prices were out of line the other way round, they did the opposite. Then they waited until the futures expired, and cashed in their profits. They did not have a problem of storage and transport because the commodities were electronic. It was easy to obtain the cash to fund their trading, because they could borrow it against any future profits. As long as they spent hundreds of millions of pounds buying futures, shares and bonds, they would be guaranteed tens of millions in profit.

When US investment banks discovered this in the mid-1980s, it was a revelation. Financial trading had always involved taking risks to make money. If you believed share prices were rising you could buy shares to back your hunches. If you were good enough at spotting trends in the market you would make money. But you always ran the risk of being wrong. Arbitrage trading was different. It did not require an expensive bet on whether shares were rising or falling. It made no difference. An arbitrage trader did not take a view of markets but simply exploited inefficiencies. The best thing in the early days was that few banks understood this, and wide gaps persisted between futures and cash markets. The US banks could see that if they recruited traders who understood how to calculate derivatives prices, and gave them the computers they needed, there were risk-free profits to be made. It was like having somebody who knew exactly the right time to pull the lever on a casino slot machine. However, these traders had to be well-educated to grasp the mathematics involved in calculating prices of some derivatives. The banks started to hire mathematics and engin-eering graduates as arbitrage traders. They became known as 'rocket scientists', and were regarded with both awe and amusement. They were different from traditional traders in banks and exchanges. Whereas traders tended to be extroverts who would battle for the best prices, rocket scientists were more introverted and spent their days studying screens for small price differences, working in a quiet and calm atmosphere similar to the universities from which many had come.

In the previous year, most of Barings' derivatives trading had been done on Japanese markets. Its chief trader in Tokyo was a thirty-year-old Californian called Fernando Gueler, a slight, enthusiastic man with a rapid-fire high-pitched voice, who headed a team of traders there and in Osaka. Gueler had an economics degree from Harvard and had joined Barings in 1988 to research derivatives. He had worked hard to develop a way of arbitraging between the Japanese stock market and futures contracts. He would watch screens to see when prices moved out of line and then he would buy Japanese shares while selling futures, or the other way round. He had perfected a system that allowed him, at the touch of a button, to buy or sell a basket of Japanese shares replicating the Nikkei 225 index. In order to buy the futures he had to place an order on a futures exchange. Here he had a choice. Futures based on the Nikkei 225 were traded on an exchange in Osaka, the second largest Japanese city. But they could also be bought and sold on an exchange in the former British trading post of Singapore. Gueler had become used to placing his orders on the Singapore International Monetary Exchange (Simex) because he could obtain better prices there. Barings had a trader on the Simex floor with an uncanny ability to buy futures quickly and cheaply. It made Gueler's arbitrage, and another type of derivatives trading called volatility trading, more profitable. The trader was a twenty-seven-year-old from Watford called Nick Leeson, who had worked at Simex for two and a half years and had gradually come to dominate the exchange.

Leeson was a slight-framed young man with thinning blond hair, and a ready grin. He was a far cry from a rocket scientist, having failed mathematics A level, but it did not matter, because a floor trader on an exchange like Simex was not there to make arcane calculations. His or her job was to get the best possible prices for customers, rather than bothering about the reasoning behind it. Leeson had joined Baring Securities six years before as a settlements clerk whose job was to settle trades after they were agreed by traders. This involved paying money to other banks and ensuring Barings received all the financial contracts it had agreed to buy, a tedious but vital task carried out in what was called the 'back office'. He quickly established a reputation as a hard worker who could be relied upon to sort out foul-ups quickly and meticulously and had got his break in 1992, when Baring Securities decided to start trading on Simex. He was sent to set up and run a small offshoot called Baring Futures (Singapore), that he managed virtually single-handedly, with some Singaporean women working in the back office. Banks usually separated traders from the back office to prevent fraud. Traders were often tempted to cheat or cover up mistakes, and this was usually caught by the back office. But it had not seemed worthwhile to have both a head trader and somebody in charge of the back office at Baring Futures. Baring Securities simply wanted someone to buy and sell futures for its traders, or for customers such as other investment banks. What was the point of employing two managers, for trading and for the back office?

So Leeson was given two jobs. He spent each morning on the trading floor at Simex, buying and selling futures. When the bell rang for the end of trading at 2.15 p.m., he would walk over to a grey tower block nearby called Ocean Towers, where Baring Securities had its office. He would take the lift to the office of Baring Futures on the fourteenth floor and spend a few hours settling his trades and updating the trading records, helped by the Singaporean clerks. Simex was an open outcry exchange similar to the two large futures exchanges in Chicago, on which young traders wearing coloured jackets to represent their bank or trading house bought and sold using shouted bids, reinforced with a set of hand signals. Most banks on Simex had red jackets because it was considered a Chinese lucky colour, but Baring Futures jackets were in dark blue and yellow vertical stripes. Leeson was a powerful figure at Simex. He would sit on a five-legged metal stool at his trading booth, taking orders over the telephone. In the loud maelstrom of the trading pits – octagonal hollows in the trading floor where contracts such as the Nikkei were traded – he could switch from a quiet demeanour to the aggressive posture of the futures trader. He also looked the part now, having put on weight from nights drinking in the brightly painted waterfront bars on Boat Quay. He was watched carefully by others because he often bought and sold in such large amounts that he would move prices. From the calm of his arbitrage desk in Tokyo, Gueler could hear the roar of the Simex pits as Leeson took down over the telephone line his orders to buy and sell.

But for the past year and a half Leeson had been doing far more than simply carrying out the orders of the Osaka and Tokyo traders. He had proved himself such an efficient floor trader that in late 1993 he had been encouraged to develop his own trading activity. Leeson had started to exploit the differences between prices on the two futures markets in Singapore and Osaka. He did not have to be physically in Osaka to do so because it was an electronic exchange. Barings had assistants in Osaka who could buy or sell futures on trading screens for him. Leeson told Gueler that he could make money for Barings by switching trades between Singapore and Osaka. Most customers wanted to buy futures in Singapore; it was cheaper than in Osaka, because Simex did not require them to deposit as much cash for collateral. But Simex was a small exchange, so any large orders tended to move prices. When Leeson went into the pit with a big customer order for Nikkei futures, it would drive up the price before he was able to fill the order. Leeson told Gueler that there was a great opportunity here. Before going to the pit, he could buy the same number of futures for Barings itself in Osaka. He could then sell futures to the customer at the Simex price from a Baring account. When these contracts were put in the customer's account, it would leave Barings short of, say, a hundred contracts at the higher price. But Leeson would also hold a hundred contracts in Osaka at the lower price. He would have arbitraged the prices on the two exchanges, leaving Barings with a risk-free profit that was equivalent to the gap between Osaka and Simex prices.

This sounded complicated but it was actually simple. It took a computer and a highly educated trader to work out if cash and futures markets were out of line. It took nothing but common sense to do the same for futures markets. The very act of trading for customers created a gap that Barings itself could exploit. Compared with what Gueler did it could hardly be flattered with the name arbitrage. It was not so much a trading strategy as a means of exploiting information about what Barings' customers were doing. It was rather cheeky, but nobody had objected. Leeson had rapidly shown that 'switching', as it became known, was enormously profitable. Occasionally Gueler had worried that he was exploiting customers. Yet nobody wanted Leeson to stop. As 1994 went by he seemed to have discovered a way of making even more money than the Tokyo and Osaka rocket scientists. The 'switching' activity had been the most lucrative part of

Baker's division, making £28 million out of the £53 million revenue from derivatives trading. Baker's ascendancy at Barings owed a great deal to Leeson. It was almost too good to be true, but Baring Securities was used to one or two people earning a large proportion of its profits. In the 1980s most of its money had been earned by a group of traders who dealt in Japanese share warrants, a type of derivative. When those ran out of steam, it was rescued by a young Malaysian trader in Tokyo who started to make big sums from trading options, another type of derivative. Leeson was only the latest trader to have the golden touch.

Best of all from Barings' point of view, these profits were coming from trading that did not require risk-taking. With Leeson's switching, it seemed to have found a way of obeying Revelstoke's dictum while making large profits. Leeson's switching involved buying huge amounts of futures on Osaka and Simex, but he was taking no risk from market movements. If the Nikkei fell, the hundred futures he had bought for Barings on Osaka would fall in value. But he also had what was known as a 'short' position on Simex because he had sold one hundred contracts. This would rise in value as the Nikkei fell, exactly cancelling out the Osaka position. Each time he did some switching Leeson ended up with a matched position. There were only a few obstacles. One was that trading had to be funded. On exchanges such as Simex and Osaka futures lasted for three months. A bank might not be due to settle with an exchange for a month, but it was clear every day how much it stood to gain or lose. To protect themselves against a bank not being able to meet the final bill, exchanges used a system known as margining. Each day they would tot up a bank's futures contracts and demand cash to cover any existing short-fall. These demands were known as margin calls. But exchanges did not pay out cash daily to banks whose positions were in profit. This meant arbitrage traders had to pay large sums to fund loss-making contracts and wait for the profitable ones to pay off. In the previous few months Barings had had to pay £740 million in margin calls to the Singapore and Osaka exchanges to cover loss-making contracts in Leeson's switching account.[3]

In addition Leeson was now devoting so much effort to trading that he appeared to be losing his grip as back office manager. There had been a disturbing incident in which Leeson and the Baring Futures clerks seemed to have failed to collect £50 million owed to Barings by one of its customers, a US investment fund. The gap in the accounts had been questioned by its auditors, and Leeson had admitted to making a mistake in not collecting the money. Bax had written to Norris to say that Leeson was now so busy that he should no longer be in charge of both trading and settlement.[4] As a stop-gap, Tony Railton, the deputy head of derivatives settlement in London, had flown to Singapore at the start of February to help sort out the back office. It was now vital to ensure that Baring Futures was running smoothly. Not only was it making a huge amount of money and absorbing cash, but Leeson's trading was attracting a large degree of attention from other banks. Each day the Osaka Securities Exchange published figures to show how heavily each bank was trading. The number of futures held by Barings had risen sharply in January and February, and wild rumours were flying around. Some banks thought that Barings must be in trouble because it held so many loss-making futures on Osaka. Another rumour was that Barings had a large customer who was taking a huge bet on the Nikkei index rising. The bank's senior managers had discussed the rumours in London and reassured themselves that every loss-making future was matched by a profitable one. But they had none the less asked Leeson to reduce his switching.

At the board meeting, held in a long room whose windows over-looked the gleaming Lloyd's of London building and whose walls were hung with portraits of the Barings, the directors had approved the accounts for 1994 without even discussing Singapore. The accounts did not show exactly how much Leeson had made and his name was not mentioned. Now, as dusk fell, Norris was working in his office. He had other things than Leeson on his mind. It was gratifying at the moment but it would no doubt diminish soon as other banks moved in. That was always the danger. As soon as you discovered an easy source of profits others would rush to seize the same opportunity. He had visited Singapore in mid-February to resolve a problem with an Australian merchant bank in which Barings had a stake. While there he had met Leeson. Leeson had come to the glass-fronted office where he had been sitting and they had briefly talked over his trading. It was the end of a tiring day and Norris was tired. Leeson was sweating despite the air-conditioning, and he launched into a long, rambling explanation of his business, full of jargon that Norris did not understand. Norris had grown impatient, and hustled Leeson out as fast as possible. He had not liked Leeson much. He seemed like a typical trader: loud and boastful. Not that it mattered. People like Leeson came and went, hardly visible from the top floors of 8 Bishopsgate.

Whether the Barings directors had heard of Leeson or not, he had helped to bring them large rewards. Pay in merchant banks and broking firms had risen sharply in the 1980s as the million-dollar bonuses of Wall Street crossed the Atlantic. Barings had one of the most generous profit-sharing schemes. Each year the bank paid just under half of its operating profits to staff in bonuses. The Baring Brothers directors justified it as the reward for having given up shares in the bank when the Foundation took ownership in 1985. Baring Securities' staff had always been used to big bonuses because Heath had shared out a quarter of the profits made by his firm each year among its dozen founding members. The largest share went to Heath himself. This year would see the biggest-ever hand-out of bonuses. Barings had made £204 million operating profits in 1994 and at the end of the week would start to hand out the first instalment of £102 million in bonuses. Leeson would get a £450,000 bonus, while Baker would get £880,000, Norris and Peter Baring would both get £1 million, and Tuckey would receive £1.65 million.[5] Norris had expressed some doubts to Baker about paying Leeson that much. He seemed immature and Norris thought it might spoil him to be overpaid. Yet there did not appear to be much choice. There was talk of other investment banks in Singapore trying to recruit him. The fact was that Leeson seemed to be making a large amount of money, no matter what scruples Norris had. Without a few star traders around Barings might not keep its pride of place in the City for another two centuries.

CHAPTER 1

At 4.00 p.m. on Thursday 23 February an unexpected visitor arrived at Peter Norris's office. It was Tony Gamby, Barings' head of settlements, who had walked round from 8 Bishopsgate to see him urgently, bringing disturbing tidings from Singapore. In his efforts to sort out payments and trades at Baring Futures, Tony Railton had become more and more worried at what he was discovering. The records were in an even worse state than had been feared. The Baring Futures office was on the fourteenth floor of a block called Ocean Towers. It was a fifty-foot-long room with a set of desks at which the trades were settled. It was in an isolated spot at the end of a long, featureless corridor, which a visitor had to take a detour to find. Baring Securities' main office was on the twenty-fourth floor. To get between the two required two lift journeys: one set of lifts stopped at the seventeenth floor and another went up from there to the top. The senior clerk, Norhaslinda Hassan, was away on maternity leave, so Railton had been forced to try to make sense of the records himself. He had spent a few days sorting through them, becoming ever more baffled. There did not appear to be enough cash to pay the sums owed by Baring Futures. Leeson also seemed to have put less money on deposit at Simex than he had claimed in margin from London. Railton had worked out there was a cash shortfall of about £95 million. He thought he must have missed something, but Leeson was the only one who could explain where he had gone wrong. He had started to try to pin him down to explain it but it was a hard task. Leeson kept saying he was unwell and postponing meetings.

Eventually Railton had become frustrated and gone to Simex to confront Leeson. He found him as usual near the pits. Amid the noise and crowd Railton had tried to force some answers from Leeson, but he was a moving target. As Railton talked Leeson kept darting over to buy and sell futures. Railton left when Leeson promised to go over the whole thing that afternoon. But by then, things were even more confused. A fax had arrived from London asking why Leeson had requested $45 million overnight for margin calls, given that he was supposed to be reducing trading. Leeson had finally gone to the Baring Futures office and started talking to Railton and Simon Jones, but after twenty minutes he had got up to leave. He said he had to visit his wife Lisa, who had suffered a miscarriage. He would return shortly, he said. But he never had. Railton and Jones had stayed into the evening, trying to make sense of the accounts. At 9.30 p.m. Jones had decided to go home and carry on working on the problem the next day. He saw no reason to talk to anybody in London about it. After he left Railton had phoned America Square before returning to his hotel for the night. Gamby was very concerned that Leeson had not returned. It could mean that he had been hiding trades or defrauding Barings. As he listened to Gamby's tale, Norris started to suspect the worst himself. The memory of Leeson sweating and blustering in front of him in Singapore the previous week started to assume sinister overtones. He began to feel physically sick. But Norris was not going to panic. He asked Sacranie to gather a group of managers to sort it out without any more delay.

By 6.30 p.m. half a dozen executives had been summoned to Norris's office. George Maclean, a soft-spoken Scotsman who was Baker's direct boss, had also arrived. Baker himself was on a skiing holiday in the Swiss resort of Verbier. Norris had not bothered to summon Hopkins, although he was the head of risk. There were four desks set around the room, including those of Norris, Sacranie and Richard Greer, the head of research, as well as a two-seat blue sofa opposite Norris's desk and chairs in a matching fabric arranged around a wooden table in the centre of the room. They settled down to debate where Leeson could have gone. There was confused chattering, and Norris interrupted it briskly, believing that he had to take charge if they were to get anywhere. Instead of Baker, he had called Mary Walz, a thirty-four-year-old American who had been recruited by Baker to head equity derivatives trading. She was a forceful and articulate woman and an ally of Baker's. She and Baker sometimes moaned to each other about all the flaws of Barings, Baker reserving his most withering scorn for Tony Hawes, the treasurer, whose job was to organize funding for operations such as derivatives trading. Hawes was a plump man of fifty with bushy eyebrows, who lacked the personality to stand up to Baker. Instead, he would try to fend off any criticism with an ingratiating smile. It had not done him any good. Baker had become so frustrated by his recent encounters with Hawes that he had nicknamed him 'Forrest Gump' after the recent film about an *idiot savant* who could perform miraculous feats.

Walz had already received unsettling news about Singapore that afternoon, having been told that Simex had made a $45 million margin call. This made no sense to her since Leeson was supposed to be reducing his trading. She had rung Hopkins to talk it over. Then she had telephoned Gueler at home in Tokyo, waking him up at 2.00 a.m. Walz had told him about the $45 million margin call and said he should try to find Leeson. 'This must be a joke,' Gueler thought to himself. Brokers and traders at Baring Securities were always playing practical jokes on each other. The irreverent tone had been set by Heath, who loved ringing colleagues and pretending to be someone else to fool them. Greer, the first head of the Tokyo office, had kept a record of things that amused them all as meticulously as he researched Japanese companies and had started a 'joke file' in 1984. A decade later the joke file comprised eight thick folders. Gueler had reason to think Walz's call was just another entry for the joke file. Just before he had left the office that evening Gueler had been rung by Norris to tell him that Barings was so pleased with his trading in 1994 that he was to be appointed a director of the new investment bank formed out of Baring Brothers and Baring Securities. When Walz called Gueler he thought it was probably an initiation test for new directors. But when he realized she was serious he had spent an hour trying to reach Leeson on his mobile telephone in Singapore. There was no reply and Gueler eventually went back to sleep.

Walz racked her brains for a way of locating Leeson. Then she remembered that Leeson had stayed with his parents-in-law on past visits to Britain and a secretary had their telephone number in Kent. Walz found out the number, then went over to America Square to join the others in Norris's office. When she rang, the telephone was answered by Patsy Sims, Leeson's mother-in-law. Walz did not want to alarm Mrs Sims, so she said that she was about to go out to Singapore and wanted to speak to Leeson to ensure that he would be there when she arrived. Mrs Sims was an outgoing woman who was proud of her daughter, and of her son-in-law's growing success. She chatted happily to Walz, saying she had been worried because Lisa had recently had a miscarriage. But Lisa had just rung her to say that she and Nick were going to the resort of Phuket in Thailand for the weekend. Walz hung up and reported to the others what Mrs Sims had said. The confirmation of Lisa Leeson's miscarriage was greeted with awkward relief. It was consistent with what Leeson had told Jones. The managers decided that they might have misjudged the trader, who was just taking care of his wife. Leeson was known to be deeply attached to Lisa, a former Barings back office clerk, whom he had met when he was sent out from London to sort out a settlement problem in 1991. They could understand him letting Baring Futures' back office get a little out of hand if he had been worried about his wife's health. All might yet be forgiven.

But they still had to track Leeson down. By now it was 2.30 a.m. on Friday in Singapore. Norris knew Hawes was due to have arrived there that night on a flight from Tokyo. Hawes had gone to Singapore with Railton three weeks before to launch an initiative known as the 'Singapore Project', the grand title for an effort to improve Baring Futures' settlements and to get more information about the margin calls Leeson was making. Since the previous autumn, Hawes had been doggedly trying to find out why Leeson needed so much cash but it was hard to pin the trader down. Leeson kept explaining to Hawes how Simex calculated margin calls but Hawes found it difficult to understand. It was embarrassing to have to question him again and again, and he was acutely aware that he had been a far less successful trader than Leeson when he had run foreign exchange trading for Barings in the 1980s. Hawes wanted to be clear how much cash was being used for Gueler's trading, and how much was for customers, but fresh questions occurred to him after each time he talked to Leeson. Leeson was respectful, but he made it clear that it was very tedious to keep going over it. Hawes hoped he could finally lay the issue to rest on this visit to Singapore. It was becoming urgent because Leeson's cash demands were so big that Hawes had just had to go to Tokyo to set up a new credit line with Sanwa Bank. Hawes had just arrived at his hotel in Singapore, and was unpacking when the telephone rang at 2.34 a.m.[1] It was Norris, who told him briskly that he should find Railton and return with him rapidly to the Baring Futures office in Ocean Towers.

Norris also called Bax, a calm, efficient manager whom he respected, and asked him to get hold of Jones and go over to Ocean Towers. Bax rang Jones but there was no reply, so he drove to the financial district alone. It was deserted when he arrived, with only a few lights burning in surrounding office towers. But there were still lights on the fourteenth floor of Ocean Towers. It was not unusual. Leeson's trading was so complex and heavy that clerks had to work at night to reconcile trades. Bax found two women clerks in one corner working on the day's trading returns while on the other side of the room Railton was showing Hawes statements from Citibank, Baring Futures' clearing bank. The papers were stacked neatly in a cupboard, open for inspection. The worst possibility seemed to be that cash had been siphoned from Baring Futures into a secret bank account by Leeson. Hawes came upon a highly suspicious transaction. Barings had a Citibank account for its own trades and another for those of customers. On 2 February £50 million had been transferred from one account to another and then credited back again later that day. It seemed as if Leeson had attempted to conceal a hole in one account by double-counting the £50 million. This was the amount he had claimed to have failed to collect from the US investment firm, and, though he had said it had been reclaimed, the statement indicated that the cash was still missing.

Bax put a call through to Norris's office and was asked to call Singapore hospitals to see if Lisa Leeson had been admitted after her miscarriage. As activity in Singapore became more frantic the phone on Sacranie's desk rang. It was Alex Murray, a Barings manager in New York, who had been Norris's assistant before Sacranie. He had rung to talk to Sacranie about something else, but as they spoke, he could hear Norris talking loudly in the background: 'Somebody go out and get some hamburgers. And buy me two packets of Marlboro.' Murray realized that something must be wrong, because Norris had given up smoking six years before. Norris had started to be gripped by fear. As he looked around the room he could see nearly all those responsible for Leeson. It struck him this would be the first time they had actually seen the Simex statements themselves. Everyone had relied on Leeson to tell them what he was doing. But he was no longer there, and they were in the dark without him.

At 8.00 p.m. (4.00 a.m. Singapore), Hawes was beginning to find out the enormity of what they had missed. After the shock of reading the bank statements he sat down at Leeson's desk to recover. In front of him he noticed a pile of folded computer paper listing all the positions Baring Futures held on Simex that day and he started leafing through it. Some trades were in an account numbered 92000, used by Leeson for switching. Even more were in an account of which Hawes had never heard. It was an error account, which was an account often used by traders as a storing place for unreconciled trades. As Hawes worked his way down the statement, he realized this was not an ordinary error account. The account seemed to hold most of Leeson's trades instead of just the odd one. It was called Account 88888.

Singaporeans are superstitious because of their Chinese roots, and numbers are chosen for portents. On the face of it 88888 was the luckiest number possible for a five-digit Simex account because eight is a Chinese lucky number as it sounds like the word 'prosper'. But five eights are far from lucky because the number five in Chinese sounds like 'never'. Hawes had discovered the 'never prosper' account. It had lived up to its name. The computer print-out showed that it held a huge number of futures based on the Nikkei and Japanese government bonds. The Nikkei futures alone were equivalent to more than £3 billion of Japanese shares. Virtually every one was long, and the Nikkei would have to rise well above 18,500 for them to be in profit. The further it dropped, the more Barings owed. But the Nikkei had been dropping since the week after an earthquake had struck the port of Kobe on 17 January, disrupting production in Japan's industrial heartland. The index had closed the previous evening at 17,830, and was expected to keep falling. Hawes started to tot up what Barings owed. He scribbled down the numbers on a piece of paper as Bax stood nearby, phoning Norris to tell him of the discovery. Hawes's rough calculation came to $250 million. He pushed the piece of paper under Bax's nose as he spoke. If he was right, Barings could face losses of at least £200 million, including the £50 million hole in the accounts. Those in London were dumbstruck. Their chief trader in Singapore had been operating a secret account. But what on earth had he been up to? He had no profits to embezzle in the five eights account. What had he been doing?

Norris told Hawes to fax across the five eights account. Broadhurst and Sacranie cleared a space on the round desk in the middle of the room and tried to make sense of it. Since Leeson had been supposed to have matched contracts they started looking for a short position in Osaka. The previous Friday the account held 21,000 Osaka futures, worth £2.3 billion of Japanese shares. They matched the Osaka positions with Simex ones. But it made no sense because all the futures were long. Every single contract they could identify was losing money. Norris was now pacing the room, waiting for them to add up the futures. He looked over their shoulders to see what they were doing, and saw them trying to match the positions. 'Bloody hell, you can't assume that. Just add it up!' he said. He started adding them himself. They came to over £3 billion. The futures in five eights were completely unhedged. Even a small drop in the Nikkei 225 would increase the loss by billions of yen. Using Barings' precious capital, Leeson had taken the largest losing bet in history on the Japanese stock market. Norris sat down at his desk and tried to think dispassionately. Leeson had clearly been deceiving the bank for months but that was irrelevant now. The challenge was to save Barings. It could have lost more than £200 million already, but the frightening thing was that Leeson had pushed it into a bottomless hole. The Nikkei was falling and Barings' bill was growing ever bigger. It did not have much capital. The Baring Foundation's shares had a balance sheet value of £308 million and it had a further £101 million in loan capital. If Leeson's losses ate through this Barings was finished.

Even as Norris considered the next move a further blow came from Singapore. The futures in account 88888 were an extraordinary discovery. But as Hawes leafed through the computer print-out, he found Leeson had not only been trading futures, and phoned Norris to tell him. His voice was usually quiet and measured but now it was quivering with fear: 'I've found options. We haven't even counted them. There are thousands here.' This was even worse. Options were a type of derivative Leeson was allowed to buy and sell for Barings' customers but barred from trading for Barings.

Options got their name from the fact that they allowed the holder a choice. Futures were agreements that always resulted in one side losing and the other gaining. They were simple bets, like placing money on the toss of a coin. But options were sold by one trader to another. A trader who held an option had the right to buy or sell something at a set price in the future, without the obligation to do so. If a market moved in the right direction and he could make a profit by buying at that price, he would do so. But he was not obliged to fulfil the contract. If the market went against him, and the asset was selling for less than the price at which he had an option to buy it, he would do nothing. The option would simply expire at the end of three months without being exercised and the trader would escape the loss.

Options were similar to a man offering you the right to sell him 1,000 oranges in a week's time for 10p each. If oranges were selling in a local market for 10p each it was not worth buying them today only to keep them for a week and sell them to him for exactly the same price. But the price of oranges was likely to change during the week. It might be higher than 10p or lower. If you agreed to sell the 1,000 oranges for £100 and waited until a few days later to buy them at the market, there was a risk. You would gain if the price of oranges was lower than 10p in the market that day, but lose money if it was higher. If the price had risen to 11p you would have to spend £110 buying the oranges and only receive £100. Thus a futures contract would carry risks. The price in the cash market would have to move in the right direction for you to make money; if it did the reverse you would lose. However, if the man allowed you a choice of whether or not to sell him the oranges, it would eliminate the risk. If oranges cost 11p each in the market that day, you would tell him you were not going to complete the bargain. But if they cost 9p each that day, you would buy them and then sell them to him for 10p. He would have given you an option, which you would exercise. The fact that you held an option meant that you did not run any risk of loss. Conversely, the man who had given you the option would be taking a big risk. The best outcome for him would be that he would not lose money. But if the price of oranges fell below the 10p option price he had given you, he would have to buy 1,000 oranges at an artificially high price.

That was the difference between futures and options. In a futures contract both sides took an equal risk. But the person who granted an option was taking a potentially far greater risk than the person who held it. As a result options were not just traded freely between those who thought a market would rise and those who thought it would fall. They came at a price. In order to obtain an option you had to pay a fee known as a premium. If this premium turned out to be more than the amount you could make by exercising the option, you lost money, but if the premium was lower, you gained. The seller of the option took on the risk of market movements in return for the premium. If the market moved too far against him, he could be left having to pay a large bill. The trick was to sell the option for a big enough premium to offset the risk. But this was a very difficult matter as risks were hard to calculate because the value of options depended on how much prices in the market tended to fluctuate and the time left before the option expired. Nobody had been able to value options consistently until two mathematicians in the US, Fischer Black and Myron Scholes, invented a method in 1973. But theirs was a complex equation. Working out the right premium for an option was the sort of task only a mathematically sophisticated trader like Gueler could do properly. Without Gueler's education, and his computers, it would be reckless to sell options. Yet that was exactly what Leeson had been doing, according to the records of the five eights account. What was more, he had been selling vast numbers on behalf of Barings for at least a year.

At 6.30 a.m. in Tokyo (10.30 p.m. London) Gueler was woken once more by a telephone call from Walz. He had slept fitfully since her earlier call, worrying about Leeson's disappearance and the unexplained margin call. Walz told him that they needed him to assess some of Leeson's positions and he should go to Barings' office in the centre of Tokyo immediately.

When Gueler arrived there he called Norris. Norris was now too worried for niceties. 'Sit down, Ferd. Listen to what I'm going to say, and don't interrupt,' he said briskly. Norris told Gueler that Leeson appeared to have options in an account that he had hidden from Barings and they had to value them. Hawes would send him details of the options and he should work out what exposure they gave Barings to market movements. Gueler should not tell anyone in the Tokyo office about it. 'But those can't be ours. They belong to Customer X,' Gueler said immediately. He and the other Tokyo traders had watched as Leeson had sold enormous numbers of options over the closing months of 1994. Leeson's options selling clearly had nothing to do with arbitrage trading or the switching account. It had to be for a customer and Leeson had dropped hints that this was so. The traders in Tokyo and Osaka had speculated constantly over who Leeson's customer could be. It must be a large bank or investment fund that had a strong view on the Nikkei. They had dubbed the mystery trader 'Customer X' and it became a challenge to discover who he was. Leeson would not tell them directly, but he talked of a secretive investment fund, run from the Bahamas by a Frenchman called Philippe.

Gueler started to calculate the risk of the options. The print-out Hawes had found did not disclose the premium Leeson had gained for selling them, so he could not tell whether they were in profit or loss, but the strategy behind them was obvious. The options had been sold in pairs, called 'short straddles'. The buyer of a straddle gained money from one option if the market rose and from the other if it fell. The seller of a straddle gained if the market was stable because he kept the premium, without losing on either option. Selling short straddles was particularly risky because a seller lost from any change in the market, up or down. But it was lucrative in the short term: the seller received two sets of premium. The options Gueler was examining were recognizably the ones the Tokyo traders believed Leeson had sold to Customer X. The previous autumn Customer X had appeared to be placing a huge bet on the Nikkei staying stable. For a long time it had worked. The Japanese economy was depressed and the Nikkei stagnated. What was more, Customer X was buying so heavily that he was cornering the market. Other traders were too intimidated to bet against him and the Nikkei grew flatter. Customer X was single-handedly squeezing the Nikkei. Then the Kobe earthquake struck and even Customer X had been unable to fight against it. The Nikkei dropped steadily, and with every point the straddles had lost value. Now Norris was telling Gueler something inconceivable: these options did not belong to Customer X. Leeson had simply sold them for Barings. 'We're not sure yet, but we think we own them,' said Norris.

Then Norris told Gueler to do something else. He should find the details of all the futures contracts which Leeson had bought on the

Osaka exchange, and calculate how much Barings would owe if they were not matched by Simex futures. This bewildered Gueler even more: surely they must be matched, he thought. But he did as he was told. By now others were filtering into the office for the start of the day's trading. Gueler went to the back office to find the details of the Osaka futures and came back to his desk to enter them into a computer spreadsheet. He could now see what they were worth. Since all the Osaka futures were long they were in loss before the market opened. The Nikkei jumped 60 points as trading started, reducing the loss. But the relief did not last long. Gueler could hear traders near him selling Japanese shares, and watched the Nikkei slumping. It dropped through 17,800, then 17,700 and kept going. He waited for a correction. Traders seek the moment that a market corrects, where enough traders are buying to outweigh the sellers. Then a market will bounce back upwards. But that was not happening this Friday morning. The Nikkei just kept falling. As it did so, the loss was escalating by the second. The futures in the five eights account were so volatile that each point the index changed made £100,000 difference to the amount that Barings owed. The initial rise of 60 points reduced the loss by £6 million. As the Nikkei fell again, the loss spiralled upwards at an almost dizzying speed. If these futures were not matched by others, Gueler could see that they were all in terrible trouble.

In the midst of this activity one man was still oblivious. Andrew Tuckey had left 8 Bishopsgate earlier in the evening to drive home to west London. One of Tuckey's neighbours had died of cancer, and he had gone to a memorial dinner at the family's house opposite. He had walked home with his wife and put on some music. His directorship of the Royal Opera House was matched by his devotion to music. He had gone to bed after an hour but at 11.05 p.m. the telephone woke him up. 'Andrew, this is Peter Norris. I have George Maclean with me,' said the voice at the other end. Norris quickly outlined what they had discovered: the damage could be over £100 million, but they had not yet worked it out. 'We have lost a huge amount,' Norris said. Tuckey listened calmly, asking a few questions about what Norris and Maclean knew so far. He had advised so many troubled companies that he was trained to think coolly and analytically in the worst times. But he had little to contribute. Tuckey had never met Leeson. He was a merchant banker not a trader. His working life was spent with chairmen and chief executives of large companies, not among futures traders. He could grasp rationally that it made sense to combine a merchant bank with a stockbroking firm but he did not have an instinct for markets and trading. He left that to others. Now he realized that those others had made an enormous error. He told Norris to call him back when he knew more, and tried to return to sleep. But as the night wore on he could doze only fitfully. He knew that a calamity probably faced him when he rose.

In Tokyo Gueler was feeling frightened and alone. He was sitting on a floor where traders gossiped as they watched the market rise and fall. A market was the expression of thousands of individual decisions to buy and sell shares, but it felt as if it had a life of its own, like a wild creature. Now he was watching this creature savage Barings and he could not even warn anybody. 'You're looking white as a sheet,' said a trader sitting nearby. Gueler laughed nervously, saying that he was still recovering from the night before. He went to a room off the trading floor to phone Norris to tell him about the loss. 'This is the most aggressive strategy I have ever seen in my life,' Gueler said. As far as he was concerned, the fact that Leeson had lost so much money was not the most extraordinary thing. It was the way he had done it, by taking a naked bet against the market. It was almost as if Leeson had wanted to lose the cash. Traders like Gueler were trained to protect themselves if a market moved against them. The first thing they did when one of their positions started losing money was to buy or sell futures to offset it. If you were losing as a market fell, you would buy short futures to gain from the fall. This would stop your losses before they got out of control: literally hedge your bet. It was called dynamic hedging and was a routine strategy for options traders. Often dynamic hedging was blamed for making markets more unstable. But Leeson had been doing the opposite. As the market had fallen, he had bought more and more long futures. What could he have been thinking? It was almost as if he had been seized by a death wish.

In London Norris now knew that Barings faced enormous losses on both the futures and options. The five eights account showed a shocking disparity between what they thought Leeson had been doing and the truth. Not only had Leeson been taking bets on the Japanese stock market without telling them but he had also been selling options without them having the least idea. The daily reports they received from him had been a complete fiction. Several of those in his office had met daily and had solemnly discussed the profits and supposedly tiny risks of Leeson's trading. But all this had been a fantasy. Several of the unhappy group were overcome by exhaustion and despondency in the middle of the night. At 4.00 a.m. Maclean tried to catch some sleep on the blue sofa opposite Norris's desk. Others kept picking over the records of the five eights account. As dawn started breaking Norris gazed out of the windows at the light coming up over City rooftops. 'We have broken the bank,' he said half in despair, half in wonder that they had fallen victim to such a bizarre deception. At 5.30 a.m. Tuckey rang. He had just risen after a fitful night, hoping against hope that the £100 million had been found. Norris told him how much worse the losses had become, and that they were now unsure whether the bank could be saved. Indeed, it might already be too late. If Barings had lost more than its equity of £308 million, it might technically be insolvent already. It would then be under a legal obligation to stop trading immediately before it bought shares or assets it knew it could not afford. It might be impossible to open for business in two hours' time.

Tuckey told Norris to start calling Barings' directors to 8 Bishopsgate. They had to decide immediately whether to declare Barings insolvent. Norris told Gamby and Brenda Granger, who was Railton's boss, to fly to Singapore to help to clear up the aftermath. Then he took a shower and braced himself for the phone call he dreaded most. At 7.15 a.m. he rang Peter Baring at his home in Notting Hill to inform him that the 1890 crisis in which his family's bank had almost collapsed was being repeated. Baring was known for not spending any longer than necessary on the telephone, even sometimes hanging up when the conversation was over without saying goodbye, leaving a baffled caller at the other end. 'It must be serious if you are calling me at this hour,' said Baring, when Norris rang. Baring listened to what Norris had to say without displaying any emotion. Then he walked to the underground station near his home and boarded his customary tube for the City.

Others were also getting telephone calls at home. Hopkins was finally telephoned by Norris and Maclean. Hopkins wondered what was so wrong that Norris would bother to summon him. He had already come to the conclusion that his career at Barings was over. By removing him from the management committee Tuckey had indicated clearly that his authority was being diminished. Hopkins had spent the previous evening discussing with his wife what to do about it. They had decided he should seek early retirement, and he was planning a meeting with Peter Baring that morning.

At 8.30 a.m. the directors met in the boardroom on the eighteenth floor of 8 Bishopsgate next to Tuckey's office. It was a square room with a large round oak table; a painting called *Philosopher with Perspective*, showing figures in a ruined landscape, hung on one wall. Norris was the first to speak. He told them that Barings had sustained such a heavy loss that its capital might have been wiped out. The damage had been done by a single trader in Singapore, who had disappeared and could not be found. Peter Baring had asked two lawyers from Slaughter and May, Barings' law firm, to the meeting. One of them was an expert in insolvency. Baring asked him to tell them whether he thought that Barings could carry on trading, or should go into liquidation immediately. The lawyer said that he believed the bank could legally carry on until the end of the day. The extent of the loss was uncertain, and the weekend was approaching. Financial markets would then be closed and Barings might have enough time either to sort out the mess or be rescued. This was the first piece of good news Norris had heard for fourteen hours. At least it gave them a chance to rescue Barings. If it had to be sold, Barings could probably do a good job of that. Selling companies was something that Baring Brothers knew a lot about. It would be selling itself this time but the same principles applied. The depressed mood started to lift slightly as the directors realized they could at least do something. They were no longer condemned just to sit there hearing ever worse news about Barings' plight.

The next step was to inform the Bank of England. The Bank had just celebrated its 300th anniversary and its white stone edifice in the heart of the City on Threadneedle Street had been floodlit every night for several weeks. It was only 300 yards away from 8 Bishopsgate and Barings' directors could gaze down on the Bank's roof. Like other British banks, Barings was supervised by the Bank of England. This meant that Bank officials received monthly reports on its activities to check it was not taking undue risk, and could tell it how much capital it needed. The Bank's job was to ensure that banks did not collapse and lose the money lent to them by depositors. The supervision department was headed by Brian Quinn, a brisk, silver-haired Scotsman, who was nearing retirement but still bustled energetically around the corridors of the Bank. Quinn and the supervision department had been heavily criticized for failing to spot fraud at the Bank of Credit and Commerce International before they closed it down four years earlier, and Quinn had been implementing reforms to try to ensure it was not caught out again. Apart from its supervisory role the Bank tended to act informally as the City's protector, stepping in whenever a big crisis threatened it. The most notorious of these was the Barings crisis in 1890. When the first Lord Revelstoke had left Barings exposed in Latin America he had appealed for help to William Lidderdale, the governor of the Bank. Lidderdale rescued Barings by persuading leading banks, including rivals such as N. M. Rothschild & Sons, to contribute £17 million to a guarantee fund.

Peter Baring rang the Bank and asked to see Eddie George, the governor. George was an affable figure who had none the less earned the nickname 'Hard Eddie' for his tough management of the Bank while he had been deputy governor. He was determined and unafraid to fight his corner against the government when he disagreed with the Chancellor of the Exchequer. A chain-smoker, he usually took his most important decisions in a fog of tobacco smoke. But George was not there to take Peter Baring's call. That morning he had set off for a skiing holiday with his family at the French resort of Alvoriaz in the Haute Savoie. Instead the Bank arranged an appointment for 11.00 a.m. with Quinn and the deputy governor of the Bank, Rupert Pennant-Rea. Pennant-Rea, a tall, gangling man who, like Tuckey, had been born in Rhodesia, was not an average Bank official. Until 1993 he had been editor of *The Economist* magazine, and was a free-thinking intellectual who often wore coloured V-necked pullovers under his suit jackets. He had been chosen as a counterfoil to George by Kenneth Clarke, the chancellor. Just before 11.00 a.m. Baring and Tuckey walked down to the Bank, set around a grand courtyard designed by the architect Sir John Soane in the 1770s, with French windows leading from the governor's office on to it. Like every visitor to the Bank, they had to tell their business to the footmen dressed in pink tailcoats and red waistcoats with silver buttons before being led around the long, echoing corridors to see Pennant-Rea and Quinn.

Peter Baring told the story of what had happened while Quinn and Pennant-Rea listened in silence. It was a huge surprise. The Bank was supposed to detect if Barings was running untoward risks, but this was a bolt from the blue. How could it have been allowed to happen, they wondered. But Pennant-Rea faced a more immediate task than finding out. He had to decide whether to repeat Lidderdale's action in November 1890 when he persuaded Lord Salisbury, the prime minister, to give government backing for the rescue of Barings. There was good reason to slip from the back door of the Bank and catch a cab over to Downing Street, as Lidderdale had done. The Bank had since put in money to support banks when it believed that their collapse could lead to financial panic, with frightened depositors withdrawing cash from other financial institutions. It had done so in the property collapse of 1973–4 and again in 1991–2, when it secretly supported about forty small banks. On the face of it few banks were more obvious candidates to be rescued than Barings. Not only had the Bank already done so once a century before, but Barings was a cornerstone of the financial establishment. The Earl of Cromer had been managing director of Baring Brothers when he was appointed governor of the Bank in 1962. For the past year Peter Baring had been chairman of the London Investment Banking Association. Many overseas banks took it as read that Barings would be supported by the Bank in a crisis. If it failed to aid Barings, what would happen to the other merchant banks such as N. M. Rothschild & Sons and Schroders?

Yet Pennant-Rea realized that, according to its own principles, the Bank should not rescue Barings this time. Peter Baring had told them that a single trader in Singapore had blown Barings apart. If that was so, there was no reason for depositors to think that because Barings collapsed, other banks might too. What had happened was so extraordinary that it was by definition unrepeatable. That meant the Bank should allow Barings to collapse, no matter how shocking that would be. He told Baring and Tuckey that he could not commit the Bank to a rescue, but it would do its best to save it by any other means possible. The two men left to return to Bishopsgate, and Pennant-Rea set about finding George to tell him the extraordinary news.

In Alvoriaz, as George walked up the steps of his skiing chalet he was greeted by a woman attendant telling him he was wanted on the phone. It was the first time he had managed a family holiday since being appointed governor, but as soon as he heard what Pennant-Rea had to say, he knew it was over before it had begun. He apologized to his wife and called a taxi to take him to Geneva airport. There was only one Swissair flight back to London, and although it was full, he argued his way on to it. As it cleared the clouds leaving the mountains behind, he reflected on what should be done. Like Pennant-Rea he could see no logical reason why a fraud perpetrated by one man should make depositors of other merchant banks believe that they too were likely to collapse. If Barings was sinking, the Bank would have to let it go down.

Back at 8 Bishopsgate Norris now knew for certain that Nick Leeson was not coming back. He had left a confused trail behind him. When Leeson's fellow floor traders had arrived for work at Simex in the morning, they had found a fax from Leeson saying that he and his wife had flown off to Phuket for the weekend to celebrate his birthday. But at 3.00 p.m. (7.00 a.m. London) Bax received a hand-written resignation note from Leeson, faxed from the Regent Hotel in Kuala Lumpur, 200 miles north-east of Singapore. 'My sincere apologies for the predicament that I have left you in. It was neither my intention or aim for this to happen, but the pressures, both business and personal, have become too much to bear and after receiving medical advice have affected my health to the extent that a breakdown is imminent,' Leeson wrote. The trader said he would contact Bax and Jones early the following week 'to discuss the best course of action'. Norris instructed Bax to fly to Kuala Lumpur and locate Leeson. Bax rushed to Singapore airport without any luggage and caught the first flight. In Kuala Lumpur he was driven to the Regent Hotel, speaking to Norris on a telephone as he went. When he arrived at the hotel he quizzed staff and found that Leeson and his wife had left three hours before the fax had been sent, leaving instructions for it to be transmitted later. Bax checked into a room there, buying a change of shirt and underwear from the hotel shop. He rang Norris to tell him the trail was cold. Norris told him to return to Singapore the next morning, and Bax lapsed into an exhausted sleep.

As Bax slept, the Bank of England was moving into action. Pennant-Rea and Quinn waited until the London Stock Exchange closed at 4.30 p.m., then sent out an alert. They knew many bankers would

33

be heading homewards for the weekend early on Friday evening. At 4.30 p.m. Bank officials started calling the fourteen biggest UK clearing banks and merchant banks, asking their chairmen or chief executives to attend a meeting at 5.30 p.m. No details were given of what it was about. A call went to Schroders, one of the most distinguished and reputedly best-managed merchant banks, which had had a good year in 1994. Like Barings, Schroders had done well in the 1980s, building up strong operations in Asia and restoring itself to the first tier of merchant banks. Unlike Barings, it was still largely owned by its founding family. It had been started by a German merchant, Johann Heinrich Schroder, in 1802 and about 40 per cent of the shares were held by Schroders and their relatives. It took a perverse pride in the shabbiness of its office block near the Bank on Cheapside, with lifts that hardly seemed to move and fraying carpets. The bank's chairman, George von Mallinckrodt, also had German roots, and was married to the sister of Bruno Schroder, the largest shareholder. Mallinckrodt was a trim, immaculately dressed man with a mischievous sense of humour, who loved his role as an ambassador for Schroders and the City, where he was known universally as 'Govi'. Like Barings, the bank had a non-family member as chief strategist. In Schroders' case it was Win Bischoff, the chief executive, a South African corporate financier who smoked large cigars.

Mallinckrodt and Bischoff were in a tricky meeting, deciding on the bonuses they would pay executives for 1994, but realized immediately the phone summons meant that it must be something serious. Bischoff wondered if Clarke was going to resign as chancellor because of some rift with John Major. The other obvious possibility was that a large bank was in trouble. The first thought was that it might be S. G. Warburg, a relative newcomer among merchant banks, having been founded by a German Jewish *émigré*, Siegmund Warburg, with his partner, Henry Grunfeld, after the Second World War. Warburg had grown into the biggest merchant bank by the early 1980s, with ambitions to stand alongside US investment banks such as Goldman Sachs. It had gone into a grand merger with two broking firms called Rowe & Pitman and Mullens, and a jobbing firm called Akroyd & Smithers in the mid-1980s. But Warburg had over-extended itself and become bloated. A few months before its profits had fallen because of rough financial markets, and it had tried to rescue itself by merging with Morgan Stanley. That merger had collapsed, and Lord Cairns, its chief executive, had resigned. Its chairman, Sir David Scholey, who in 1992 had been considered a possible rival to Eddie George to become governor of the Bank of England, had been forced to take up the helm. Mallinckrodt and Bischoff wondered if Warburg was in such a bad way that Sir David now needed help.

A call was also made to Sir Evelyn de Rothschild. Rothschild, an autocratic, short-tempered man, who had taken control of Rothschilds after a bitter row with his cousin Lord Rothschild, had a personal fortune of £1 billion and was the last of an old breed in the City. He not only controlled the majority of shares in his family's bank, N. M. Rothschild & Sons, through a Swiss company, but he also chaired it like a nineteenth-century merchant banker. Barings and Schroders might bear some of the characteristics of the family-controlled merchant banks, but N. M. Rothschild embodied them. Unlike the Barings and the Schroders, Sir Evelyn had not chosen a talented outsider to lead strategy. Perhaps as a result, Rothschild was no longer as powerful a rival to Barings as in the early nineteenth century, when the two were the strongest dual forces in the City. In 1818, Byron answered the rhetorical question in his poem *Don Juan*: 'Who hold the balance of the world? Who reign o'er congress, whether royalist or liberal?' with the line: 'Jew Rothschild, and his fellow-Christian, Baring'.[2] N. M. Rothschild & Sons had been founded by Nathan Meyer Rothschild, a dominant nineteenth-century City financier, in 1808. In 1890 his grandson 'Natty', the first Lord Rothschild, had at first resisted paying money to the Bank of England's guarantee fund, but had eventually given £500,000 under pressure from Lidderdale. So it was natural for the Bank to call on Sir Evelyn to seek help in rescuing Barings again. But, by coincidence, he was in Singapore on an Asian tour, and the call was taken instead by Bernie Myers, the bank's managing director.

The offices of N. M. Rothschild & Sons were still in New Court in St Swithin's Lane, where they had been since shortly after the bank was founded. It was only a stone's throw from the Bank of England so Myers put on a coat and set off on foot to find out what was going on. As he drew near he could see familiar faces converging on the Bank. One was Sir Chippendale Keswick, the deputy chairman of the family-controlled merchant bank Hambros. Like Bischoff at Schroders and Tuckey at Barings, 'Chips' Keswick was the non-family outsider who ran Hambros' merchant bank. The two men fell in step and started talking about what the call might mean. It must be a rescue, they agreed. But which bank was going down?

At the Bank the knot of bankers were shown to an elegant octagonal room on the first floor called the Committee Room, by the Court Room where the Bank's directors meet. Both rooms were designed by the architect Roger Taylor in 1774, and had been on the ground floor in Soane's original Bank of England. When the Bank was enlarged in the 1930s, they were taken apart and rebuilt on the first floor. The Committee Room was ornately decorated, with a twenty-three-foot-high ceiling. It had plastered walls decorated with three friezes of Roman figures called Honos, Moneta and Securitas Publica and was dominated by a thirty-five-piece chandelier made in 1770, which hung low over a blue baize-covered table. It was an intimidating place and the air of tension was heightened by the loud ticking of a gold-leafed clock set in the wall above the Egyptian marble fireplace.

The bankers gathered in the room were the heart of the City's establishment. They included leaders not only of the merchant banks but the clearing banks such as Barclays and National Westminster, which had also contributed to the 1890 rescue of Barings. Scholey was there, which reassured those who had wondered about Warburg. But what else could it be? The bankers did not have long to wait. Pennant-Rea and Quinn walked briskly into the room with two officials. 'I have some sad news,' said Pennant-Rea. He outlined what had happened, and said the Bank was likely to call on them again to save Barings as their forerunners had done a century before. They were asked to leave telephone numbers where they could be contacted the next day, and after just half an hour the meeting finished. Quickly the bankers dispersed back to their offices. It was tempting to carry on gossiping but they could not stand around on Threadneedle Street without attracting attention and they had work to do. Several knew they might be at risk if Barings collapsed. Some traded on the Singapore and Osaka futures exchanges and others had lent money to Barings. They had to find out the risks to which they were exposed. The merchant bank chairmen knew they had the biggest problem. They were grouped together with Barings in the minds of investors and depositors. If Barings collapsed, who would want to lend money to another merchant bank or own its shares? Mallinckrodt and Scholey returned to their separate offices from the Bank worrying about what damage might be caused to them by Barings' failure.

As the City started to buzz with the bizarre news about Barings, Tuckey and Peter Baring had reached a decision on the eighteenth floor of 8 Bishopsgate. The two men had returned to the Bank at 3.00 p.m. to meet Pennant-Rea and Quinn again. Pennant-Rea had told them the Bank would not put up public money to save Barings. Now Baring and Tuckey knew it was time to abandon their last faint hope that Barings could stay independent. A team of corporate financiers had been working all day to gather information about Barings for potential buyers. As evening fell Tuckey was sitting in his office with Baring. It was a large room with a set of green armchairs and a sofa to receive guests. Tuckey had a painting next to his desk of a young girl in a light-blue dress clutching at her hat on a cliff-top. It was a carefree image, a reminder of calm in moments of stress. By his sofa were two glass cases containing wooden models of a ship, the *Norman Court*, the last trading vessel owned by Barings, which used to sail from Britain to Yokohama in Japan, via Hong Kong, in the nineteenth century but had sunk off the Welsh coast in 1870. Tuckey picked up the telephone and rang Jan Kalff, the chairman of the Dutch bank ABN Amro, which had old ties with Barings. Barings had formed links in the eighteenth century with the Dutch merchant bank Hope and Co., which became Bank Mees and Hope, owned by ABN Amro.[3] It also owned the London broking firm Hoare Govett, and Tuckey knew that Kalff was interested in buying a merchant bank to create a fully fledged investment bank.

Kalff was not in his office because he was on the way to catch a flight for Asia, but Tuckey caught him on his car telephone as he neared Amsterdam airport. Kalff was very enthusiastic. This could be the chance he had been looking for, and he told Tuckey he would send some managers overnight to London. Tuckey thought the Dutch were likely to be congenial owners but, as a precaution, he also called Smith Barney and Merrill Lynch, two large US investment banks that wanted to expand in Europe.

At the Bank Pennant-Rea had his own worries. Although the Bank was a grand force in the City, it was not the all-powerful body it seemed. George had been trying to gain more independence but the

Bank remained under the control of the Treasury. It could not take its own decision on whether to rescue Barings with public cash. An argument had broken out between the Bank and the Treasury in 1984 after the Bank committed money to rescuing a bank called Johnson Matthey Bankers before consulting the Treasury. The senior civil servant at the Treasury was Sir Terry Burns, a northerner who had been brought up near Sunderland and who got on well with Kenneth Clarke, partly because both prided themselves on being blunt outsiders. They also shared an interest in football: Burns supported Queens Park Rangers, the west London team, while Clarke was a fan of his home-town team, Nottingham Forest. The two had arranged to go to a match that weekend between the two teams at QPR's ground, and Burns was looking forward to his day out.

At 4.30 p.m. Pennant-Rea had phoned Burns to brief him. Burns took the call in his high-ceilinged office in the Treasury, opposite the Houses of Parliament. Pennant-Rea told him the Bank was unlikely to ask for public money to rescue Barings. Instead it was going to try to persuade British banks to cooperate in a private rescue. That was a relief for Burns, but he realized none the less that the government could face a serious crisis. If Barings collapsed, there might be a crisis of confidence in the City. Not only might other banks be at risk but London's reputation might be damaged and there could also be damaging repercussions on Britain's relations with Singapore. Both Clarke and John Major, the prime minister, would have to be told as quickly as possible. There was no problem with Major. Burns met Alex Allan, Major's principal private secretary, every Friday at 5.30 p.m. to review the events of the week and discuss things that were coming up. It was generally a relaxed affair, though this time it would be different. Letting Clarke know was more tricky. The chancellor, a carefree politician who preferred to think on his feet rather than spend hours worrying over every problem, had sped off to Dorneywood, his official residence in Buckinghamshire, for the weekend. He was due to return on Sunday and meet Burns at QPR's ground so they could watch the football match together. But Clarke was driving his own red sports car, which had no telephone, so he was out of contact for two hours. Burns told Treasury officials to relay the news to Clarke as soon as he arrived at Dorneywood.

The mood was even more worried at the headquarters of the other merchant banks. When Mallinckrodt returned to Cheapside, he went to Bischoff's office to tell him the news. The two men reflected on the consequences for Schroders. It too relied on the mystique of being a City merchant bank. Like Barings, it did not have a lot of capital. If Barings was shown to be fragile, Schroders could suffer a loss of confidence. Mallinckrodt decided to test the waters to see if the merchant banks could rescue Barings. Meanwhile, Scholey had returned to Warburg's headquarters at Broadgate. He called some executives to his room to investigate how badly Warburg was exposed to Barings' collapse. Then he went to his bookshelf and pulled out a City history to remind himself of what had happened in 1890. His father, a City financier, had often told him the story of how Barings was only rescued when Lidderdale forced Lord Rothschild to contribute. That piece of history was also on the mind of Bernie Myers. He sat and waited in his office until 11.00 p.m. (7.00 a.m. in Singapore), when he could wake Evelyn de Rothschild in Singapore. Unlike most of those involved, de Rothschild owned a large part of his bank, so any money put up for Barings would be his own. But this time the Rothschild family did not hesitate. Just after midnight Scholey was woken at home by the telephone. It was de Rothschild, who had just spoken to Mallinckrodt after receiving a call from Myers. The two men had agreed that if necessary the merchant banks would try to rescue Barings themselves. 'If capital is needed, I am there with £50 million,' de Rothschild said.

By the early hours of Saturday 25 February Tuckey and Peter Baring were back at their homes trying to catch a few hours' sleep before resuming the effort to rescue Barings. They rose early to return to Bishopsgate. At 8.00 a.m., they met again in Baring's office. As merchant bankers they were accustomed to being called to advise companies in crisis. Now they had to seek help, and the obvious place to look was at another merchant bank. Baring picked up the telephone and rang Win Bischoff at home to ask Schroders to be Barings' adviser for the weekend. By 9.30 a.m. two corporate financiers from Schroders had arrived at Bishopsgate for a summit with Baring, Tuckey, Norris, Pennant-Rea and Eddie George. It was the first chance for George to find out at first-hand what was happening. He had arrived home at 11.30 p.m. the previous night and poured himself a stiff drink. The futures losses now stood at £385 million after a further fall in the

Nikkei index on Friday afternoon. The good news was that Hawes had now located the full profit and loss statement for the five eights account, which seemed to show that Leeson had gained more than enough initial premium from selling the options to offset these losses since the Kobe earthquake. They remained in profit by £1.3 million, although a further fall in the Nikkei could put them into loss. It appeared unlikely Barings could keep its plight secret for long since most London bankers now knew about it. As news spread it might lead to panic on the Tokyo market on Monday. Unless something was done by then Barings stood to lose millions more on the contracts Leeson had abandoned.

There was no chance that the bank could be rescued by its owners because the Baring Foundation was a charitable trust; nor was there a chance of British taxpayers footing the bill. George made it clear that he agreed with Pennant-Rea that a rescue would have to be carried out without government assistance. That meant persuading someone to buy a bank that probably had no capital left. They had until midnight on Sunday night to do it, because that was when the Tokyo market opened. It looked like a hopeless proposition but there was one thing on their side. Earlier that week many banks would have jumped at the chance to buy Barings. If they could neutralize the mess left by Leeson and find a temporary means of keeping Barings afloat, they could probably find a buyer. This involved three tasks: finding some capital to replace the Baring Foundation shares, dealing with the five eights account, and locating a buyer to take Barings over permanently. They agreed to split the tasks: Schroders would raise the money to recapitalize Barings. It would contact the bankers who had met the previous evening and try to persuade them to band together to lend money for fresh capital. Tuckey and Peter Baring would negotiate with potential buyers, who had started arriving at 8 Bishopsgate. A group of executives from ABN Amro had just been shown to the eighteenth floor and been presented with twelve boxes of information on Barings, which included all the customary charts and figures on earnings and profits for a buyer to do 'due diligence', but with all the figures recalculated to exclude Baring Futures.

This left the futures and options in Account 88888, which were the worst problem. Something had to be done to bring these losses under control. Without that it would be impossible to get banks to inject fresh capital, because it would be swallowed up immediately as the Nikkei fell. But how could that be done? The most obvious way was to find the banks and investment funds that held the other sides of the futures. They had already made large profits from betting against Leeson. If the Nikkei fell further, they would make even more money. But George thought the Bank might be able to cajole them into closing the contracts, rather than undermining Barings further. It would only work if there were just a few banks involved and the Bank could contact them easily. If that failed, they would have to persuade someone else to take over the futures. The likeliest candidates were funds which already invested in the Japanese market and would have most to lose from the Nikkei falling further. George said that the Bank might be able to sound out Japanese pension and investment funds through the Bank of Japan, the country's central bank. Finally, there was an outside chance that somebody could be persuaded to take a bet that the Nikkei index would bounce back, and Leeson's futures would be worth holding. But since there were almost bound to be some further losses, whoever took such a bet would demand to be paid enough to make it worthwhile. It would be like selling an option on the Nikkei. In return for an initial fee the investor would take on the risk of a further fall in the value of the futures and options.

It looked pretty far-fetched that they could pull off such a coup within thirty-six hours but they had to try. In the meantime Norris would organize a means of transferring the futures to an investor with an appetite for risk, helped by Baker, who had arrived back from Verbier, still wearing brightly coloured ski gear and a pair of padded boots. By this time Norris had recovered from his initial shock and despondency, and the challenge of mounting a rescue was starting to revive him. It would require an astonishing deal involving the switch of a massive futures and options portfolio. 'If we pull it off, it will be the greatest derivatives trade the world has ever seen,' Norris exclaimed to Baker as they started work. Who could they persuade to take on such a huge risk? Few people in the world could contemplate it. They had to find somebody with a lot of capital and a lot of nerve. Although large banks had the capital to absorb such a risk, they had little appetite for it. More likely were the 'hedge funds' run by investors such as George Soros, which were given money by rich people, mainly millionaires in the US, on which they tried to make high returns.

Soros's Quantum Fund had become world-famous after he took a huge bet that sterling would be forced out of the European exchange rate mechanism in September 1992. The only other possibility seemed to be one of the world's richest investors, such as an oil billionaire. A single investor could take a rapid decision, which was vital. Barings had a head start because it had an asset management arm which earned money by managing the money of big funds.

But even if such an investor could be found, Barings would have to devise a way of managing the five eights account. Whoever took the risk was unlikely to want the fuss and bother of actually holding the derivatives and paying margin calls. Instead, the futures and options could be managed by an investment bank, with the risk passing to the investor through a contract known as a 'swap'. This was an agreement in which one side agreed to take over from the other the variable risk of a portfolio in return for a fixed reward. In this case, it would be an 'equity swap', because it would be based on the Nikkei. The bank would take on the futures from Barings and make all the margin payments as the Nikkei went up and down. It would agree a swap with the investor. If the futures lost money, he would pay the bill; if they gained money, the bank would pass on the profits. It would be a perfectly orthodox deal for any bank with experience of derivatives. The difficulty was that it would be one of the largest equity swaps ever agreed and it had to be struck within thirty-six hours.

Baker's first port of call was Chris Goekjian, the chief executive of Credit Suisse Financial Products, the biggest specialist derivatives firm in the world, based in Canary Wharf in the London Docklands. Baker knew Goekjian, a quiet, methodical man, who had worked with him at Bankers Trust, a US bank that made its name through pioneering complex derivatives. If anybody could manage the futures and options that Leeson had taken on, it would be an expert like Goekjian, who knew as much as any rocket scientist. Baker told Goekjian he had to discuss a large derivatives trade. 'Fine, just call us on Monday morning,' replied Goekjian. 'No, we must meet now,' Baker insisted. Goekjian did not want his weekend to be interrupted but agreed reluctantly to come into the City with another CSFP executive. They met Baker and Norris in Baker's office at 8 Bishopsgate at 6.00 p.m., to be told about Leeson's trading. Goekjian was astonished. He was used to dealing with large derivatives positions but not ones like this. The trading risk on Leeson's options alone from movements in the Nikkei was ten times greater than CSFP's entire limit for risk. That was before considering the futures. 'This is so big. It's unbelievable,' Goekjian said out loud. He wondered how a small bank relatively new to derivatives could have let any trader take risks on such a scale. It did not say much for the two men now standing in front of him, who had been in charge of Leeson, but Baker and Norris seemed unabashed. Norris was excitable and jittery. He kept coming up with new suggestions for the futures, like a corporate financier advising on a take-over. Baker was behaving as if he was absolutely confident that Barings would survive. He hinted that the Bank of England would not let the City's oldest merchant bank go down. 'We have a very close relationship with the Bank of England. We've been around for 200 years,' Baker kept saying. He told Goekjian that Barings was searching for an investor to take on the risk. He had been in contact with Bankers Trust as well. Would CSFP and Bankers Trust join forces on an equity swap?

Meanwhile, Win Bischoff had set to work trying to raise the money to keep Barings afloat for the next few weeks. He had been given a desk in 8 Bishopsgate and was settling down to the task, puffing at a big cigar. Bischoff had been told that the Leeson losses stood at £385 million, so he rounded it up to £400 million and pondered how to divide up the sum among the banks on his list. Clearing banks such as NatWest were a lot bigger, so they could afford to contribute much more. But the merchant banks had more to lose than Barings. Bischoff decided to ask the large banks for twice the amount the merchant banks would have to provide. Then he got on the telephone with the list of numbers provided by the Bank. He soon got into the swing of it. Passers-by could see him with his feet on the desk, working his way through the chairmen and chief executives of banks. He seemed to be enjoying himself enormously. Although Bischoff sympathized with Peter Baring and Andrew Tuckey, this was the most exciting drama in the City for years, and he was at the heart of it. He cajoled some chairmen and appealed to the loyalty of others. Soon the pledges were mounting up nicely towards £400 million. Many bankers had their own ideas for rescuing Barings. A few mooted buying parts of it. John Craven, a tough South African who chaired Morgan Grenfell, the merchant bank owned by Germany's biggest bank, Deutsche

Bank, said that he thought Baring Asset Management could fetch £600 million. Morgan Grenfell might even be interested in buying BAM, he added casually. In any case, he could be counted on for a contribution.

That afternoon David Verey, chairman of the small merchant bank Lazard Brothers, received a phone call at his home in Wiltshire. It was Nicholas Baring, Peter's elder brother, who had worked at the bank up to 1989 but had left to become chairman of the insurance company Commercial Union after Peter was made chairman over his head. Nicholas Baring was a more outgoing, imaginative man than Peter. In the 1970s he had sometimes been frustrated at the slow growth of Barings and had championed new ventures overseas. Hesitantly Baring said there was a problem he wanted to consult Verey about and asked whether he could drop by. When Baring arrived it transpired that he was in an odd position. He was the only trustee of the Baring Foundation around. His cousin, Lord Ashburton, chairman of the bank before Peter, was on holiday abroad. Nicholas asked if Lazard Brothers would act as the financial adviser to the Foundation. It was normal for a company's main shareholder to get financial advice from a merchant bank in the case of a take-over or a crisis. In such times everything normally turned on what the shareholder wanted, because it was the owner. Barings was different. Although it was owned by the Foundation, the executive directors retained voting shares which put them in control. Barings had paid out enough cash to the Foundation to allow it to distribute £67 million to charity since its formation in 1968.[4] But the directors had absolute freedom to run their own affairs. Verey began to realize that his new client had a great deal of interest in Barings' destiny, but virtually no power over it.

By mid-evening Bischoff was pleased at progress. He had gained pledges for £400 million from the bankers he had rung. It seemed that fresh equity could be provided to replace Leeson's losses. Those trying to solve the futures losses were in more difficulty. The Bank of England was losing hope of being able to reach a deal with the banks that held the other side of the futures contracts. An official who had flown out to Singapore had found that too many banks were involved to be able to strike a rapid agreement. There was no sign yet of an investor or hedge fund willing to take on the futures. Nor

44

were CSFP and Bankers Trust happy about undertaking such a large deal. Usually a bank making a swap with an investor would examine his credentials carefully to ensure he would not default on the deal. But with only twenty-four hours left until a deal had to be signed, Barings had not even located a potential investor. Other things worried Goekjian as well. He and his colleague had finished their meeting with Baker and Norris by 8.00 p.m. and left Bishopsgate. In the lift on the way down they started to confide their fears. Neither was sure they should deal with Barings. Baker and Norris had been responsible for allowing Barings to collapse. How could CSFP be sure the two men were trustworthy? Even if they were not implicated in Leeson's trading, they might be about to be dismissed. Furthermore, CSFP only had the word of Baker that the Bank of England was involved. It could not take on to its books a stunningly risky portfolio of futures and options just on the say-so of two discredited executives of a failing bank.

The two CSFP executives were ushered out of a rear door of 8 Bishopsgate as reporters and photographers gathered at the front of the building. The news about Barings' troubles had not taken long to filter out. Early editions of the *Sunday Telegraph* were going on sale at news-stands in central London with the first details. Newspapers were frantically trying to piece together what had happened. But on the eighteenth floor Tuckey and Baring were still not sure. Even a day after the discovery they could make no sense of it. Sometimes traders made losses which they tried to hide for a time, but they always confessed when the sums got to frightening levels, usually a few hundred thousand pounds or even £1 million. Nobody went blindly on as Leeson had done, as losses mounted into hundreds of millions. The hidden trading must have been deliberate. But why? It would have been easy to explain if Leeson had taken money from Barings, but Hawes had found no sign of cash being transferred out of Baring Futures. It brought them back to the story of Customer X, with which Baker and Norris were familiar. It had now assumed sinister overtones. Perhaps Leeson had been trading futures and options for him, and when the deals went wrong, they had been transferred to a Barings account. Customer X might have paid Leeson to ditch the futures and abscond before they were discovered. Or perhaps he had reached a deal with Customer X. Leeson would hide loss-making trades in Account 88888 and Customer X would take all the profits. They might even now be sharing the proceeds.

At 8.00 a.m. on Sunday morning Peter Baring, Tuckey, Bischoff, Norris and Eddie George met again on the eighteenth floor at 8 Bishopsgate to discuss progress. There was still no solution for the futures in the five eights account. But they had not given up. George was awaiting word from the Bank of Japan on whether investment funds in Tokyo would take them. There was better news from Bischoff, who was confident that the British banks would contribute £400 million to prop up Barings. Bank chairmen and chief executives had been called to another meeting at the Bank of England in a couple of hours' time to hammer out a final agreement. But Bischoff's tidings did not get the enthusiastic reception he had anticipated. 'Thank you very much, but it may be academic now,' said George. Another shock had just come from Singapore. Hawes had been analysing Baring Futures' accounts, and had found that the options in Account 88888 were more threatening than they had seemed initially. Leeson's straddles were in loss by about £200 million because of the fall in the Nikkei. This sum was more than covered by the premium he had got for the sale of options, so the Simex accounts showed a £1.3 million profit. But it now transpired that Leeson had been using the option premium to balance losses in the five eights account. He had counted the premium as pure profit, without adjusting the figures to show the sum he would eventually have to pay to traders who had bought options from him. Barings would have to pay the bill not only for £385 million of futures losses, but for a further £200 million of options losses Leeson had concealed in the accounts.

Bischoff knew immediately this was very bad news. It was not only that the losses were 50 per cent higher than had been estimated. As importantly, it would undermine Barings' credibility with the bankers they were due to meet at 10.00 a.m. When he had talked to the bankers the previous night, several had emphasized that they would only put in money if they were certain it would not be eaten up by further losses. 'We must know this is not the tip of an iceberg,' Craven had said. It could also undermine efforts to sell Barings. The executives from ABN Amro were still at 8 Bishopsgate and seemed to be interested in buying the bank, but the discovery might also put them off. But there was nothing Bischoff could do. The meeting at the

Bank was approaching fast. He had no time even to adjust Schroders' charts drawn to show how Barings could be rescued, which referred to a £385 million loss. One of Schroders' corporate finance team hastily scribbled a new sum on the relevant page. Meanwhile, the Bank of England had received its own setback. The Bank of Japan's governor had rung Pennant-Rea to say the Japanese authorities could not organize a rescue. The Ministry of Finance, which might have twisted arms to ensure that Japanese pension funds took on the futures and options, did not want to risk Japanese public money and was not convinced that the Nikkei would fall drastically as a result of Barings' collapse. The odds appeared to be shifting away from a rescue. With only a few hours left until the midnight deadline, Barings urgently needed a helping hand from the City's most powerful banks once again.

Despite these problems there were still faint hopes that an investor could be found to take over the futures and options. The news had spread round the world and Barings was now getting some strange offers of help. One was from a small London investment firm that claimed to be acting for Tommy Suharto, son of the president of Indonesia. It said Suharto had 1,260 tonnes of platinum held with Union Bank of Switzerland in Basle, worth $17 billion.[5] The precious metal could be used as collateral against loans to recapitalize Barings. Norris was bemused at the idea but agreed to see Suharto's representative. Another possibility, which also seemed highly unlikely, was the Sultan of Brunei, an enclave on the Borneo coast, 600 miles east of Singapore. Brunei's oil reserves had given the Sultan a fortune of $30 billion. Baring Asset Management had invested some of the money managed by the Brunei Investment Agency in the past. It had voluntarily given up the contract in 1994 because the BIA had asked fund managers to bear the risk of keeping its investments in custody. But Roger Davies, a partner of Allen & Overy, the City law firm which carried out work for the BIA, had rung Barings after reading about the fraud in the Sunday newspapers to see if it could help. He had now set off for 8 Bishopsgate and was talking to John Bolsover, the chairman of BAM, on his car telephone. When Davies arrived he was moved briskly to the head of the queue of potential buyers and financial advisers collecting in the corridors of 8 Bishopsgate.

Bankers had already been gathering around the City to prepare for the 10.00 a.m. meeting. Several had been asked to come to the back door of the Bank in Lothbury so they would not be seen entering, but when Scholey turned up at the large iron gates he found them firmly locked. He went round to the front door, joining others now entering the Bank. Once again they were escorted to the octagonal Committee Room, where a few bankers who could not be located at short notice on Friday were already gathered. They included Andrew Buxton, the chairman of Barclays, a tall, shy man, who had only just survived a crisis at Barclays two years earlier when it made a loss of £242 million because of poor property lending. It had been humiliating but he had hung on, and he took his place near the head of the table as befitting the chairman of Britain's biggest bank. There were about twenty-five bankers, most of whom had known Baring and Tuckey for years and respected them. They were all aware disaster could strike anywhere. Patrick Gillam, chairman of Standard Chartered, had been appointed in 1993 after the bank lost £293 million in a securities fraud in India. But there were some tensions. Clearing bankers and merchant bankers were suspicious of each other. Clearing bankers thought of merchant bankers as snobbish, overpaid financiers, still living off a glorious past; in contrast, many merchant bankers saw clearing bankers as bureaucratic money lenders who were lacking in imagination and flair.

At 10.00 a.m. George walked in with Quinn, followed by Baring, Norris, Tuckey and Bolsover from Barings, and the advisers from Schroders and Lazard Brothers. The City's attempt to repeat the 1890 rescue of Barings had begun. George opened with an apology that the Bank could not provide its usual grand lunch because the kitchen was closed and so were the sandwich bars in the City, but it would try to lay on something. Then he described what they knew so far: Barings appeared to have been the victim of a 'rogue trader' in Singapore. The bankers already knew about the losses discovered on Friday. These had now worsened and stood at £600 million. Despite an intake of breath from around the table, George said he believed all the losses had now been discovered and added that they needed to do three things: sort out the futures and options, provide new capital for Barings and make sure depositors did not withdraw their cash on Monday. The last of these was easiest because the Bank was prepared to stand behind Barings' deposits, provided that Barings had been recapitalized.

The first appeared to be hardest. George explained that the Bank had been trying to find someone to take on the futures and options but without success. Negotiations were now taking place with what he called 'an Islamic investor'. Bolsover and Tuckey had told him about the Brunei Investment Agency, although it seemed highly unlikely that a deal would be struck. George emphasized there was no guarantee of a deal. They had to discuss first whether the banks would take on Barings' derivatives.

With the loss already so big, George explained Barings could not afford to pay more than £200 million to whoever would take on the futures and options. This was equivalent to a 4 per cent movement in the Nikkei. In effect, whoever took them would be making a bet that the Nikkei would fall less than 4 per cent when the Japanese stock market opened at midnight. All it needed was strong nerves, and deep pockets. By this time the bankers were deeply worried. Some were from merchant banks and others from high street banks but they had one thing in common: they knew very little about derivatives. Barings had already lost a lot of money and stood to lose more when the Japanese market opened. Some had seen a report on the Bloomberg financial news wire saying the Nikkei could fall 10 per cent. The losses had risen by £200 million already and who knew how much higher they could grow. Murmurs of disquiet rumbled around the table. Then David Band, the Scots chief executive of the investment bank Barclays de Zoete Wedd, spoke up from between Buxton and Scholey. 'If we stand behind an open-ended position like this, we will just get shot at by hedge funds,' he warned, and reminded them of what had happened in September 1992 when George Soros had bet massively against sterling and made a huge profit. The funds would know the futures were held by the banks, and it would encourage them to take opposing bets, forcing down the Nikkei and escalating the losses. The vision of Soros fighting against them only unnerved them further. After a short discussion they ruled out taking over Barings' derivatives.

George accepted the decision without arguing. He had not thought the banks were likely to relieve him of his most difficult problem. The vital task was to persuade them to chip in not only the £400 million they had already informally promised but a further £200 million as well. If they would lend Barings £600 million for three months, that would give it time to find a buyer and repay the money with interest. But no bank was going to lend money without being sure they would get it back, so the bankers had to be shown that Barings was still worth that amount. George introduced Peter Baring, who opened his mouth for the first time since coming into the room. Baring quietly thanked them for coming, and told them that Norris would explain Barings' corporate finance and stockbroking arms and would be followed by a summary of BAM by Bolsover.

Norris referred to a set of charts drawn up by the corporate financiers of 8 Bishopsgate which explained the earnings of Baring Brothers and Baring Securities during 1994. By this time he had been awake for seventy-five hours. He had recovered from the initial shock of the discovery and was operating on adrenalin. His natural self-confidence had revived, and he wanted to show what a fine investment bank Barings had become. But Norris was making a bad error. Like all bankers being asked to lend money to someone who has wasted it, the chairmen gathered around the table wanted to see a bit of humility. Some of those under them had dealt with Norris in the past and found him insufferably arrogant. Now they wanted to hear him apologize for what he had allowed to happen.

They did not get that satisfaction. Norris seemed completely unabashed as he talked about how Baring Brothers and Baring Securities had grown, and enthused about the 'superlative and growing' corporate finance business. It was too much for several bankers to stomach and they listened in icy silence. But this irritated mood turned to outrage as they looked at the figures on the first chart. They showed that after taking out Leeson's profits, Barings intended to declare a pre-tax profit of £83 million for 1994 while paying bonuses to its staff of £84 million.[6] This seemed utterly unbelievable to the heads of clearing banks. Their suspicion of merchant bankers had been confirmed more strongly than they could have imagined. The directors of Barings were paying themselves and their staff more than they declared in profits. Even the heads of other merchant banks were taken aback. They were used to handing out between a quarter and a third of profits in bonuses. John Manser, chief executive of Flemings, a family-owned merchant bank that had always been a rival of Barings, idly estimated how much he would have had to pay his own staff under Barings' formula.

After Norris had finished, Bolsover started his presentation. He was a tall, energetic figure who had built up BAM into a leading British fund manager after being recruited by Tuckey in 1976. He, too, was outspoken and had as big a reputation for arrogance as Norris. He also made an upbeat presentation on its strengths, emphasizing that BAM would have to pay bonuses, due on Tuesday, or its star employees would leave and the value of the business would fall.

Even as the bankers were digesting this, they were given an even larger shock. Some were wondering if the problem of the futures could not be solved quite simply. All Leeson's futures and options were in an account at Baring Futures. Why not just cut it adrift and refuse to pay? Baring Futures would collapse but the rest of the Barings group would survive. Manser asked Norris whether this could be used as a way of escaping from further losses, but Norris explained that it was impossible because Barings had already met margin calls on Leeson's trading of more than £700 million. The bankers were amazed. They had been told that Leeson had hidden all his futures and options in a secret account but here was the man in charge of investment banking saying they had paid £700 million to cover trading they did not even know had existed. What sort of outfit was he running? By this time, most of the bankers' previous goodwill towards Barings had evaporated. They were being asked to risk their shareholders' money to rescue a bank which had paid inflated bonuses to directors who were so ignorant of what was going on under their noses that they had handed £700 million over to a crooked trader to help him defraud them. Some of the clearing bankers reflected that if this was how the City's merchant banks ran their affairs, perhaps it would be better to let them collapse. When the questions finished it was getting on for 12.30 p.m., and George said that they would leave the bankers alone to decide on whether they would lend the cash. His staff had rustled up some sandwiches that would be served next door.

Meanwhile, George and Pennant-Rea had an appointment with the chancellor, who had driven back that morning to Downing Street to decide what to do about Barings. Like Lidderdale in 1890, George and Pennant-Rea drove over to Westminster to see the chancellor. They met Clarke and Burns in the chancellor's private flat at the top of 11 Downing Street at 1.15 p.m., with other Treasury officials. It was quickly established that the Bank was not going to ask the Treasury for public money to rescue Barings. George said the Bank had not found a way to deal with the derivatives, even if the banks were willing to lend £600 million. It now seemed likely that Barings would fail, with unknown consequences for the City of London. There could be a loss of confidence in other merchant banks and the Bank would have to try to persuade depositors not to withdraw their money. A collapse could also disrupt other banks in Singapore that had traded with Leeson. That might damage Singapore's relations with Britain, which were touchy at the best of times because of its history as a former British colony. This incident was almost bound to embarrass and damage not only Barings but the City, and probably the Bank of England and the government as well. It was a gloomy prospect but Clarke was determined not to let it ruin his day. The Bank of England still had a few hours to try to rescue Barings and no decision was likely until at least 8.00 p.m. That meant that he had a few hours spare before the crisis erupted. He and Burns might as well spend their time enjoyably by watching football.

Back at the Bank the bankers had returned to the Committee Room after lunch. At first there was an awkward silence and some shuffling of papers as they wondered how to proceed. Most were used to being in charge but in this meeting everybody was on an equal footing. After a few moments Buxton decided he should try to organize things since he was chairman of the biggest bank. He asked if the others would go ahead with lending £600 million in view of everything they had heard. By now there was little enthusiasm for Barings but most agreed to try, if only for their own good. Scholey and the other merchant bankers knew how much damage could be caused by the collapse of Barings. Buxton started trying to fix the sum that each should contribute. On a scrap of paper he divided those in the room into clearing banks, and large and small merchant banks. He reckoned that they would have enough if the clearing banks gave £60 million each, big merchant banks gave £30 million each and small merchant banks gave £10 million or £15 million each. Then he started to work his way around the table. All went smoothly until he got to Patrick Gillam of Standard Chartered. Gillam was not a banker by training, having been managing director of British Petroleum before coming to Standard Chartered, and did not think much of a bankers' club

52

rescuing one of its own, using shareholders' money. He said he could not promise any money for Barings because he lacked authority from his board of directors. Despite Buxton's urging he refused to commit more than £10 million, although his bank was among the larger ones.

Undaunted, Buxton carried on round the table. Then he came to Lord Rockley, chairman of Kleinwort Benson, one of the oldest merchant banks. Rockley was genial company but he was tougher than he seemed. One of his first acts on being made chairman had been to persuade his chief executive to resign. Now Buxton faced a distinct problem for it seemed that even a fellow merchant bank was unwilling to help. 'We would prefer not to participate,' Lord Rockley said.

'Not for any amount?' Buxton asked.

'Perhaps a small sum,' Rockley replied.

There was a pause as the other bankers waited to see if Kleinwort would be allowed to get away with this. 'Right,' said Buxton firmly. 'Well, for small, I will read £30 million.'

He scribbled the sum down on his sheet of paper and passed on to the next banker in line. With that the tension in the room eased as others realized it would be too awkward to follow Rockley and Gillam's example. Buxton finished his impromptu whip-round and added up the figures, putting down £30 million for Standard Chartered. It came to £640 million, which was plenty to provide fresh capital for Barings. But after hearing of how Norris and the others had failed to control Leeson, the bankers did not want to rescue Barings, they wanted to take it over and ensure it was run properly. They agreed to replace Peter Baring as chairman of the bank with somebody they knew and trusted, such as the former chairman of Lloyds Bank, Sir Jeremy Morse. They also agreed to appoint their own directors. Whatever happened to Barings, by Monday it was not going to be managed by its current directors.

Schroders had suggested a generous reward for the banks taking part: they would get an immediate fee of 5 per cent and 1 per cent extra for each month it took to find a buyer, giving them a £48 million fee for a three-month loan. Baring had then appealed to the bankers and suggested this reward should be enough. If they sold it for more than £600 million after thee months, all the extra money should go to the Foundation. But the bankers did not have any patience with a shareholder, even if it was a charitable trust, that had let the management ruin the bank. They rejected this, deciding to keep any profit. Then they talked about the bonuses that had irked them. Some clearing bankers did not want to pay bonuses at all, but the merchant bankers said that would be foolish. Craven argued that if the bonuses were not paid, all of the staff would leave and Barings would be worthless. 'Well, if we pay them on Tuesday, they'll leave on Wednesday,' said Myers. The bankers agreed that bonuses would be paid in stages and executives such as Tuckey would not get anything. Manser then suggested they reach a gentlemen's agreement not to try to poach employees from Barings, since they would be its new owners, but others dismissed the idea, saying it would merely allow foreign banks to recruit the best ones instead. The era of being able to enforce gentlemen's agreements in the City had long gone, if it had ever existed. 'Only a suggestion,' said Manser, accepting defeat. The City's bankers had dug into their pockets to finance a rescue of Barings, but they would only do so on terms that brought them handsome rewards.

Over in west London Clarke and Burns were arriving at Loftus Road for the football match. Burns had driven them in his car because it had a phone that allowed them to keep in touch. Just before they parked Burns had been speaking to the Bank of England and had detected a shift in the atmosphere. Suddenly the notion that Barings would be rescued was becoming less far-fetched. News had reached 8 Bishopsgate of the bankers' offer of £640 million. But more importantly, the Sultan of Brunei had turned from an outside hope into a real chance. Davies, the lawyer from Allen & Overy who represented the Brunei Investment Agency, was sitting in Tuckey's office talking about taking over the futures for the £200 million fee the Bank had suggested. The BIA was also thinking of going further and taking part in the rescue package. The agency might contribute £300 million towards the £600 million needed to recapitalize the bank. In return it would have the right to convert its loan into a 50.1 per cent equity stake after three months. It would be able to buy out the banks' £300 million loan, making the Sultan Barings' sole owner. But this news was not going to stop Clarke watching football. He settled contentedly in his seat in the directors' box as the whistle blew for the kick-off at 4.00 p.m. Burns was feeling less at ease. The match was being televised, and Burns wondered about the headlines the next morning if the

Chancellor of the Exchequer was observed by millions of television viewers cheering on Nottingham Forest while a City merchant bank fought for survival.

At 8 Bishopsgate the mood lightened as news of the Brunei Investment Agency's interest spread. ABN Amro seemed to have cooled off after being rebuffed earlier at the Bank of England. Its managers had tried to take part in the bank meeting but Buxton had refused permission because they would not promise to contribute to the rescue fund. As dusk fell, all efforts concentrated on ensuring that the world's richest man rescued Barings. The first problem was to draw up an agreement. Given the sums involved and all the complications, it would take hundreds of pages to describe the deal fully. The Sultan might have to be woken up to approve it because it was already the early hours of Monday morning in Brunei, but his advisers did not want to bore him with details. Meanwhile, it was being considered by a four-man committee led by the Sultan's younger brother, Prince Jefri Bolkiah, the finance minister of Brunei, who was known as an international playboy. The Sultan was forty-nine and had been trained at Sandhurst, the military academy. The Brunei royal family was still close to Britain, although Britain had ceded full sovereignty in 1984. The Sultan's father had even built a museum to Sir Winston Churchill, the wartime British prime minister, in Brunei. Between them, the Sultan and his brother owned three large houses in Hampstead, one of which was being transformed into a gymnasium. Prince Jefri had also paid £55 million to buy the former Playboy Club in Mayfair in 1992, which he was converting into a home. There was at least some hope that the Sultan would splash out on a merchant bank as well.

Half-time in the match came at 4.45 p.m. and Burns hurried to the telephone to check on progress. He got through to Pennant-Rea, who could hear the huge QPR crowd roaring in the background as he spoke. Pennant-Rea told Burns that there might be a breakthrough. The only obstacle was that CSFP and Bankers Trust had insisted on the Bank of England standing behind the deal because Goekjian wanted to be insured against the possibility of the Sultan pulling out. Pennant-Rea told him of the terms on offer and said he would fax over details in an hour. Clarke would then have to decide if it was an acceptable risk. Clarke and Burns mulled over the development as they waited for the second half to begin. It still seemed improbable that Barings would be rescued by the Sultan, but then nothing in this affair so far had been very likely. In any case they did not have to make an immediate decision. They could watch some more football.

At 8 Bishopsgate the mood on the eighteenth floor was improving rapidly. The advisers from Schroders had written the terms of agreement on the single sheet of paper wanted in Brunei and it had been sent by fax. There appeared to be a decent chance that the bank would escape collapse. Jim Peers, Barings' company secretary, started to feel so confident that he went to the twentieth floor to tell the team of receivers from Ernst and Young, the accounting firm, who were standing by ready to take over management of the bank if it was put in administration, that they would probably not be needed after all.

In the office of the Baring Foundation, the feeling was less buoyant. Lord Ashburton had now returned and several trustees had gathered to discuss what to do. In theory, they could attempt to assert their will by going to court and arguing for control of the bank to be transferred to them. But that would be an open declaration of hostility, pitting two members of the Baring family as trustees against another as chairman, and the option was rejected with little discussion. It was alien to all the Baring family stood for to lapse into a squabble when crisis struck. They had instead tried to keep in touch with what was happening two floors below. Verey was by now sending one of them to the lavatory every fifteen minutes to pick up snippets of gossip. It was a bizarre position for Ashburton, who had selected Peter Baring to succeed him as chairman of Barings, but he did not let any resentment show. It had been a grey day, but as twilight fell, the sun sank in flaming red over the Bank of England. Verey and Ashburton stood looking out over the City, reflecting on the strange fact that a bank that had survived so long might disappear overnight. At 5.00 p.m. the trustees met Peter Baring, Tuckey and Eddie George on the nineteenth floor. It was a restrained occasion. Lord Ashburton talked calmly about the legal position of the Foundation if Barings collapsed. There was no flicker of recrimination or anger that Peter Baring had allowed the disaster to occur. Outsiders looked on as Peter, Nicholas and John Baring courteously discussed how to dismember the bank that had always borne their name.

At 5.45 p.m. the QPR–Nottingham Forest match ended with honours evenly distributed in a 1–1 draw. In the directors' box Clarke and Burns awaited a fax from the Bank. The details were not yet complete, and they had to hang around until 6.30 p.m. before the terms of the agreement with Brunei came through. It was now fast approaching the deadline for a deal. Burns and Clarke took the paper, and set off eastwards across London towards Downing Street. As they drove, Clarke agreed on the telephone that the Bank could guarantee the deal if the Sultan assented. At 7.00 p.m. the chairmen and chief executives of the British banks returned to the Bank of England and reconvened in the first-floor Committee Room. Eddie George walked in looking a lot more cheerful than when they had last seen him. He outlined the deal now on the table. The 'investor', as he called the Sultan, would contribute £300 million to a rescue and the banks would only have to provide £350 million. Attractively for the banks, his cash would be written off before theirs if any further problems were uncovered. Buxton went round the table again, scaling back contributions. Patrick Gillam of Standard Chartered still protested, but most bankers were content at the new arrangement which involved less risk. By this time George had also obtained money from the two Scottish banks, Royal Bank of Scotland and Bank of Scotland, which had not been at the morning meeting, having managed to persuade George Mathewson, the chief executive of Royal Bank, during a telephone conversation as Mathewson drove to Edinburgh from his house in Perthshire.

Now all the elements were in place for a deal. All that was required was assent from the Sultan. There were only a few minutes until the first deadline of 8.00 p.m., when the Sydney stock exchange opened. All hopes were now pinned on Brunei. The alternatives had failed. Around the world, banks waited to find out whether Barings would be saved or chaos would break out in the financial markets. At 8.00 p.m. the answer came back: no. Prince Jefri and his group believed the risks were large and there wasn't time to consider a deal properly. The Sultan was fast asleep and they had decided not to wake him up. At 8 Bishopsgate, advisers watched directors of Barings disappear into Tuckey's room to be given the news that the bank had collapsed. Peers returned to the twentieth floor to find the administrators from Ernst and Young, leading them down to see Peter Baring, who told them that he intended to seek a court order to put Barings into administration. At 8.36 p.m. George returned to the Committee

Room with Peter Baring, as the bankers were debating the principle of a rescue. David Band of BZW was arguing that to rescue every bank in trouble merely encouraged sloppy management. Band was cut off in mid-sentence. 'I am sorry, gentlemen, but our investor has decided not to proceed,' said George. Baring stood up to make a brief speech, thanking them for their efforts. He seemed as calm and considered as ever, even in the moment of collapse. All their efforts had come to nothing. As he left, Peter Norris leaned forward in his chair near where Baring had been speaking, buried his head in his hands and wept.

The reaction was harder-headed among the brokers and traders of Baring Securities at America Square. The fourth-floor trading room was by now crowded with people, most of whom had enjoyed working at Baring Securities, especially in its heyday in the late 1980s when earnings from Japan had been so large that several of them had earned annual bonuses of more than £1 million. They had been good at spending it too. Heath had always quizzed potential employees closely to find out if they liked spending. He did not want employees who put their earnings in the bank. Big spenders would be eager to earn more and would work harder. The firm had been a glittering example of the excesses of the 1980s. But now the party was over. At 9.00 p.m. somebody shouted the news across the floor that Barings had collapsed. It caused pandemonium. The traders were used to reacting instantly to shifts in markets. Now the job market had changed. All of them could be out of work tomorrow, seeking jobs at other firms. Their livelihood was in the investors to whom they sold shares, and the research documents on companies and markets that littered their desks. Panic broke out as they realized that administrators might be on their way at that moment, ready to impound the precious papers. There was a rush for the lifts and a crowd of traders streamed out into America Square clutching boxes full of files. On the fifth floor Norris's office now stood abandoned. The desk at which he had sat contentedly only three days before was still littered with papers and faxes from Singapore, displaying the secrets of the five eights account.

Norris himself had returned to 8 Bishopsgate. He had spent the last days in a desperate attempt to save Barings. Now his last act as chief executive was over and he had lost his company. All around him there was chaos in the corridors of the eighteenth floor. Barings' advisers, trustees and potential buyers mingled in a crowd with directors of the bank and hangers-on. A judge arrived to set up an impromptu court to hand ownership to the administrators. The bankers were dispersing into the night outside the Bank of England, hurrying back to their offices again to see what would happen when the stock market opened in Japan. Clarke and George were by now ensconced back in the chancellor's flat in Downing Street, waiting for news to emerge. The Bank of England was preparing a statement to explain why Barings had not been saved and to try to reassure financial markets. At 10.10 p.m. the news hit the financial wires. Burns could see it on his laptop computer which he was using to monitor all the news services. 'Barings has been the victim of losses caused by massive, unauthorized dealings by one of its traders in south-east Asia,' the Bank's statement started.

At home in Kensington Christopher Heath was following the news on television with a colleague who was visiting from the US. Despite the manner in which he had been treated by Barings, Heath was shocked and subdued at the news. Not everybody felt that way. The pair rang Andrew Baylis, who had been Heath's right-hand man in the 1980s and had been expelled at the same time. He was less dismayed by what had befallen Barings. 'They deserved everything they got,' he said.

CHAPTER 2

All Christopher Heath wanted was to have fun and make money. He was not getting much of either. There was a world of excitement out there somewhere, but it was hard to imagine from a desk in the plastics division of Imperial Chemical Industries. It was late 1968. Heath was twenty-two and itching to break free of the confines of ICI, Britain's biggest chemicals company. It felt like the last place an ambitious young man should work in the London of the swinging sixties. After four years at ICI he was getting paid £850 a year. At this rate he would never make real money. He could only watch in frustration as his school friends made their way in the City. That was where the real rewards lay, among the merchant bankers and money men. But the City was a stuffy place, full of men in pin-striped suits speaking the secret language of broking and jobbing. Heath had his eye on something that sounded a great deal more rewarding. Bernie Cornfeld's Investors Overseas Services, the financial phenomenon of the 1960s, was near the height of its fortunes. Who better to work for than the American whiz-kid who had amassed a fortune with a team of financial salesmen touting high-return investments? Newspapers carried photos of the bearded Cornfeld dressed in casual clothes, surrounded by glamorous dolly-birds. He was the financial world's equivalent of Hugh Hefner, whose Playboy empire was also expanding at the time. Cornfeld's IOS was now the largest fund management firm in the world.[1] Heath wondered how he could throw in his lot with this financial buccaneer.

Heath had joined ICI almost by chance. At Ampleforth College, the Catholic public school in Yorkshire, he had enjoyed himself but had not been particularly academic. His chief talents were for practical jokes and mimicking teachers. He had a short attention span and he used to amuse his friends by clowning around. He became an avid horse-racing fan and loved betting. Heath had no interest in going to university. He wanted to start earning money as quickly as possible. It was not just self-interest. He was an only child, although there were five children from his father's first marriage, and he wanted to support his mother, whose life had been very tough. She was the widow of General Sir Louis Heath, an army officer who was trapped with her in Singapore when the Japanese invaded in 1942. Christopher had not yet been born but the couple had a baby daughter. Lady Heath and her daughter were separated from her husband and locked up with other wives and children in Changi, a prisoner-of-war camp. Japanese soldiers treated even the families of prisoners-of-war extremely harshly. Lady Heath and her baby were so badly starved in Changi that the baby died, and Lady Heath herself weighed under five stone when she was released.

General Heath had fared even worse under the Japanese. He was transported with 2,600 prisoners to a camp called Kwarenko on the island of Formosa.[2] There were appalling conditions at the camp, which was rife with dysentery. General Heath was fifty-seven years old but was treated as ruthlessly as any of the younger prisoners. The Japanese guards insisted that, whatever the condition of the prisoners, they should always salute them. Those who failed to do so were beaten. As the result of a First World War injury General Heath had a withered arm that did not hang straight. One day a guard lost his temper and beat him with a bamboo cane for lack of respect in not straightening the arm to attention. He was so badly hurt that the blood vessels of one eye ruptured and he nearly lost it.

The couple were reunited after the war and Christopher was born in 1946, but General Heath never fully recovered from his treatment at the hands of the Japanese and died in 1954, leaving his wife £2,500. Lady Heath worked as a school matron to support herself and Christopher. They were assisted by being given the use of a grace and favour apartment at Hampton Court. Despite everything Lady Heath was not broken by her wartime experience. She was a strong-minded woman, who kept Christopher firmly in hand. He had no memory of the war, and one day was invited to a New Year's Eve party at the Japanese embassy. He enjoyed himself, drinking sake and mixing with Japanese expatriates. The following day he casually told his mother about his experience. She was appalled that he had supped with the old enemy. 'Christopher, how *could* you?' she asked despairingly.

When Heath was in his last year at school, a friend of his father's, Field Marshal Bill Slim, asked him to lunch at the Athenaeum in London. Slim, who had acted as a father figure to Heath after his father had died when he was eight, brought the conversation round to what Heath wanted to do with his life. The truth was that he had no idea. Slim promised that he could find Heath a job at National Bank of Australasia. If that did not interest him, there might be an opening at ICI. Heath was already armed with the results of a Vocational Guidance Association test that indicated that he had an accounting ability as high as a fully trained professional. It was enough to get him into ICI. He took an eye test and was pronounced colour-blind. Unable to work in the paints division, he had joined plastics. And there he was still, answering inquiries about chemicals and chasing payments. It was rather dull, and the idea of making a mark by selling shares for IOS was more appealing. Heath was on the edge of taking the plunge, when one day he was invited to a dinner party by the father of a girlfriend. He was seated next to a City stockbroker who started quizzing him on what he was doing and his ambitions. Heath confessed that he had been thinking of trying to join Cornfeld. 'That organization is going to go bust,' said the man briskly. Heath was intrigued at being given what sounded like an invaluable piece of inside information. The broker introduced himself as Denis Russell, a partner in a small stockbroking firm called George Henderson & Co. He said he was looking for new recruits and asked if Heath would be interested in joining. For a frustrated young ICI clerk it was a perfect opportunity. Within two months Christopher Heath was a stockbroker.

The firm that Heath joined in February 1969 had been formed by George Henderson after the 1914–18 war. It was jointly owned by its partners, who shared its profits between them. Denis Russell was the senior partner, partly through the good fortune of having married George Henderson's daughter. The offices of George Henderson & Co. were in Old Jewry, near the Bank of England and the Stock Exchange. It was a typical small broker which earned money by selling shares to investors. Brokers earned a fixed commission on every share they sold. George Henderson was an institutional broker, which meant that it mostly sold shares to investors such as pension funds or insurance firms, rather than to individuals. If one of these funds wanted to buy shares in a company like ICI, it would ring up a salesman at George Henderson and place an order. But the salesman could not just buy the shares from another investor and pass them on. In the 1960s the City was still working according to an intricate division of labour, devised in 1908, called 'single capacity'. To obtain shares, a broker would have to go to the London Stock Exchange and buy them from another type of City firm: a stockjobber. Jobbers such as Akroyd & Smithers and Pinchin Denny worked at octagonal booths on the Stock Exchange floor called pitches, at which they traded shares. A jobber quoted a bid (the price at which it would buy a company's shares) and an offer (the price at which it would sell them). Jobbers made money by holding shares that rose in value, and from the gap between the two bid and offer prices, called the bid–offer spread.

The gulf between brokers and jobbers was wide. Although both types of firm bought and sold shares, only one was taking risks in doing so. Brokers' fixed commissions meant they gained a steady income whatever the price of a company's shares. The most important thing for brokers was volume; they had to get a steady flow of orders from investors. When the markets were busy, they made a lot of money. When they were slow, the commissions fell and the partners of the firm would have less to share out among them at the year-end. Although brokers were salesmen it was a more respectable occupation than selling cars or cosmetics. The City was still a closed world dominated by the old school tie and introductions from old army chums. Virtually all brokers were men who had been educated at public schools. Jobbers' lives were different. It was a rougher, riskier business in which both the profits and losses could be enormous. Jobbers bought large blocks of shares and then tried to sell them at higher prices to make a profit. When a market was stable or rising, it was easy enough. But if it fell, a jobber might have to sell shares for less than he had paid. Jobbers were traders who needed good instincts and strong nerves. This was the other half of the City, where public school charm mattered less than the ability to survive the rough and tumble of the Stock Exchange floor. The 'blue buttons' who acted as messengers and assistants for jobbing firms were often indistinguishable from

East End barrow boys who pushed barrow-loads of meat around nearby City markets such as Smithfield.

George Henderson & Co. was a quintessential City stockbroker. Its partners were a jolly bunch who did not take life too seriously or work too hard. The less assiduous turned up for work at about 9.00 a.m. and telephoned a few clients to get some orders. Then they went out for lunch to pick up the gossip. By about 5.00 p.m. it was time to clamber back on the train to the suburbs. Most of the George Henderson partners had known one another at school or in the army. Heath felt he had made the right choice almost as soon as he arrived. Each February, the partners handed out bonuses for the previous year. Heath had been told by Russell that he would be too late to qualify since he was only joining on 17 February. But within a few days Heath was called down to the room shared by the partners and joined a small queue outside. When he entered the room one of the partners handed him two cheques, face downwards. He found they added up to £250, nearly a third of his annual salary at ICI. It was his introduction to the City bonus and he was favourably impressed. Heath became an apprentice to Denis Russell, who had decided that he needed an assistant as he got close to retirement. Russell gave him a desk next to his own and told him to listen to all his telephone calls. Heath could hear him ringing up his favourite customers such as Legal & General, the insurance company, which invested huge sums on behalf of policyholders. At 4.00 p.m. he would be quizzed on what he had learned. After three weeks Russell told Heath he would not be coming in on Fridays any more. Heath could handle his calls.

As the 1960s drew to a close the City was nearing the end of an active few years. The uncertainties of economic life under the Labour government of Harold Wilson, culminating in the 1967 devaluation of sterling, had not dampened the stock market. The Financial Times 30 index had been rising steadily, driven by take-overs. General Electric Company's bid for Associated Electrical Industries and Thorn's bid for Radio Rentals both excited the City and gave brokers plenty of opportunity to sell shares in a rising market. Bernie Cornfeld was not the only one earning a fortune. From his vantage point in the City Heath could see a new breed of British entrepreneur making their mark. There was Jim Slater, whose holding company Slater Walker was buying companies cheaply and delighting its investors by boosting earnings. In the same mould was the Wiles Group, run by James Hanson and Gordon White, which was developing its buccaneering style. There was scandalized talk of 'asset strippers' buying up companies to sell their assets and make immoral short-term gains. Heath did not agree. In his opinion men like Hanson and Slater were to be admired and emulated. They were not members of the tired British establishment which was happy to sit back and watch the country's genteel decline; they were self-made men who were not just becoming millionaires themselves, but were giving the same chance to those who worked alongside them. That was the way to lead your life, Heath thought. Not sitting out your days as a wage-slave, but having the nerve to stake your own money.

There were many brokers who did just that. Most partners and salesmen at George Henderson would invest their own money in shares to supplement their income. This was known as 'personal account', or 'PA' trading. The brokers would buy some shares in companies they liked the look of. Sometimes they would be acting on gossip or a tip from a friend picked up at lunch; often they had inside information. Twenty years later the government cracked down on what was by then known as insider trading, but in the late 1960s it was still seen as a perk of the stockbroker's life to trade on information he had picked up about a deal or take-over that would be announced shortly. Such gossip might come from a merchant banker advising a company or a broker arranging its share issue. A broker could buy some shares for his personal account and sell again at a higher price when the deal was done. In times of low activity in the markets, when firms were making only small profits on commissions and the annual bonuses were low, many brokers made more from their PA trading than from their normal business. Heath started to dabble in PA trading. For someone who loved gambling it was thrilling to buy some of a company's shares and watch them move, trying to spot the right moment to sell. There was a large board near Russell's desk on which share prices were plotted by an assistant who walked up and down listening to a telephone on a long lead. Heath did not even have to go to a bookmaker to monitor his bets.

With such stimulation Heath was soon enjoying himself more in the City than he had ever done at ICI. But he was not making much of a mark. Although he was a competent salesman, he was too distracted by his social life to devote himself to broking the shares of British companies. Now he had some money in his pocket, Heath was starting to enjoy himself around town. His ready charm brought him plenty of girlfriends, who would be taken home to meet the disapproving eye of Lady Heath. But the late nights on the town took their toll. Heath occasionally slunk into George Henderson well after Russell, who arrived at 9.00 a.m. One or two partners started to talk about how Heath should apply himself. One morning he arrived to find Russell looking at him sternly. 'Christopher, you are going to have to make up your mind. Do you want to be a stockbroker, or a lounge lizard?' Russell demanded.

Despite these doubts Heath was a well-liked figure because of his love of practical jokes. He specialized in ringing someone up in charac-ter and fooling them. When the father of one of the partners died and the man put an advertisement in a newspaper offering to rent out a house that had belonged to his father, Heath rang up, pretending to be an Arab prince anxious to find a large mansion in the country. The partner was very excited and started quoting higher and higher rents. Heath agreed, but finally said that the house was too small to accommodate all his wives. The others who had listened in were so amused that they made Heath ring up the next day and say he would be interested if he could put up a tent in the grounds for his wives.

As the 1970s wore on life became tougher at George Henderson. Almost from the moment Heath had joined, the stock market had fallen. Russell's views on Bernie Cornfeld proved to be prophetic. IOS collapsed in the middle of 1970, not helped by revelations that some of its directors had lent themselves and their associates $30 million of company funds. By 1973 Britain was gripped by industrial relations strife and the failure of the incomes policy of Edward Heath's Con-servative government. The oil crisis of October 1973, when Middle East producers cut supplies to western countries, led to the government declaring a state of emergency. The squeeze affected the City heavily. George Henderson started trading at a loss during 1974. Other brokers were closing and a drastic step was needed to save money. It came in a merger. Keith Barlow, a former army major who was by then senior partner of George Henderson, was close to a firm called Fenn & Crosthwaite. Unlike George Henderson, Fenn & Crosthwaite was a private client firm. It bought and sold shares for people with money to invest, rather than the investment funds that George Henderson favoured. But it too faced hard times. The firms agreed to merge. A cheaper office was on offer on the northern side of the City where Bishopsgate petered out into Shoreditch and Spitalfields. The newly formed partnership of Henderson Crosthwaite & Co. opened for business in reduced circumstances in a big Victorian building next to a pub called Dirty Dick's and opposite a public lavatory early in 1975.

For Christopher Heath the City was losing some of its allure. The get-rich-quick era of the late 1960s now seemed distant, and brokers were struggling to make a living. By late 1974 he was twenty-eight years old and nearing the time when he would be considered for a partnership at Henderson Crosthwaite. If he failed to achieve that, he would have to look elsewhere. But Heath had not shone in his five years at George Henderson. It was hard to stand out in such a gloomy time. Heath needed a spark and he found it one evening at home. Since 1971 he had been sharing a flat in Knightsbridge with James Nelson, one of his oldest friends, who had been at a preparatory school called Avisford, near Arundel in Sussex, with Heath, and then at Ampleforth. For the past year Nelson had been working at Foreign & Colonial, a fund management firm in the City. Such firms invested money on behalf of individuals or institutions, buying shares through brokers like Henderson Crosthwaite. As its name suggested, Foreign & Colonial was founded as an offshoot of the British empire in 1868, and was originally an investment trust, which put money in investments in British territories in Asia such as Hong Kong and Singapore. In 1884 it had bought bonds in Hong Kong for the first time. Since 1961 Foreign & Colonial had been putting British money into Japanese companies. That had been Nelson's speciality since joining Foreign & Colonial. He had spent several weeks visiting Japan and other Asian countries, learning about their economies and identifying firms he believed would grow rapidly and whose shares were worth buying.

Flying out from the depressed economy of Britain to Asia, Nelson had been excited at what he saw. He was particularly impressed by Japan. Japan had none of the feeling of a country in decline which hung over Britain. Quite the reverse. Japan had recovered from the humiliation and devastation of its military defeat by the US, and had achieved fifteen years of rapid industrial growth. American assistance after 1945 enabled its industries to borrow technology from the more advanced US economy. But Japan had better labour relations and innovative forms of industrial management. Its workforce was well-educated and disciplined. It had a highly effective form of national planning, dominated by the powerful Ministry of International Trade and Industry. It also saved a far higher proportion of income than the US or Britain, re-investing savings in industrial production.[3] By 1960 it was achieving annual economic growth of 13 per cent, a rate which it managed to sustain throughout the decade.[4] In 1961 Ikeda Hayato, the prime minister, set a target of doubling national income within ten years. The target was hit within seven, as industries such as steel, shipbuilding and petro-chemicals were nurtured by the authorities. Japan also started to produce high-quality cameras, television sets, motorcycles and cars. These consumer goods were the engine of growth in the 1960s, as Japan imported raw materials, such as iron ore and oil, and exported finished products. Nelson could see it was not just the quantity of its output that was rising; Japan had started to produce higher-quality, longer-lasting consumer goods than the US.

The Japanese economy was so strong by the early 1970s that it weathered the 'Nixon shock' of August 1971, when Richard Nixon, the US president, tried to boost the dollar by ending convertibility of gold, and placing a 10 per cent surcharge on imports. Between January 1971 and January 1973 the Nikkei index shot up from 1,900 to 5,400. This meant an investor in an average Japanese firm more than doubled his money within two years. However, the economy was badly affected by the 1973 oil shock, which hit Japan hard as the country relied entirely on imported oil. Government efforts to curb inflation after the oil crisis depressed both the economy and the stock market. By October the Nikkei had fallen back to 3,300. Despite this Nelson could see that Japan had much more potential than Britain. When growth resumed, an investor in Japanese companies would make more money than someone who placed cash in British ones. One night in their Knightsbridge flat, when Heath and Nelson were discussing Heath's stalled City career, Nelson listed all the factors that made him excited about Japan: its growth rate, its low inflation, the quality of its industrial output. Heath reached for an envelope and scribbled down what Nelson was saying. It made a punchy list of reasons why his investment fund customers should buy Japanese shares. Heath was enthused by the idea of selling Japanese shares. There was a simple story to tell and it was one of optimism rather than the familiar one of decline. Not only that, but the entire Japanese economy seemed to be so vibrant that almost any share might rise rapidly.

Even more importantly, it would be something different. Heath had a chance not just to follow the herd at Henderson Crosthwaite but to develop his own niche. Nobody else there was selling Japanese shares to City funds. It cost more to buy foreign shares because the government had imposed exchange controls to encourage domestic investment and there was also still a lot of anti-Japanese sentiment in the City. But Heath did not share that feeling. He started his Japanese venture with three investment trusts launched by fund management firms in 1972, including Crescent Japan, run by Edinburgh Fund Managers, and GT Japan, which was managed from Hong Kong. These allowed British investors to pool their money in trusts which used the money to buy shares in Japanese companies. Their shares had been issued at £1 each on the London Stock Exchange in 1972, but the drop in the Japanese market had led to a rapid fall in 1974 and they were trading at only 35p each. Heath realized there was an opportunity here. Because of the falling Japanese stock market, each trust was holding a high proportion of capital in cash rather than shares. Heath thought that anybody who bought them was almost bound to make a profit. He decided to bounce the idea off a natural sceptic, a partner called Noel Pace, who had been a prisoner-of-war of the Japanese Army and had suffered from ill-treatment and malnutrition during the construction of the Burma Railway. Heath explained his theory. 'Well, I don't like the Japanese, but it sounds like a good story, and we should make some money,' said Pace firmly.

Heath started to ring up fund managers to try to sell them shares in the three Japan trusts. He found it hard going at first. But Heath was a good salesman. He painted a glowing picture of this economy growing on the far side of the world and his efforts started to pay off. The shares in the three investment trusts began rising, driven by their new advocate in London. The Henderson Crosthwaite partners watched with bemused admiration as Heath for the first time showed his true talent. He also came to the notice of other brokers with an interest in Japan. These were led by Vickers da Costa, the longest-established foreign broker in Japan, which had an office in Tokyo. For a time Heath was only a minor irritant, but he thrust himself into a bigger league in May 1975. By then shares in Crescent Japan had risen to 140p. Edinburgh Fund Managers showed its gratitude when it decided to issue more shares in the fund. In order to do so, it had to appoint brokers to sell shares. The traditional method was to appoint a few brokers and allocate them blocks of shares which they would have to sell on the morning of the issue. Graham McLennan, the man in charge, turned first to the old-established names of Vickers da Costa, Grievson Grant, and Messel & Co. as brokers, but he decided to give a break to Heath by including him as well. But the other brokers were not keen on flooding the market by raising the £1.7 million that Edinburgh Fund Managers wanted. The day before the issue, Grievson Grant and Messel both rang up McLennan and pulled out, saying regretfully that they did not believe they could sell the shares.

That left only Vickers and Heath. Early the next morning Vickers also withdrew. McLennan became so irritated at their tactics that he decided to hand over the whole deal to Heath. At 8.00 a.m. Heath got a call. 'You are on your own,' McLennan said. Heath had a choice. He could withdraw also, and avoid a large risk of humiliation, or he could take over the whole issue. Heath's natural ebullience won through. He had talked the previous day to one of the larger City fund managers, who had expressed enthusiasm about the issue, so at 9.10 a.m. he called him. 'I must apologize, Christopher,' he said. 'I have checked, and Japan is not a class of asset that we buy.' This was a body blow. Heath's favourite prospect had collapsed. He picked up the phone and started calling all the fund managers with whom he had done business. He made slow progress, and had sweated his way up to selling 60 per cent of the shares by midday. Then the phone rang. It was a fund manager who had earlier turned down Heath. 'Have you got any of those Crescent Japan left?' he asked. He had not got any shares in Japan in his portfolio and, having decided it was time to expand, single-handedly bought the shares that were unsold. Heath had won. He rang back McLennan at Edinburgh Fund Managers to give him the news. McLennan was so delighted that he told Heath that he would not buy fresh shares with the £1.7 million through Vickers. Heath could have all the business. This was a wonderful break. For the first time Heath would actually buy shares in Japanese companies himself.

McLennan gave him the name of two Japanese brokers in London through which to buy the shares. He dutifully rang up Yamaichi Securities and Wako Securities and passed on the orders. In theory a British investor could go straight to a Japanese broker, not bothering with intermediaries like Heath. Japanese firms knew more than a British broking firm about their own country, but many British investors did not trust Japanese firms to advise them. This was partly because of Japanese culture. A Japanese company regarded it as a source of shame when a broker advised investors to sell its shares. Brokers would write short notes, often on a single side of a piece of paper, in which they would analyse a company and then say whether it was worth buying its shares at their current price. Because Japanese society placed such emphasis on politeness, brokers virtually never issued 'sell' notes on companies; they would almost always recommend buying. This made their advice next to useless. Another problem was that Japanese brokers would be allocated blocks of shares by their Tokyo offices to sell and would push those they had just been given, like a cosmetics salesman pushing the latest product. This meant there was a place for the knowledgeable outsider like Heath and he grabbed his opportunity with both hands. The Henderson Crosthwaite partners soon noticed a change in his behaviour. He no longer came into the office at 9.00 a.m. Instead, he arrived promptly at 6.00 a.m., a good couple of hours before the earliest of the others, and set to work, looking out on a gloomy courtyard surrounded by high buildings.

By the time he arrived, the Japanese brokers would have been allocated blocks of shares from Tokyo, and Heath would ring round to find out what was on offer. By 9.00 a.m. he would be on the phone to his customers, selling the shares. It was not a sophisticated operation. Heath had not even visited Japan by late 1975, and he had little idea of the companies he was peddling. But it did not matter too much. The fund managers liked to deal with him. He always had an amusing story or an imitation of the Japanese brokers. As his business grew his encyclopedic memory and facility with numbers came into their own. He had an exact recall of which fund manager had bought any block of shares. If another was keen to buy a company's shares, Heath would always know where they could be found quickly. It was not just his work habits that changed; he also lost some of the geniality that had characterized his earlier years. Those around him started to see a tougher and fiercer side of Heath as he battled to establish his place. Sometimes they would hear him shouting down the phone at the Japanese brokers, and abusing them viciously if they gave him too few shares or cut him out of a trade. Some thought that Heath was bound to alienate the Japanese brokers, who were always impeccably polite and discreet, but to their surprise, the Japanese usually jumped to attention when exposed to the rougher edge of Heath's tongue. Many of them came to respect the energy of the young British broker who hectored them, and he struck up close working relationships with several of his Japanese counterparts.

Nomura, the largest Japanese broker, helped him gain some first-hand knowledge of Japan by offering him a place on a trip it organized in spring 1976. Each morning he would be picked up at his hotel and taken to visit several companies. Heath found it all a bit strange. If a broker went to a British company, he could usually get some inside information by firing a few awkward questions at the finance director, but meetings at Japanese companies were stiflingly formal, and any harder questions would be politely evaded. At the end of his trip to Japan Heath spent a week in Hong Kong visiting fund managers with whom he had started to do business. As he wandered around, one broker advised him to visit the fund manager who had started the GT Japan investment trust. He was called John Bolsover, and he had just started up a fund management firm owned by Henderson Administration, the British fund management firm, Sanwa, the Japanese bank, and Baring Brothers & Co., the British merchant bank. Heath did not have much interest in Baring Brothers. As far as he was concerned, it was a rather stuffy merchant bank. But he reasoned that if Barings was interested in Japan, he might do some business in London. He made an appointment to go and see Bolsover. The meeting turned out a disappointment. Bolsover listened to Heath's sales pitch impatiently and threw some abrupt questions at him. He gave the impression of not having any interest in another unknown broker. 'I suppose we might do something with you,' Bolsover said grudgingly, emphasizing that Heath would have to come up with some fresh ideas.

It was a minor setback. Heath's Japanese venture had already worked well enough to earn him a partnership in Henderson Crosthwaite. Barlow had his doubts about how long enthusiasm for Japan would last, and he had proposed that instead of becoming a full partner in Henderson Crosthwaite – putting into the pot all his earnings and receiving an annual share of profits – Heath should be treated differently. He could keep a commission from Japanese broking and receive a smaller share of the profits. The firm would set up a special vehicle for Heath called Henderson Crosthwaite & Co. (Far East). This arrangement suited him well. He liked the idea of having a stake in his own business, and he was convinced that his tiny arm of the firm had more potential than the rest. Although James Callaghan had just succeeded Harold Wilson as prime minister, Britain appeared little closer to solving its economic problems, and the FT 30 index had fallen steadily since April. In contrast, Japan was starting to forge ahead again after the 1973 oil shock.

As a partner Heath was entitled to assistance. A trainee called John Bonfield was assigned to help him. Bonfield, a quiet young man from Rossall in Lancashire, was out of place at Henderson Crosthwaite because he had not been to a public school, and had been teased when he first arrived for wearing brown shoes, considered a *faux pas*. Heath was soon doling out the same treatment to his assistant as to the Japanese brokers, shouting viciously at Bonfield if he could not find the shares that Heath wanted to sell. Sometimes he would apologize for having gone too far.

Heath was progressing steadily by 1979 when the City was struck by a political event that was to transform it. After five years battling hopelessly to restore the economy, the Labour government called a general election in June and was defeated by the Conservative party led by Margaret Thatcher. Although City brokers were relieved to have a Conservative government, Thatcher caused unease. She had little time for the public-school network that still ruled the City. But one of Thatcher's first reforms helped Heath enormously. She abolished exchange controls, which meant investors no longer had to pay a premium of up to 30 per cent to buy Japanese shares. The floodgates lifted and investment started to pour into Japan. Heath soon needed new recruits. He had strong ideas about who he wanted around him. Heath liked insouciance, a devil-may-care attitude. Broking was a dull business unless you had a laugh or two along the way. Heath liked Catholics. He was one himself and he found them congenial company. He also favoured single children, believing that it fostered drive and self-reliance. He had not met the children of his father's first marriage and considered himself an only child. Most importantly, he liked people who were greedy. The City was not an intellectually exciting place. In the end everything came down to money. So Heath wanted people around him who liked to spend money. That would impart a drive to earn more and to work harder. 'Are you hungry?' he would always ask, as he peered at any potential recruits. That was what he wanted around him: an army of Christopher Heaths.

He soon found his ideal recruit. Diarmaid Kelly was a plump twenty-one-year-old, with dark, slicked-back hair, who smoked French cigarettes. He was a Catholic and an only child. Kelly was as keen a raconteur as Heath, with an inexhaustible fund of stories, and could rattle out historical allusions for every event. He had also been educated at Ampleforth, but had not managed to stay the course. At the age of seventeen Kelly had been caught smoking marijuana and had been expelled. The Ampleforth authorities had also reported him to the police. This had left him with a drugs conviction that, to his immense frustration, meant that he could not visit America. Despite it, he had been employed as a blue button by Pinchin Denny before joining Henderson Crosthwaite. Kelly neither knew a great deal about Japan nor spoke Japanese, but Heath recognized a fellow spirit. Kelly had filled in for Bonfield when he was on holiday, and he joined Heath full-time in 1981. Like Heath, Kelly was eager to make some money. He had been so poorly off in his early days at Henderson Crosthwaite that he had joined the Honourable Artillery Company to earn some extra cash. It had not been sufficient to make ends meet. One evening he was so broke that he accepted a £100 bet from a group of friends that he could not drink a bowl of bitingly hot Phal sauce that had been brought to their table in an Indian restaurant in London. He succeeded in drinking the sauce despite the pain, but he vowed to find a way of earning enough money not to have to do it ever again. He had all of the qualities that Heath wanted and soon emerged as Heath's favoured assistant.

By the time Kelly joined Heath's group, it was racing ahead. The other parts of Henderson Crosthwaite had picked up considerably from the dark days of 1974, but trade in Japanese shares was much brisker. On a good day Heath would earn £10,000 in commission. It was equivalent to more than £2 million a year. The rest of Henderson Crosthwaite was being overtaken by an offshoot run from a corner of the office. Kelly was not slow to rub in the growing disparity. An

74

order book was kept at Henderson Crosthwaite to record orders from investors. Kelly would try to fill up a page each morning before the others in the office had sold a single UK share. It amused him to demonstrate how energetically the tail was starting to wag the dog. Heath was making more than he would have done as a full partner. He was no longer an impoverished young man but he was still to make what he considered a decent sum. He had at last found a bride of whom Lady Heath approved, a businessman's daughter called Maggie Wiggin, who was almost as strong-minded as Heath's mother. She also suited Heath because she shared a love of horse-racing and of country pursuits such as fly fishing. Friends of Heath observed that Maggie was one of the only people capable of keeping him in line when he was excited by a wild idea. They married in June 1979 and moved into a large house in Kensington, but it was not all Heath's money. Maggie Heath was still better off than her husband, and insisted they bought the house jointly. She was cautious about spending money, fearing that Heath was inclined to fritter it away.

Yet, unknown to his wife, Heath was about to discover something that would eventually make him very rich indeed. Like other turning points in his life, it occurred by chance. One day he went to lunch with a fund manager who told him about a new financial instrument that had surfaced in London, called an equity warrant. These warrants were not like shares in Japanese firms that Heath had been buying and selling and were not even traded on the Tokyo Stock Exchange. Instead, they were sold in London on what was called the Eurobond market. Eurobonds were like other bonds issued by companies as a means of borrowing money, pieces of paper which promised to pay their bearer an amount of money as well as interest payments on the debt. Instead of being bought and sold in a single country, Eurobonds were stateless. They were issued offshore by companies from around the world and held by investors who did not want to pay tax in their own country. Eurobonds had been created in 1963 after the US president, John F. Kennedy, imposed a tax to stop US citizens buying bonds in foreign companies. Like British exchange controls the tax was intended to stimulate investment in domestic industry, but it led instead to the creation of the Eurobond market based in London. Bonds were issued in dollars by companies of all nationalities and sold through London merchant banks. The first Eurobond was a $15 million issue by the Italian road-building company Autostrade. It was handled by S. G. Warburg, which was a key factor behind Warburg's rapid rise to pre-eminence among London merchant banks.

By 1982 Japanese companies had become heavy users of the Euro-bond market. They needed to borrow money to finance their growth and it could not all be raised by issuing shares. They had been drawn towards instruments that made borrowing cheaper than a standard Eurobond. The key to achieving this was the rise of the Japanese stock market. The Nikkei had risen steadily through 1980 and 1981, reaching 8,000 by August 1981 from its 1980 low of 6,500. It provided a chance for companies to lower the cost of borrowing by paying less in interest on the Eurobonds they issued. The first method they used was to issue bonds that could be turned into shares, called convertible bonds. In return for lending $1 million to a company, an investor received a piece of paper entitling him to be paid $1 million plus a set interest rate. But he could also exchange the paper for a fixed number of shares. The number was set at a level where the investor would only gain from converting his bond into shares if the company's share price rose to about 20 per cent above its level when the bond was issued. The rise of the Nikkei meant investors knew there was a decent chance they would gain from conversion, and so they would accept a lower interest rate payment on the bond. In January 1982 a new way for Japanese companies to raise money was found. Instead of a convertible bond, a company called Mitsubishi Chemical issued a $50 million Eurobond with equity warrants. These were separate pieces of paper that entitled the bearer to buy its shares for 20 per cent above their current value at any time over the next five years.

In 1982 the term 'derivative' had not been coined on financial markets. But warrants were derivatives. In fact, they were equity options granted by the company itself. Not many brokers could see the point. City brokers were used to dealing with bonds and shares. They were now being offered something that might have a value if the company's share price rose enough, but did not seem to be worth anything at the moment. None of them knew of the Black–Scholes option pricing model, and not many could have understood it if they had been shown it. So most traders had decided to ignore warrants. They stripped the warrants off the bonds and traded the bonds alone. But Heath learned over lunch that the discarded warrants appeared to have a hidden value. A warrant with a face value of $100 gave its holder the right to spend $100 on buying a firm's shares at a 20 per cent premium to the current price. If the shares had been worth $1 and had risen 20 per cent to $1.20 each, you could buy eighty-three shares for $100. They would be worth only the $100 you had just spent on them. This meant the warrant was worthless, because the holder could not gain anything from exercising it. But if the firm's share price rose to $1.45, then the eighty-three shares would sell for $120. This gave the warrant a value of $20. And if the share price doubled to $2, the eighty-three shares could be sold for $166, valuing the warrant at $66. In other words, a warrant worth $20 when the shares were selling for $1.45 rocketed to three times the value if they rose a further 65 cents. This meant that warrants were what brokers called 'geared' to the underlying shares.

Until a company's shares rose to a certain level above their original price, warrants were worth nothing. When the shares reached that level, a warrant was worth its face value. If the shares rose further, it led to a steeper rise in the value of the warrant. This meant warrants were risky but had potential for huge rewards. Few people realized that potential in 1982. Warrants were so little valued by Eurobond traders that warrants with a face value of $100 were selling for $15. Anybody who was bullish about Japan had an opportunity for a cheap flutter. Heath was excited by the discovery, and he went to see a Henderson Crosthwaite partner called Martin Riley, who was good with numbers. Riley set out to investigate. He found that four other firms had issued bonds with warrants in February. They included a small trading company called C. Itoh and a textile firm called Toray Industries. All of these warrants were selling at bargain basement prices. 'These look like quite good value,' Riley told Heath. Riley wrote a note for Heath setting out the theoretical value of the warrants, and Heath set about selling them with his usual vigour. It did not work as planned at first. The Japanese market went through a dip, and the Eurobond market was more uncomfortable than ever about warrants. By spring 1982 Eurobond traders were not even bothering with them. For some time the bonds were selling for almost the same price, whether or not warrants were attached. A $100 warrant could be bought for $1. Yet Heath persevered with them. He was an eternal optimist about Japan and he knew that warrants had potential.

Heath was expanding in other directions. He decided that to carry on growing, he needed an outpost in Japan. It was ambitious, but Heath was now making enough money to finance a cautious expansion. He sent Patricia Anderson, an analyst he had recruited, to Tokyo to work from the Daiwa Securities office there. But he had grander plans in mind. While on a visit to Tokyo the previous year he had come across a young man called Richard Greer, a tall twenty-six-year-old with a suave, self-assured manner who worked in Tokyo for the trading company Jardine Matheson. His father was the Bishop of Manchester and he had impeccable credentials. He had been educated at Winchester and Corpus Christi College, Cambridge. He also had a wilful streak. He rejected the idea of working in the City as too dull. Instead, he had gone to Hong Kong and from there to Tokyo. His job was selling ski-wear and sports clothing. He enjoyed life in Tokyo to the full. He frequented the nightclubs of the Roppongi district and wore a T-shirt with the inscription 'Mr Roppongi'. Heath was keen to hire him but first wanted to make sure he spoke Japanese as well as he claimed. He devised a characteristically Heath-like test to find out. Having by now hired an Australian called Rosemary Morgan who spoke Japanese, Heath told her to ring Greer at the Tokyo office of Jardine Matheson, pretending to be a Japanese woman who had met him in a bar one night. When she got through, Morgan kept asking Greer in Japanese if she would see him again. She got mystified responses, but they were in fluent Japanese. Greer was recruited.

In January 1983 Greer and Anderson opened the Tokyo office of Henderson Crosthwaite (Far East). The venture was not glamorous. Tokyo was a very expensive place to live and work in, and Heath did not want to risk too much money. Greer solved this by finding space in the office of a trading company called Dodwell's in a building used partly as an office and partly as a warehouse. It was stacked with sewing machines and tins of dog food, a new product Dodwell's was trying to introduce in Japan. The office was run on a shoestring. They did not have a machine that would show the up-to-date share prices on the Tokyo Stock Exchange, so they relied on ringing a woman whom Greer knew at Flemings. They were not allowed to ring the London office direct because calls from Tokyo cost so much. They would instead call the number of a telephone on Heath's desk, let it ring three times to signal that they wanted to speak, and someone in London would call them back. Greer was seeking lively recruits and came across a renegade figure at a small Japanese firm, a twenty-two-year-old called Alex Murray who had just left University College, Oxford. He was the son of a diplomat, and his mother had acted as a judge in Japanese war crimes tribunals. He was a chubby man with a deep, cultured voice, who liked hanging out in bars and was impressed by Greer's ability to get invited to the most glamorous parties. Though Murray had a gloomy streak and tended to see the worst side of everything, he was clearly capable of spending his evenings in restaurants, which both Heath and Greer regarded as vital.

From the start, no matter how threadbare the office might be, they had taken hospitality very seriously. The filing cabinet near Greer's desk had one drawer marked Companies, a second one marked Sectors, and a third marked Entertainment. This meant taking care of the fund managers who were now flying out from London to see the companies in which they were buying shares. There were several firms of brokers in Tokyo competing for lucrative business, and Heath drummed into Greer early on the need for absolute devotion to fund managers' whims. 'This is a service industry, and we are servants. Never forget that,' he would insist. Henderson Crosthwaite might not have access to Tokyo share prices, but Greer made it the best host in Japan. When someone arrived on a long flight from London, a car would be waiting for him at the airport. There would be a telephone and fax machine at his disposal. When he was dropped at his hotel, he would find a vase of fresh flowers in his room with a hand-written note from Greer. There would be notes on the city, showing him how to find any restaurant or shop he might want to visit. Each evening he would be taken to dinner. He would be accompanied after this to a club, if he wanted. There was an element of bribery in all this hospitality, but it had a deeper purpose. Greer and the staff he recruited did not want to let a visiting fund manager out of their sight for any longer than necessary. Left to his own devices he might wander off and visit another stockbroker and this had to be prevented by filling up all his waking hours.

By the time Murray was recruited in late 1983, Henderson Crosthwaite (Far East) was rapidly growing apart from its parent. Heath's operation was now producing 60 per cent of profits and was attracting a novel degree of attention from larger firms. As investors' money flowed ever more rapidly out of Britain into Japan, Heath's operation was becoming an attractive prize. Scrimgeour Kemp Gee, one of the oldest broking houses in the City, approached Barlow to suggest a merger, but talks between the two firms failed because Henderson Crosthwaite's partners were cautious. Instead of Scrimgeour they went for a merger with a small broking firm called Beardsley Bishop Escombe, which had offices in several county towns including Hereford and Cheltenham and dealt with private clients. The merger took place in the middle of 1983, making Heath one of twenty-eight partners in the enlarged firm. He was not happy. His firm was going in the opposite direction to his ambitions. He now wanted to expand into areas that Barlow was not willing to allow. In particular, Heath wanted to start trading, as well as broking. Any firm could be a jobber of Eurobonds. It was an international market without the strict demarcations of the Stock Exchange, and Flemings, in particular, had taken advantage of this by trading convertible Eurobonds. Heath had discovered that Flemings was making a lot of money from trading in the Japanese bull market. It meant that every bond which Flemings bought to trade would rise in value before it was sold. It was becoming more rewarding to trade than to stick to its traditional role of broking shares and bonds.

The bond trading desk at Flemings was run by a gravel-voiced City veteran called John Galvanoni, who was known as 'Galvo'. Heath had been courting Galvanoni to join him. But a broker needed plenty of capital to trade bonds. The risks were much higher because the firm would have to hold stock and take a risk that it would fall in value. Barlow had made it plain that Henderson Crosthwaite had no interest in going into Eurobond trading and would not commit capital to it. Heath realized that if he was going to expand the way he wanted, he would have to find a new partner with a more go-ahead attitude. He had a showdown with Barlow. 'It's not just a question of you going and getting into bed with anyone,' he said. 'I want to have the choice.' Barlow did not like being addressed this way, especially when Heath called him 'sunshine' during a fierce exchange, but he knew he could not resist Heath's will, since the Japanese arm of Henderson Crosthwaite was growing apace. He agreed to give Heath the voting right over his firm. That meant Heath could not be forced into a merger he did not like. Heath also won the right to seek a new partner for Henderson Crosthwaite (Far East). If Heath could find a firm willing to pay a decent price, the other partners would let him go. With this decision reached in principle, he set about bolstering the firm he would be trying to sell. He was not looking for young people any more, but for a few experienced brokers who could help him run the firm. In return Heath could offer them the chance to be founding partners in a business that would at last be run just as he wanted.

He found one recruit at the stockbroker W. I. Carr, which specialized in markets such as Japan. Andrew Baylis was a thirty-seven-year-old doctor's son who had been educated at Cheltenham College and then studied philosophy and sociology at the London School of Economics in the 1960s. Baylis was hardly a typical student in the left-wing hothouse of the LSE. 'How could you tell Baylis at the LSE? He was the one wearing the suit,' the joke soon ran at Henderson Crosthwaite. He had gone into the City after university, thinking that it seemed like a place that would provide plenty of action. He was a salesman at Carr, working with a trader called Colin Ring. Baylis had all the loquaciousness of his Welsh roots, speaking in long, flowing sentences with many verbal flourishes. He camouflaged his shyness with a hard wit, often at the expense of others, but he was loyal to those he trusted. Baylis, who had known Heath socially for a long time, rapidly emerged as his right-hand man. He was not as good at selling as Heath or Kelly because, despite his oratorical skills, he lacked their warmth and charm. But Baylis had something that was badly lacking in Heath's group; he could get to grips with adminis-tration and make sure the outfit ticked over properly. Soon after his arrival Baylis slipped into a managerial role and became immensely useful to Heath because he was willing to do the tough things from which Heath instinctively shied away. Heath might bark a lot but he hated actually to bite.

The final recruit in August 1983 was a different animal. The Honourable Alexander Andrew MacDonell Fraser was a tall, hand-some man who worked as the London representative of Sun Hung Kai Securities, a Hong Kong broking firm. He was the only son of a judge from Perthshire who had been appointed a law lord in 1975, taking the title Baron Fraser of Tullybelton. Fraser had been educated at Eton College and St John's College, Oxford, which gave him a combination of laid-back charm and patrician haughtiness. He got along well with Heath, sharing his love of gambling. His first job after Oxford in 1968 had been at Kleinwort Benson, the merchant bank. He had not blazed a distinguished trail there, being known as much for a dark-blue velvet suit that he owned as for his merchant banking skills. Fraser spent evenings at the New Casanova Club, a casino off Grosvenor Square, and was inclined to gamble to the limits of his means. He had gone to Hong Kong in 1970 as an analyst with Vickers. Like Heath with Japan, Fraser had been struck by the vitality of the colony compared with Britain at that time. He felt an immediate affinity with the money-making culture and with the Chinese love of gambling. In 1977 he came back to London with Sun Hung Kai. His job was to buy shares and bonds in the London market for Sun Hung Kai's customers. Fraser had done well, partly because many of them wanted to trade gold and London was the centre of the world market. Heath thought Fraser's contacts in Hong Kong could come in useful selling Japanese shares.

Baylis, Fraser and Ring all joined on the understanding that Henderson Crosthwaite (Far East) was only a temporary home. By late 1983 Heath could be seen around the City lunching at various brokers and advertising his business for sale. He did not just want capital to start trading convertible bonds. He now had his chance to emulate Bernie Cornfeld and the entrepreneurs of the 1960s like Jim Slater, who had made millionaires of their followers. Heath knew his business was worth several million pounds to the right buyer. Most of it would have to go to Henderson Crosthwaite, but if he hung on to a share of the business, he could create his own partnership. This was the moment for which he had been waiting. It could vindicate his efforts of the past fifteen years. But Heath did not just want to sell to the highest bidder; he also needed a good name. Greer's outfit in Tokyo was a representative office with no power to buy and sell shares. Heath wanted authorization from the Japanese Ministry of Finance for a full branch in Tokyo but the ministry would only license a respectable firm. Heath started talking to Garantia, the largest Brazilian stockbroking firm. Though Garantia was keen to buy, Heath was looking for a firm whose name would be better known. Hoare Govett, the stockbroking firm, sounded like a better bet. Heath talked over his ideas with its partners. But the right offer did not come. The others waited while Heath talked and mused. Nothing seemed quite to fit what was wanted. Then one day Heath got a call. Would he care to come and have lunch at Baring Brothers?

CHAPTER 3

When the twenty-one-year-old Honourable John Baring told his father that he wanted to try his hand at banking the reaction was sceptical. 'I don't know why you would want to go into the City now. I think that it is all over,' said the sixth Baron Ashburton. It seemed he had a point. It was 1950 and there was little of the past glory of Baring Brothers & Co. evident at 8 Bishopsgate. Clement Attlee's Labour government had just nationalized the Bank of England and the utility industries, and it appeared that banks would be next. The City was a moribund place, and many of his friends from Eton and Trinity College, Oxford were taking jobs in industry instead. The merchant bank that John Baring joined was a genteel place, still run by a group of partners appointed by the second Lord Revelstoke before the war. The sons of the Baring family were allowed to have a go at merchant banking if they wanted, although it was not compulsory. Unlike the Rothschilds, no Baring got anything from the family bank unless he worked there. Some needed to do so. Although there were then four peerages in the family, the 1890 crisis and the depression of the inter-war years had taken a toll. John Baring's father had joined Baring Brothers in 1923 because his own father had been a spendthrift. Appearances were as distinguished as ever at 8 Bishopsgate. The partners ran the firm as a gentlemen's cooperative, working alongside each other in the partners' room with its open fire in the hearth and large oak desks. But the deals they did were as nothing compared with the fireworks of Baring Brothers' past.

Even in straitened times, Baring Brothers still occupied the heart of the City. The firm had been founded on New Year's Day 1763, when the house of John and Francis Baring & Co. opened in Queen Street.[1] Francis Baring was then twenty-three years old. He was a sharp-featured man who talked lucidly and impressed those who worked with him. But he was hard to penetrate. 'His manner was cold and his disposition reserved,' wrote one observer. His father, John, was born in Bremen and emigrated to Exeter in south-west England in 1717 with £500 of capital. He was among the German and Dutch merchants settling in Exeter to buy cloth before dyeing and finishing it for their home markets. He became British after five years and married Elizabeth Vowler, daughter of a trader in groceries. The merchant house opened in London by his sons was involved in the textile trade and took speculative 'adventures' by taking stakes in cargoes of raw materials, such as indigo and cochineal, that were being transported round the world, often from Asia to Europe. London houses soon developed a financial offshoot of trade by backing other merchants. A foreign trader might want to sell a spice cargo to another in London whom he did not know well. If he simply accepted a bill of exchange from the buying merchant, it might be worthless. So smaller merchants started paying well-respected houses such as Barings for the use of their names. In return for a commission they would 'accept' a bill by putting their name on it, and would promise to pay it, taking the risk of not being paid in turn by the merchant.

Bills issued by London houses gradually came to be used for all purposes. Until after the US Civil War, settlements between Boston and Philadelphia were carried out with sterling bills.[2] Six months after the American revolution in 1766 Francis Baring dissolved the partnership, and the firm was rechristened Baring Brothers & Co. in 1807. Francis started to establish a network of agents in foreign centres, and formed an alliance with the Amsterdam merchant house of Hope & Co., despite an early setback over an effort to corner the European cochineal market in 1787. They tried to buy up all the supplies so they could set the price themselves, but fresh supplies arrived from Mexico and the venture collapsed with losses of 2 million guilders. Baring quickly built up his trade with governments, supplying food for the British Army in the American War of Independence, and then supplying both the British and the enemy side in the French wars. Between 1793 and 1815 it was a leading force in raising £770 million in the London market for the British government to finance war and imperial expansion. Its operations also grew into America, and it raised $15 million in London and Amsterdam for the US purchase of the

Territory of Louisiana from the French in 1803. It was an 1818 loan of Fr264 million to the French government to pay off war reparations – after Francis Baring's death in 1810 – that placed the firm alongside Rothschilds as a leader in international finance. The Duc de Richelieu commented famously that: 'There are six great powers in Europe: England, France, Prussia, Austria, Russia and Baring Brothers.'

By then, the Barings were moving from traders and mercantilists to pillars of the British establishment, symbolizing a shift that not everyone appreciated. The writer William Cobbett objected angrily to *The Times* describing Baring Brothers as City pillars in 1810. 'Dealers in papers and funds,' he said. 'I look upon the life of Sir Francis Baring . . . as being of no more, if so much, value to England, as that of any one of your apprentices or plough boys.' In 1817 Alexander Baring, one of Francis Baring's sons, paid £136,600 for Grange Park, next to Stratton House in Hampshire, which had been bought by his father in 1801 for £150,000. A few years later Cobbett observed gloomily in *Rural Rides* that: 'The Barings are now the great men in Hampshire. The small gentry are all gone, nearly to a man, and the small farmers along with them.'[3] In 1834 Alexander Baring became the first Lord Ashburton. Britain was changing and the City was driving that change. By the 1840s, London was the first port of call for foreign governments and companies needing money to fight wars, or build railways and roads. One man's voice ruled the City: that of Thomas Baring, Lord Ashburton's cousin, who by 1853 was the leading partner. A railway tycoon from America visiting London observed: 'Ask about anything, and the reply is, "What does Mr Thomas Baring say or think?"' Baring Brothers was a leader in financing America's industrial infrastructure. After being one of five banks to raise cash for Ulysses Grant's first re-funding loan to rebuild after the American Civil War, Barings was responsible for managing 29 per cent of all bond and share issues by US railroad companies.

Baring Brothers met its fate in Argentina. The country had already given it problems in 1828 by defaulting on interest payments on a £1 million loan raised by Barings to build a port at Buenos Aires. British bondholders agitated for their cash, and the Argentine government even offered the Malvinas Islands – over which the two countries would later fight a war – as recompense. By 1859 interest payments were resumed, and the thirty-five-year-old Ned Baring, a nephew of Lord Ashburton, was sent on a tour of the Americas to report on prospects. By 1885 he was made a peer in Gladstone's dissolution list, becoming the first Lord Revelstoke. He bought the estate of Membland in Devon, berthing his 150-ton yacht, *Waterwitch*, nearby. An impatient and vain man, Ned Baring was by then the dominant partner in Baring Brothers and pushed enthusiastically into Latin America. Nemesis arrived in the form of the Buenos Aires Water Supply and Drainage Company, the concession for which was being sold by the Argentine government for $21 million in coined gold. In return for building the works, an investor would receive £10 million of shares and debentures. From the first issue of stock in London in 1890, Barings faced trouble. It had little idea of the size of the engineering task and the work was dogged by delays. A crisis finally erupted when the Argentine president resigned and the government threatened default. By coincidence the Russian government chose the same time to withdraw £2 million of deposits from Barings. The partners' capital was insufficient to meet their commitments, and Baring Brothers faced ignominious collapse.

Only Lidderdale, the governor of the Bank of England, saved Barings. He persuaded George Goschen, the chancellor, to allow it to start a guarantee fund to stand behind Baring Brothers on 14 November. When Rothschilds joined the fund, he managed to raise £10 million within twenty-four hours, and the final pledge was £17 million. Among the contributors were not only merchant banks but their new rivals, joint stock banks such as London and Westminster. Barings was saved, but its pride was dented. 'There really is no excuse for Ned . . . He might at least have guarded our good name. But it has all gone, offered up to his insatiate vanity and extravagance . . . Verily "A great Nemesis overtook Croesus,"' wrote Tom Baring, Lord Revelstoke's brother. The Barings' partnerships had been unlimited and they had to sell everything to meet commitments to the guarantee fund. Membland went, and French paintings and furniture were stripped from Revelstoke's town house. The Barings were not finished, though. By the end of November £1 million of fresh capital had been raised from family members who were not partners, and they could limp back into merchant banking with a new firm, called Baring Brothers & Co. Ltd. The Ltd was the important change; the Baring family fortunes would not be risked again. John Baring, who became the second Lord Revelstoke on his father's death in 1897, displayed better judgement in slowly building a second firm to rival the first. Barings once more got the ear of overseas governments, and by 1902 was even raising money for capital for Argentina again, starting with a £1.5 million issue.

The influence of the second Baring Brothers had spread to Japan by the start of the twentieth century. It was a leader of a £5.1 million loan raised for the Japanese government in 1902 that was four times oversubscribed because of investors' enthusiasm for Japan. Barings capped it by covertly participating in a further loan to Japan during the 1904–5 Russo-Japanese War, despite its links with the Russian government. Within a few years it had re-established its place as the leading London bank for foreign borrowers. Revelstoke bolstered the firm by recruiting outsiders. One was Sir Edward Peacock, a Canadian financier from Dominion Securities, the Toronto firm. Peacock was a taciturn man who was still at the helm when John Baring joined in 1950, and was known as 'the dead hand' for his aversion to risk. That was also the attitude of Gaspard Farrer, an expert on American securities, who joined in 1902. Farrer expressed clearly in his letters Baring Brothers' attitude after 1890. 'We are not capitalists, cannot undertake the business of a capitalist, and are only prepared to act as intermediaries between the borrower and the public,' he wrote in 1906. 'We cannot compete with the big capitalists, and it is silly and dangerous to pretend we can.' By that time it was clear who the big capitalists were. London's place as the world's leading financial centre had passed to New York. The leading banker of the age was J. P. Morgan, who was starting to compete strongly with Barings in Latin America. The two banks even talked briefly of merging and closing down J. S. Morgan & Co. in London, but the talks collapsed.

Baring Brothers was now struck by an event that was even more momentous than 1890 in changing the nature of the bank. The outbreak of war in Europe in 1914 in effect closed down the world of international trade and finance on which Baring Brothers had made its name and fortune in the nineteenth century. By the end of the Great War the old world of the City of London had died. Baring Brothers' links with Russia had been cut off by the Bolshevik revolution, the only consolation being that it could hold on to £3.5 million left in its vaults by the Russian government. It was no longer needed by the great foreign powers. The worst measure was the embargo on foreign loans made by the Treasury in 1918 to protect sterling and prepare for the gold standard. The firm was forced to look closer to home for work. Peacock came on board to expand corporate finance, a promising area of new business, which involved issuing new capital for growing companies and advising on the restructuring of older industries. Barings had already had a sensational experience of raising capital for British companies in 1886, when it had led a £5.2 million flotation of Guinness, the family-owned drinks company. There had been bedlam at Bishopsgate as it was besieged by people wanting shares. In the slump of the 1920s and 30s, this was a less exciting field. Peacock helped Montagu Norman, the Bank of England governor, to restructure industries. Between 1929 and 1933, he advised on the merging of a hundred mills to form the Lancashire Cotton Corporation.[4] Barings also raised capital for growing industries such as brewing and public transport.

The Second World War only reinforced Baring Brothers' attachment to caution and progressing at the steadiest of paces. When war broke out it lost £562,000 due from companies in Germany. It had been forced to hold credits to Germany steady throughout the 1930s after Standstill Agreements to prop up the ailing German economy were introduced in 1931. But by then Barings had taken most of its money out of Germany, after a partner called Arthur Villiers toured the country and decided it was unsafe. The bank acted more swiftly than rivals such as Schroders and Kleinworts, which were badly caught. It was still fresh in the partners' minds when John Baring joined. Despite the pessimism of his father, who was still a director, John Baring found corporate finance work interesting. Financial predators were starting to emerge in post-war Britain. In 1953 the East End entrepreneur Charles Clore mounted a hostile bid for J. Sears & Co. after discovering it had underestimated by £10 million the real estate value of its 900 shoe shops. It set the tone for a number of hostile bids.[5] In 1958 twenty-four-year-old Nicholas Baring joined, followed a year later by his younger brother, Peter. Their father, Francis, was a partner in the bank in 1938 at the age of twenty-nine, but had been killed in the retreat to Dunkirk in 1940. Their great-great-uncle had been the first Lord Revelstoke. The two had been educated identically, both going to Eton and Magdalene College, Cambridge, but Nicholas was the leader by both temperament and age. He was much more outgoing and played with ideas more easily than Peter.

Nicholas could walk into a cocktail party and engage any guest in lively conversation about the state of the world. Even as a young man Nicholas had been more cosmopolitan than Peter. At Cambridge he had been interested in relations between Britain and its fading empire, and spent a year as *aide de camp* to Evelyn Baring, the governor of Kenya, before joining Baring Brothers. Nicholas was soon discontented at what he saw as the parochial and conservative spirit that had overcome Barings. In 1961 he went to Argentina to take over what remained of its Latin American business. To be a Baring in Buenos Aires was still something to be reckoned with, even half a century after the great days. Barings still raised money for big projects, but it no longer risked its own capital to any great extent. When it backed a project, it would pass on most of the risk to other banks. After a couple of years Nicholas moved to Washington, where he joined the World Bank, which financed projects in developing countries, much as Barings had done in the nineteenth century. Back in London there were the odd relics of the past. In 1963 it was in London that the government of Japan raised its first international loan since the war, and naturally turned to Barings. But the bulk of Barings' time was taken up with the 1960s wave of mergers and acquisitions. Baring Brothers' work on industrial restructuring in the inter-war years had given it one of the best lists of corporate customers in the textile, brewing and transport industries.

In December 1961 ICI made a £200 million hostile bid for Courtaulds, the producer of the fabric rayon. Courtaulds was a customer of Barings, and a partner called Andrew Carnwath helped to repel this bid in March 1962. The ICI–Courtaulds bid was a turning point for Baring Brothers because it showed the importance of corporate finance compared with banking. It was not as well paid as it became in the 1980s, but neither did it put much capital at risk. Soon Baring Brothers was starting to direct its most talented directors away from banking towards advisory work. Apart from Carnwath, there was Wally Giles, a Scotsman who had joined in 1959. Giles was a shrewd, energetic man who rapidly built up an active business advising brewing firms on the never-ending stream of mergers and acquisitions in the industry during the 1960s. He was a kind man who did not mind explaining what he was doing to less experienced directors such as John Baring, but he did not always encourage the young. 'You're a thruster,' he once muttered darkly to Nicholas Baring. It did not appear to be a compliment. Giles and Carnwath established a new place for Baring Brothers in the 1960s but it no longer dominated London merchant banks. Newer houses, such as Morgan Grenfell, had stronger businesses. Above all, S. G. Warburg was chasing the grandest firms, having beaten the City establishment in the 1958 hostile bid by Tube Investments and Reynolds Metals Corporation for British Aluminium. Warburg also pioneered the Eurobond market, the sort of financial innovation that had typified the buccaneering nineteenth-century Baring Brothers.

The modern Baring Brothers dabbled only cautiously into Euro-bonds, not wanting to risk its capital. It was now content to earn a modest living without risk. That aversion to risk was spreading to the very capital structure of the bank. Since the election of Wilson's 1964 government John Baring had fretted at the possibility that a partner might die, and inheritance tax might be levied on his share of the firm's net assets. In theory, this could be a serious blow. It had also become a serious risk. Peacock had stayed on the board until he was eighty-three and Arthur Villiers had only retired at seventy-one. The partners' capital totalled £25,000, and if one died in office, he would in theory only be taxed on his share of this amount. But Baring was worried that the Inland Revenue might instead choose to tax a partner on his share of the £20 million of net assets held by Baring Brothers. That could force it to bring in outside capital, and possibly go public. Some of its rivals had done so already. J. Henry Schroder Wagg & Co. had been transferred to a public company called Schroders in 1959, and S. G. Warburg & Co. came under Mercury Securities. But Baring did not fancy the idea of answering to public shareholders because he thought it would create pressure to raise profits each year and go into riskier undertakings. So he and Wally Giles devised a different way to retain the firm's traditions, while keeping Baring Brothers privately owned. They set up a trust called the Baring Found-ation, and gained agreement from the directors that they would hand over 74 per cent of the partnership equity to the Foundation.

On the face of it this was hardly in the directors' best interests. They jointly owned a company that was worth £20 million between twelve of them, including five Barings. Nicholas Baring had been made a director in 1963 and Peter had joined him in 1967. John Baring's father, Lord Ashburton, was still on the board, although he was now seventy and was taking little part in the day-to-day running of the bank. In theory, the fifth Baring, the third Earl of Cromer, was now in charge. Rowley Cromer, as he was known, was top of the list of directors published in the slim annual accounts, indicating that he was the most senior. But Cromer was actually not running things. He had been appointed governor of the Bank of England for a five-year term in 1962 and had only returned to Baring Brothers the previous year. He was having some trouble fitting back in, since he had become used to the staff who had been at his beck and call at the Bank. He no longer wanted to work alongside the younger directors in equal partnership. Within three years he had departed again to be British ambassador to Washington. So the bank was run by a triumvirate of John Baring, Carnwath and a third partner called John Phillimore, who had worked in Latin America before the war. The partners agreed to hand over 74 per cent of the £20 million and distributed £500,000 of capital reserves among themselves as compensation. They did so because they did not regard the bank as truly theirs. Baring Brothers & Co. was a business built up over time and handed down over generations, as the family had always done.

With Baring Brothers expanding gradually as more business flowed in during the merger years of the 1960s tensions surfaced among younger and older partners about how aggressive it should be. Nicholas Baring, who had returned from the World Bank, was keenest for it to revive some of its former daring. He had made a sortie into France with a research organization called Eurofinance which he set up with other banks including Dresdner Bank and Credit Suisse. Eurofinance researched French and German companies and helped one or two of Barings' brewing clients to buy companies in Europe. It was an interesting idea but it did not make much money. A more promising venture was a bank that it owned jointly with two US banks and a Swiss bank called London Multinational, which lent money to large companies. This was not enough for Nicholas, who was frustrated at Barings' lack of Eurobond activity. An opportunity soon presented itself through Sanwa Bank, the fourth largest Japanese bank, which was looking for a way to enter the Eurobond market. A partnership with Sanwa seemed to be a good solution because it fitted with Barings' historic connections, and Sanwa had a balance sheet big enough to absorb the risk. There was only one problem. Baring Brothers had abstained from trying to get work from Japanese companies because it worked for the Japanese government. Nicholas had to argue to get Baring Brothers' other partners to agree, but finally they did. Sanwa Financial Services was set up in March 1973 as a joint venture to underwrite Eurobonds in London.

Whatever the others' qualms about venturing overseas, there were not many alternatives by 1973. The 1960s take-over boom had finished, and Barings faced just as gloomy prospects in the wake of the October oil price shock as George Henderson & Co. did around the corner in Old Jewry. The parlous state of the economy was brought home to them forcefully by Barings' venture into property development in December 1973. The partners had decided that the Norman Shaw building at 8 Bishopsgate had to be reconstructed. Although it was cosy and familiar, its warren of small rooms did not seem to befit the modern merchant bank that Barings was making modest efforts to become. They started trying to arrange a redevelopment deal. Then the partners became concerned that their hands were about to be tied. The Victorian Society had just been formed, and it seemed Bishopsgate was in danger of being listed. John Baring was not a sentimentalist about such matters. He arranged for temporary offices in Leadenhall Street and ordered the demolition of 8 Bishopsgate. This would have been a canny move but for one thing: the 1974 property crash. Almost as soon as the site was reduced to rubble it became impossible to redevelop. From Leadenhall John Baring silently thanked God that Barings' balance sheet was so conservative as the FT 30 index sank. It was not the most propitious time for him to become the first chairman of Baring Brothers & Co., but this happened in March 1974 when Carnwath retired.

With the British economy in crisis and the City depressed, Nicholas Baring's enthusiasm for overseas expansion was becoming shared by others. Latin America, Barings' traditional strength, did not appear to offer many prospects as most Latin American countries were either unstable or being run by military regimes. There were better prospects in Asia. The Sanwa partnership gave Barings a link with Japan, but John Baring could not summon up much enthusiasm for the Japanese economy. He was more at home with the former British empire in Asia, having spent some time in Hong Kong in the 1960s. That was also the region where Baring Brothers had obvious reasons to take an interest. Among its British clients were shipping companies with links to the east through Singapore, such as Ocean Steamship and Metal Box. It advised companies that owned rubber plantations in Malaysia, such as Guthrie and Harrisons & Crosfield. It also worked for some of the Hong Kong hongs – 'big companies' in Chinese – such as Inchcape. Since the war these companies had been more interested in their British operations, but by the early 1970s they were once more expanding in Asia and wanted a partner to help them in their efforts. Baring Brothers had long-standing links with one of the oldest and most powerful hongs of all, Jardine Matheson. The name Baring resonated in places such as Hong Kong and Singapore. The firm now wanted to escape from the gloom afflicting Britain and to rediscover its eighteenth-century merchant banking roots. It was most likely to do so in Asia rather than Latin America.

That was the idea but it was not easy. Barings' obvious partner in Hong Kong to match its link with Sanwa in Japan was Jardine Matheson, but in 1971 Jardine Matheson had joined with Barings' rival Robert Fleming to form a Hong Kong investment bank called Jardine Fleming. This had been a nasty blow and was seen by Barings as the result of having disagreed with the Keswicks, the family that was fighting for control of Jardine. In the late 1950s the last of the Jardines had decided to sell the 30 per cent stake his family still held in the business. The Keswicks persuaded Barings to join forces in buying the stake for £2 million. Barings split the 15 per cent of Jardine Matheson it now held with Flemings and another investor. Wally Giles had cultivated Barings' relationship with Jardine during the 1960s and had got on well with the Scots establishment in Hong Kong. But in 1971 an argument had broken out over who should be the next *taipan* (literally 'big boss'). The Keswick family wanted to install Henry Keswick, while Giles had put Barings' support behind a rival candidate. Barings lost the debate after the Keswicks appealed to other share-holders, including Flemings. Within a few months Flemings had been rewarded for its loyalty, and Barings had suffered for the stand taken by Giles. It tried to retrieve the loss by seconding a director to Hong-kong and Shanghai Bank. This also failed when Hongkong and Shanghai eventually set up a merchant bank called Wardley. It was clear by 1972 that Barings had to do something to establish itself in Hong Kong.

The man whom John Baring chose for a vital and delicate task was just twenty-eight and had worked at Barings for four years. Andrew Tuckey was the second son of an army colonel who emigrated to Rhodesia with his wife and three sons in 1951, after rebelling against his demob life at a rivet factory in Sheffield. The family bought 4,000 acres of empty plain a hundred miles from Salisbury, then the capital of the British colony, for tobacco farming. For three years, while they built a house, they lived in a mud hut with a canopy formed by a tarpaulin slung over a branch and cultivated the land. For the three young boys it was an amazing adventure. When they went exploring in a Land-Rover, they would cut marks on trees to show them the way back to their property. They were educated at a school called Plumtree by the border with Botswana, which had been founded to teach children of workers on a railway line. Life on the plains had its risks. One day the boys were helping to push the Land-Rover out of a ditch when it rolled back and crushed the top of Andrew's index finger on his right hand against a rock. He was driven in pain to a doctor, who snipped off the finger at the joint with a pair of scissors. Tuckey came back to Britain at the age of nineteen, and became an articled clerk to a friend of his father at the accountancy firm Dixon Wilson. He then went to work for British American Tobacco for two years before joining Baring Brothers. He was interviewed by Peter Baring, who was impressed by his intelligence and sang-froid. He joined the corporate finance department, already marked out as a future partner.

Andrew Tuckey flew out to Hong Kong in August 1972, the month he turned twenty-nine. He was officially to be finance director of Inchcape's Asia operations. He was to get the lie of the land, and see whether it was possible to form an Inchcape Baring to rival Jardine Fleming. He had been chosen because the partners were struck by his knack of gaining the trust of company chairmen despite his youth. Even crusty old sticks like Lord Inchcape respected the polished and confident young man. When he arrived, Hong Kong was presenting its liveliest face. Hong Kong had been founded in 1843 as a Crown Colony after the Treaty of Nanking. Despite its strategic value to the old empire, its repute was not high in the London of the 1970s. Its factories were known for turning out cheap, shoddy goods, and the motives of British people who lived there were often questioned. 'A place in the sun for shady people,' ran the City phrase. But in contrast to the Britain of 1972, Hong Kong was a place of enthusiasm and energy. It was in the middle of a raging bull market, with the Hang Seng index jumping from 270 in 1971 to its peak of 1,750 in March 1973. It seemed a place Baring Brothers should re-enter after a century away. The idea of a joint venture with Inchcape turned out to be impractical, and Tuckey tried to find an alternative that would not cost Barings too much. The choice became obvious when Barings joined forces with Sanwa in March. The banks in London Multinational were also interested in Asia, and together with Barings and Sanwa set up a joint venture to explore the Far East.

In October 1973 Tuckey became the first chief executive of the cumbersomely named Baring Sanwa Multinational Bank and a director of Baring Brothers. The chairman was Shichiro Murai from Sanwa. After the 1973 oil crisis Japanese banks were restricted by the Ministry of Finance from expanding in Asia but Sanwa was permitted to put up 40 per cent of the initial $5 million of capital, with Barings taking another 40 per cent. It allowed Sanwa to learn the western art of merchant banking. Three Japanese executives were sent to Hong Kong to work with Tuckey. While two of them worked, the third appeared simply to take notes. After a few days Tuckey asked what he was doing. 'He is writing investment banking manual,' came the reply. BSM's business gradually expanded around the rim of the Pacific as Tuckey pursued Barings' clients, remaining impeccably cautious. An even more diluted joint venture was started in Malaysia with a local bank called Bank Pertanian Malaysia in May 1974. By 1975 BSM felt confident enough to open an office in Singapore. It had achieved full independence ten years earlier by withdrawing from the Federation of Malaysia, and in 1970 Lee Kuan Yew's government had started its attempt to become the leading financial centre of south-east Asia. It established a rival to the Eurobond market in the Asian dollar market. Business could be counted in what were called Asian Currency Units, and only taxed at 15 per cent. It was also attractive because the body that supervised banks, the Monetary Authority of Singapore, was tough and efficient at stamping out malpractice.

The man sent to open the Singapore office was Geoffrey Barnett, who was already working for BSM from Hong Kong, covering Malaysia and Thailand. Barnett was the son of Air Chief Marshal Sir Denis Barnett, who had worked in Bomber Command during the war. Barnett had military neatness and precision, and a hesitant manner. He had seen Asia as a young boy, visiting his father who was stationed in India and Japan. He was educated at Winchester and Clare College, Cambridge, joining Barings in 1971. In May 1975 he opened Barings' office in Singapore, on the fifth floor of the Ocean Building, alongside which Ocean Towers was later erected.

It was a good time to live in Singapore. The government was only then starting to knock down the historic districts of what was known as the Garden City to make way for flats and shops. It was a delightful place, Barnett thought: well ordered and neat, without the squalor of Hong Kong's poor Chinese districts. There was much to do. Barings was among twenty-one merchant banks in Singapore. Jardine Fleming had opened an office and Schroders had formed a partnership with a large Singapore bank. Barnett was busy with share issues and flotations, and even the odd take-over. By now Tuckey had returned to London and his place at BSM had been taken by John Dare, an American who had been working for London Multinational. Dare was a tall, soft-spoken man with clear blue eyes and a deliberate manner, who diligently continued the expansion of BSM. By 1976 it was making a small but useful profit of HK$4 million.

Fund management was an activity that Baring Brothers had not taken too seriously as a means of earning money. Until well into the 1950s it managed the funds of private clients – known as 'special accounts' – without charge, simply receiving a share of the commission if they bought or sold shares. It had plenty of distinguished clients. Lady Diana Cooper wrote to Bishopsgate from the Dorchester Hotel in 1942 with the honest appeal: 'We are in financial straits. Can you help us out by selling our worst shares? If I don't get £2,000 soon, they will put me in jug.'[6] It also managed some of the funds of the Queen. Only in 1955 did Barings start advising the trustees of the pension funds of companies on how to invest their money. By 1976 this was still only a moderately profitable activity. There was one notable exception, which had fallen into Barings' lap in 1975. After the oil price crisis of 1973 Arab countries were flush with cash, known as 'petrodollars'. The Saudi Arabian royal family had put its $170 billion of petrodollars under the management of a body called the Saudi Arabian Monetary Authority. In 1975 it appointed Baring Brothers and the US investment bank White Weld to manage this money. It was a highly rewarding contract, and a series of Barings' younger managers were sent out to Riyadh and Jeddah to work at the SAMA offices there, some even learning Arabic to fit them for the role.

Barings' investment department in London was sleepy and invested most of the pension fund money it managed in British shares. Tuckey was frustrated that he could not persuade it to put more money into Japan and Asia. Then, in 1976, he came across someone in Hong Kong who was to help transform Baring Brothers' fortunes in the 1980s: John Bolsover. Bolsover was a fund manager at Henderson Administration Pacific and was both highly ambitious and self-confident. He was a dishevelled figure with a piercing gaze and an abrupt manner, who had little respect for old British institutions like Baring Brothers and had gone out to Hong Kong to escape what he saw as Britain's depressing decline into socialism. Bolsover, the son of a doctor, had attended Repton, the public school, and then done a business degree at McGill University in Montreal. He had been offered two jobs on graduating: as a fund manager or as a spy for MI6. He was discouraged from becoming a spy by his father, and the alternative was to be a fund manager in Hong Kong. He was now running a venture in Hong Kong backed by Henderson Administration, a London fund management company that had no connection with Henderson Crosthwaite. He had set his own terms in a meeting in London with the chairman of Henderson Administration, demanding a seat on the board and the right to be paid more than the chairman himself. 'I entirely agree with you about the salary, old boy,' the chairman had told the twenty-eight-year-old Bolsover. 'But it might take me until lunch tomorrow to get you on to the board.' By September 1975 Bolsover was back in Hong Kong, in charge of a new firm.

Bolsover wanted to attract some British pension fund money and the simplest way was by reaching an agreement with a British bank. It was a meeting of minds with Tuckey. The two men set up yet another joint venture called Henderson BSM Management in March

1976. On April Fool's Day it launched its first investment trust, the Henderson BSM Japan Fund. After a year Bolsover persuaded Barings and Henderson to create a single company called Henderson Baring Management. Bolsover had lost none of his ambition and laid down as a condition that he and his fellow fund managers should share in the profits. Baring Brothers and Henderson agreed that the employees of HBM could take a third of the profits each year in bonuses.

By the end of the 1970s the elaborate network of joint ventures through which Barings had tiptoed back into Asia had unravelled. In late 1977 London Multinational broke up when two shareholders, Credit Suisse and Chemical Bank, announced at the same board meeting that they were pulling out. A year later Sanwa and Baring parted company. Even the most cautious of the partners could see that Baring Brothers Asia, as BSM duly became in November 1978, provided an alternative to being a parochial British merchant bank. Andrew Tuckey had proved himself by building for Barings an international venture that not only sounded interesting but actually earned money. In July 1980 Tuckey was appointed to succeed Nicholas Baring as chairman of Baring Brothers Asia, recognition that an outsider had succeeded in restoring Barings' place in Asia.

Tuckey had been recognized as the most talented of the partners, probably even a future chairman. His talents were now switched to revive a domestic business that had faded during the 1970s partly because so much energy had been devoted to Asia during that time. Many of the brighter young recruits had been sent to work alongside Tuckey there. As well as Barnett and Dare, George Maclean had worked in Singapore and Hong Kong for three years. Maclean was a neat, dapper man who had joined Baring Brothers in 1966 after studying law at Edinburgh University. He spoke gently and had an open and enthusiastic manner, but could also be extremely obstinate. Maclean's strength was in playing safe rather than taking risks. His talents had fitted well with the cautious Barings of the twentieth century. When he returned to London in 1979, Maclean joined Barings' banking arm, which lent money in a cautious manner and underwrote Eurobond issues. Tuckey could see that banking was now stuck in a rut and made too little money. Even worse, corporate finance had faded from its best days in the 1960s under Giles and Carnwath. It was run jointly by Peter Baring and a partner called Robin Broadley, a former City lawyer. The City was growing more competitive as US investment banks attempted to break into the preserves of merchant banks. Banks had to come up with more ideas. Although Peter Baring was careful and dedicated as ever, he lacked the spark of the best merchant bankers. Some of Barings' oldest customers, including Guinness, had drifted away to Warburg.

Tuckey turned his attention first to pepping up Barings' bond underwriting side. It was not long before he had a stroke of luck. The biggest Eurobond issuer in the world was the World Bank, where Nicholas Baring had worked in the early 1960s. Until exchange controls were lifted, the sterling bond market had been quiet. The World Bank preferred to issue bonds in Swiss francs or dollars rather than in sterling. Barings had led two sterling issues for the World Bank in 1952 and 1971, being nominated for the second one by the Bank of England because it was the least aggressive of City merchant banks, and was acceptable to the others. Early in 1981 the World Bank decided to issue a £100 million bond. This was a highly prestigious venture, and Nicholas's contacts brought Baring Brothers a chance to lead it. The World Bank's treasurer rang Nicholas and arranged a meeting. By then Tuckey had moved Norris across to work on bond issues. He was clearly the brightest of the younger generation and grasped all the technical details easily. When they met the World Bank treasurer, Tuckey listened with admiration as Norris reeled off details of Eurobond settlement methods. The World Bank issue in April 1981 was an important step for Baring Brothers, marking the return to its old role as a City fund-raiser for overseas institutions. As the bond business picked up steam, Barings felt so confident by December 1984 that it took a stake in a jobber of government – or 'gilt-edged' – bonds called Wilson & Watford. It became a fully fledged bond trading firm for the first time in its existence.

The man chosen to take charge of this unfamiliar new activity for Baring Brothers was another member of the family. Michael Baring was the great-great-grandson of Henry Baring, one of three sons of Sir Francis Baring who worked at Baring Brothers. Henry Baring was a wayward character whose first wife Marie bore three sons and two daughters before he divorced her in 1824 for adultery, a rash step for the time. He then remarried, and had Ned Baring who became the first Lord Revelstoke. He was a talented gambler, who broke the bank at L'Enterprise Generale des Jeux in Paris, and a very good shot. While some of the descendants of his second marriage were determining the bank's destiny for the next 150 years, the line from his first family meandered down uneventfully. Michael Baring's father, Raymond, lived the life of a country gentleman on inherited family money. He was a keen fisherman, and his most prominent role in public life was as secretary of the Test and Itchen Fishing Association. One son became a soldier, the second a farmer and the third was Michael. After Eton and Oxford, Michael joined Baring Brothers as a trainee in 1970, and in 1977 went to Jeddah to help manage the Saudi Arabian Monetary Reserves. Michael chain-smoked with a distracted air, and was often to be seen hunting in his pockets for matches. He was an easy-going and charming man, who inspired affection, but not an outstanding banker. He was intelligent and analysed succinctly what had to be done, but often seemed too disorganized to do it himself.

By now Baring Brothers faced large questions about its future strategy in the City. Although she was an advocate of free enterprise, Margaret Thatcher had an uneasy relationship with the City. She found its old boy network elitist and alienating, riddled with restrictive practices in much the same way as British industry. Nothing much was done about that in her first term of office. The FT 30 index had risen during 1982 and 1983 as the outlook for an economic recovery brightened. In the election of June 1983 the Conservatives defeated Labour, which among other campaign pledges had promised to re-impose exchange controls, and Thatcher's government was re-elected with a 144-seat majority. The election followed Britain's defeat of the Argentine attempt to recapture the Falkland Islands – which Argentina had offered to hand over in 1843 as recompense for defaulting on its 1824 Barings loan. The Conservative victory was a happy event for merchant banks like Barings and brokers like Henderson Crosthwaite that gained a growing share of income from cross-border investment. But the City did not emerge unscathed. The Office of Fair Trading was pursuing the Stock Exchange about fixed commissions for brokers, which it saw as anti-competitive. Shortly after the election, an agreement was reached between Cecil Parkinson, the Trade and Industry Secretary, and Nicholas Goodison, the chairman of the Stock Exchange, which led to the abolition of fixed commissions and the fall of the division between jobbers and brokers. The big jobbing firms feared that they would lose business unless they could be brokers as well.

The Exchange's rules had already been changed to allow outside firms to own up to a third of brokers and jobbers. Large banks in Britain and abroad rushed to take up the opportunity. As the flow of international finance resumed at a pace unseen since 1918, many of them wanted to get into the City. Union Bank of Switzerland bought the broking firm Phillips & Drew; the US bank Security Pacific bought a stake in Hoare Govett; Barclays formed BZW from the broking firm de Zoete and Bevan and the jobber Wedd, Durlacher Mordaunt. The most ambitious move was an attempt by S. G. Warburg to form the largest British investment bank from itself, the broker Rowe & Pitman, the jobber Akroyd & Smithers and the government gilt broker Mullens. As walls between City firms came down merchant banks started to worry that they could not exist alone. They had always used independent firms of brokers to sell the shares and bonds of companies they advised, but if all independent brokers were snapped up, how would a merchant bank survive alone? Such concerns occupied the Barings partners throughout 1982 and 1983. They could hardly ignore what was dubbed 'Big Bang' in the City, for Baring Brothers played a role in advising other banks in their purchases of brokers. The corporate finance department advised UBS on buying Phillips & Drew, and Paribas, the French bank, on its purchase of Quilter, Goodison, the broking firm headed by Nicholas Goodison. It was the largest rush of work in a consolidating industry since the take-overs of the 1960s.

There were plenty of grand schemes about, but Sir John Baring, as he had become, was not convinced that Baring Brothers should join the rush. If there was any stockbroking firm that Barings might fit well with, it was Cazenove & Co., a venerable blue-blooded firm formed in 1823, that was broker to the Queen, just as Baring Brothers was known as her merchant bank. Barings had always had extremely close links with Cazenove, and relied on it to be Barings' eyes and ears in the Stock Exchange. If Cazenove was to sell itself, it would be a blow for Barings' chances of remaining as an independent merchant bank. A meeting was held to mull over the idea of a merger. But the senior partners of Cazenove said firmly that it was going to stay independent. With that reassurance that Barings could still work with Cazenove, it did not appear to John Baring that there was any need for a grand merger in the style of Warburg. When he looked at the partners around him, he saw men who were well suited to a small partnership but he doubted whether they were the right material to manage a large investment bank with a hierarchy. There was talk of S. G. Warburg competing with the Wall Street giants such as Goldman Sachs. It would be pie in the sky for Baring Brothers to think in such terms, Sir John felt. It would only end up being bought by another bank and losing its independence. If it wanted to do that, it could just as well simply auction itself among the clearing banks now. It would be far better to stick to what it knew in its cautious manner, and trust there was a future for an independent merchant bank.

But Sir John was not opposed to the odd smaller venture where it made sense and would not alter the whole character of the bank. Wilson & Watford was an example of that. Another one soon popped up. Baring Brothers Asia had been underwriting share issues by Asian firms and had also gained work at Japanese companies through its former joint venture with Sanwa. John Dare had returned to London in 1979 to take charge of Barings' Japanese business. In the early 1980s this had become more profitable as the Japanese economy expanded. Dare had helped Japanese companies, including Nissan and Toyota, to issue convertible Eurobonds in London. Barings had no capacity itself to distribute Eurobonds and tended to use Vickers to sell them to investors. Citibank, the large US bank, had approached Vickers' partners and offered to buy the firm. Vickers asked Barings to advise on the offer, but it also asked if Barings itself would be interested in buying it. When the partners considered it, buying at least one bit of Vickers – the part that sold Japanese and Asian shares – made sense. If Vickers was not available to work with Barings any more, its Japanese business might suffer. But they did not want the whole firm because that would require the sort of big London merger they had rejected. Vickers made it clear that it was all or nothing and went on to sell out to Citicorp. The need to do something about distributing Barings' Japanese Eurobonds and shares was now urgent. Dare and Michael Baring wanted to find a firm that could do that instead of Vickers. It did not need a big deal; a small broker would do.

As they talked about the idea with one of the directors of Vickers da Costa, it emerged that there might be another suitable candidate.

There was a tiny Japanese broking operation being run out of Henderson Crosthwaite by a chap called Christopher Heath. It only employed twenty people, compared with the 830 of Baring Brothers, so there was not likely to be a huge management problem controlling it. John Dare set about arranging a lunch at 8 Bishopsgate with Heath.

Dare, Michael Baring and Christopher Heath got together at the round table in the boardroom next to Tuckey's office in November 1983. The lunch went well. Dare was impressed by Heath's enthusiasm and excitement about his business. He appeared to have a similar vision about the growth of Asia and Japan and the almost limitless possibilities of the Far East. Heath made it clear he was already talking to others about being bought out from Henderson Crosthwaite. 'My partners don't even know where Japan is,' he said, with a laugh. He would need a substantial partner with some capital to get the business moving.

'Look, we might be interested,' said Dare.

For his part, Heath was taken with the sound of Barings. You could not have a much better name than Barings as a broker in Japan. It would provide some capital to start trading convertible bonds. All the ingredients seemed to be there. Dare introduced Heath to Tuckey, an encounter that also went well. By the start of 1984, Dare and Heath were negotiating for the latter to join Barings, and bring along with him all the others at Henderson Crosthwaite (Far East) in Bishopsgate and Tokyo.

Baring Brothers did not strike everybody at Henderson Crosthwaite as the perfect fit. Baylis had doubts. He believed that Barings was too cautious and lacked an appetite for the ups and downs of stockbroking. 'If we make one slip, they will be in here like the Red Army,' he said warily. But Heath's partners recognized it was his decision where they went. The important thing was to make sure that they could carry on doing what they wanted without interference and that they would have a stake in the business. They had joined Heath on a promise that they could be partners, not just earn salaries. So, like Bolsover before him, Heath told the Barings partners that a condition of them buying Henderson Crosthwaite (Far East) was that he and his fellow directors retained a stake in the business. It took some working out, but eventually they reached a complex deal. Baring Brothers agreed to pay £5.8 million to the partners of Henderson

Crosthwaite to buy Heath's business from them. It arranged with Heath to set up a company called Baring Far East Ltd, which would be the owner of a new broking firm called Baring Far East Securities Ltd. Baring Brothers would hold 75 per cent of shares in Baring Far East, while Heath and the partners of Henderson Crosthwaite (Far East) would get 25 per cent. The shares would be worth little to begin with, but they could start to be exchanged for cash after four years, at a price determined by the profits they made.

This quarter share in the firm was divided among the partners by Heath, with a little haggling. Heath got 28 per cent. Baylis, Bonfield, Greer, Ring and Fraser each had 10 per cent, and Kelly 9 per cent. Anderson got 5 per cent, Murray 3.5 per cent and Christopher Derricott, one of the first analysts, 3 per cent. Roy Johnson, who was in charge of settlement, got 1.5 per cent. Only 90 per cent of the shares were allocated, to allow for others to join later. This meant that if everything went according to plan Heath would eventually get 7 per cent of operating profits, while senior directors like Baylis would receive 2.5 per cent each. That would be a good reward under the projections drawn up by Dare and Heath. These stretched for seven years, and the 'likely case' was that operating profits at the new firm would grow from £2.2 million in 1984 to £6.8 million in 1990.[7] That would mean £550,000 would be set aside to pay the partners in 1984, and in seven years' time they would earn £1.7 million between them, with Heath getting £470,000 for that year. Dare was mildly worried at the idea that Baring Far East Securities could be more successful. These were only numbers drawn from the air after all. Of course, it would be a good thing if it worked well, but Dare wondered what would happen if it made double what they were expecting in seven years' time. That would mean that Heath could earn £1 million in one year. The Baring Brothers partners were not worried so much by the principle as by the practical effect of paying people so much. Dare confessed he was concerned that the directors might lose their drive if they became so rich that they did not have to work again, and suggested to Heath they should put a limit on the sums that could be paid out through the profit-share.

'What happens if you make £10 million, and we pay out £2.5 million. Won't your people just take the money and go home?' Dare asked.

Heath looked at him in wonder. 'You don't understand these guys,' he said. 'In our world, somebody who gets £1 million just wants to make £2 million. These are people who make money, and spend it.' He explained his recruitment method: how he always asked potential recruits about the lives they led. 'If he spends money on parties and racehorses, I say "fine" because he will want more. I want a guy who lives well, and is hungry.'

It was a lesson for Dare in how alien the world of broking was to merchant banking. He and Tuckey agreed to give their new firm plenty of independence. They knew they did not yet understand it, and worried that they would only crush it by imposing their own ideas. Dare would become non-executive chairman, Heath managing director, and the executive directors would be the five partners with shares of 9 per cent. Barings nominated three non-executive directors, including Tuckey and Michael Baring. A deal was struck in May 1984, and a drinks party was held on the nineteenth floor of 8 Bishopsgate to celebrate Baring Brothers' cautious entry into stockbroking. During the talks Heath's business had been code-named 'Harrier' to preserve secrecy, and Heath had been referred to as 'Biggles'. Dare presented Heath with a leather flying helmet, and he donned it to laughter and applause. There was a note with it: 'To the pilot. With best wishes for a smooth flight. From your new Air Controller.'

CHAPTER 4

In early 1985 it was bitterly cold in London. The heating was not working properly in the building to which Baring Far East Securities had just moved from Bishopsgate and Diarmaid Kelly sat at his desk in the new office wearing a coat, hat and gloves. The gloves made it hard to work the terminal in front of him. When he punched one of the square buttons to get a direct line to the Tokyo office, his gloved finger would press down another button as well. Apart from the temporary difficulty Kelly was satisfied. For several months following the signing of the deal Heath and his colleagues had carried on working in Bishopsgate. In November they had moved to a block nearby in Bury Street. There Kelly sat, surrounded by empty desks. Heath had ambitious plans for growth. The firm was already doing better than anticipated. Profits of £2.2 million had been predicted for 1984, but it had actually made £4 million. It was a good start, and they were truly on their own as Barings had agreed not to interfere for fear that it could crush its new offspring by mistake. Tuckey and Dare agreed that it was only a small thing and should be permitted to flourish in its own way, with Heath simply passing on information as he saw fit to Dare. There would also be formal board meetings four times a year. Heath devised a method of making sure these were simply a formality. The day before they took place, the directors of Baring Far East Securities would meet in London to discuss what was going on at a 'pre-board' meeting. At the end, they would agree on a bowdlerized version to present to the Brothers the following day.

The most important thing Heath reported to the March meeting was that Baring Securities was on the point of trading Japanese convertible bonds. Heath had failed to entice Galvanoni away from Flemings, but had sidestepped him and gone directly to Doug Hanney and Doug

Atherley, the two-man team on the convertible bond desk at Flemings. The 'two Dougs' absconded for double their Flemings salary and the promise of becoming directors within six months if everything worked out. They started trading in May. It was a tense time. Heath had eagerly pushed them to start without even waiting for telephone lines to be installed at their desks. Greer and Murray were warned that the bond traders should be the first priority. They should be told any news about companies whose bonds they were trading. For the first time, Baring Securities would not just earn commission for selling shares, it would be taking risk.

After a couple of weeks of successful trading the market moved against the two Dougs one day, and they lost some money. Heath saw Atherley looking depressed. 'How did we do today?' Heath asked.

'Not too well, Christopher. We were down a bit,' replied Atherley.

Heath appeared puzzled. 'Why's that? You were busy, weren't you?' It was as if he could not bring himself to accept that a higher return involved a higher risk. Fortunately he did not have to suffer many reverses. The market was moving steadily upwards. If the Tokyo staff passed on a titbit about a company that looked a good bet, the two Dougs would soon be trading the company's bonds in London.

Heath was not put off by the odd mishap in convertible bond trading. Far from it. Trading was rapidly becoming the engine of Baring Securities' profits. There were few competitors, and it could set a wide gap between bid and offer prices for convertible bonds, as well as making money on the steadily rising value of the bonds. Monthly earnings at Baring Securities started to outstrip Heath's projections by an impressive margin. But Heath had a further trick up his sleeve. Warrants had by now been trading long enough for the shares of companies that first issued them in 1982 to rise well above the level where the warrants were worth money. Investors who had bought the original warrants of Japanese companies at their lowest in 1982 had made hundred-fold profits because the warrants had risen from $1 to $100 or more. Galvanoni's best asset was now a team of warrant traders led by Trevor Sliwerski, a thirty-four-year-old trader who had been in the Boy Scouts with his son. A tall, gangling man who loved to talk endlessly about warrants, Sliwerski had worked at the Stock Exchange after leaving school with three O levels. That autumn Sliwerski rang Heath and suggested that they met for a drink.

He had become sick of Galvanoni vacillating over whether to go himself. 'I want to make net what Galvo gets gross,' said Sliwerski ambitiously. Sliwerski soon arrived at Baring Securities with three other traders, leaving Galvanoni in tears on the Flemings trading floor. By hiring Sliwerski Heath was taking even more risk. Warrants were more volatile than even the notoriously volatile Japanese stock market.

As Heath stepped up the level of risk, Baring Far East Securities was turning into a far bigger firm than Baring Brothers had anticipated buying. Its financial year ended in September and by then it employed seventy-five people. Its earnings had burst through the most optimistic projections for the decade already: Baring Securities had been expected to make £3.3 million in 1985, but had made £10 million. The original agreement with Baring Brothers was beginning to appear ludicrous. The seven-year buy-out formula had already been met, and Baring Brothers owed Heath's partners £400,000. Some arrangement had to be devised to replace it. Baring Brothers now wanted undiluted ownership of Baring Securities. Sir John Baring agreed with Heath that he and his partners should share in the profits instead of having a 25 per cent stake. Baring Brothers would take half the profits of Baring Securities each year and would also charge Heath's firm interest on the Baring Brothers capital it had used during the year. This would leave the rest – probably between 40 and 45 per cent of profits – to be shared out among staff. Heath devised an arrangement for splitting this money. It would be divided into three 'pools'. The C Pool was to pay the bonuses of all but the eleven founding partners. The B Pool, which would only exist for two years, was an annual payment of £200,000 that would be divided among the partners as a compensation for giving up their entitlement to a share in Baring Securities. The rest of the money would be shared among the élite profit-sharing pool – the A Pool.

The A Pool comprised the original eleven partners of Baring Securities. Heath had been vigilant in avoiding dilution of the partnership, although three other directors were eventually admitted to it. There was no legal deal determining how much cash went into the A Pool, but Heath sent its members a letter saying he 'hoped' the A Pool would get 25 per cent of operating profits each year. This was to be split in similar proportions to the former deal. Heath would now get 7 per cent of profits each year in cash, while those such as Fraser and

Baylis would get 2.5 per cent each. Heath's partners were not the only ones now sharing in profits. By 1985 the Baring Foundation had owned 74 per cent of Baring Brothers for seventeen years. But John Baring was becoming concerned about how to protect his family's legacy. Baring Brothers could now be worth about £400 million, which meant the partners' 26 per cent could fetch £100 million. During Big Bang, partners of some of the oldest City firms had gained millions by selling the firms to large banks. Baring was now fifty-seven and approaching retirement. He did not want to part with his share of the nominal £25,000 capital only for the next generation to sell theirs for millions. He wanted Baring Brothers to remain independent while preserving a tradition of partnership. The only way he could see of doing so was to hand the ownership to the Baring Foundation, and replace it with profit-sharing.

In November the 26 per cent stake of the thirty-two partners was bought for £12.5 million in preference shares by a new company called Barings plc, wholly owned by the Baring Foundation. This massively undervalued the partners' shares, but in return the firm introduced a profit-sharing deal. It applied to partners and sixty senior managers. It was similar to that of Baring Securities. Half of Baring Brothers' profits would go to Barings plc each year, and it would also have to pay for the use of its capital. The rest of the profits would be divided among participants in the profit-sharing scheme.

Barings was not the only firm paying its senior employees more. The City was changing. As new capital flooded in, an old honour code was breaking down. City firms had been partnerships that worked as a single unit. Brokers and merchant bankers would patiently wait their time to be partners and would then amass a decent wealth before retiring. Now the cult of the individual was growing, part of the ethos becoming known as 'Thatcherism'. Norris left Baring Brothers at the start of 1984 despite being appointed a director. Goldman Sachs had promised him a $60,000 salary and the guarantee of a $130,000 bonus. The deal with Heath had ended the last traces of poverty at Baring Securities. It was spent on the things they had always coveted. Bonfield bought a Porsche with his first big cheque. 'I never thought I'd have the money, but I swore if I did I'd buy one,' he told those who teased him.

However good life was by the end of 1985, the Japanese government was about to ensure that Baring Securities' partners had more money than any of them had ever dreamed about. In September, leading industrialized countries agreed to push down the dollar against other currencies. By January 1986 the yen was rising steadily and the Japanese government reduced interest rates. This set off an explosion in the value of property and shares. Between January and August 1986 the Nikkei rose from 12,800 to 18,900, adding a third to the value of the average company. Companies had to raise capital to grow, which they had traditionally obtained in the form of loans from banks. There was now an alternative. Their shares were rising so rapidly that it was cheaper for them to issue bonds with equity warrants. It led to a sudden rise in equity warrant issues in London. In 1985 Y679 billion (£3 billion) of warrants were issued, but in 1986 this rose to Y2,006 billion (£8.5 billion).[1] Bedlam broke out in the corner of the trading floor where Sliwerski worked. The phones rang off the hook as Japanese broking firms rang up with warrants to trade. Fund managers realized that they could make money faster by buying warrants rather than Japanese shares. Sliwerski had come to Baring Securities on a prediction that his team could produce £4 million in revenue in the first year, doing forty or fifty trades per day. By September the group had brought in £23 million, and was making more than 500 trades per day. Other brokers chased into warrants, and Flemings and Barings had to reinforce their teams. By the end of 1986 warrant trading had become one of the City's most profitable and aggressive markets. Baring Brothers might have hoped for a gentle venture into broking, but it was now grasping a tiger by the tail.

Warrant trading was not for the cautious. It was a 'knock-for-knock' market, which meant that traders had to guarantee to buy or sell a block of at least a hundred warrants in any Japanese firm if asked. This made it easy to be caught long of warrants that were falling in value, or short of warrants that were rising. Games developed among traders, who would try to catch each other short of warrants in a particular company. If ten traders rang Sliwerski and bought a hundred warrants each in Asahi Chemical, he would be 1,000 short. If he phoned a couple of other traders to buy them, word would go round the market that he was short, and other traders would keep ringing to squeeze him further. Trading ended at 3.30 p.m. each day, and the last quarter of an hour became known as 'the cutting zone', because it was when traders desperate to escape from their positions would buy and sell at large losses to extricate themselves. Traders often did not pick up the phone because of what might happen to them. Traders at Flemings had devised a technique similar to the start of the Oxford and Cambridge boat race to stop themselves being trapped in a squeeze. They might need to buy a warrant simultaneously from ten other traders before word got out that they were short. Ten would ring up other market-makers, and when each one got through to a counterpart, he or she would raise an arm to signal they were ready while passing the time chatting idly. When all ten arms were in the air at once, one of the senior warrant traders would give a signal, and they would all buy a block at the same time before word could get out.

Despite ups and downs the warrant trading business was hugely profitable. Because the warrants were rising so fast investors usually made healthy profits on anything they bought. It meant that they did not cavil at a wide bid–offer spread. Sliwerski could also make a profit by running his book long. At the height of the market Sliwerski had a £25 million warrant book. This meant that £25 million of Barings' capital was at risk. The warrant book was more volatile than an equivalent holding of shares. Warrants tended to be four times geared, gaining and losing value four times more rapidly than shares. This risk was not hedged by other shares or futures. It was never clear that Baring Brothers understood these risks fully, yet it was happy enough to reap the profit. In 1986 Sliwerski's team made £23 million profit. This was two-thirds of Baring Securities' £33 million profits, with £6 million more coming from convertible bonds.[2] Its profits were eight times the size predicted two years earlier. Barings' annual report for 1986 noted 'an outstanding year of achievement' for its offshoot, adding a reference to the 'generally favourable' trading conditions. It did not disclose that Baring Securities actually contributed £16 million of Baring Brothers' £25 million operating profits. This left £14 million in bonuses to share out among Heath's staff. The A Pool members were not just well off; they were rich. Richest of all was Heath, who collected £2.5 million for the year. It was not on view from outside. Baring Securities was registered in the Cayman Islands and did not have to publish what it paid its directors. But the A Pool were sitting on a gold mine.

Heath's firm was growing apace and signs of strain were emerging.

One of the first places to feel this was the back office. Many financial markets were caught in the middle of an awkward transition from paper certificates to electronic settlement, and the growth of Baring Securities was placing the firm's back office under severe strain. Heath tried to keep costs at a minimum in the early days, and the back office had not been his first priority. The worst problem was with warrants issued by Japanese firms in Switzerland to cash in on the private wealth there. There was an odd system for settling Swiss franc warrants, and a backlog soon built up. When it did a trade, Baring Securities sent a form to a bank in Switzerland with instructions to transfer the warrants to a customer's account. But electronic forms in the Swiss clearing system lacked space for all the information, so warrants were often put in the wrong account. By autumn 1986 there was a backlog of up to a year in sorting out the foul-ups. Other firms had also been badly affected. It could only be solved by reconciling every one of the trading slips with the faxed forms that came back from Switzerland. Neil Andrews, the thirty-one-year-old head of Eurobond settlement, was asked to sort out the mess. He was horrified. The firm was at risk of having to bear all the costs of unreconciled trades, and there were hundreds of errors running into millions of francs. Andrews rented extra space on the floor below and hired twenty temporary staff who reconciled all the trades but two. Baring Securities ended up losing only Sfr80,000.

There was no time to pause. Heath was driving Baring Securities ever faster onwards. By November 1986 it had burst out of Bury Street and moved to a new office in Portsoken Street, 200 yards from America Square. It was now expanding in all directions. In June it had joined the London Stock Exchange and officially changed its name from Baring Far East Securities to Baring Securities. Heath had been appointed to the board of Baring Brothers as recognition of his achievements and the Brothers were starting to regard Baring Securities as more than a tiny offshoot that simply dealt in the shares of Japanese companies. Heath and Tuckey agreed that Baring Securities should set up a team to research and sell European company shares, which fitted well with Baring Brothers' ambitions to turn itself into a pan-European merchant bank. The flow of cash from warrant trading was so strong that it could finance the growth of Baring Securities across Asia. This became Andrew Fraser's domain and he started to open offices everywhere from Hong Kong to South Korea. But despite a glimmering of cooperation in Europe, Baring Securities and Baring Brothers mostly kept their distance. Heath had little interest in working with the Brothers in Asia, although he was treading a similar path to Tuckey the decade before. When it opened an office in a new Asian city, Baring Securities would often pick a different building from the Brothers. Heath was happy for whoever headed Baring Securities in Seoul or Bangkok not only to ignore the Brothers, but to build their own empire within his firm.

Apart from Asia Heath's most significant offshoot was created in the middle of 1986 with the opening of an office in New York. It had been coming a long time, but Heath had waited to snare his man. His chosen ambassador in America was Jim Reed, a burly man who was born to a half-English, half-Irish father and a Japanese mother. He had been to Marine officer-training school, and he treated his fellow brokers at Vickers, where he worked, like a platoon who had to give him unquestioning obedience. Reed had first met Heath in 1983 when Heath was scouting for a potential head of a New York office, and he had been uncharacteristically abashed by the meeting. As usual Heath was staying at the Hotel Pierre on 61st Street. The hotel's meeting rooms were all booked, so he had been forced to take the ballroom instead for the interview. When Reed arrived at 9.00 a.m. to find a solitary figure sitting at a table in the middle of a vast ballroom, he was taken aback. 'This guy must be powerful,' he thought. But Reed was unimpressed by the idea of working for an outfit called Henderson Crosthwaite, and instead took a job at Nomura in San Francisco. By spring 1986, however, he was ready to join. It was enough for Reed that Barings had financed the Louisiana Purchase. That was a good story to tell clients. But when he met Heath for lunch in a Beverly Hills restaurant, Reed complained that he had just bought a house on the west coast and would lose $80,000 if he moved to New York. Heath took out a cheque book and wrote a cheque for $30,000. 'If we have a good year, I will reimburse the rest,' he said.

By 1987 everybody in the A Pool had money to throw around. One way they spent it was taking bets on financial markets themselves. Baring Securities' internal rules insisted that staff had to carry out P A trading through the firm so that it was visible for inspection, and they were barred from buying some instruments, such as warrants. But within limits they could risk their new-found wealth. One of the most active PA traders was Fraser, who was still a keen gambler. His favoured market was Hong Kong, where he had worked before joining Heath. In July 1987 Baring Securities became a member of the Hong Kong Futures Exchange. By autumn that year most of the world's stock markets were in the later stage of a prolonged boom. Wall Street was in its fifth year of a bull market, and the FT-SE 100 index was rising. Hong Kong was full of frenzied speculation over which firm faced the next bid. Fraser had been through a profitable summer trading on his own account, and he was feeling very confident. In the middle of October a rumour swept through Hong Kong that Cheung Kong Holdings was about to bid for Hong Kong Land, which was partly owned by Jardine Matheson. A bid was bound to push the Hang Seng index up further, and Fraser decided to take advantage. He took his bet on the Hong Kong Futures Exchange, the most straightforward means of gaining from a rise in the market. Fraser bought $100,000 of long futures for his own account. This was a calculated bet. He believed the worst he was likely to suffer if it went wrong was a 50-point fall in the market, and a loss of $20,000.

He had reckoned without the biggest stock market crash since 1926. On Monday 19 October, the Dow Jones Industrial Average fell 508 points to 1,738, its worst-ever fall, as investors lost confidence after a rise in US interest rates. The fall was mirrored round the world. The Hang Seng dropped 2,100 points, forty times the fall Fraser had discounted. The Hong Kong Futures Exchange closed because several of its most powerful members could not meet margin calls. Not only had Fraser lost an appalling amount, but he was unable even to quantify the damage for several days, because the exchange stayed closed. When it finally reopened, he faced a bill for $1 million. It was not a happy prospect since he had just bought a big country house in Scotland. At first it appeared that Fraser might be unable to pay. Heath sounded out the Baring Securities directors to see whether they would take part in a whip-round to bail Fraser out. The idea was not greeted with unanimous approval. Heath took Atherley on one side: 'We have got to help him out. He has just bought a large property, and he is one of us.' Atherley did not see why traders in Japanese warrants and bonds should help out Asian equity salesmen. They were making most of the firm's money already. In the end the crisis was resolved when Fraser came up with the money to pay the $1 million himself. A few days later somebody plucked up the courage in the office pub, known as The Boardroom, to raise the subject in front of Fraser. There was silence while everybody waited for his reaction. 'Until you have lost a fortune three times, you are not a man,' he replied airily.

The October crash was a problem not only for Fraser. In Tokyo the Nikkei had been rising so fast in an inflationary bubble that Japanese companies could not just cut their cost of borrowing with warrants but push it below zero. Bonds with warrants could be issued at a yield below long-term interest rates. In effect companies were being paid to borrow. The Nikkei had escalated from about 18,500 in January to 26,646 in mid-October. It fell 3,836 points on that Monday, removing £5 million from the value of Baring Securities' warrant book. Sliwerski was in Tokyo, and found himself arguing with Baylis over whether to pull out of warrant trading altogether. Sliwerski was so obsessed with his own product that he was later quoted in a *Financial Times* travel article talking about warrants on holiday. He offered Murray £100 not to show it round the office, but failed. 'This is too good to miss, Trevor. It shows you're even a bore on holiday,' Murray said. Sliwerski won the day. It turned out to be a sound decision for Baring Securities. By the end of October warrant trading was back in profit and was entering an even more profitable phase. Up to 1987 it had sold warrants mainly to overseas investors because of restrictions on Japanese investors buying them. But as overseas investors started to sell Japanese shares and warrants, Nomura and the other Japanese brokers stepped into the market to buy the warrants to resell them to Japanese people. Nomura's 500 branches in Japan were soon selling warrants to Japanese investors as fast as the firm could buy them in Tokyo.

This massive show of confidence in the Japanese market soon pushed the Nikkei back up. By January 1988 it was close to its peak the previous October. Sliwerski and the other foreign brokers were busier than ever, taking part in a vast repatriation of warrants. But if Baring Securities recovered itself rapidly, the same was not true of Baring Brothers, for Baring Brothers had been badly hurt in the October crash. It was caught along with other banks in the disastrously timed flotation of British Petroleum, one of the Thatcher government's flagship privatizations of public companies. Barings had been given a role as 'gate-keeper' to the issue, which meant its job was to oversee the work of other merchant banks and brokers involved. Because this work brought only a small fee, it was given a big slice of the £7.2 billion shares to underwrite. But the price at which it had to take on BP shares was set at 330p before the crash. The crash left them trading at 280p, and the government faced an appeal from some of the US underwriters to abandon the sale. It refused, and all those involved took heavy losses. Barings sustained a £9 million loss. It was a bitter blow for a bank that prided itself on not taking risks, and its merchant banking profits were heavily reduced. The banking arm lost £5.3 million for the year, only just balanced by a £6 million corporate finance profit. In contrast Baring Securities made a £60 million operating profit, of which £30 million came from warrant trading. After distributing £30 million to its staff in profit-share Baring Securities still had enough left over to contribute £27 million to Baring Brothers.[3]

It was a turning point. Baring Brothers could no longer pretend Baring Securities was merely a minor offshoot. It had to face the awkward fact that in the second year of its profit-sharing arrangement for its directors, its bonuses had been largely earned by Baring Securities. This was noted carefully at Baring Securities, where resentment of the Brothers was stirring. Heath's fellow directors were now coming to view the Brothers as a dead weight on their firm. It was unnerving for Baring Brothers as well. Heath's firm had been more successful than they could have envisaged and they were worried it might go to his head. 'We need you to hang on to his coat-tails,' John Baring told Heath's wife Maggie at a dinner. The rampant success of Baring Securities and the A Pool had largely gone unremarked, because Barings could hide it within its slim, opaque accounts. Heath's share of the A Pool for 1987 had brought him £4 million, but the accounts of Barings simply showed the overall group had made a £4.5 million profit after transferring money to its hidden reserves. It might have concealed the truth for some time given that Baring Securities did not publish accounts. But Heath had been appointed as a director of Baring Brothers in March. It was hard to avoid given that his outfit was now earning the biggest share of the profits. This meant that his earnings were disclosed in the Baring Brothers annual accounts. The 1986 accounts were placed in Companies House in October, with details of his £2.5 million earnings that year. Before long it was spotted by a researcher.

Heath was visiting Tokyo to try to sort out the aftermath of the crash the day the story broke in British newspapers: Baring Brothers was employing Britain's highest-paid businessman. When he returned to his room in the Imperial Hotel he found sixteen messages to ring people in London he had never heard of. The first turned out to be a reporter from the *Evening Standard*. By the next morning, when he came out of his hotel bedroom there were two photographers standing in the corridor. Meanwhile, Maggie Heath was besieged by reporters at their house in Kensington. Their life changed overnight. Not all of this change was pleasant for Maggie Heath. They received one kidnap threat on their son William, and one day when she went out to the local shops, she was pinned against a wall by a beggar who hissed at her: 'Give me some money, you rich bitch.'

For Heath, though, having so much money was a dream come true. He had waited a long time for it. Now, for the first time in his life, he had plenty of money to throw about. He set about doing so. The first priority was horses, with which Heath had always been fascinated. He and Maggie had already bought a flat racing horse called Buzzler. He now started building up a stable of hurdlers. He hired a trainer called Oliver Sherwood to help him. It was not hard to find candidates. With the news out about his wealth, Heath was offered a place in every syndicate going to buy horses. He gradually built up a stable of twenty-five horses, which he raced at courses such as Kempton in his wife's colours of orange and blue. Heath was in seventh heaven at being a racehorse owner.

Like the Barings before him in the nineteenth century, Heath ploughed part of his earnings into becoming a country squire. In 1986 he and his wife had jointly bought Ashe House, a Grade II-listed Georgian country house in Hampshire, with eight bedrooms, five bathrooms, tennis court and swimming pool, near Newbury race-course. It was now augmented with the 391-acre estate and a full-time butler and maid. Heath filled Ashe House and the Kensington home with oil paintings by English painters such as Stubbs and Seymour. He collected English furniture from the seventeenth and eighteenth centuries. He acquired two vintage Bentleys and a chauffeur-driven office limousine; he bought a stretch of fly fishing on the River Lochy near Fort William. There was a 148-foot yacht that he shared with a member of the Baring family called Oliver Baring, who worked at Warburg, but which he later took over in full himself, mooring it off the Côte d'Azur in summer. Maggie Heath, who had always been accustomed to having money around, became alarmed at the rate at which her husband could spend it. She had to fight to dissuade him from buying a helicopter and an aeroplane, although he still chartered planes occasionally. Even the everyday spending on wines and fripperies ate through money. His annual bill for cut flowers was £7,000. At Annabel's, the nightclub in Mayfair, Heath would entertain to his heart's delight with champagne and the best of wines for all his companions. This was the life of which Heath had always dreamed, and he enjoyed his good fortune to the full.

All this unnerved Maggie Heath, who wanted to ensure there would be some money left when these boom times were gone. She was a strongly independent woman, who was liked by the directors of Baring Securities for keeping her feet firmly on the ground throughout. She watched her weight carefully, and Heath bought her as a joke for one birthday the registration plate 2 FAT, which she put on a Mercedes estate and drove proudly around. Maggie Heath was not idle herself. In December 1987 she was the chairwoman of the Save the Children Fund annual carol concert in the Albert Hall, to which Margaret Thatcher came as the guest of honour. The photograph of 'the two Maggies' together passed into the folklore of Baring Securities as a symbol of how far it had come. But Thatcher was not impressed with the sight of empty seats in the hall because companies that held debenture seats to entertain their clients had not bothered to fill them. 'You are going to have to do something about that, my dear,' she said to Maggie Heath. Maggie Heath promptly went out and paid £10,000 to book the Albert Hall for a night the next year, then sat down to think how she could use it. She came up with the notion of a Joy to the World charity event, and efficiently wrested away two members of the Save the Children committee to help her. Save the Children was a little upset to have its event hijacked so effectively by an insider, but Maggie Heath had learned some lessons about business from her husband. She made up the tiff by giving the charity the proceeds of the first two years of the Joy to the World event.

By 1988 the country had woken up to the fact that wealth was not only being created in the City, but distributed among those who worked there. It fitted the spirit of the times, in which Nigel Lawson, the chancellor, and Thatcher painted a picture of Britain as an 'enterprise culture' in which old wealth was being elbowed aside by entrepreneurs. No one embodied it better than Heath. He was a beneficiary of both Thatcher's financial deregulation and Lawson's tax cuts. Heath afterwards counted Budget Day in March 1988, when Lawson cut taxes, reducing the top rate to 40 per cent, as one of the high points of his life. That afternoon Heath was at Cheltenham to see two of his horses romp home winners in separate races. He had a £500 each-way bet on each. As Heath celebrated, Lawson reduced his annual tax bill by £500,000. It started to seem that Heath was leading a charmed life.

By now Baring Securities had 560 employees, many of them young and eager to make money. Anybody could make their mark by catching Heath's eye. A notable example was Warren Primhak, a twenty-three-year-old trader who joined Baring Securities in 1985 as a back office clerk. Primhak, the son of a taxi driver, was lean and pale with a mop of ginger hair. He rapidly became its mascot. His cockney vowels could be heard across the trading floor, cajoling a stuffy fund manager into buying Japanese shares. He would be first in The Boardroom when the day was done. Heath said he got a hangover just looking at the amount of drink that Primhak got through.

In 1988 Primhak was sent to Tokyo to work as a trader and salesman. Heath and Kelly arranged a send-off for him. They persuaded Primhak that he needed to pass a medical before going to Tokyo because the Japanese financial authorities were very strict about the lifestyle of traders. They called a 'strippergram' service of the kind that was becoming popular in Britain. A woman turned up in a nurse's uniform and Kelly showed her to the company boardroom, where Primhak was waiting. When she persuaded him to take down his trousers the rest of the Japanese sales desk burst in and took his photograph. It hung on the wall of the trading room as a memento as Primhak flew to Tokyo.

Before Primhak arrived there had been a strict divide between the Japanese and British brokers, exemplified by the breakfasts that Alex Murray and others had on the trading floor. They would order British breakfasts of bacon and eggs that they consumed with relish on the floor. The smell was such anathema to the Japanese traders that these were eventually banned. But Primhak quickly struck up a friendship with the head of Japanese equity sales, a short, round man called Yusuke Fujiwara, and the other Japanese brokers. They would often spend evenings in a bar called Prego, to which Primhak would drive in his Toyota jeep, while Fujiwara would arrive in a convertible Jaguar XJS. As he drove there he could chat from the Tokyo streets to the London trading floor on the phone.

By the late 1980s traders in the Tokyo office were getting annual bonuses of $500,000 and upwards. By this time the A Pool had been squeezed from 25 per cent to 18 per cent of the operating profits to share out more for other bonuses. Heath made up by allocating the unused portion to raise shares within the A Pool, with his own rising to 33 per cent. In his early days at Baring Securities, Primhak had been rescued from trouble by Heath. He had overspent on a credit card, and run up a £2,000 bill. He was taken to court and agreed to pay it off at £50 a month. When Heath heard about this, he pulled £2,000 out of his pocket and gave it to him. In London, although not on the scale of Heath, Primhak imitated him as a spender of money, buying two horses, as well as a five-storey Georgian house in Limehouse and a house in Portugal. In Tokyo he went further. He paid $500,000 of his own money for two precious memberships of golf clubs. His expenses for entertaining customers were $100,000 a year. He and Fujiwara loved gambling. One year he placed a rolling bet of $2,000 on the New York Giants to win the Superbowl. The bet rolled up to $75,000 by the time they reached the final – and lost. Primhak and Fujiwara also flew to Las Vegas twice a year to gamble in the Nevada desert. On one trip Primhak took $50,000 in cash with him and he had to pay tax on it when he was stopped at San Francisco airport. On the way back he hid his winnings in his bags to avoid a repeat. The Japanese airline then lost the bags, which were only returned after a fraught few hours.

By the late 1980s Primhak was only one element in a Tokyo office that was becoming frenetic. The Japanese city lent itself to such fever. Night in Tokyo was a mass of flashing billboard lights and deafening noise. In the small, claustrophobic world of foreign brokers and invest-ment banks there was little to do but spend the vast amounts of money being thrust into their hands. Baring Securities in Tokyo became a supercharged version of the culture Heath had created. Traders thought little of spending £1,000 on an evening out. One trader fell asleep in a taxi one evening and his colleagues told the driver to take him to Yokohama. He did not have enough cash on him and had to spend the night in a police cell. Many nights passed at Solemn, an expensive restaurant whose decor was modelled on Arabia, which had a model camel in its lobby. This was kidnapped one night by one salesman as a practical joke. The atmosphere was scarcely less hysterical on the trading floor. While in Las Vegas Primhak had picked up terms that became his chief criteria for judging people. Aggressive gamblers with the guts to place big bets were 'eagles', while 'pigeons' were cowards. 'You're a pigeon!' he would sneer at those he thought lacked nerve. He also picked up a Goldman Sachs description of weak players in markets as 'fishes'. Some mornings Primhak would stroll to his desk after a night out spent drinking. Some of the traders around him would applaud ironically. 'I'm going in! I'm going in! Kill the fishes! Kill the fishes!' he would shout as a rallying cry.

Even in this highly charged atmosphere some valuable work was being done. Baring Securities joined the Tokyo Stock Exchange in June 1988, and on its first day of trading it bought and sold shares equivalent to a third of the turnover of the London Stock Exchange that day. Heath's idea that he could become the leading foreign broker of Japanese shares had seemed far-fetched fourteen years before, but it was now coming true. Under the influence of Greer the research by the analysts of Baring Securities on Japanese companies was now pre-eminent. Vickers da Costa had faded under the ownership of Citicorp. In London Baring Brothers wanted to find a way to illustrate Baring Securities' legitimacy. The directors had been shocked by the publicity over the amount paid to Heath. After a century of discretion they were facing the unpalatable fact that Barings was best known for paying Heath millions. The directors needed to find a way of promoting a new image for their subsidiary. Peers came up with the idea of applying for the Queen's Award for Export Achievement. It was only an honorary award, but it would associate Baring Securities with something more lofty than a profit-sharing arrangement. The award was duly made in April 1988, and the framed certificate was hung in the head office of Baring Securities. On it the Queen and Margaret

Thatcher declared their recognition of 'the outstanding achievement' of Baring Securities in increasing British exports.

The award gave Baring Securities an image of respectability. Yet its directors were still prone to mishaps that would have frightened the Brothers had they known. One involved Kelly, who was in the habit of PA trading on the London Traded Options Market. If Kelly believed that shares in a company were likely to rise, he could buy what were known as 'call options' in that firm's shares. They were options that allowed him to buy shares at close to their current price at some time in the future. It created a problem in September 1988 when he bought £10,000 of options in the shares of Consolidated Gold Fields with a colleague. Kelly had heard rumours that the firm was about to sell off its South African assets, which would raise its share price. They bought the options on Monday 19 September. Two days later the shares rose by over £3 to £14 each when Minorco, an investment vehicle of the Oppenheimer family's mining empire, launched a £2.9 billion hostile bid for Consolidated Gold Fields. The bid brought them a profit of £40,000, which Kelly regarded as pretty good for two days' investment. But it also brought them to the notice of the Department of Trade and Industry. There were accusations of widespread insider dealing in the company's shares and options, and Kelly was interviewed along with hundreds of others in a DTI invest-igation. Kelly was cleared of any impropriety, though the DTI later concluded that some other City professionals had probably been involved in insider trading.

By the late 1980s the directors of Baring Brothers were starting to get worried at how little they knew of what went on inside Baring Securities. Dare and Tuckey had tried to avoid interfering too much in their subsidiary. But they were now uneasy at the lack of information about its revenues and costs. It was not just that they were not given much data; there did not seem to be much about. Heath was still insisting there was no need for conventional management controls. He still wanted to run the business as he had in the old days. He did not want a management committee, nor a finance director. He preferred to run a collection of fiefdoms, to which only he was privy. To give everyone information about exactly where the profits were being made and what everyone else earned would only provoke jealousies and rivalries. So it was not only Dare and Tuckey who were in the dark.

With the exception of Baylis, the directors of Baring Securities were as well. When it came to calculating C Pool bonuses, Heath would simply tot up what he reckoned to be each salesman's contribution, and compare it with the revenues. The figures would usually match well enough. Baring Brothers went along with this for a time. But it was worried. In the reconstruction of November 1985, John Baring moved Peter from heading corporate finance to become the group's first finance director, and allow Tuckey to become head of corporate finance and capital markets. Peter Baring had pressed in his restrained way for a finance director to be appointed at Baring Securities.

Heath eventually conceded the point, and in September 1987 Ian Martin was appointed as finance director. He was a thirty-five-year-old accountant, a thin man with large ears and protruding front teeth, whom Fraser had christened 'The Weasel'. Martin had been finance director of County NatWest, National Westminster Bank's unsuccessful attempt at an investment bank. He had failed his 11-plus exam and gone to a secondary modern school in Horsham, Sussex, but he had obtained a place at the University of Essex to study mathematical economics, and then had joined the accounting firm Arthur Andersen. He was not a devil-may-care salesman of the kind Heath and his fellow directors respected, and they would imitate him behind his back. Kelly was shocked to receive a memorandum from Martin one day. He thought that was an evil innovation. They had just chatted amongst themselves before; nothing was written down on paper. It was an unhappy sign of the modern world of bureaucracy and controls intruding on their enchanted firm. Kelly and Fraser were also put out by Martin's assumption that he had joined their inner circle; just because he had a grand title did not mean he was one of them. In practice his arrival did not transform the quality of financial data. Martin collected it more efficiently than Heath had done, but he did not distribute it. Martin's place in the privileged élite was ensured by having secrets that he would share only with Heath and Baylis. At board meetings he would disclose hardly anything. It did not matter to the others; they were doing so well that nobody felt like asking questions.

Martin had a stronger impact on the back office and operations side of the firm. Until he arrived nearly all such work had been done by Roy Johnson. But Johnson was overstretched, and the Swiss warrants episode had showed that settlement had to be taken more seriously. Martin took over the job and spent the next nine months recruiting more people to work on settlements and financial controls. The head of settlements was a tall, amiable man of thirty-eight called John Guy, who had just joined Baring Securities from Kleinwort Grievson, the stockbroking arm of Kleinwort Benson, and was getting to grips with its flaws. However, Martin had ambitions beyond running the invisible machinery of Baring Securities. It was still expanding rapidly and moving into countries with unfamiliar stock exchanges and settlement systems. The expansion into Asian countries under Fraser was continuing. The traditional method used by Baring Securities when going into a new country was to set up a temporary office – often in a big hotel room – from which an analyst could work. When the analyst had visited enough firms, he or she could write a report for fund managers on, say, Thailand or Malaysia recommending some shares. Then the sales desk would buy and sell them through local brokers for a while, finally setting up as a full member of the country's stock exchange. It was the model that had been used so successfully in Japan, and was now being spread into developing Asian countries as western investors became attracted by the rapid economic growth rates of what were dubbed the 'Tiger' economies of the Pacific Rim.

All this was fine in principle, but the problem with these countries was that their stock exchanges were still small and illiquid, used to turnover of a few tens of thousands of shares a day. When an order came from US or UK pension funds, it was for hundreds of thousands. Exchanges and brokers could quickly seize up under the pressure. Besides that, it was not always simple just to roll into town, because many countries had restrictions on foreign brokers and the authorities had to be cultivated. It was an opportunity for Martin which he seized. He came up with the idea of a Business Development Group, which would go into unfamiliar markets to square regulators and set up an infrastructure. Martin liked to talk about it in glamorous terms as a commando group that would knock a clearing in the jungle for other troops to follow. The Baring Securities directors found the idea of a fighting force of grey-suited accountants laughable, but at least somebody else would do the boring work. Martin began to recruit a team of accountants for BDG, who were known as 'Martin's henchmen'. The henchmen had another function. They would carry out internal audits, a conventional practice in a large company. Instead of relying on annual inspections by accountants, Martin would send a henchman to local offices to check on the managers and examine the books. It was supposed to be a safeguard against Heath's fiefdoms running out of control, but it did not always work. One henchman who turned up in New York was thrown out of the office by Jim Reed, who insisted he would not brook interference.

If all this was an irritant to the other Baring Securities directors, Martin gained respect for sorting out a way of making their capital go further. Baring Securities was now growing so fast that it needed more capital to support its far-flung operations. Every branch and membership of a stock exchange not only added to expenses, but required a block of capital to be set aside to satisfy local regulators that Baring Securities would not collapse. Despite the vast sums now being earned through warrant and share trading, there was a dire shortage of capital. So much of the firm's profits was taken out in profit-sharing for Baring Securities' directors and employees that not enough was being left to provide a base for growth. Baring Securities could not issue either shares or bonds because it was a subsidiary. So Martin devised a means of manufacturing capital. Normally a loan does not count as capital because a bank can demand it back instantly, unlike shares or bonds. But Martin got around that by setting up two subsidiaries called Baring Securities Financial Services and Baring Securities International Holdings. These borrowed the cash from ten banks to fund Baring Securities' expansion. Once he had the money, Martin used it as capital to inject into Baring Securities' local subsidiary companies around the world. It was a rickety structure. If the banks lost confidence in Baring Securities and withdrew their money, it could all tumble like a pack of cards. But it was legal, and there did not seem much danger of that. The firm was making a lot of money, and its parent had deep pockets.

By 1988 the senior executives of Barings had other things on their minds. Sir John Baring was coming close to retirement and the decision was approaching as to who should succeed him as chairman. In terms of precedence there was little doubt it should be Nicholas Baring. Of family members working there only Peter and Nicholas were directors of Barings. Nicholas was the elder brother, with much wider experience of the international breadth of Barings' businesses than his brother. Nicholas was the chairman of Baring Asset Management and had been appointed deputy chairman in 1986. In contrast Peter had worked only in corporate finance before becoming finance director. Yet despite his range of interests Nicholas's record of making money was not very distinguished. He had been made deputy chairman partly to compensate for losing executive control of Baring Asset Management in 1986. The task of managing BAM had passed to Miles Rivett-Carnac, a former navy commander with a bluff manner that concealed a keen intelligence, who had joined Baring Brothers in 1970. Rivett-Carnac decided BAM could produce ten times the profits of £3 million it was then bringing in. The main difficulty was that it was an internally divided business. Bolsover had returned to Britain in 1985, but had refused point blank to amalgamate his operation with the domestic fund management arm, which he regarded as dozy and badly run. Bolsover was just as keen as Heath on keeping his distance from Baring Brothers, and just as aggressive in doing so. But Rivett-Carnac gradually won Bolsover over by sending him hand-written notes and trying to plant ideas in his mind, and the two sides of BAM finally merged in 1989. Profits grew rapidly.

In 1987 Nicholas fell ill with cancer and took six months off to recover before returning. By the time a choice had to be made on John Baring's successor, Nicholas was not a shoo-in. Indeed, Rivett-Carnac was seen by some as a good alternative. John Baring wanted above all to keep Tuckey. He was not old enough to be chairman, but Baring wanted him to take over Baring Brothers. He was the outstanding talent in the firm, and it was critically important that he could work with Baring's successor. Baring took a long time to decide, consulting most of Barings' senior directors. Several of them, including Tuckey, were opposed to Nicholas. Peter emerged as the best candidate, despite his diffidence about it. He was a safer pair of hands. Even after selecting Peter, John Baring asked others if he should be a non-executive chairman with Tuckey as chief executive. In the end he made Peter executive chairman with Tuckey and Rivett-Carnac as his deputies. Nicholas left Barings to become chairman of the insurance firm Commercial Union. The accession of Peter Baring had little effect on Baring Securities except to make Heath even more confident in his independence. He had respected John Baring, who had a dry sense of humour and a knack for knowing what was going on under the surface. Heath did not think that Peter Baring's instincts for potential trouble were as finely developed as his cousin's.

Heath was more concerned with keeping the earnings flowing at Baring Securities. Warrant trading had picked up again, but the firm was having to fight harder to remain a leading foreign broker in Japan and Asia. US investment banks were moving into the region and would try to poach its staff because of its strong reputation. US banks had an edge on Baring Securities in one respect. They were accustomed to selling futures and options in the sophisticated US market and had brought this expertise to Japan. The futures market there was poorly developed, but US banks were selling futures and options based on the Nikkei, both in Osaka and Singapore. Baring Securities was in the business in a small way. It joined Simex in 1987 but only as a non-clearing member. This meant it did not execute trades on behalf of its customers, but would place orders through other brokers. Heath and Baylis, who was now virtually a full-time manager and had moved to an office away from the trading floor, wanted to remedy Baring Securities' weakness in futures and options. Baylis's first move was to hire a futures and options broker called Rupert Lowe from Phillips & Drew to set up an operation that would allow Baring Securities to buy and sell derivatives on exchanges around the world. It was a grand scheme that soon turned out to be impractical because most investors did not regard Barings as a global broker. They wanted to buy derivatives in London and Chicago through other firms. The only markets in which they were inclined to buy futures and options through Barings were in Japan and Asia.

The man picked by Greer to sell futures and options in Tokyo was a thirty-five-year-old American called Mike Killian, who worked on Simex for Chase Manhattan, the US bank. Killian was a born-and-bred futures salesman. He had an MBA from the University of Chicago, and had sold commodity derivatives for the US bank Continental Illinois. Killian cut a rather mysterious figure when he arrived in Tokyo. He was a wiry man with a weathered face and walrus moustache, who resembled a nineteenth-century cowboy. He had a quiet, mesmeric voice and a laid-back manner accentuated by his New Age beliefs. He believed in negative and positive vibrations, and had used crystals to predict the level of the Nikkei. He also tucked a long magnet down the back of his trousers, aligned with his spine, to cure a back problem. But Killian had a tough side as well. His nose had been broken twice during arguments on trading floors. Primhak and others regarded Killian as sneaky and tight-fisted. He went out of his way to make the most of his reputation. Eating in Tokyo was expensive but he found an Indian restaurant where he could buy lunch for less than £5. Killian's isolation had other causes than his personality. He traded with investors, such as hedge funds and small US brokers. These were different from the big British funds that provided the backbone of Baring Securities' business. The brokers thought that he was running a slightly shady bucket shop, and Killian would emphasize constantly that he was a force unto himself. 'I could run this business from a hotel room,' he said, in answer to any criticism.

Whatever its antecedents it was soon clear that Killian's operation was a useful addition, though this was less to do with the commission he earned than the cash his customers deposited with Baring Securities. The Osaka and Simex exchanges required brokers to put down a cash deposit called 'initial margin' if they bought futures and options for customers, but they allowed brokers to net customers' contracts before handing over initial margin. Barings might have two customers, one of whom was 200 futures long and another 200 short. Barings could demand cash from these customers to cover the initial margin for 400 futures, but it did not have to hand it to the exchange because these positions netted. The firm was left with surplus cash that it could deposit at a bank. This interest provided most of the income from futures and options sales. (Later, in 1990, futures and options would earn £27,000 in commission and a further £61,000 from cash deposits in a single week.[4]) It meant that derivatives profits were peculiarly dependent on the back office. Baring Securities needed to collect cash as efficiently as possible and deposit as little as it could with exchanges. Killian started to build up a futures and options sales desk in Tokyo. Baylis hired a twenty-eight-year-old Malaysian called Su Khoo, who was the brightest mathematics specialist taken by Barings up to that point. After leaving school Khoo sat a national mathematics exam and was top in the country. She had worked as an actuary, calculating obscure probabilities for insurance companies. Khoo would sit silently at her desk in Tokyo studying futures and options prices.

The success of futures and options was not simply a matter of Killian's salesmanship. It was helped by the bizarre state of the market in Japanese derivatives. Just as warrants had been completely mispriced in their early days in 1982, so Japanese equity futures and options often sold for completely the wrong price in the late 1980s. The Japanese tended to undervalue options that gained from a fall in the market because the country was gripped by a euphoric belief in the Nikkei's indefinite rise. Japanese investors also liked to sell options because they liked being paid cash immediately, and deferring their risk. Khoo would sit with four screens showing futures and options prices and just by looking at these screens she could spot huge bargains. Investors were underestimating the risk of volatility by selling options too cheaply. Anyone willing to pay the option premium could place a bet that they were wrong. They could buy a call option that gained if the market rose more steeply than expected, and another – known as a put option – that gained if it fell. This was known as volatility trading. A trader who was 'long volatility' gained if the market moved around. Investment banks often traded volatility as well as arbitrage, because it could only be done properly by traders who understood option pricing. Markets tended to be full of mispriced volatility because it was not well understood by many people. In mid-1989, 'implied volatility' in the Tokyo market stood at 5 per cent. This meant that you would make money from buying options if the market moved by more than 5 per cent upwards or downwards within a month of the deal being struck.

That seemed to be a very good bet, and so it proved in July when a salesman called Robin Cohen, who worked with Khoo, sold what was called a 'short strangle' to the Kuwait Investment Office. The KIO was in charge of investing the oil revenues of the Kuwaiti royal family. Cohen persuaded it to buy a set of options that put it long volatility on the Nikkei. The Nikkei had drifted between 33,000 and 34,000 up to the Japanese general election on 23 July, and the country was widely expecting the defeat of the long-standing Japanese ruling party, the Liberal Democratic Party. Traders in the cash markets mostly waited for the result. But by going long volatility, the KIO gained whether the market went up sharply on an LDP victory, or fell on a Socialist Party victory. The Socialist Party took over the majority in the Upper House from the LDP, but the result had been so discounted that the market started rising again, bringing big profits to the KIO. The 'Barings strangle' was described admiringly in the financial press as an example of new-found sophistication in financial trading. More importantly for Baring Securities, the KIO's success also galvanized Su Khoo into becoming a trader. She had been in Tokyo for over a year and had watched many clear opportunities for profit-making flash up on her screens. Cohen told Diarmaid Kelly that the Japanese options market was the most extraordinary he had encountered in his life. If you knew what you were doing, there was little risk involved. You could buy or sell options at their advertised prices and be guaranteed a profit. It was like shooting fish in a barrel.

In fact, Heath and Baylis's thoughts were already moving in this direction. They had started to become worried at the entry of US banks into the warrant market. It was becoming hard to gain returns that had been easy before. This was the time for Baring Securities to start trading futures and options as well as warrants. Already Sliwerski was becoming exasperated at people telling him that a new world was on its way. 'If anybody else mentions volatility to me, I'll punch him,' he said with feeling one day. Even some old hands such as Kelly were getting in on the act. At the same time as the KIO had bought its strangle in Tokyo, someone in London had pointed out to Kelly and Sliwerski an option on the Nikkei being offered at what appeared a very cheap price. It was a put option on Nikkei futures that would pay out money if the Nikkei fell below a certain level. Kelly was uneasy at the listlessness of the market, and thought it might not be a bad thing to buy some insurance. After all, an uncomfortably large proportion of Baring Securities' profits rested on the Japanese bull market. The put option was on sale for £500,000, and Sliwerski and Kelly got Baylis's and Heath's approval to buy it. Baylis was now keen to expand into derivatives trading. They were looking out for opportunities, when one arose from an odd quarter. Martin was interviewing an accountant called Richard Johnston, who seemed a good candidate to be one of his henchmen, when it became clear that he knew more about futures and options than anybody else currently in the London office.

Johnston was a talkative Ulsterman of twenty-eight who had been to Manchester University before training as an accountant. He was a keen fan of the cult Manchester band Joy Division and had even worn black the day the lead singer, Ian Curtis, committed suicide. He had learned about derivatives while working at Bankers Trust. His first task was to examine the settlement of futures and options in London, which he discovered was in a mess. But after finding someone to sort it out he was soon dispatched to Tokyo to scout out whether there was a potential derivatives trader lurking there. When he arrived, he found two potential hopes, whom he took to lunch. One was Su Khoo and the other was Fernando Gueler. Gueler was then twenty-four years old and had been working at Baring Securities for a year, researching derivatives and doing odd jobs like helping to automate warrant trading. Gueler was the son of a trader of fork-lift trucks in California, who was a whiz-kid at mathematics as a teenager. He gained the maximum score on the Advanced Placement test at school before going to Harvard. Gueler was bounding with enthusiasm, but his potential had not yet been fully recognized. This was partly because he was so excitable. Sometimes words tumbled out of his mouth so fast that he was difficult to understand. For the time being Khoo struck Johnston as a better bet. She was well organized and had clear ideas about making money. Johnston thought it would make sense to give Khoo a chance, with Gueler backing her up, and by October 1989 she was a futures and options trader.

It turned out to be just in time. Khoo started gradually by buying options that made her long volatility. She was never a purely mathematical trader and did not use computers to carry out calculations, but instead would write her trades on sheets of paper in red and black ink. Yet Khoo had a sound instinct. She bought volatility throughout late 1989, making modest amounts to re-invest in her trading. Then at the end of December the world changed decisively. On 29 December 1989 the Nikkei index reached an all-time peak of 38,915 after a fifteen-year bull run. When Christopher Heath had become interested in Japanese shares in 1974, the Nikkei had stood at around 4,200. It was virtually ten times that level on the eve of 1990. Its last gasp brought Heath a final deluge of money. Baring Securities made £61 million in warrant trading in 1989. Its operating profits for the year were £97 million and Heath took home £8 million. But the Nikkei was not to reach 40,000. Political and economic uncertainty in Japan finally punctured the speculative bubble that had buoyed up the Nikkei for so long. The index started to fall. It was bad for most of those in Baring Securities' Tokyo office. The equity salesmen and traders faced a harder task with the Nikkei in retreat. The problems were worst on the warrant desk as they depended on a rise in the Nikkei for warrants to keep gaining in value. Without a bull market warrant trading was painfully exposed. The engine that had driven Baring Securities for six years started to splutter. It was now awkwardly dependent on its put option and Khoo's venture into options trading.

Khoo hardly appeared to be a likely saviour of Baring Securities. She was not in the mould of Primhak, who believed in trading by instinct and having the guts to lead the market. Primhak would look over at Khoo in her corner of the room, silent and unsmiling. 'Come on, say something,' he would mutter. The futures and options sales desk was a flock of pigeons as far as he was concerned. People like Khoo and Gueler were utterly different from Primhak, who was in the tradition of the jobbers of the Stock Exchange. They were the bright pupils in the classroom despised by the rough boys at the back. They did not live the wild life of the equity salesmen and traders, spending money like water around Tokyo. Each lunchtime Khoo, Gueler and Johnston would repair to a cafeteria in the same building as the Baring Securities office. Khoo and Gueler used to call it the 'doom and gloom room'. Gueler had a beef curry and Johnston a steak sandwich, while Khoo picked away at a fish curry. Theirs was an arcane and technical world. Often they talked the mathematics of futures and options, where different risks were known by Greek symbols: 'delta' was the rate at which a future or option changed in value as a cash market moved, 'gamma' was the rate it altered for a given move in the market. Volatility traders were often known as 'Gamma geeks' by the uninitiated. One of the Baring Securities brokers came up with a nickname for the futures and options desk that expressed their other-worldliness. He referred to them as the 'Technopeasants'.

The put option soon started paying dividends. The £500,000 premium was rapidly regained, and as the market fell below 29,000 in April it started to pay out millions of pounds. Even more cash was soon flowing from Su Khoo. She had bought volatility cheaply at the end of 1989, which brought enormous profits as the Nikkei slumped by a quarter. By April the market had become so scared that there was a panic rush to buy volatility, so that investors could somehow protect themselves from the débâcle. The volatility being implied by option prices shot up from 5 per cent to about 100 per cent. Khoo then went short volatility and the market promptly evened out at

33,000 between May and July, bringing her yet another bonanza. Then in July volatility again became very cheap. Khoo decided to buy it once more. She had just positioned herself heavily long volatility when on 2 August Saddam Hussein, the ruler of Iraq, invaded Kuwait, starting the Gulf War. Over the next six days the Nikkei dropped 3,200 points to 27,600 as shares in Japanese companies that were dependent on oil supplies dropped. As war news came through daily, with setbacks and victories for the Allied troops, the Nikkei bounced up and down erratically. It was the perfect moment to be long volatility. Khoo sat at her terminals as the Gulf War progressed, exhausted by riding the wave of volatility. She got neck ache from the sheer physical stress and tension, but in a single month she earned $16 million in revenue. She was afraid to tell Johnston how much she had made because she thought she was bound to lose some of it.

By the end of the year the balance of power at Baring Securities was shifting away from those such as Sliwerski and Primhak who had made money in the Japanese bull market. Profits from warrant trading halved to £27 million in the year to September 1990, while Khoo's options trading produced £11 million. She and the put option propped up Baring Securities' profits at £81 million. It had been forced to hunt outside Japan for earnings, expanding to Bangkok, Kuala Lumpur, Jakarta, Korea, Manila and Taipei, and now its best bet appeared to lie in repeating in Asia in the 1990s what it had done in Japan in the 1980s. Recession had struck western economies again, and fund managers were looking to invest in Asian economies. Heath had mixed feelings about it for Asia was the domain of Fraser and relations between them were strained. Apart from the loss on the Hong Kong futures market, Fraser was blamed when three of the Asian sales desk left to go to Flemings in March 1989. The animosity was mutual. Fraser had lost patience with Heath over his spending habits. Heath had also started having an affair in 1989, which Fraser thought was hypocritical since Heath had made a point of not recruiting people who had been divorced. Asia had never made as much money as Japan in the 1980s, and Fraser had been made to feel it. Now the earning power was reversed, and Asia was starting to boom. Those on the Asian sales desk in London were not only making money, but winning awards just as the Japan operation had done in the 1980s. In July 1991 the desk was voted top of two polls by London fund managers, and fifteen of them decided to celebrate in true Baring Securities style.

They picked an Italian restaurant in Fulham for their night out. It was a sunny evening and they sat outside at a garden table next to a wall. Fraser turned up resplendent in his cream-coloured St John's College, Oxford rowing blazer. As he arrived he warned the others, who were already drinking strawberry daiquiris, that nobody should spoil his blazer. Carl Strutt, the head of Asian sales, took the challenge by bribing a waiter to spill a tray of daiquiris all over the blazer. He went to the lavatory after this triumph and returned to see the others all eating their starters. On his plate lay one lettuce leaf and a live snail, which someone had taken from the wall. 'We'll give you £50 to eat your starter,' someone said. After bargaining it up to £100, Strutt put the snail in his mouth, but he was so disgusted that he spat it out. 'You're a wimp!' shouted Fraser. He reached over for the snail, dropped it in a glass of red wine and swallowed it. The evening became louder and wilder. Strutt still wanted to have his own back on Fraser and bribed one of the equity saleswomen called Libby Hankin – whom he later married – to crawl under the table and catch Fraser by surprise. She made her way on her hands and knees down the line of legs until she reached Fraser and then popped her head up in his lap, shouting 'Boo!' Fraser was so shocked that he toppled over backwards, taking two others down with him, and landed heavily on his left wrist. The next day he appeared at work with his fractured wrist in plaster. The good times at Baring Securities had started to take their toll.

CHAPTER 5

In Baring Securities' seven years of existence, Heath had been its unquestioned leader. He had a way of gaining loyalty by making people feel they did not work for an ordinary firm. One of Heath's first employees, called Alex Stewart, became so intrigued by Japanese culture that he wanted to go to the country to study the ancient art of the tea ceremony. Heath had helped pay for him to go. Despite his sins, some of his employees regarded Heath as a spiritual leader. He might be a spendthrift, but he had a moral quality. As far as the health of the firm went, they were forced to put their faith in him because there was no alternative. By 1991 Baring Securities employed 1,100 staff. Only three – Heath, Baylis and Martin – knew its financial structure in depth. The others had not cared too much as long as the money flowed in, but now they were starting to worry that the collapse of the Japanese stock market had damaged their firm badly. Doug Atherley had become convinced that Baring Securities had grown too large, and was losing its touch, but he could not find Heath to confront him with his worries as Heath was spending more and more of his time flying around the world. Even when he was in town, he was hard to pin down. One day Atherley finally got hold of him and was attempting to explain why he was worried when a light for an incoming call flashed on a nearby desk. Heath reached across to pick it up as he was talking. Atherley lost his temper. 'For God's sake, Christopher, it has taken me five months to get five minutes with you,' he said. 'Just talk to me.'

When Atherley finally decided to leave, he could not even get hold of Heath to tell him the news. After several weeks of trying, he finally tracked Heath down to a Singapore hotel and faxed his resignation across. Later that day Atherley's wife picked up the phone at home.

'Get me Doug,' said an irritated voice at the other end. 'Christopher, I don't work for you. You can at least be polite,' she said. When Atherley picked up the phone, he heard an apoplectic Heath. 'What the hell is this?' he said, refusing to accept his resignation. As far as Heath was concerned, nobody just walked out of his firm. He made it clear that Atherley could do what he wanted as long as he did not resign. Perhaps he wanted to work in Tokyo or New York instead. What did he fancy? Atherley and his wife soon found themselves on a first-class flight to New York, then chauffeured to a suite at the Hotel Pierre. Jim Reed was not happy about having Atherley thrust on him. He did not have a high regard for the British at the best of times, whom he felt were lousy managers scared to sack people. Now he was being asked to take a guy from London just because Heath was afraid to lose him. 'You're a lazy fuck!' Reed would tell Atherley at every opportunity. Within a few months Atherley had left after all.

Fraser, in particular, irritated Reed intensely. Reed had dismissed one of his own staff for buying Hong Kong futures without authority just before the October crash. The man, who had lost his life savings of $500,000, was an old friend of Reed's but that was too bad. Rules were rules. From then on Reed started calling Fraser 'the Left Dishonourable'. He did not put up with any nonsense from Heath either. One day, the two had a blazing row in the Tokyo office over Reed's insistence on salesmen in Tokyo not ringing US investors directly. Reed insisted it was illegal because it broke the rules of the Securities and Exchange Commission, the US regulator of financial firms, but Heath suspected it was more a matter of Reed protecting his turf. 'You're always whinging, Jim,' said Heath. 'Why can't you be a team player?' Nobody talked to Jim Reed like that. 'Fuck you! I'm not going to be responsible for people breaking regulations,' shouted Reed. He walked out, and when he returned to the office after three hours, Heath apologized.

By 1991 discontent had spread widely. Everyone knew the firm was not doing well. Khoo was still supporting the edifice, but it could not last for ever. The truth did not seem to have dawned at Baring Brothers. John Dare still chaired the quarterly board meetings amiably, listening to the latest stories of achievement. 'Well done, well done,' he said. Reed used to laugh at him. 'Dare thinks we're a piece of steak,' he would say. But people were getting worried. Warrant trading had not recovered since the Tokyo crash, having gone from a profit of £27 million in 1990 to a loss of £1.6 million in 1991.[1] Khoo's trading only brought in £11 million to compensate and the broking business lost £2.8 million. Operating profits dropped from £81.5 million in 1990 to only £36.5 million in 1991. The A Pool profit share dropped to £6.6 million, hardly the largesse to which they were accustomed.

As these worries spread Tuckey and Peter Baring were wondering how to bring Baring Securities into the fold. They wanted to tame Heath in the same way as Bolsover. Tuckey talked of it as a stool with three legs. If Baring Brothers, Baring Securities and Baring Asset Management could be brought under control, Barings would have a solid business. They first had to persuade Heath that his destiny lay with Barings as a whole, which meant appointing him a director of the holding company. However, there was an obstacle. The Barings directors all took part in the same profit-sharing scheme set up in 1985. Once money had been shared out to managers in each of the businesses, some of the rest was allocated to the directors by Peter Baring. It did not produce the same spectacular sums as Baring Securities, but it was not to be sneezed at. In 1990 Tuckey had been paid £814,000. Tuckey thought that it could only work if Heath gave up part of his A Pool share to join the Barings profit-sharing scheme. In September 1990 he took Heath to dinner to discuss the idea. He raised the problem of Heath's profit-share. 'Well, there is a way out of that,' said Heath. 'You can buy me out.' They agreed Heath would become a Barings director once a third of his A Pool share was bought out by Barings. Heath used Warburg to value his share, which estimated it to be worth £22 million. Tuckey's valuation was £16 million. They split the difference at £18 million, which meant a third of it was worth £6 million. By 1991 it turned out to be a generous offer given that the firm's profits had halved, but Tuckey and Baring stuck to the arrangement.

The disclosure that Heath alone was being offered a lifeline out of the declining A Pool caused outrage among the others. Baylis, Fraser and Kelly all demanded that the same offer should be made to them at the same time. They had become used to living well from the proceeds of the A Pool, and a boost in what was promising to be a meagre year would come in useful. 'How can you offer this to one shareholder and not the others?' Baylis asked Tuckey angrily. But Tuckey and Peter Baring were firm: they saw no need to buy off the others to get Heath on the board.

Rivett-Carnac tried to broker peace. 'Couldn't you split it with them?' he asked Heath.

'I wish I could, but I need the money,' Heath replied. He was now so used to living regally that he was already counting on the £6 million to support his lifestyle.

Finally, Tuckey faced down Baylis, Fraser and Kelly by telling them that if it was really a point of principle, they would call the entire deal off. Confronted with the ultimatum they backed down and Heath got his money, joining the Barings board with Bolsover and Dare in November 1991. The experience reinforced Fraser's view that Heath was forfeiting his place as the undisputed leader of Baring Securities. He was already resentful of the way in which Heath deferred to Baylis. Fraser and Baylis were not a happy mix and had come to dislike each other cordially. Kelly's reaction was less pronounced. He remained close to Heath because of their long association, and Heath's wife was also fond of him. But Kelly thought Heath had been selfish to take the money. It was not in the spirit of Baring Securities.

Unfortunately for Tuckey and Peter Baring their effort to draw Heath into the fold had come too late. Already there was a split between them and Heath over how Baring Securities should proceed. Heath and Baylis had become convinced that Baring Securities needed to find a new engine for growth. Broking was no longer a profitable enough business in itself to make the sort of returns Baring Securities had come to expect. Brokers such as Henderson Crosthwaite in London had traditionally survived on the system of fixed broking commissions that had remained in place until Big Bang. When these went the profits of broking declined. This process of decay had been seen in the New York market, where broking firms gained half their income from commissions in 1975 but only 18 per cent by 1989. The large US firms had responded by injecting more capital into financial trading. It was not something they talked about loudly, since it sounded rather disreputable to make most of your profits from a sophisticated form of gambling, but they had little alternative. Baring Securities was in the same bind. It had always earned more money from trading than selling shares. In 1986, it had earned just £3.5 million from equity broking, against £23 million from trading warrants. At its peak in 1989 equity broking had brought in only £19 million of the £97 million operating profits. It was not something it had ever emphasized too hard to Baring Brothers, but in its six-year existence, 82 per cent of its profits had come from trading. Since warrants had run out of steam, Heath and Baylis reasoned that derivatives trading was the way ahead.

But derivatives trading was an expensive affair. You needed to invest in technology and have plenty of capital to take large bets. The harsh truth was that Baring Securities had run out of money. So much of its profits had been extracted in bonuses that it was already painfully reliant on the bank loans obtained by Martin. It was borrowing £31 million from banks to support the business, and had committed £33 million more to growth around the world, such as opening a Korean branch and offices in Frankfurt and Paris. That meant it was £64 million short of capital before even investing in new forms of trading. In the 1980s it had been able to divert money from warrants into growth without consulting Baring Brothers but it could not do that now because the earnings were not there. Nor could it borrow from banks. Martin had seen the writing on the wall. The European Commission was preparing a directive that would compel all banks to hold adequate capital. It was only due in 1996, but it would prohibit the sort of capital structure he had devised, in which bank loans were used as an artificial form of capital. This meant there was only one place to go for more capital: Baring Brothers. Heath was as confident as ever about that. Barings had done well from Baring Securities, gaining £170 million from it in six years. He told Martin he had an understanding with Peter Baring that he could claim back some capital if needed. Then one evening in November Martin was at his desk when he heard an explosion of anger from the next office. Heath entered his room in a rage. 'Those bastards have spent our money!' he shouted.

Tuckey had just phoned Heath to explain that Barings was paying $78 million to buy a 40 per cent stake in Dillon Read, the Wall Street investment bank. Baring Brothers had formed links with the merchant bank Kidder Peabody in the nineteenth century, but these had faded and Tuckey was now looking for a way for Baring Brothers to gain a foothold on Wall Street. Barings was helping Dillon Read's partners to buy back their firm from Traveler's Group, the US insurance company. Tuckey had demonstrated that the priority for capital was Baring Brothers, not Baring Securities. The following day he dutifully went round to Baring Securities to face the music. Baylis was even more angry than Heath. 'You are buying a stake in a clapped-out broking house,' he said. It was too late. The blow came just as they were on the point of needing capital for derivatives trading. Heath had been trying to lure Stephen Posford, the star trader at Salomon Brothers in London. Posford had made a lot of money by trading Japanese and German bonds and futures using mathematical techniques. But in September 1991 Salomon was plunged into crisis when it admitted rigging US Treasury bond auctions. It caused a wave of defections, and Heath had persuaded Posford to have lunch with him, Tuckey and Michael Baring. Tuckey rang Heath the next morning to say he was impressed, but the problem was that Posford traded bonds not equities. If he was to join, he would have to work in the treasury and trading side of Baring Brothers. 'We are very clear about the boundaries, and you will have to be careful to watch them,' Tuckey told him.

Posford was not interested and the talks broke down. The Dillon Read episode persuaded Baylis that words were not enough. Barings had to be shown the urgency of the problem. He and Martin drew up a thirteen-page paper setting out their arguments for more capital.[2] In addition to the £64 million capital shortfall, they estimated that Baring Securities was in need of £55 million to be injected into the balance sheet to support derivatives trading. This meant that it was £119 million short of capital. They argued that the firm could generate £45 million more revenue a year with the fresh capital, which would include £3.4 million a year from index arbitrage and £13.5 million from arbitraging warrants and convertible bonds. Greer tried to press home this view on 12 December when Peter Baring visited Tokyo. Baring was introduced to Primhak, who was dressed in a loud waistcoat to be interviewed for a CNN broadcast. He came across Khoo, who told him she had earned $1 million that day. He looked pleased. Baring listened as Greer told him they needed to step up derivatives trading not only to grow but to survive. He admitted that in the past Barings had 'never understood your business' and had to make more effort to do so. Despite such expressions of good intent, Baring Brothers and Baring Securities were fast reaching an impasse. Baring and Tuckey now knew that Baring Securities was deeply troubled. The old ambiguity about how it earned money had been stripped away by Baylis and Martin. Now it was clear that Barings owned a broking firm that was heavily reliant on trading and had little confidence in its own survival unless it gambled even more heavily.

Tuckey did not relish the idea of Baring Securities becoming a trading outfit like Salomon Brothers. He did not think much of Baylis and Martin's paper either. If you were going to ask for £120 million, you had to come up with something more than thirteen pages of vague description of what you might do with it. 'If you think that this constitutes a business plan for £120 million, you've got another think coming,' he said sharply. It soon became clear that his misgivings over Baring Securities were shared by some of its directors. Tuckey decided he needed to keep a closer eye on it, and took over from Dare as chairman in late 1991. The first board meeting chaired by Tuckey was on 21 January. The meetings up until then had remained in the format established early on by Heath: Martin handed out a few figures and there was some polite discussion. On that Monday things changed. Willie Phillips, the managing director of Baring Securities in Hong Kong, had flown in for the meeting. He was a forty-one-year-old diplomat's son, talkative and full of energy, who worked with Fraser on Asian share trading, and he was wound up by the idea that it was starting to be weighed down by losses in Tokyo. What exercised him most was the accounts. The forty-three directors were responsible for the firm, but forty of them knew little about its inner workings. He had an ally in Sliwerski, who had been worried by criticism of non-executive directors of Maxwell Communications, the company run by the tycoon Robert Maxwell, for failing to prevent him plundering the group's pension funds.

The usual pre-board meeting was held that morning, and at lunchtime Phillips talked angrily about the mess Baring Securities was in. At the meeting in the afternoon Tuckey was startled to witness an open revolt.

'These figures don't tell us anything. Do they mean we're making a profit or not?' Phillips asked.

There was an awkward silence.

'I don't think this is an appropriate forum for that debate,' Martin said carefully.

'This is a board meeting. If we can't discuss it here, where can we do it?' argued Phillips.

'That is a very good question,' Tuckey interjected. 'Are we making a profit or aren't we?'

To the dismay of Baylis and Martin, who had hitherto kept a lid on such questions in front of the Brothers, the directors were soon discussing openly how little they knew. Sliwerski protested that he was entirely in the dark. 'I'm not saying anything untoward is going on, but we've all read what Maxwell did, and think: "How the hell did the non-executives let him get away with it?" The fact is that 90 per cent of us don't know what is going on 90 per cent of the time,' he said.

Heath listened to the insurrection without breathing a word. Dare chuckled as he walked out of the room with Tuckey. 'Welcome to the chair,' he said.

It was a warning shot for Heath, who decided the need for more capital was urgent. If the Brothers were not going to supply it, he would have to look elsewhere. He already had an idea. On a visit to Mexico City he had bumped into a customer called Faud Sayeed, an Egyptian property magnate, whose £2 billion fortune was invested by a Geneva-based company called Unifund.

Heath had explained his problem to Sayeed, who had offered to buy a stake in Baring Securities. Heath believed the £100 million he wanted could be raised by selling a quarter of the firm. Heath suggested the idea to Tuckey but got a guarded response. Tuckey was coming to think that Baring Securities had been running out of control. The last thing he wanted was another shareholder, allowing Heath and Baylis to divide and rule. But Heath did not give up. On 26 March Baylis came to a weekly meeting of directors of Barings to outline his latest scheme. This time it involved establishing a separate company with up to $400 million of capital to sell derivatives. An outside party would provide all the capital for the company in exchange for up to 50 per cent of the profits, while Baring Securities would manage it. This idea did not get a much better response from Tuckey or Peter Baring, who asked for further details. Heath now tried to get on with his strategy despite the lack of enthusiasm from Bishopsgate. He found a trader at Salomon Brothers called Jonathan Waxman. He was not such a star as Posford, but he had made money for Salomon with a type of long-term arbitrage known as 'basis trading'. He searched for long-term disparities in derivatives and bond markets and then took positions that gained when the markets moved back in line. It was not clear what Waxman would do at Baring Securities but he was hired on a guaranteed salary and bonus of £1.5 million over two years. The problem was that Heath and Baylis still had not found the capital to enable him to trade in the style of Salomon Brothers.

In the meanwhile, the internal divisions within Baring Securities were widening. The firm had moved to America Square, but discontent prevailed. By the board meeting on 27 April Alex Murray had become so disenchanted that he decided to resign. That morning he told his fellow directors what he was going to do. Jim Reed was pleased to hear that one of Heath's detractors was leaving. 'Good! If you feel that way, you *should* go,' he said.

Murray went to see Heath in his office on the fifth floor, taking along his resignation letter.

Heath was in subdued mood. 'Do you think I'm the problem?' he asked.

'I think you probably are,' Murray replied.

'Should I resign?'

'Yes, you probably should,' said Murray remorselessly.

As ever, Heath wanted to avoid open conflict. Despite Murray's harsh words he persuaded him to stay, promising that Murray could help him reshape the firm. Reed was outraged at this British manoeuvre to avoid bloodshed, and wanted Heath to throw Murray out. 'Get rid of the guy. This is your chance to show who is in charge,' Reed urged Heath.

But Heath was punch-drunk. 'I've got to keep Alex. I am under pressure.'

The pressure soon intensified. As the put option ran out and Khoo's trading profits declined, the firm had no supports left in the Japanese bear market. By May 1992 Baring Securities had dipped into loss for the first time in its short existence, losing £1.3 million in May and £1.5 million more in June. It could no longer deliver the profits that had enabled Heath to keep the Brothers at arm's length.

Heath and Baylis had elicited a promise of £10 million more capital if they could justify the outlay but they were rapidly overtaken by events. Barings directors started to understand the fragility of the capital structure devised by Martin. When they examined the affairs of the two intermediate companies closely, they found that Baring Securities' outstanding loans were governed by an agreement that allowed the banks to withdraw their loans if there was a 'material adverse change' in Baring Securities' finances. Making operating losses clearly fell in this category. If these loans were withdrawn Barings would have to find capital to replace them or risk the collapse of Baring Securities. For a merchant bank that prided itself on conservatism it was an enormous shock. Furthermore, it was becoming clear that Baring Securities would not have enough money to pay the annual bonuses to which its traders and salesmen had become accustomed. It was expecting to make operating profits of about £10 million for the year to September and it was due to pay £18.5 million in bonuses. Unless Baring Brothers picked up the tab, it could start losing its best employees. Tuckey decided urgent action was required. He suggested to Heath that a full review of how Baring Securities spent and made money was required. Tuckey had his own candidate for the job: Peter Norris. Heath did not have the energy left to resist, but suggested a last compromise. He asked for Greer to come back from Japan to work alongside Norris.

Norris had returned to Baring Brothers from Goldman Sachs in May 1987. Although he had an exciting time, he missed Barings. Goldman Sachs was a relentless place that fostered internal competition. 'The thing that you never doubt at Barings is the motives of your colleagues,' he told Peter Baring when he arrived. Tuckey was pleased to have got him back. 'It's so nice to hear Peter's laugh again,' he would say. Norris had been sent to Hong Kong in October 1987, returning to London briefly in 1988 to help wind up a business he had started with his first wife in 1980 called Duff & Trotter. His marriage had by now broken up. The business was named after the high-class emporium in P. G. Wodehouse's books and it sold up-market food and delicacies through five shops. It worked in the 1980s, when people had plenty of cash to throw around, but in 1988 it started to lose money. It got into serious trouble the following year when efforts to dispose of leases on its shops failed. Duff & Trotter had to be wound down, and Norris spent £400,000 to buy out the leases and cap the loss. It was only his earnings from Baring Brothers that enabled him to meet the bill.

In Hong Kong Norris had taken over Baring Brothers in the only part of the world where it had struck up a working relationship with Baring Securities. Phillips had worked with the Brothers on deals including the $1.5 billion flotation of Cathay Pacific Airways, the largest issue Hong Kong had seen. He had also helped Barings win the lead role in the $6 billion flotation of Hong Kong Telecom, which Norris went on to handle in relative harmony with Phillips.

The sort of business they did in Hong Kong was becoming all the rage among big investment banks. In the past companies had been owned by investors in their own countries. A US company wanting to go public would hire one of the big Wall Street firms to sell its shares to US investors. But companies had now realized that the most effective way to raise capital was to tap not only domestic investors but the different capital markets around the world. An investment bank would coordinate a global offering of shares in Asia, Europe and the US. The role of managing such an issue was highly rewarding. The lead manager might get a fee of £10 million. In Hong Kong, Norris and Phillips worked together and shared out the proceeds between Baring Brothers and Baring Securities. In other parts of the world relations had been less easy. The brokers at Baring Securities tended to think they could manage share issues as well as the Brothers, if not better. There had already been spats over the matter. Greer had made a push to take over all such activities from Baring Brothers in Tokyo the previous autumn. Dare had written to Heath insisting that Greer had to respect the boundary, and complaining that his actions had been 'extremely diverting, and created considerable strain on some of our key people'.[3] However, Hong Kong was an oasis of good relations amid such bickering. Fraser and Kelly had come to regard Norris as one of the few Brothers who knew what he was doing. His reputation was such that they were happy for him to return early in 1992 to work on international share offerings at America Square.

There was one problem. Baylis and Heath had employed a former Scotland rugby player called Jeremy Campbell-Lamerton to do something similar. A compromise was reached and Norris became co-head of a new department with him, but the pairing was not a success.

Campbell-Lamerton underwrote a share issue by a cement company in Pakistan without informing Norris, which inflamed tensions. Then there was an upset over Barings' role in the flotation of the phone company Teléfonos de Mexico. It was due to get a $3 million fee, but was dropped after Baring Securities' research reached US investors, in breach of regulations, for which Campbell-Lamerton was held responsible. Nor did Norris endear himself to other investment bankers. His largest transaction was the £2.5 billion sale of shares in the pharmaceuticals company Wellcome by the Wellcome Trust, which owned it. Flemings was advising the Trust, and had taken great pains to prepare for the global offering of shares. It hired a banker called Ian Hannam from Salomon for the task. Barings advised Wellcome. Hannam and Norris did not get on. Norris maintained he was entitled to the details of where Flemings intended to sell shares, but Hannam said that this was privileged information. Norris was given access to records but outraged Hannam by getting them photocopied. Flemings insisted on the photocopies being returned, and rumours began to circulate in London investment banks that Norris had committed a breach of trust. Baylis and Heath lapped this up eagerly, and Norris soon became known as 'Captain Xerox' among his detractors at America Square.

In early summer 1992 Greer flew back from Japan, and began working with Norris on the project in America Square. The work was shrouded in secrecy. On 14 July Norris sent a memorandum to senior directors setting out the terms of the review. They would look at ways of saving costs, how the capital should be structured, and how Baring Securities was managed 'in the shortest possible time-frame'. Staff should not be told what was going on. The story would be that they were developing initiatives for derivatives trading. They would report weekly to Tuckey and Heath.[4] Considering they came from opposite sides of the fence, Norris and Greer got on well. They were both bright and analytical, and the work progressed rapidly. Norris quickly grasped where the firm was losing money. It was clear that its Australian arm, which was losing £3.7 million a year, should go, and so too should Frankfurt. Japan was more delicate, since Greer was in charge there. Norris and Greer compromised on a modest cut of fifteen jobs and savings of £3.7 million. Apart from the offices that were being closed down, London would bear the brunt of the cuts, with seventy-four jobs lost. By the time the savings were added up around the world, they came to 180 jobs lost, and £20 million a year saved. That was not enough in itself. Norris realized Baring Securities' bank loans had to be replaced. The loans had become known as 'the black hole' because of the possibility of collapse if the banks withdrew funding. Barings had pondered trying to issue more capital, but the timing was not propitious. Investors might be scared off by the disclosure of losses at Baring Securities.

Instead, Barings borrowed $75 million privately. It was lent the cash by Prince Khalid Abdullah, a member of the Saudi royal family, for which Barings had managed petrodollars in the 1970s. Prince Khalid was given a good return. Barings had to pay much higher interest on this loan than it had been paying to the banks. Barings had enough money to inject £80 million into Baring Securities. However, the financial change was not enough for Norris. He believed Baring Securities could no longer be run as Heath's fiefdom with its other directors largely kept in the dark. He drew up plans for a fifteen-man management committee that would meet weekly. The A Pool would be replaced with a profit-sharing arrangement that included everybody on this committee. Since Baring Securities was not going to be able to fund bonuses itself in 1992, Barings would provide £15 million to do so, but in return for this Baring Brothers was taking control. The profit-sharing would be under its control, and could be varied as Tuckey determined. Greer did not contradict Norris, but his heart was not in it. He was loyal to Heath, who was now talking about selling out to another firm. Baylis went round to Bishopsgate to urge Tuckey to let them go. 'Make yourself a hero. You can walk away looking brilliant,' Baylis said.

Tuckey was not going to be browbeaten. 'You do not understand. Barings does not sell things,' he retorted firmly.

In fact, Barings was more pragmatic than this suggested. Tuckey and Peter Baring had pondered the idea, but they did not want to be forced into a sale at an inopportune time, and Tuckey believed that the problem could be brought under control.

Tuckey instructed Norris to warn the directors of Baring Securities that if they tried to sell themselves without permission, they would breach their legal duties as directors. It was not enough to stop Baylis. If Barings was not willing to let them go, they would have to force

Tuckey to accept it. In August Baylis and Heath called a meeting of Baring Securities directors at Ashe. Martin was on holiday in the south of France and had to fly back from Toulouse to attend it. After they had chewed over the issue once more Baylis suggested there was only one way forward. They would have to go to Tuckey and Baring and threaten to leave *en masse* unless they agreed to bring in another shareholder. As long as they stuck together a mutiny could force Barings to back down. But by this time the divisions within Baring Securities were running deep. Fraser and Kelly both believed the management had to be opened up and power taken away from Baylis. Baylis's record as a manager was patchy to say the least. He had been responsible for Australia and Europe, which both lost money. Now he was hiring people like Waxman at vast expense. 'We cannot just resign. It would be absurd,' said Fraser. Kelly backed him, and the threat of a mass mutiny receded. They agreed instead to go to Barings one last time to press for what they wanted. Martin flew back to resume his holiday. When he returned, he went with Heath and Baylis to see Tuckey and Baring. They took along financial projections and details of their plans for how the capital could be used. It was useless. The answer was an unambiguous 'no'.

Heath was taken aback. He had convinced himself the financial case was so sound that nobody would reject it. 'I can't understand. It was a no-brainer,' he kept saying to Martin. Events were moving out of his control. On Wednesday 13 August Norris and Greer presented their draft reorganization to the A Pool. Norris explained it and said it came as a single package, all or nothing. Unless they agreed to the cuts and management changes there would be no extra capital and no money for bonuses. He was afraid an arch-debater like Baylis could keep arguing until Christmas if given any leeway. Despite that, they wrangled for two weeks over details, with Baylis and Norris locking horns constantly. By the end of August it had been agreed, except for one thing. Tuckey believed Baring Securities needed a full-time man-ager to run it. Its administration and controls were still very weak. He would have preferred a chief executive, with Heath as chairman. But it was too tricky to take the title of chief executive away from Heath so Norris came up with the idea of a 'chief operating officer' instead. It sounded more like the person who ran the nuts and bolts rather than the more glamorous side of things. Heath could step up to be executive chairman, preserving honour on all sides while giving Baring Brothers a tighter grip. It hardly needed stating that Norris would be the chief operating officer. That was certainly what Tuckey wanted as it would allow him to give up the chairmanship of Baring Securities without worrying about what Heath was up to. In Tuckey's mind Norris would be chief executive in all but name.

Since Heath had seen the first draft of Norris and Greer's review, the other Barings directors had found him depressed and lifeless. On 10 September Tuckey told Heath that the time had come to hand operational control over to Norris, and become chairman. 'Should I resign?' Heath asked. Tuckey said he should not. Heath's spirits appeared to rise a little, with the uncertainty resolved. All seemed set fair, and Tuckey and Baring crossed their fingers that it would work. On Thursday 24 September, the same day it disclosed its half-year results, Barings announced that it was restructuring Baring Securities. An internal paper sent to staff by Heath said he was transferring 'day-to-day management responsibilities' to five managing directors who would run operations: Baylis would be in charge of derivatives, Fraser of Asia and Europe, Greer of research, Kelly of Japan and trading, Reed of the US and Latin America. Norris was joining from Baring Brothers and would take over administration previously shared among Heath, Baylis and Martin. When they arrived for work, those being sacked were told to take one of the two Art Deco lifts to the second floor, where the news was broken. The humorists of the trading room dubbed it the 'Auschwitz lift' because those who entered it did not survive. The final figures showed a £10.8 million operating profit for the year to September and a bonuses bill of £18.5 million.[5] These problems were exacerbated by having to write off the £3 million fee it had given to an insurance broker for taking over the lease of its previous office. The broker had taken the money and then failed to move.

Slowly and painfully the new Baring Securities started life. The markets were still bad with the Nikkei index continuing to fall. It had dropped from 23,800 in January to 14,300 in August, the lowest level it had hit for six years. Although there was some relief in London that the worst might be over, the cuts had been so small in Tokyo that employees there immediately started speculating about when the next round would come. Every Wednesday at 1.00 p.m. in America Square, the management committee would gather in the boardroom, with a telephone link to overseas members such as Reed, to chew over the latest bad news. The cuts had pushed the firm back into operating profit but there was little optimism about the future. Heath found the process agonizing. The meetings seemed to go on for ever. There would be squabbles among directors in charge of different things, which was what Heath hated most. He could not see the point in allowing tensions to arise by giving everyone a lot of needless detail to quibble about. But as far as Norris was concerned this was a long-overdue airing of tensions. It might be hard at the moment but that was just a teething problem. These people were coming to terms with having to manage their firm for the first time. In the meanwhile, he could get on with trying to improve the administration. It was tough work that often felt like wading through treacle. There were still fiefdoms that he lacked authority to penetrate, such as Reed's empire, but slowly improvements were made.

Despite the appearance of reform underlying tensions among those at the helm had not disappeared. Fraser was still angry with Heath for letting the business run out of control and for not being firm enough to deal with Japan earlier. His disquiet was also shared by some of the up-and-coming directors of the firm, among them Richard Katz, a thirty-six-year-old trader who had been trading investment funds that bought equities in Asian countries such as Korea. He and Khoo had been virtually the only traders making good profits in the previous year. Katz had an old-fashioned City background, having worked for the jobbing firm Smith Brothers in the late 1970s. He was born into a north London Jewish family, and his father ran a clothing business in the East End. When he had arrived at Baring Securities, he had made a joke of the fact that he was joining a Catholic-dominated firm. 'I want to take all Jewish holidays off,' he replied when Baylis asked him if he had any requests. For a time Katz and Primhak had sat next to each other, and their part of the trading floor had been dubbed 'the Gaza strip'. Katz was ambitious and had gained a place on the committee. Because the committee now included people such as Katz who did not owe their advancement solely to Heath, his old ability to run Baring Securities just as he wanted was undermined. Soon he became harder than ever to track down and stopped appearing at the weekly meetings, or only phoned in from overseas. It was preferable to work in the sunny optimism of Asia than the grim bureaucracy of America Square.

Part of Heath's disenchantment stemmed from the fact that the things that always excited him most, hiring new people and venturing into exciting new areas, were now denied to him. There was hardly any spare capital with which to entice derivatives traders and even those they had were heavily curtailed. Waxman, who had been dubbed 'the Mad Hatter' at Salomon because he wore a Jewish skull cap, had been used to dealing on a large capital base at Salomon but was stranded at his new employer. He had little chance to display his skills, and instead was confined to taking simple bets on movements in markets. One of these caused consternation when he bought a currency position that depended on a rise in sterling just before 16 September, when Britain was forced out of the European Exchange Rate Mechanism and the pound fell dramatically. Other traders, including George Soros, had bet so heavily against sterling that Waxman was forced to cut the position. But it tarnished his reputation in the eyes of Kelly and other directors. Meanwhile, the warrant trading business sunk further into loss. Sliwerski was so frustrated that he wrote an anguished memo to Katz and Kelly complaining that 'with the way things have unfolded over the years, I have effectively lost control of my department . . . We have this paranoia that if the house of Goldman Sachs does something we have to run and cut. Sod Goldman Sachs!'[6] He suggested that he should return to the trading desk and try to inject a bit of spark into the younger traders. But his memo did not have the desired effect.

The tensions between Norris and Heath finally erupted in mid-October when Heath was on a visit to Hong Kong. He arrived to find Phillips worried that some local managers who had just been made directors of Baring Securities in Hong Kong might have been offended as Norris had ruled out paying the customary salary increase for such a promotion. US investment banks were expanding rapidly in Asia, and Phillips thought there was a danger of them leaving. It was 11.00 a.m. in London, and Heath rang up Norris from Phillips's office to instruct him to pay the money. Norris said it would be wrong, and they should discuss it later at a management committee meeting. It was 7.00 p.m. in Hong Kong, and Phillips and Heath were about to go out to Happy Valley racetrack with a director of

Hongkong and Shanghai Bank. Heath explained he could not participate in the committee meeting. 'You will be responsible if these people leave,' he said firmly.

It was too much for Norris, who exploded with anger. 'All you fucking do is please yourself!' he shouted. He was so enraged that he did not realize Heath had dropped his receiver in shock, and he carried on hurling abuse into the empty air.

The argument was quickly smoothed over by Tuckey, who phoned Hong Kong the next day to talk it over with Heath. Soon afterwards there was a second call from Norris, who apologized: 'It was very insensitive of me.' But the damage was done. Despite the attempts to paper over the cracks with the formulation of Norris as chief operating officer, he and Heath were already fighting.

Bonuses were paid in part on 15 October. The next day Phillips resigned to join Salomon Brothers in Hong Kong. It was the first defection of a director in 1992, despite Murray's attempt earlier. Phillips was partly disenchanted with Baring Securities, believing that Heath no longer had his old grip on the firm, and partly wanted to avoid returning to London to replace Norris as head of equity capital markets. It was a crack in the fragile public consensus and it made everyone re-evaluate. Greer sent a note to Heath on 19 October urging him to assert his authority. He talked of 'a spreading crisis of confidence in the company which in part is inevitable given the current business conditions, but in a large part also stems from the new style of management'. It would be exacerbated by the departure of Phillips. He said that both Norris and Fraser needed to be 'reined in', and others had to be prevented from leaving. Morale needed to be restored. 'You are the only person who can ensure this happens,' he ended.[7] But if Heath had any energy and confidence left to achieve this, it was knocked from him in November when Baylis discovered that he had cancer of the bone marrow. Heath wept openly when Baylis told him. And Baylis's problems were not confined to having cancer. He was also a Name at Lloyd's of London, the insurance market, which was facing large bills from claims related to asbestosis in the US. Two of the worst-affected syndicates were called Gooda Walker and Feltrim and Baylis had joined both of them. Heath's closest lieutenant throughout the 1980s faced financial ruin and death.

There were soon further problems for Heath. Late in 1992 a hidden tax liability relating to Japan was discovered. It had been accumulated on bonuses that were deferred by employees working in Japan in order to avoid tax. If they took their annual bonuses immediately they could face Japanese income tax of about 50 per cent on the money. Most foreign investment banks in Tokyo used the same method for getting round this. Instead of employees being paid their bonuses, they would simply be told what the sum was and the capital would be retained by Baring Securities. When they finally left Tokyo to return to London, they would be paid the money in a lump sum and because they were no longer resident in Tokyo, the Japanese tax authorities would then only levy a 20 per cent tax on the money. It meant being paid between leaving Japan and becoming resident once more in London. But Baring Securities now discovered it had miscalculated its own tax liability as the employer, a serious matter since it owed tax on accumulated bonuses over several years. It found that instead of owing $60 million to cover all the unpaid bonuses, it might owe $70 million. The result was that Sajeed Sacranie, who was then working in the internal audit department, was sent to Tokyo to carry out a full audit. One day Greer returned from a trip to find Sacranie in the office talking to people. Sacranie did not find any further holes in the books. But internal audits devised by Martin involved not just examining the accounts but looking into how the office was organized and run, and which personalities exerted the most influence.

Sacranie rapidly discovered that the Tokyo office was in a severe mess. Greer was generally liked but had lost authority that year. He was known as 'Mr Yes' for his willingness to concede requests for higher bonuses and perks. Sacranie discovered one or two cases of impropriety, such as two members of staff who were living together in one apartment and renting the other one while claiming a housing allowance. More generally, he found an office that was split by rivalries, dominated by a faction led by Fujiwara and Primhak. He wrote some of the more lurid discoveries in a note that he faxed to Norris in London, although the formal audit report did not contain them. But it was enough to further inflame the feeling among those in London that Heath had allowed the firm to run out of control. The mood in the management committee was changing from feeling sorry for Heath to outrage at what had gone on in secret. Murray had by now been appointed as personal assistant to Norris and had not lost his earlier indignation at Heath's methods of management. Katz was also irritated at the stalemate at the head of the firm. Heath no longer had enough support to take it in the direction he wanted but he was still powerful enough to block alternatives. Fraser was the most antagonistic to Heath, as he believed Heath was undermining Baring Securities by encouraging a split. Meanwhile, Norris had become convinced that Heath, Baylis and Reed were in a cabal, still plotting a breakaway. By the early part of 1993 the senior management of Baring Securities had reached the point of stasis.

The deadlock was broken on 26 February. The cost savings of September had resulted in the firm making an operating profit of £8 million in the last months of 1992. On 26 February it announced to employees the bonuses they would get for the three-month period, so Baring Securities' year-end could be adjusted to December. There was £2.6 million to pay out, and directors in charge of different parts of the firm started to tell individuals what they would get. Tuckey was in his chauffeur-driven car on his way to an afternoon appointment when he was called by Fraser, who told him that he had listened all day to complaints from staff. They believed that Baring Securities was in chaos and that there was no longer an effective management. 'It is a shambles here. The place will fragment if you don't take a decisive step,' said Fraser. 'You have fudged it up to now.'

In the same week Murray and Katz came to see Norris with another director called James Remington-Hobbs, and told him things could not go on as they were. Norris went round to 8 Bishopsgate to tell Peter Baring that there was no alternative but to get rid of Heath. He did not expect a response, but Baring had clearly been pondering the same question. 'Actually, I agree,' he said. 'We will have to do it.'

Once the decision had been reached in principle, they moved fast. On Sunday 28 February a small group of Baring Brothers' directors, including Peter Baring, Michael Baring, Peter Norris and Geoffrey Barnett, who had been appointed Norris's counterpart as chief operating officer of Baring Brothers, met at Tuckey's house to mull over what ought to be done to end the stalemate.

At the first meeting, there was merely a general discussion of the awkwardness of what they faced. All these men were veterans of Baring Brothers. Norris was the youngest, and even he had been at Baring Brothers for nearly a decade before Heath's arrival. The Baring

Brothers partners were summoning up their nerve to reassert their grip on the company. The following Saturday the same group met again at Tuckey's house, and this time came to a firm decision. They would ask Heath to leave. It would mean expelling Baylis and Reed as well because they were the closest to Heath. Martin was not in the same league, but he was definitely in their camp and he would have to go too. It was easy enough to select those whom they no longer wanted to have around; the question was whether they could carry out traumatic surgery on Baring Securities without killing the patient. There was deep loyalty to Heath. No matter how much staff might complain now about uncertainty and lack of management, it was not clear Baring Securities could survive without its founder and creator. They could now be certain enough of backing from some key figures such as Fraser but others were an unknown quantity. Greer appeared so close to Heath that he would inevitably defect. It was impossible to tell which way Kelly would go because he was in many ways the closest of any of them to Heath. But there was no means to sound out Kelly without letting him know what was intended. They simply had to take the gamble. Baring decided to appoint Kelly and Fraser as joint deputy chairmen to give Kelly an enticement to stay.

Norris would become chief executive, but he feared that if Tuckey became chairman it would seem too much like a take-over from Bishopsgate. He went to see Peter Baring to talk it over. 'I am sorry to put it like this, but Andrew can't be chairman. It just won't work,' Norris said. Baring came up with a reasonable alternative. Rivett-Carnac had just retired as chairman of Baring Asset Management. He seemed a good choice to restore peace. Baring went to visit him to explain what was brewing. 'It's going to be a very difficult human situation. Will you take it on?' he asked. To get all the problems out of the way at one go, a former warrant trader called Vanessa Gibson, who headed derivatives under Baylis, was added to the list of those to be ejected. There had been rows over the way she managed the operations. With the decisions made, all that remained was to carry out the deed. On the afternoon of Friday 12 March Kelly was phoned by Peter Baring, who asked him to come over to 8 Bishopsgate at 5.30 p.m. When he got there he found Tuckey and Bolsover in Baring's office. Baring told Kelly they had decided to ask Heath to leave because they could not have someone in charge of Baring Securities who was trying to sell off the firm. Kelly was shocked and confused. He asked whether Heath could not stay as a non-executive chairman, but this idea was dismissed. Kelly was not sure what he should do, but he felt vulnerable. He agreed that Reed, Baylis and Martin had overstayed their welcome. He also felt a responsibility to stay and hold Baring Securities together. He agreed to the *fait accompli* presented to him.

The following day Heath was at home with 'flu when he was called by Peter Baring, who was his usual brisk self on the telephone: 'Ten a.m. tomorrow, 8 Bishopsgate.'

'Why?' asked Heath.

'I do not want to discuss matters like this on the telephone,' said Baring.

The next day Heath turned up at Bishopsgate.

'I would like your resignation. We want to give the new management a chance, and they feel inhibited with you around,' said Baring.

Despite the trouble that had brewed for a year, when the showdown came Heath was taken aback. He quietly accepted the deal on offer, but seemed in a state of shock. Bolsover had been asked by Tuckey to be there to console him because the two men were friends. They had spent weekends together and Bolsover shared Heath's restless spirit. Bolsover had found the previous two weeks agonizing because, as a director, he had participated in the decision to eject Heath. 'You must think I'm the biggest shit in the world,' Bolsover said when they met.

Baylis and Martin were next to arrive and neither was as shocked as Heath. 'Do you still believe what you told us last September, that there's no future for the firm without extra capital?' Baring asked Martin. He confirmed he still did, and Baring said they wanted him to leave. Early in the afternoon, Tuckey phoned Reed in New York to break the news. 'Things have got to change. You're an innocent bystander, but I am aware of your loyalty to Christopher,' Tuckey said. He told Reed that he had sent a group over to New York to see him, led by Norris and Peers.

It was an ill-fated expedition. There was a snowstorm over New York and their plane was diverted to Chicago. Norris called Reed from O'Hare airport to tell him they would be delayed. They finally got to the Baring Securities office on Madison Avenue on Monday.

Peers made the formal offer to Reed: that he should accept severance and not disrupt the business in the US. They were nervous that Reed was liable to be the loosest cannon. Reed agreed terms, but was not going to go quietly. 'You are the most unethical son-of-a-bitch I have ever met in my life. What you've done to Christopher is totally wrong,' he told Norris. He insisted that they had to let him address his employees. 'If I don't say something, you're totally fucked,' he said. He made a brief speech to about 110 staff, ending in tears.

By that evening Heath was feeling better. He telephoned a friend and said it was probably all for the best. He also rang Kelly to congratulate him on being made a deputy chairman. Kelly was upset and guilty that he had allowed it to happen, but Heath reassured him. Both men were in tears. Baylis, who had been ejected at his moment of greatest vulnerability, was not so phlegmatic. He was contemptuous of Tuckey and Baring, and his feelings were not helped by his perilous physical condition.

One surprise survivor of the coup was Greer. He was due to return to London as head of research, and had been scheduled to tour Latin America with Norris the previous week. When he had arrived in New York he had heard Norris was not coming, and the news set off alarm bells. On the Saturday morning Greer had phoned Kelly from Chile. 'For God's sake, what is happening?' he asked him.

'Something's going on, but I can't tell you about it,' said Kelly.

By now it was Saturday night in London, and Greer rang Heath from Santiago airport. 'I have just been summoned to see Peter Baring,' Heath said.

Greer flew on to Argentina, and called Heath when he arrived. 'I am out,' Heath told him.

'What the hell should I do?' asked Greer.

'Well, don't just resign on principle. You'll be out of a job.'

Greer heard nothing all day, and finally rang Peter Baring at home on Sunday night, waking him up. 'Andrew was trying to get hold of you,' said Baring.

'I have heard what has happened,' said Greer.

'What do you want to do?'

'I want to stay.'

There was a long pause, as Baring absorbed these unexpected tidings. 'I am very pleased,' he said finally.

Like Kelly, Greer could not think what he would do if he simply walked out. He had no doubt where his loyalties lay but he was a pragmatist.

With Kelly and Greer on board, the coup had gone as well as could be expected. The news of Heath's departure was splashed across newspapers on Tuesday. He was dignified in defeat, refusing to display any anger at his treatment. He was not bitter, he said. It had just been a difference of view.

CHAPTER 6

The usual Christmas party had not taken place at Baring Securities in December 1992 because nobody had the heart to organize it amid all the turmoil. So the Christmas party was held in July instead. Norris spent most of his time talking to the settlements people, which was noted as a novelty. Heath's idea of a good time had never been to hobnob with back office staff. By then Norris was back to his normal ebullient self. Not only had the worst fears of those who ejected Heath not been realized, but Baring Securities seemed to be going from strength to strength. A few people had left, which had created the odd difficulty, among them Chuck Hawk, the former operations manager in New York, who handled all settlements in Latin America. But by and large the departures had been fewer than expected. Tuckey took it as a sign that Heath had misjudged his own popularity. With that weight off their shoulders it was far easier to reconstruct Baring Securities. There was a huge amount to do. Norris had been gradually trying to improve the administration of the firm since the previous September, but it had been difficult to penetrate overseas empires. Now it was much easier. Takafumï Kagiyama, who had been operations manager in Tokyo, had left following the 1992 audit. Norris was starting to come to grips with Asia. The mood was changing and business was good. In fact, it was so good that it put to shame Heath's gloomy predictions about the impossibility of getting decent returns from straightforward broking. Baring Securities was not just achieving that; it was making money hand over fist.

Just as Baring Securities had made its fortune from the Japanese bull market of the 1980s, it now found itself sitting on a second huge wave of investment from London and New York into Latin America and Asia. The buzz investment phrase of the early 1990s had become 'emerging markets', the developing countries whose growth rates were far outstripping those of developed economies. Europe was stuck in recession and Japan was still suffering the aftermath of the bubble economy. The Nikkei was trading in a band between 20,000 and 21,000, almost half its peak. Furthermore, efforts by the US Federal Reserve to jump-start the economy and prop up ailing banks by reducing short-term interest rates made it less attractive for US pension funds to put money into conventional investments such as US company bonds. Low short-term interest rates reduced the yield on bonds to the point where they were inadequate to redress the $38 billion deficit in the fifty largest US pension funds. Investors in the US had been parochial, but they were being forced to look elsewhere for good returns. It was not simply pension funds doing so. Ordinary people were more active equity investors than Europeans, putting savings into mutual funds – the equivalent of British unit trusts – rather than banks. By 1993 the best-performing mutual funds were those that bought overseas bonds and equities. Americans started switching their money out of the blue chip US stocks and into Latin America and Asia. A US 'wall of money' began to hit stock markets everywhere from Hong Kong to Mexico.

Heath had astutely foreseen this trend three years before when he started opening offices across Latin America. Baring Securities was in place in Mexico City, Lima and Santiago when local stock markets started being driven upwards with dizzying speed. As military regimes across Latin America were toppled by reformist liberal governments, barriers to investment were brought down. The Peruvian stock market rose by 75 per cent during the first eight months of 1993 as investors such as Soros put cash into obscure Peruvian companies. By the autumn US interest in Asia was verging on the hysterical. US investors had billions to invest in Asia, and Baring Securities was the main overseas broker in Asian cities from Jakarta to Manila and Seoul. Carl Strutt had taken over from Phillips as managing director of Baring Securities in Hong Kong and was attempting to handle a flood of broking orders. By the time of the July Christmas party the firm was making more than it had ever done from simple stockbroking. Just as Heath's business had originally exceeded all expectations, Baring Securities was once again able to confound the sceptics. In the September 1992 restructuring Norris and Greer had set a target for the year of £45 million profits before bonuses and had laid out an 'all singing, all dancing' case of £67.5 million. In fact, it made a profit of £8 million from Asia in the first quarter of the year and a total of £14 million. That put the firm on course to hit the 'all singing, all dancing' target. Derivatives had produced only £1.5 million of that sum. Norris was heading a firm that did not need to trade derivatives to make money.

This was just as well, since derivatives trading was giving him a headache. The wrangle between Baring Brothers and Heath had left in its wake a confused and demoralized department. It bore all the signs of a Heath operation. There were traders in different offices, some doing roughly the same thing, none of whom seemed sure how they related to anybody else. Some were warrant traders who were doing their utmost to adapt to a new world, while others were rocket scientists born and bred. Among the London traders was Khoo, who had returned from Tokyo late in 1992 after her options trading had lost momentum when others had entered the market and the obvious mis-pricing had been squeezed away. 'Man, this is turning into a real job,' a trader said to Gueler as they struggled for profits that had flowed easily before. Khoo was tired of Tokyo's bright lights. She heard that Baylis was building up derivatives trading in London and she wanted to be part of that. But when she arrived the civil war was at its height and it was hard to do anything. They lacked technology or capital to trade in a sophisticated manner. The only thing left was to take a punt every so often, like Waxman's ill-judged bet on sterling. Khoo sat alongside a former warrant salesman called Jeremy Oades, becoming disaffected. Feuding at the top was replicated in a battle for control of the operation. It was being run day-to-day in London by Vanessa Gibson, who had joined to sell warrants in 1985. Now thirty-three years old, she had done a degree at the London College of Fashion, but then gone into the City where her father worked.

Gibson was headstrong and did not mind upsetting those she thought deserved it. Richard Johnston was top of the list. Johnston was good at making profits in odd ways and had spotted an opportunity in the Osaka margin rules which allowed brokers to net off futures before paying initial margin. Johnston started to net off his own trading positions against those of customers. As this allowed Barings to reduce the margin it put up to Osaka the money could be put in the bank to gain interest. It was the sort of thing only an accountant would think of, but it made money. When Gibson looked through his books, she became convinced he was making more money from accounting tricks than genuine trading. It caused acrimony between them, which increased when Johnston returned to London in August 1992. He was among staff fleeing Tokyo because they were scared the firm might be taken over by another bank that would refuse to pay the bonuses they had deferred to avoid tax. Johnston was offered a job by Baylis as risk manager for derivatives operations. Because these were now so disparate, Martin thought they should be controlled from London so that all orders from round the world would pass through a derivatives control unit on the London trading floor. Martin sold the idea to Johnston as a powerful and glamorous job, but Johnston arrived back to discover that Gibson had no intention of relinquishing power to him. Relations between them deteriorated and Johnston threw all his energy into trying to undermine her. He triumphed in March when Gibson was forced out, leaving the operation rudderless.

Norris had taken temporary charge himself for lack of a better idea. He asked Gueler to look after Japan and Asia, and Oades to watch over London. The promotion of Oades was the final straw for Johnston, who went back to Tokyo with UBS. It rapidly became clear that this arrangement would not work. Sacranie went to Hong Kong in May to examine derivatives operations there. The head trader in charge of futures and options was called Richard Magides. Sacranie was alarmed when he looked at Magides's trading book, because Magides seemed to be breaking rules by selling options without having been given authority. He was losing money, although his authorized trading was in profit. Norris told Sacranie to stop him trading. Gueler arrived from Tokyo the next day to help clear up the mess and Magides left shortly afterwards. Norris was by now wondering whether he should simply shut the whole thing down as it was so painfully difficult to manage. Furthermore, the Brothers had just had a big fight with Heath over this issue. It would be strange to go to war to prevent the business becoming a derivatives trading shop, and then adopt the strategy they had fought against. But Norris thought it was wrong to abandon the activity altogether. Financial markets were increasingly being led by derivatives, both those traded on exchanges and 'over-the-counter' futures and options, bought and sold privately by banks. Investors now demanded expertise in derivatives from investment banks. Whatever the problems of managing it at present, the firm would probably come to regret it if it abandoned derivatives trading.

Then an idea occurred to him. What about handing it all over to Ron Baker? Baker had only arrived at Baring Brothers in April 1992 but was already flavour of the month. He had helped to turn around a lackadaisical treasury and trading arm by bringing from Bankers Trust a debt trading side. Debt trading was not the same as trading equity derivatives, but they had two things in common: they both involved risking capital, and derivatives. Norris had already come to the conclusion that the business had to be handled by somebody who could understand futures and options. Unless you bandied around terms like gamma, delta and vega, you would not be respected by the Techno-peasants. They were temperamental and worse than computer buffs at dismissing the uninitiated. Baker could hold his own with them. Some people had their doubts about Baker. He was loud, could be aggressive and did not fit in with the fusty old Baring Brothers culture. He liked to listen to blues and pop music at the end of a working day, and had brought a fridge into his office so he could have cold beer. But Baker could clearly do one thing of which others at Bishops-gate appeared incapable: manage people. Baker was not just a corporate financier put out to grass with some paperwork; he could hire and fire people effectively and he handled teams of traders well. The other directors were impressed at the group of young and sparky people Baker had gathered around him.

Ron Baker was indeed unlike the average Baring Brothers executive and the way in which he had come to Bishopsgate showed how the City had opened up in the years since Big Bang. Baker was forty-one years old, the son of an owner of a building company in Melbourne. He had graduated from Melbourne University with first-class honours in economics and gained a graduate diploma in accounting. He had become company secretary of a small accounting firm in Melbourne. When the firm was taken over by a larger company, Baker became involved in sorting out the take-over, and was so intrigued with the idea of take-overs that he went back to university to study mergers and acquisitions law. After five years in Australia with Bank of America, Baker was sent to London, where he got involved in the Eurobond market. By 1986 the Eurobond market had become dominated by swaps. Bonds in a currency nobody wanted would be switched into another that was more popular, or a fixed rate bond would be swapped into a floating rate one. Baker handled several swapped issues in Australian dollars, which brought him to the attention of Bankers Trust. He joined in May 1987 and eventually became the head of Eurobond syndication. It was a quintessential offshore financing activity. Baker would find a Spanish bond trading at one price with a floating yield and swap it into an international fixed rate bond in another currency. Bankers Trust would take all the complex equations and write over-the-counter derivatives to solve them. It was like having a financial chemistry set that could recombine all the elements.

The activity was highly profitable. By 1991 the fifty people under Baker were making $45 million of revenue each year. Profits were so good because they were in a perfect trading position, much like Sliwerski's warrant trading operation in its heyday. It had all the elements for success. Baker was at the heart of a massive flow of information. He could see how orders were coming in and what prices were being bid and offered, so if there was a sudden switch in the market, he would be on top of it immediately. Bankers Trust was making its money in two intertwined ways: charging for sales to customers, and trading on its own book. It could spot mispricing in different markets and arbitrage the differences. Baker came to think of it as trading information. There were lots of inefficiencies in different countries. One would have a certain tax rate and short-term interest rate; another would be different. Baker was trading sixteen currencies of bonds in many countries. If you combined that information with inside knowledge of what investors and borrowers were demanding, you were in an unbeatable position. Baker sometimes talked of it as the 'information vortex'. All this knowledge and information whirled around him and only he, at the heart of the vortex, could fit the pieces together. Of course, you had to be careful. A customer order might be large enough to move prices in markets. There was always a temptation to delay such orders and trade for your own book first. That was known as 'front-running' and it was frowned on by all regulators. But as long as you avoided that trap information was gold dust.

Despite his success Baker was under some pressure at Bankers Trust by 1991. Allan Wheat, chairman of the London subsidiary, had defected to Credit Suisse First Boston in March 1990 and taken with him several executives, including Chris Goekjian. Wheat had supported Baker's business, but Bankers Trust lost interest following Wheat's departure. It made good money but not enough. The problem was that Bankers Trust had found a means to make higher returns with derivatives than Baker's remoulding of publicly traded bonds. The buzz word there was 'risk management', which meant going to companies and offering them complex futures and options. If a company wanted to protect itself against a lack of volatility in interest rates, Bankers Trust might sell it what it called a 'wedding band'. This was rather like a straddle sold in exchanges such as Simex, but was far more complicated. It was an over-the-counter contract with embedded options that paid the company money if interest rates rose or fell. The difference between exchange-traded derivatives and the complex OTC ones was like the difference between ready-to-wear and couture clothes. Couture fitted better but the price was higher. Bankers Trust's president, Eugene Shanks, wanted capital to be directed into this. According to computer models at Bankers Trust, this sort of operation was preferable to Baker's, which was founded on what had become a largely unprofitable Eurobond business. Baker started to feel unloved, and pondered taking his entire operation away from Bankers Trust. All he needed was $100 million capital and he could walk out of the door.

In late 1991 Baker approached Lazards, Flemings and Barings. At Barings he met Michael Baring and Tuckey. The latter was intrigued. He wanted to make more use of Barings' name and this seemed like an excellent venture. 'This is a franchise name. We can do a number of things with it,' Tuckey told Baker. Baker might also help to revitalize Barings' capital markets activities, a task that was now urgent. Bond underwriting had made money following the 1981 World Bank issue, but margins had fallen by the late 1980s. That left treasury and trading. It started trading bonds in 1984 after buying Wilson & Watford. Gilt trading never made money. Baring Wilson & Watford competed with twenty-seven others in a dismal market. By 1988 the firms were making joint annual losses of £100 million. Bond trading lurched from one problem to another and Michael Baring, who headed it, was dubbed 'Captain Chaos'. The joke was that if he lost the envelope on which he scribbled things everything ground to a halt. The worst débâcle came with a 1988 issue for the state-owned French railway company SNCF. Bond syndication was then headed by Francis Baring, a thirty-nine-year-old second cousin of Ashburton, who set a price for the £75 million of bonds that was undermined by a fall in the market. Other banks started to go short by selling bonds. Francis held firm on the price and soon found Barings had not only failed to sell any bonds, but had been shorted so heavily that it officially owned 120 per cent of its own issue. This at least allowed it to force the price back up again, but it still ended up holding most of the bonds and losing more than £250,000.

From 1987 onwards, Michael Baring had worked alongside Tony Hawes, who handled the treasury and foreign exchange. Hawes was an amiable, rather shy man who joined Barings at the age of eighteen from Merchant Taylors School. He was an efficient book-keeper, and did his best to help organize what Michael Baring wanted. He was not assertive, but he burrowed away and got on with things. However, in 1991 he became the victim of Tuckey's growing impatience with the poor record and prospects of treasury and trading. Tuckey had supported the idea of Baring Brothers continuing with treasury and trading, but he was losing patience with Michael Baring. Tuckey decided something had to be done to bolster treasury and trading, preferably by bringing in someone who knew something about the modern world of trading. The obvious candidate was Ian Hopkins, a career banker who had worked at London Multinational Bank in the 1970s. He had neatly combed receding hair and wore large spectacles. He often sailed at weekends, and had the fresh complexion of somebody used to the outdoors. Hopkins took pride in being meticulous about details and having a strong instinct for caution. His nickname at Charterhouse, the merchant bank where he had worked before coming to Barings, was 'Doctor No', and he liked to have an aura of mystique and authority. Hopkins had far more experience of trading than most at Bishopsgate, and had a grasp of futures and options.

Hopkins' first task on arriving at Baring Brothers in 1986 had been to install new computer systems on the treasury and trading floor to track risks and exposures better. He was helped by Geoff Broadhurst, a twenty-six-year-old accountant from South Africa, who had been seconded from Deloitte, Haskins and Sells, Barings' accounting firm. Broadhurst was stockily built with the look of a rugby player. He was very ambitious, and was soon promoted to financial controller of Baring Brothers when Hopkins took over as finance director. Hopkins was asked to investigate what could be done to improve treasury and trading. He wrote a paper to the management committee criticizing the controls and methods of the department. The result was his appointment as its joint head with Michael Baring. His arrival left Hawes without a clear role. Hawes found it humiliating, but would have worked under Hopkins. It was not an easy task. Hopkins hardly spoke to Hawes. Things got worse when Baring moved from being joint head of treasury and trading in mid-1992. Hopkins was left as the sole head with Hawes as his deputy. Hopkins did not respect Hawes much as a trader. He would sometimes bait him. One day Broadhurst visited Hopkins in his office, separated from that of Hawes by a glass screen. The air-conditioning control for both was on Hopkins' side. 'Would you like to see Tony put on his jacket?' Hopkins asked, twisting the dial for Hawes's office. After two minutes, Hawes started to shiver and slipped on his jacket. He finally agreed to take early retirement in March 1993.

Tuckey asked Maclean, an elder statesman who was trusted to protect Barings' capital, to interview Baker. On the face of it, this was not a match made in heaven. Maclean was proper and cautious, while Baker was punchy and informal. But to the surprise of other directors, they got on well. Maclean picked over Baker's business plan, and thought it was well supported and sound. Baker's operation had risks. Each trade involved a derivative. But Maclean felt Baker was trustworthy.

After the conflicts and tensions of Bankers Trust, Baker found Bishopsgate a relief and his wife liked the fact that he worked for a British bank whose name people recognized. Baker took one look at the fifteenth floor trading floor and decided it was moribund. But even though Barings was hardly the most dynamic place, it had the shell of what he required. It had a treasury and offices in London, New York and Tokyo for him to use as bases. He quickly recruited a team from Bankers Trust and felt an almost paternal responsibility to them to make his Barings venture work out. Among them was Mary Walz. Green-eyed, with short chestnut hair, she had a brisk manner and could swear like a trooper when provoked, but she was not as confident as she tended to act. She came from Michigan, and had an MBA from Wharton, the business school of the University of Pennsylvania. She was interviewed by Maclean together with Heather Nicol, another Baker protégée. He was impressed by both. They were tougher than the women Maclean was used to, but he reflected that perhaps they had to be tough to succeed.

Baker set to work and quickly made a success of the asset trading business. In the wake of the bubble bursting in Japan, there was an overhang of assets being sold by Japanese investors to prop up balance sheets. It was like 1987, when Nomura repatriated all the Japanese equity warrants, in reverse. There was a steady flow of bonds that Baker could package up, turn into a different form and sell to one of the many European banks that were seeking assets. It was a simple but profitable business. Falls in interest rates and rises in bond prices helped. Most assets that Baker held on Barings' books rose in price with the passage of time. He could take on a bond, package it up with derivatives and hold it for a while before a buyer was found, and that would earn him money by itself. By 1993 it was going so well that Baker's twenty-six traders made an £11.1 million operating profit from debt trading. He was soon getting plaudits from Tuckey and Rivett-Carnac. Baker felt properly appreciated for the first time since Wheat had left Bankers Trust. He had originally wanted to stay at arm's length from Baring Brothers and even thought of running the entire operation through an offshore subsidiary in Dublin to save tax, but Tuckey had persuaded him to regard himself as a full member of the Baring Brothers management. Occasionally he would be asked if he wanted to take on something more. The experiment with bringing in an outsider seemed to Tuckey and Maclean to be running exceptionally smoothly. Baker had brought to Baring Brothers everything it had lacked for so long.

Baker's main concern after his arrival was to get debt trading running. By the middle of 1993 he felt he could turn his attention to the next step. In August Baker wrote a plan for Baring Brothers to start trading emerging markets debt, in addition to its developed countries debt operation. He estimated that it could make £6.25 million profit in 1994. It would involve working with Baring Securities and using its research.[1] This interested Norris. Baker was thinking already of the overlap between the derivatives trading operations in Bishopsgate and America Square. His plan included using derivatives to sell bonds paying a return linked to equities. If Baker was thinking of breaking down boundaries in that way, maybe he should take over the whole thing. In September Norris asked Baker to do this. They mulled over the idea of Baker taking over Killian's futures and options sales team as well, but Baker did not press for it. He was more interested in the trading side of the operation. It seemed to be a good opportunity. His star was rising at Baring Brothers and it would give him greater prominence at Baring Securities. His background was in debt and he did not know much about exchange-traded futures and options. However, he was feeling confident. He had started up a debt trading operation from scratch and made it work. He could probably find someone to handle the operation and report to him. Baker accepted Norris's offer, and went on what he regarded as a well-earned holiday in Melbourne for a rest after a hectic eighteen months.

By the autumn, Baring Securities was doing better than ever. It was even starting to work with Baring Brothers. Despite old tensions Fraser and Kelly wanted to ensure the Brothers lead managed as many international share issues as possible. Investors wanted Asian and Latin American shares, and markets were so buoyant that there was a short-age. An investment bank that managed a share issue could keep its customers happy by allocating them a good slice of the shares. Tuckey had stepped up firepower in mid-1992 by transferring a group of corporate financiers from Bishopsgate to America Square. It had pro-vided a reason to take Michael Baring away from treasury and trading. The group quickly managed to pick up work and by 1993 was steaming ahead. Although other investment banks were rushing into emerging markets, Barings already had a foothold. In January it led a $352 million issue by Grupo Carso, a Mexican conglomerate, and in November lead managed a $72 million issue of shares by a glass company in Shanghai that was part-owned by Pilkington, the St Helens glass-making company. Michael Baring was happier in his new role, and it helped to have an actual Baring call on company chairmen in Latin America and Asia. It had been a long time, but the name of Baring still reverberated powerfully in Buenos Aires or Santiago. Barings was returning to its old business as an international financing house. The activity of raising money for Grupo Carso on international capital markets in the 1990s was essentially the same as that for which Baring Brothers & Co. had gained its reputation in the nineteenth century.

That was how Peter Baring felt when he surveyed the business Barings was becoming once more. The shutters that had gone down after the 1914–18 war were opening up again. It seemed to be a world of vast, almost limitless potential. Barings had a handful of people in India, a country of a billion people where new projects and companies were blossoming constantly. How many might it need in a decade's time? Five hundred? A thousand? It felt like picking up a lump of soil and seeing green shoots still there, alive after nearly a century. The British merchant banks had a culture of internationalism and adventure. It had been buried for decades in a world of socialism and trade barriers but now it was returning. Peter Baring delivered a speech in Mexico in April 1994, during which he showed a slide of an investment portfolio. Thirty-seven per cent of it was invested in the UK, 27 per cent in the US, 12 per cent in Chile, 6 per cent in Argentina. Then he put up another slide, showing a portfolio with money invested around the world from Hong Kong to Japan and Asia. The first slide was Baring Brothers' own investment portfolio in 1900, when it was run by the second Lord Revelstoke, Peter Baring's great-uncle; the second was the recommendation of Baring Securities in 1994 on how investors should spread their money. He showed another slide of a certificate for twenty shares in the Chilean Mining Association held by Barings for a Swiss investor. The certificate dated from 1825, only seven years after Chile became independent, but it was just the sort of investment that Baring Securities was recommending to investors 170 years later.

'It is difficult not to be impressed that, with sailing ships and quill pens, our predecessors nearly 170 years ago were doing international business similar in form to what we do today,' he told investors who were celebrating the centenary of the Mexican stock exchange.[2] Baring questioned whether the flood of money into emerging markets was a passing fad. His answer was no, that the flow of capital to countries around the world was 'the natural order of things'. It was 'a natural process and, clearly, a highly creative process'. It had simply been interrupted for a while by 'a long, painful and ultimately unsuccessful experiment with socialism' that was now coming to an end. That would allow investment to flow again from developed countries to developing ones, as 'in the nineteenth century when, despite massive economic volatility, huge sums of money found their way around the world to what were then emerging markets, like the United States, Canada, Australia, Russia and Japan'.

As 1993 passed by it was difficult not to be carried away with the feeling that investment banks were riding a long wave of prosperity and investment. On 13 September Peter Baring paid a call on Brian Quinn at the Bank of England to discuss the progress Barings had made in restoring Baring Securities to health. It was a routine chat, although supervisors had been worried by the drop in profits in 1992. During the conversation he described the recovery in profitability at the stockbroking arm as 'amazing', adding wryly that it did not 'seem terribly difficult to make money in the securities business'.[3]

With such a fair wind behind them, it seemed a propitious time to combine the two firms. There were corporate financiers working in America Square, and Baker was about to take over derivatives trading at Baring Securities. Tuckey thought Baring Brothers could combine with Baring Securities to form an investment bank specializing in emerging markets. He and Peter Baring decided to create a new entity called Baring Investment Bank with a single management to be housed in America Square. This caused a flutter of consternation among directors. Baring Brothers had been at 8 Bishopsgate for 200 years and it would be a wrench to leave. Despite the location the Brothers were clearly going to take charge of Baring Investment Bank. Neither Baring nor Tuckey were fans of management in itself. The tradition at Baring Brothers was for management to be done by corporate financiers like Tuckey in their spare time, or full-time by those who did not make the grade as revenue earners. US banks might have fearsomely high-powered chief technology officers, or chief financial officers, but Baring Brothers was a partnership at heart. It would have five parts: corporate finance, international finance, banking, equity broking and trading, and operations. Maclean would be in charge of banking, which included all trading operations such as Baker's; Fraser would head equity broking, with Kelly as his deputy; Norris would be in charge of all five divisions as chief executive of investment banking, and he would also join the board of the Barings group, putting him in the running to be chairman of Barings one day.

Operations was the most uncharted territory. It included all the back office and settlements that came under Ian Martin at Baring Securities. The chief operating officer selected to take charge of all this was Geoffrey Barnett, the Baring Brothers stalwart who had opened the Singapore office in 1975. He had spent three years away from Barings as director general of the Takeover Panel, before returning to corporate finance in April 1992. He was transparently decent and well intentioned, and was liked by everyone, but a younger generation was running corporate finance and there was no obvious place for him. Instead, he was diverted to be chief operating officer for Baring Brothers. He was well-organized and hard-working, but a far cry from an aggressive executive who could drive through painful changes. Under Barnett settlements were to be handled by Tony Gamby, the thirty-five-year-old head of settlements at Baring Brothers. Gamby was hard-working and energetic, and had joined ANZ Bank after he left school. He was personable and popular with his staff. There was clearly plenty to be done. Baring Securities was running into further settlement problems. The flood of US orders was so strong that its settlement systems in Latin America and Asia were acutely strained. Gamby and Norris met to discuss what needed to be done to update settlements. 'There's a massive task,' Norris said. It was not made easier by the upheaval after Heath's departure. Only Simon Jones was now left of the four operations managers formerly employed to run Baring Securities' back offices around the world.

Strutt was complaining from Hong Kong that settlements there were heavily overstretched. By far the worst problem was New York, which handled settlement for Latin America, because virtually all the settlement staff had followed Hawk when he left. The work was being done mostly by temporary employees. The longest-serving of the 120 back office staff had been there for five months. When Gamby flew to New York to examine things, he got the fright of his life. The Securities and Exchange Commission had just audited Baring Securities and was now threatening to remove its broking licence because settlements were in such a mess. Andrews had sent five staff from Tokyo to help. There was a backlog of unsettled trades across Latin America. Stock exchanges and brokers had not been able to cope with the influx of investment from the US. Some trades had been unreconciled for two years. Citibank had claimed $1.5 million in interest on shares in Telefónica, the Spanish phone company, which Baring Securities had borrowed in 1992 and failed to return. Norris did not want to halt trading. Baring Securities was racing along, making more than ever in Asia and Latin America. It had to reap profits in the markets as they were booming. The problems in Latin America had to be sorted out without closing down its operations. The alternative was admitting publicly that it could not cope with the pressures of operating in the emerging markets in which it specialized. Gamby and those around him would have to fix the engine of Baring Securities while the vehicle was racing along at the highest speed it had ever travelled.

One of the most difficult pieces of re-engineering was the funding of Baring Securities. Since the fright over bank loans in September 1992, a high priority had been to find an easier way of funding. A committee called the Group of Nine, which was led by Maclean, had been wrestling with this issue. The problem was that Baring Securities could only fund trading through bank loans or by borrowing cash from Baring Brothers. But Baring Brothers was only allowed to advance a fixed amount because Bank of England rules limited how much capital a bank could risk in a broking arm. Funding had been tightly squeezed during 1992 because of the firm's troubles. Even with a return to healthy profits the growth in futures and options trading was exerting a squeeze. A lot of cash had to be put up in margin payments at the Singapore and Osaka exchanges. Baring Brothers had gained a 'treasury concession' of £150 million from the Bank of England in 1992 which meant it could advance up to £150 million to its broking arm, but it was running up against this limit by 1993. The obvious way around it was to persuade the Bank to treat it more leniently. In March 1992 the Bank's rules had been changed to allow room for any bank with a securities arm to be treated as a single unit. This was known as 'solo consolidation', and would mean the removal of the £150 million limit on the amount of money Baring Brothers could put into Baring Securities to fund trading. However, solo consolidation had not actually been granted to any bank yet, and it would require work to get Baring Securities into a fit state.

By the time of the coup in March 1993 Tuckey and Maclean were agreed that Baring Brothers should try to gain solo consolidation from the Bank. They needed somebody to do the work, and Maclean had suggested Tony Hawes. It seemed to be a neat solution to a difficulty. Hawes was now simply serving out time at 8 Bishopsgate and this would give him something useful to do. The only impediment was rank. Broadhurst was now finance director of Baring Securities. He had gone to America Square after he also had fallen out with Hopkins. Although they had got on well when they both worked as finance specialists, relations had deteriorated after Hopkins moved over to treasury and trading. The two men had disagreed over the accounting of treasury and trading profits. Broadhurst regarded what Hopkins wanted as wrong and refused to back down. After fifteen months things had got so bad that he went to see Peter Baring. 'I want a change, because an individual is making my life hell,' he said. He did not name Hopkins and Peter Baring was too discreet to ask. But in February 1992 he was moved across to Baring Securities under Martin. Hawes's arrival was awkward because he had always been senior to Broadhurst but now would be reporting to Broadhurst on solo consolidation. Broadhurst took it up with Hawes immediately, suggesting that he could report directly to Norris if that would make it easier. But after two days pondering the question Hawes told him that no face-saving would be required. 'I work for you, and I will report to you,' he said, to Broadhurst's pleasure.

In fact, Hawes was pleased to have a new task and a reprieve. He had been due to retire in March 1993 and had been given a full pension, but now he could earn money in addition. The task he was taking on was complex and difficult, but Hawes was a hard worker and he settled down to it. The main complication was to unravel the balance sheet of Baring Securities and its overseas subsidiaries to produce one firm that qualified for solo consolidation. There were a number of conditions, one of which was that the firm had to be wholly funded by Baring Brothers. This created a difficulty because Baring Securities wanted the freedom to use bank loans to help with the funding of futures and options trading. There would not be any weakness in doing so, because the cash would be used for straight funding rather than capital, but it meant a separate firm had to be created to borrow from the banks and pass on the cash to Singapore and Japan. There was a further cosmetic problem. If Baring Securities was consolidated as it stood, it would simply become a branch of the Brothers. That could cause waves at America Square. To avoid that, a funding vehicle had to be created that could be solo consolidated with Baring Brothers under a different name. Instead of arranging the figures to allow a balance sheet to be produced every day, as the Bank required, Hawes had to produce three separate balance sheets. This involved splitting all of Baring Securities' operations in London into these firms. He then had to ensure that everything had been allocated correctly and no figure was being double-counted or ignored.

Meanwhile, Broadhurst had his own problems. He got on well with Norris because the two men shared an impatient and demanding side. Since Norris's appointment as chief operating officer in 1992, he had relied on Broadhurst to trouble-shoot around the world. Broadhurst would take four trips each year to Asia and the US. The exodus of operations managers following Heath's departure had affected Broadhurst as well as Gamby. By the end of 1993 he lacked experienced operations managers in every regional centre apart from Singapore. Singapore was a trial in a different way because, although Simon Jones was intelligent and highly committed, he was very difficult to deal with. Jones was half-Japanese and half-Welsh and defended his territory with intense passion. He was an old-fashioned manager who would summon subordinates to his desk by shouting out a name, and would often humiliate a person in front of others. After arriving in 1992 Broadhurst had treated Jones with respect and Jones responded well to this. On his visits to Singapore Jones was hospitable. He would take Broadhurst to dinner and they sometimes played squash. He none the less unnerved Broadhurst sometimes because he seemed to be permanently on the edge of exploding. Once the two men had been playing squash in a club on the twenty-fifth floor of the Westin Plaza hotel in Singapore. When they got down to the underground car park, Jones found he had left behind the token that would enable them to get out. The attendant refused to raise the barrier and Jones flew into a rage against her, abusing her until she gave in.

Apart from the trials of having to re-engineer Baring Securities at high speed, the main difficulty with Baring Investment Bank was that it was not clear when it would exist. Tuckey had decided there was little point in trying to combine the businesses fully while people were split between two buildings. He told staff that integration would take place when Baring Brothers moved to America Square, which in all probability would be September 1994. Meanwhile, most people carried on in their old jobs, while thinking about their new ones. To add to the uncertainty, Tuckey also decreed that parts of the structure should come into being immediately, notably the banking group under Mac-

1. Executive Directors of Barings, from the 1991 Annual Report:
(*standing, left to right*) Robin Broadley, John Dare, John Bolsover, Christopher Heath;
(*seated, left to right*) Miles Rivett-Carnac, Peter Baring, Andrew Tuckey

2. Barings' logo

3. Peter Baring takes the morning tube

4. Lord Ashburton
(formerly Sir John Baring)

5. Nicholas Baring

6. Andrew Tuckey

7. Ron Baker

8 and 9. Peter Norris before and after Barings' collapse

10. The founding partners of Baring Securities:
(*foreground*) Christopher Heath; (*background, left to right*) Andrew Baylis, Diarmaid Kelly,
Andrew Fraser and John Bonfield

11. Ian Martin

12. The office of Baring Securities at
America Square

13. Christopher Heath at the races

14. Maggie Heath

15. Richard Greer in Tokyo, 1988

16. The Singapore financial district

Baring Securities (Singapore)

17. James Bax

18. Futures traders on the floor of Simex

19. Nick and Lisa Leeson on their wedding day

20. Nick Leeson, Danny Argyropoulous and Rob Leaning at the Baring Futures trading desk, 1994

21. Nick Leeson returns to Singapore

22. Lisa Leeson tries to present a petition to the Prime Minister for her husband's extradition to Britain

23. The Sultan of Brunei and Prince Jefri Bolkiah

24. Kenneth Clarke, the Chancellor of the Exchequer

25. Eddie George, the Governor of the Bank of England

lean. In spite of these ambiguities, there was plenty of work to be done simply preparing for the move and Barnett was soon occupied in sorting that out, leaving most of the restructuring below him to those such as Broadhurst and Gamby.

Amid all these distractions Baring Securities appeared to be doing better than ever. In the second half of 1993, it had made a profit of £5.1 million in Latin America and the US, and £41 million in Asia. The derivatives business was also picking up steam and Gueler's trading operations in Japan were becoming very profitable. Derivatives had earned revenue of £18 million in the last four months of the year. Baring Securities seemed to have emerged from the doldrums to huge profitability once more. It had made £105 million for the year, not only its highest-ever profit but enough to pay out bonuses of £43.3 million.[4] Within eight months of Heath's departure, his creation was firing on all cylinders.

Meanwhile, Baker had been forced to get to grips with the equity derivatives business (one of three arms of what was to be called the Financial Products Group) rather sooner than he had anticipated. While he was on holiday in Melbourne in October he had received a phone call from Mary Walz telling him there was a fuss in London. She said Katz was stamping around America Square complaining about two derivatives traders in Hong Kong who were breaking their limits, and asking everyone what Baker was doing about it. Katz had been on a tour of Asia, and while he was in the Hong Kong office, he had come across a pair of traders, Mani Arora and Eric Wong, who had taken over from Magides and were supposed to be trading volatility on the Hang Seng index. However, Katz had looked at their books and discovered they were not simply trading volatility and hedging their book against overall market movements. Instead, they were buying and selling futures that constituted bets on the index rising or falling. Because of the lack of an overall head of derivatives trading in London, Gueler was supposed to be taking charge of Arora and Wong from Tokyo, although he had not wanted this responsibility. Tokyo was Katz's next stop, and he confronted Gueler when he got there. 'I don't know what they are doing, but they're not running an arbitrage book,' Katz said. Gueler had then rung Norris to insist that he could not be in charge of Hong Kong any more. All this had broken out within a week of Baker leaving London.

Baker was on holiday, and as far as he was concerned he was not even in charge of equity derivatives trading yet, so he laid low. Two days later he was rung by Norris about the Hong Kong incident. 'Sorry, I am not doing the job yet,' Baker said.

'What do you mean?' asked Norris.

'All we've done is agreed the thing in principle. We have not even defined the job yet.'

But Norris was not going to be manoeuvred into having to solve this headache himself. 'Well, I've put the notice on the board now. You know what people are like. They want to see what you're made of. It will be an important test for you,' he said firmly.

So at the end of his holiday, Baker flew from Melbourne to Hong Kong to see what was going on. As the plane descended to land at Kai Tak airport he thought about what he should do. It was his first task as head of equity derivatives trading, and it would not do to be lax. It would send the wrong signal to all the other traders. 'Unless there's a really good reason not to, I should fire these guys,' he thought. When he arrived he examined the books and reached the same conclusion as Katz. They were breaking limits and concealing trades. Baker called Norris to tell him he wanted to sack them. 'We cannot condone this stuff,' he said. With Norris's agreement, he told Arora and Wong to stop trading. Then he spoke to Gueler, who insisted that he could not cope with Hong Kong any more. Baker agreed it was impractical. 'You should go to Tokyo and stay there. Forget about Hong Kong from here on. We'll get somebody else in place,' he said.

When Baker returned to London he went over to America Square to see what else he had inherited. He found a demoralized operation that was officially being run by Oades but in practice was largely a free-for-all. Baker sat on the trading floor to observe it. He hated what he saw. Traders were trying to piece together deals to compete with Bankers Trust, but lacked the capital or know-how to achieve it. He made up his mind quickly that he would have to revamp the whole thing. Some would have to go and others might transfer to Hong Kong. Instead of dismally failing to match Salomon Brothers on its home ground, Baker thought they should run a market-making book from Hong Kong, and offer the funds investing in Asia new forms of debt linked with equity by using derivatives. It would at least be something original. 'It's going to be awful here. I'd advise you to go to Hong Kong,' Baker said to Oades. The next step was to find someone who could run the business under him. He decided Walz was the best person. He worked alongside her easily and they empathized with each other. The only problem was that Walz was so headstrong that she would probably refuse to take it on if he simply asked her to do so. He had just hired another derivatives specialist from Bankers Trust called Tarek Mahmoud, and he invited them both to his house to choose who would take it on. Baker decided to play on Walz's natural obstinacy by suggesting Mahmoud did equity derivatives while Walz took charge of something else. The ploy worked. Walz insisted on taking equity derivatives.

In early December Baker organized a weekend meeting for the Financial Products Group in Bruges, north-west Belgium. He had brought with him from Bankers Trust the notion of 'off-site meetings'. The idea was to gather a group of people together for one or two days to analyse what they were doing. Hopefully, they would bond together over a drink in the evenings. Baker was a believer in offsites. He was running a global business in which people were stuck on opposite sides of the world and never saw each other from one month to the next. The best way to break down the barriers was to bring them all together and let them thrash out what they wanted. If people let their hair down a little, so much the better. Baker liked to get a bit of a revivalist spirit going at the offsites. He would make a speech congratulating the highest achievers and urging everyone else on. He tried to hold his offsites at an impressive location: for Bruges, he had chosen a hotel in a thirteenth-century fortress. The offsite had been mainly for Baker's debt trading team to celebrate a successful year, but he also invited a few people from equity derivatives, including Gueler, to welcome his new recruits aboard. It gave him the chance to get their measure informally before he came to grips with what they did. Baker had already come across Gueler in Hong Kong. He found him likeable and open, but had doubts about him as a manager. He was excitable, and his explanations during the Bruges weekend of how the Tokyo traders made money for Baring Securities were sometimes hard to follow.

This view was reinforced in January, when Baker completed the last part of his fact-finding tour by flying to Tokyo to examine how the most profitable part of the equity derivatives trading operation worked. When Baker arrived in Tokyo Gueler rattled away thirteen to the dozen as he described what he did. Whatever Baker's reservations, he was running a profitable operation. Gueler explained that it had two main parts. He and an assistant trader in Tokyo called Benjamin Fuchs arbitraged the Nikkei cash and futures markets, while another trader called Adrian Brindle, who had an assistant called Jeff Goodman, ran a volatility book from Osaka. The more volatile the Nikkei, the more opportunity that Gueler and Fuchs had to make money. Volatility opened gaps between futures and cash markets that they could exploit. They had done well in the past couple of months because the Nikkei had fallen to around 17,300 during November and December after staying between 20,000 and 21,000 for most of the year. As the index had dropped, volatility had risen. One month volatility – the band within which the index had traded during the month – had doubled from 10 per cent in November to 20 per cent in December. Both the Tokyo and Osaka traders had begun to earn more money. Baker chatted away with Gueler, probing for any hidden ways in which he made money. As they talked Gueler started to refer to a trader in Singapore called Nick Leeson, whom he had already mentioned briefly in Bruges. Leeson was clearly becoming very important to the Tokyo and Osaka traders.

As Gueler explained it, Leeson was not officially part of the trading side at all. He was formally a member of Killian's futures and options sales team, and his job was to execute orders from customers of Baring Securities who wanted to buy on Simex instead of Osaka. That had become much more common in the past year since the Japanese government had imposed tighter restrictions on futures trading through Osaka, making it easier and cheaper to trade through Simex instead. Leeson also bought and sold futures for Gueler and his traders when they dealt on Simex. In addition, Leeson had developed a third trading activity on Simex and Osaka known as 'switching', a relatively simple operation which exploited price differences between the two futures exchanges. Because Osaka was a large electronic exchange while Simex was a smaller one where trading was done by floor traders, differences in the prices quoted for the same contracts often emerged for up to a minute. Baring Securities had an advantage over others here which stemmed from its early entry into Asian markets: it was one of the few brokers that could exploit these price differences because it was a member of both exchanges. Gueler had tried doing so briefly in spring 1992 and failed to make much money, but Leeson had attempted it that autumn and been far more successful. He would buy and sell futures on Simex, while Goodman executed the off-setting trades in Osaka. Leeson appeared to have quite a knack for it. He had obtained decent profits from switching soon after starting what was his first venture into futures trading.

The thing that had really excited Gueler was Leeson's November trading. As volatility had gone up at the start of the month, not only had Gueler's cash-futures arbitrage done well, but Leeson's switching appeared to have made a breakthrough. He made over £4 million for the month, and Gueler concluded that Leeson could make far more money from 'switching' when markets were volatile because price gaps between Simex and Osaka were bigger. As Baker listened he realized he had to rethink. If Leeson was really a trader, rather than an order filler, then he should be counted under Baker's set-up rather than Killian's. Otherwise, Baker would not be able to control him. At the very least he had to ascertain how much Leeson was contributing to trading profits.

Baker and Killian met to talk over how derivatives sales and trading fitted together. Killian was polite and deliberate, talking as ever in a hypnotic drawl, but Baker was uneasy at Killian's explanation. He did not have too much sympathy with Killian's business in the first place. Baker reckoned that the numbers only made sense because the traders were subsidizing Killian. If he ran his business in isolation, it would not make money. Leeson was a perfect example. He was officially part of Killian's team but appeared really to be a trader. Killian saw this differently. The traders were kidding themselves if they thought their money came from their own brilliance. The only reason Leeson could trade so well between Osaka and Simex was because of the flow of orders from Killian's customers, which told him the way the market was about to move.

At the end of his week in Japan Baker decided to gather everyone in Hong Kong at an off-site meeting to discuss what he had learned. Apart from serving as the usual bonding exercise, it would give him the chance to check that he was not wildly out in his understanding. A dozen traders gathered at the Hong Kong Hilton, a large business hotel in a tower block in the heart of the city, on the weekend of 22

January. Among them was Leeson. Baker had decided that he should meet this young man who appeared to be turning into such an integral part of derivatives trading in Asia. For all the talk about Leeson's control of Simex and his aggressive trading, Baker found a quiet, reserved young man who sat in near-silence during Saturday as the group discussed their operation. Only at the end of the weekend did Baker get a chance to talk to him alone. He told Leeson that he could see from the numbers that what he was doing worked but he was not sure it was entirely above-board. Baker liked his traders to 'work the client information curve' as he sometimes called it. That meant something like the trading activity he had pioneered at Bankers Trust, where the flow of customer orders from different markets allowed him to arbitrage these markets. But taking a customer order for Simex and then matching it over in Osaka on a Baring Securities trading book was another matter. If Leeson had been doing something like that on Simex alone, it might count as front-running. Baker was not sure the authorities in Osaka and Singapore would approve if they knew exactly what Leeson was doing.

Even if the authorities approved, Baker doubted that those in charge of Baring Securities in London knew what Leeson was doing. Nobody had mentioned him before Baker had gone out to examine the operation. Only in Tokyo had he realized Leeson's importance. 'I don't believe that people in London know what you're doing. Good luck to you, but we need Barings doing this, not just Nick Leeson,' said Baker. 'We will have to see if this is something that is wanted.' Leeson agreed quietly, and Baker returned to London to sort out the details of the operation he would take over.

By late February he was in a very strong position to name his terms. His debt trading group's £11 million operating profit had made him the single most profitable director of Baring Brothers. Baker had contributed half the banking group's £22.5 million operating profits. It meant that he had up to £6.5 million to share out among his twenty-six traders. But after he paid what he thought were fair bonuses to everyone, he had only used up £2 million, which meant there was £4.5 million left over. This money was to go into the pool to be shared among the sixty directors of Baring Brothers. Nobody else in the pool was contributing as much. Despite Tuckey's resistance to putting more capital into derivatives trading, a large slice of Baring

Brothers' operating profits had come from Baker's debt trading. The entire domestic and international corporate finance departments contributed only £14 million between them.[5] Even after an impressed Tuckey awarded Baker a £900,000 bonus, he was still putting into the bonus pool £3.6 million, the equivalent of £60,000 in bonus for each director.

Baker had now decided exactly which parts of the equity derivatives group he wanted to take on and which he wanted to junk. The issue came naturally to a head with the decision on how much to pay each trader in bonuses. This was now Baker's responsibility, and he drew up a list of those whom he wanted to keep and how much they should be paid. He also listed eight traders in London whom he thought should be dismissed because they were not doing anything useful. On the list of survivors were twelve traders: four in Osaka, four in London, three in Tokyo, and Oades in Hong Kong. He thought this would suffice for a refashioned equity derivatives arm. There was potential to build up around Oades in Hong Kong, but Walz could handle that in the next few months. After his tour of operations Baker put Gueler top of the list. In a memorandum to Norris, he suggested that Gueler should get £275,000 and Brindle should get £225,000.[6] Then there was the question of Leeson. When he had come back to London Baker had told Norris about what Leeson was doing, and asked him if he wanted to carry on with 'switching'. If Barings was going to be whiter-than-white perhaps it should not risk upsetting customers. However, neither Norris nor Baker thought the world worked that way. Most investment bankers acknowledged that customer business overlapped with trading. It was not something Barings was going to end single-handedly by taking a principled stand against it. The main question was whether there were official objections from the authorities.

Norris quickly came back to Baker and said he had spoken to James Bax in Singapore about Leeson. There did not seem to be any objection from the authorities there to Leeson. Quite the reverse, in fact. He was a valuable figure for the exchange. Baring Securities was bringing plenty of business into Simex and helping it to dominate Osaka. If Leeson could exploit what was Baring Securities' peculiar advantage at Simex for a while, let him get on with it. Thus reassured, Baker decided Leeson should be drawn closer into the group he wanted to refashion. He was making money for them already, but they could not just rely on a freelance trader on Simex doing as he saw fit. If he was trading part of the time, they needed to get their hands on him. He should have trading limits so that he was under strict control. For the moment he was Killian's and not theirs. But that could be changed over time if he really was as valuable a trader as he appeared. In his memorandum to Norris Baker included notes on three people who were not in his group but whom he wanted to help reward. One was a computer programmer to whom he wanted to give £5,000. The second was Gordon Bowser, who was in charge of futures and options settlement. The third was Leeson. Gueler had insisted they could not rely on Killian to pay Leeson the bonus he deserved. Baker had to contribute half. Baker thought there was no point in being stingy if Leeson meant as much as everybody said. He suggested that Leeson should receive a £230,000 bonus, towards which he would give £115,000. 'He is a star!' Baker wrote.

CHAPTER 7

Nicholas William Leeson's destiny was shaped by Baring Brothers even before the moment of his birth. He was born on 25 February 1967 to Harry Leeson and his wife Anne. Nick was the first child, followed by a second son, Richard, two years later. The Leesons lived in Watford, a town first formed in the thirteenth century as a staging post for travellers from the north breaching the gap between the Chiltern Hills on their way to London. Only in the 1930s did Watford gain its twentieth-century place as an overspill town to the north of London for families moving out of the overcrowded slums of the East End. Underground Electric Railways raised the money to build the Metropolitan District Railway through its financial adviser Baring Brothers. It was the Metropolitan railway, snaking north-west through Wembley, Kenton and Harrow to finish at Watford Junction, that achieved the transformation. Baring Brothers had even switched on the lights by raising £1.7 million for the North Metropolitan Power Station Company to re-equip its power stations at Willesden and Enfield to supply the expanding north London suburbs. But Watford was not one of the comfortable villages and towns forming the 'stockbroker belt' around London where a partner of George Henderson & Co. might have a residence. It was for the burgeoning ranks of clerks and white-collar workers, the petit bourgeois army that was sucked daily into the heart of London to fill in forms and copy transactions. In the evening that army would flow home along the rattling Metropolitan railway to Hatch End, Carpenters Park and Watford High Street.

Some of these lower middle classes, as they were categorized in the exacting hierarchy of British class, were ambitious to move up a rung. If they could not achieve it, their children could. One of those was

Anne Leeson, who was a nurse at a psychiatric hospital. She was a hard-working woman who tried to get the best for her children. It was not easy to provide. Harry Leeson was a plasterer who would find work on building sites around the country. The family did not have a large enough income to buy their own house. They brought up Nick and Richard in a small flat in Orbital Crescent, Watford. When their family expanded in 1974 with the birth of a daughter, Victoria, they moved to a red-brick council house in a terrace in a neighbourhood of Watford called Leavesden Green. The life was good enough for Harry, who sometimes wore his plasterer's overalls when he went to The Hare, a public house near the family's home, on a Friday night. Harry was hot-tempered and occasionally rowdy, but helped Anne to bring up their children. From early on Nick had qualities that could lead him out of Watford to greater things. He was a quiet child but with plenty of drive and determination to succeed. Nick liked playing football and could tackle aggressively, fighting for possession. But there was another side to Nick. He was bright and hard-working, with a sense of strategy and ambition, able to latch on to something quickly and absorb it. He also knew how to gain the trust of others. His fellow footballers saw a determined fighter; adults found a quiet, respectful boy.

Nick went to Parmiter's School in Watford. Parmiter's had a history similar to that of the clerks who followed the Metropolitan railway from the East End to Watford. It had been founded in 1681 under the will of Thomas Parmiter, a wealthy silk merchant, as a boys' grammar school in Bethnal Green, but moved to Watford in 1977. During the nineteenth century a tradition grew of Parmiter's sending some pupils to be apprenticed in the City. Nick was a solid pupil who worked assiduously without losing his status as a football-playing lad. His mother had told him he could work hard without compromising the respect of friends.[1] At sixteen he managed to pass six O levels, which was enough to join the sixth form and study for A levels. Leeson was chosen as one of thirty prefects in a year of 120. But in the sixth form Leeson's work suffered. Although he passed English with a C and History with a D, he failed mathematics, ending all possibility of going into further education. Parmiter's historic connections in the City came up with an alternative. He was advised to apply to Coutts & Co., the private bank founded in 1692 by a goldsmith in Scotland.

Polished shoes, an ironed shirt and an obedient manner landed him a job over 300 others who had applied. Coutts had its awe-inducing aspects. The senior bankers still wore dark frock-coats, and it was renowned as banker to the Queen. But Leeson's work of clearing cheques and debits was dull and repetitive. Within a couple of years he was looking for something more interesting. The chance came in June 1987 as the City was reaching the crest of its 1980s boom.

A friend told him there was a job going at Morgan Stanley as a settlements clerk. Morgan Stanley was not yet a large presence in the City but it was expanding and needed more back office staff to settle trades. The ten-person back office had doubled in the previous year but it was hard to find clerks, and Mark Harrison, the head of the department, was trying to poach from clearing banks. Technology was only starting to transform settlement and most of it was still done on paper. Trading on the London Stock Exchange finished at 4.30 p.m., and they would often work at the firm's office in the former Bourne & Hollingsworth store on Oxford Street until 10.00 p.m. settling trades. Harrison was impressed by Leeson. He took orders well and was fast and accurate. He also had imagination, could think on his feet and did not just rely on instructions. He would tackle problems himself rather than passing them on. Most importantly in the back office, where large sums hung on accuracy, he got things right and was careful about details. But Leeson was not just a boring clerk. The back office staff usually had a good time on Friday nights when the working week was over. They would pile into a pub near Oxford Street and get cheerfully drunk. One of their favoured concoctions was a snakebite with a depth charge: a shot of vodka poured into a mixed pint of lager and cider. The warm spirit foamed up in the glass and imparted a hefty kick. After a few of those it was easy to get a little loud and obnoxious, especially with women around. One night they were all banned from a pub in Soho.

But Friday nights around Oxford Street were nothing to what Leeson could get up to some evenings in the pubs and clubs around Watford. He went to Morgan Stanley on a salary of £15,000. There was no end-of-year bonus, but he got time-and-a-half for overtime. Leeson exaggerated a little, and his pay in the City sounded pretty good to his father and his brother Richard, who had joined Harry Leeson as a plasterer. Friends from Parmiter's were also impressed.

One of them was a postman, another worked for a paper company. Several had played football at Parmiter's, where Nick had captained the school team in his last year. They were close-knit, and they knew how to enjoy themselves. After watching a football game on a Saturday they might pile into a club, drinking raucously. With a few pints of Dutch courage inside him, one of Leeson's friends would often walk up to a woman he fancied and unzip his trousers, placing his genitals in her hand. It always caused an uproar but they usually got away with it. Their luck finally ran out one night when he tried this in a club near St Albans. Despite being warned to leave by the victim's boyfriend, they stayed to celebrate. A brawl erupted and Leeson was hit over the head with a chair. His jaw was broken, but he turned up for work on Monday morning, explaining that he had been in a car accident. On another occasion Leeson was stopped by the police and breathalysed. This time he did not bother to conceal what had happened from his colleagues at work. He did not appear ashamed and talked about it openly at Morgan Stanley.

Leeson's nights away from work did not detract from his drive to fulfil his mother's ambitions and he was badly affected when she died of cancer. It left him as the strongest and most successful member of the family. Harry Leeson worked just as hard after his wife's death, but the household drifted. Nick moved to a flat in Watford. He was also moving up at Morgan Stanley. By the end of 1987 he had switched to settling futures and options. Morgan Stanley had a growing business on the London Traded Options Market (LTOM) and Liffe, on which it bought and sold derivatives for customers. It was a growth area where it was easier to make a mark and Leeson quickly carved out a niche for himself. One of his talents was to absorb information and knowledge from others that he could turn to his advantage. Sometimes information could be gleaned simply by treating his bosses with respect and by responding to their requests. At other times Leeson had to use greater charm. Using different aspects of his personality was something that never bothered him. It was a matter of pride that he could slip between personae: prefect and football-playing lad; hard-drinking rowdy and industrious worker. His chameleon-like quality went beyond appearance. He seemed to live and breathe in different ways depending on where he was. The same Nick Leeson who went around clubs with a friend who placed his genitals in passing women's hands might also blush at work when somebody told a *risqué* story in front of a female colleague.

Leeson learned to make people like him, in order to gain something from them. He deployed his charm in a different manner in different settings. When the desired effect was achieved, he was secretly contemptuous of those whom he had fooled, but he was so adept that few people noted the artifice involved. He was like a spy, able almost to change his very being in order to blend in. Leeson could play on vanities and prejudices in those around him to persuade them of what he wanted, or distract them from things that he did not want them to see. His Achilles heel was his own desire to be admired. Occasionally it made him go too far. Leeson liked to boast of his footballing skills at Morgan Stanley, and would sometimes claim that he played for a semi-professional team, Hayes, in the Isthmian League. When a recruit called Tony Platt joined in futures and options settlement, Leeson told him the story, adding that he trained with Hayes on Tuesday and Thursday evenings. Platt was impressed, and remembered it when Wealdstone, the team he supported, was drawn against Hayes in an early round of the Football Association Cup. He went along but did not see Leeson anywhere although there were only 400 people in the ground. This made him suspicious, and when he went into work on Monday morning he decided to test Leeson. He turned the conversation around to the match. 'Did you get a game?' he asked Leeson. Leeson replied that he had played for Hayes at left back. 'Oh, that's funny,' said Platt. 'I was there, and I didn't see you.' After that Leeson's twice-weekly training sessions mysteriously ceased.

Leeson had learned under Richard Kunas, an abrasive man from Chicago, who drilled into him the odd discipline of making margin payments on Liffe and LTOM. It was interesting at first, but by the middle of 1989 Leeson was bored and frustrated again. One problem was pay. Leeson was earning £16,000 a year but was now accustomed to living above his means. He was running up debts and pressing Morgan Stanley for a pay rise. It was hard to keep progressing because those above him were young. What he really wanted was to cross the divide and become a futures and options trader rather than a clerk. He talked to the LTOM traders constantly and had already tested himself as a trader. He settled Morgan Stanley's trades in Japanese futures and options. Sometimes options on the Nikkei were underpriced, and he had dabbled on his personal trading account, matching himself against real traders. The best of them was James Henderson, Morgan Stanley's chief options trader. Henderson had been poached from Barclays de Zoete Wedd in January 1988, so he had the allure of the football star who had transferred from one club to another. Leeson heard that Henderson might need a runner on the LTOM floor, which would be more menial than his current role but would get him across the divide. He put in a word to one of the futures and options salespeople, and was invited to lunch by Henderson. They talked about LTOM, and what Leeson would have to do. Leeson mentioned his small gambles in Nikkei options, and how he thought he could pick up trading if he was only given a chance.

Inwardly Leeson was confident.[2] He had mastered the technical detail of margin payments on different LTOM contracts. He knew he could pick up trading easily enough if he could just work beside somebody like Henderson for a few months. He could absorb it as he had done so many other things already. The vital thing was to don the blue and white Morgan Stanley jacket and get on to the LTOM floor in the Stock Exchange building. To be a futures and options trader was the perfect job for Leeson, in theory. It required physical presence, quick thinking and a good grasp of detail. Leeson agreed with Henderson that he would even take a drop in salary to £15,000 to get the job. But there was a problem. Leeson had deliberately not told Kunas, knowing that it would annoy him. Kunas was well accustomed to settlements staff leaving to become traders. He simply refused to let Leeson go. After a series of meetings he relented to the point of saying that Leeson could go at the end of three months. It was not fast enough for Henderson, and the job went to someone else. Leeson was enraged. If he stayed, there would probably be another chance some time. But if he was going to be forced to stay as a settlements clerk, he could do that anywhere. Leeson knew perfectly well that there was a big demand in the City for futures and options settlements staff. It was an unusual discipline, and as more banks plunged into derivatives, they were crying out for people to settle trades. Even in the back office, job-hopping was endemic, and head-hunting firms called daily to lure staff away to other banks.

So one Friday in June 1989 Leeson resigned from Morgan Stanley and went to a head-hunter to seek another job. He had to work a month's notice and he knew it would be plenty of time to find a place. He was right. He sent over his curriculum vitae to a head-hunter, listing his education and background. The firm called back to say that an interview had been arranged that evening at a firm called Baring Securities. Leeson set off after work from Morgan Stanley to Portsoken Street. He was not impressed by the surroundings. He was accustomed to the bustle of Oxford Street and a smart office. Portsoken Street was on the edge of Whitechapel and Baring Securities' office was tatty and worn. It was a step down, but Leeson was sick of Morgan Stanley and was content to try it for a while. He was also taken with John Guy, who interviewed him. Guy was relaxed and easy-going as he explained what Baring Securities required. As ever Leeson blended with his surroundings easily. Guy asked about his ambitions. 'I have a low boredom threshold,' Leeson said, to explain his move from Morgan Stanley. He did not want to be just a margin clerk. Guy asked if he had ambitions to be a trader. Leeson knew better than to admit such a thing to a settlements manager. No, he said, he was not really interested in trading, he just wanted a good back office job. Guy was impressed. Leeson had the background that Baring Securities wanted and he seemed like a solid character who would get stuck in. He agreed to Leeson's terms and arranged for him to start work at Barings on 10 July 1989.

In fact, Leeson was not the only one who had dissembled a little in the interview. Guy not only wanted Leeson, he needed him. Guy was sitting on severe problems in settlement of futures and options similar to those it had earlier faced in Swiss franc warrants. Sometimes Guy got a little sick of the way Baring Securities would just rush into any market that sounded attractive without any thought for how he was going to settle all the trades it was grabbing. One day Guy had even gone over the head of Ian Martin, his boss, and spoken to Heath about it. He had complained to Heath that the firm was growing too fast for the supply lines to cope. 'The lines of communication are getting far too thin. It is like Napoleon in Russia,' Guy told Heath. Within five minutes Martin was in Guy's office asking him what he had said to Heath. Futures and options were a prime example of Baring Securities' weaknesses. Killian's futures and options sales desk had started selling futures based on Japanese government bonds and the Nikkei the previous autumn. In June they had started broking

Nikkei options, and had achieved early success with Cohen's sale of the 'Barings strangle' to the KIO. But selling the strangle was one thing; settling it was quite another. It was settling directly only on the Osaka Securities Exchange because it was not a clearing member of Simex. But Osaka was bad enough. The problem with futures and options on an exchange like Osaka was that they did not just have to be settled a single time, like a share or bond. Margin payments meant that every contract you sold had to be settled every day.

It was done as follows. Any customer buying futures and options through Baring Securities had to put down a cash deposit to cover the initial margin on its purchase. The initial margin demanded by Osaka was 9 per cent. This meant that if it was buying $1 million of futures, it had to put down $90,000. This cash was dispatched to Osaka by London settlements. The Osaka office netted all the positions, and put any spare cash on deposit in its bank to earn interest. But the difficulty was only now starting. Each broker would have a margin account at Osaka in which the $90,000 would be put. As the value of the futures rose and fell with the market, the account would be debited or credited by the Osaka exchange. There was a minimum 'maintenance level' of 8 per cent, or $80,000. If the market fell by 3 per cent the next day, the $1 million position would fall in value to $970,000. This would take the margin account $20,000 below its maintenance level and would trigger a margin call on the investor of $20,000. If the market rose by 3 per cent, $30,000 would be credited. On markets like the Chicago Mercantile Exchange, a loss on one day triggered a margin call on the next. But the Osaka rules were oddly complicated. A broker would make a margin call on a customer two days after the market moved but would only place the money with the exchange three days afterwards. If the market moved in the customer's favour, the cash was only credited four days afterwards. This meant that the credit balance in a margin account surged up and down according to a strange rhythm bearing little relation to the market that day.

This made the process extremely tortuous for a broker such as Baring Securities. It would hold margin accounts on the Tokyo and Osaka exchanges for its customers. It had to meet the margin payments on their behalf and then bill them promptly for all the money. If it failed to collect promptly it would have to subsidize them by paying out cash before receiving it. It also had to meet some margin payments for itself because Khoo was trading for Baring Securities. That meant there were both customer accounts and 'house' accounts for the firm. The result was a messy set of calculations involving huge amounts of cash. It was vital that any future or option sold by the firm was carefully tracked, but Guy knew that its computer systems were not up to the task. It had installed a system made by a company called Rolfe & Nolan, which was up to settling Liffe trading but had been defeated by the Osaka and Tokyo margin rules. The head of futures and options settlement was called Kevin Peat, a computer buff who had been left with no alternative but to make up his own program. After many evenings in the office working on a personal computer, he came up with a stop-gap solution which was dubbed 'the Kevin Peat System'. It was a piece of software written in the Basic computer language that would calculate the margin calls on Japanese futures and options. The figures would then be retyped into Rolfe & Nolan. Inevitably, the Kevin Peat System was full of bugs and would often freeze inexplicably. But it was the best that Baring Securities had.

By the time Leeson showed up Guy was living day to day in the settlement of futures and options. In April the entire department had consisted of Kevin Peat and one other person. Then Richard Johnston arrived. He had been earmarked to go to Tokyo and develop derivatives trading but had been stuck in settlements for two months trying to unravel the mess. Tempers were fraying and Peat had clashed a few times with Rupert Lowe. Johnston had stayed in the office until 11.00 p.m. some evenings as the Kevin Peat System coughed and spluttered. He talked to Martin about shutting futures and options sales until they could settle properly, because he was scared that the Kevin Peat System would expire, and the firm would be left with a mess of credits and debits that would become ever more tangled as the Tokyo and Osaka exchanges shunted out daily margin calls. He was waiting for someone to replace him so that he could get to Tokyo to do his real job. Nick Leeson was a godsend. Leeson worked hard and did not fly off the handle at any problem. He would listen attentively to what the brokers said and try to sort it out. There was no question about his ability as a back office manager and he seemed to Guy to have an ideal temperament. He was a bit shy, reddening easily when embarrassed by something, but he got on with brokers in a manner that Peat had never managed. He was also good at handling people around him; he had an air of natural authority despite his relatively junior position. 'At last, we have got somebody good,' Lowe told Guy gratefully one day.

After six months of futures and options in Portsoken Street Leeson was bored. Portsoken Street was a backwater and there was little prospect of promotion, but Baring Securities offered at least one thing: because it was a small firm expanding rapidly, there was always the chance of a trip abroad, either to set up an overseas office or to sort out some difficulty. Leeson told Guy that he needed a challenge. Guy spoke to Martin, who suggested Leeson should move to Australia, where Baring Securities was about to become a broker of equity options. Until then perhaps he could help in Indonesia. Guy came back to Leeson to explain that Baring Securities was facing settlements problems in Indonesia, and he needed a team to go and sort it out. They would go to Hong Kong first, where the Hongkong and Shanghai Bank and Standard Chartered, the two banks that cleared its transactions out in Jakarta, were based. Then they would go to Jakarta.

Leeson flew to Hong Kong with another clerk called Darren Pearson, son of a Trinidadian mother and British army father, who wore his hair in a ponytail. After four weeks in Hong Kong they flew on to Jakarta. They ran into a storm over the South China Sea on the way, and gulped back whiskies to help steady their nerves. When they arrived, they found a typical Baring Securities mess. It had opened the office there in 1990, as Heath re-invested money from the Japan warrant boom to expand in Asia. By then the Indonesian economy was growing at 7 per cent a year and western investment was starting to flow heavily into the local stock market.

Baring Securities had a settlements clerk in Jakarta called Paul Sneed, whom Leeson found boring and stuffy. Unfortunately the firm had not kept up with the paper chase that was the Indonesian stock market. It now accounted for about 5 per cent of the Indonesian market, which required delivery of shares into the hands of whoever bought them. But trading had grown so fast that it had broken down. Each share certificate had a table on the reverse, with five boxes to be filled in before a transfer was completed. The seller's broker would send it to the buyer's broker, which would pass it to the custodian – the bank responsible for safe-keeping – which sent it to the registrar of the company, which sent the share to the new owner. If everyone was in Jakarta and there were no hold-ups, it took two weeks. But Indonesia was an archipelago, and some firms were several hundred miles away. There were other problems. An investor might hold a certificate for 10,000 shares and only want to sell 5,000. The broker would send it to the registrar, asking for it to be split into two 5,000-share certificates. Meanwhile, the buyer of the 5,000 shares would get a photocopy of the 10,000-share certificate and a promissory note. But by the time he got his 5,000-share certificate, he might have sold his shares. His broker would send the buyer next in line a photocopy of the photocopy, with further notes attached. These photocopied promissory notes started to take over from share certificates as the most commonly traded items in the Indonesian market. Some transferred many times, while the certificate stayed stuck in a vault.

This went on for more than a year before the authorities investigated, and discovered that the value of the promissory notes was significantly above that of the underlying shares because people had started to forge them. At the local branches of the two Hong Kong banks, Leeson and Pearson found $100 million of share certificates sitting undelivered. Baring Securities could not claim its cash until they had sorted through its certificates, worked out who owned them, and delivered them. It meant long days working in the vaults of the banks, retracing steps in the paper trail. At the end of each day they put certificates into bags, carried them round to the offices of other banks and demanded immediate payment. It was hard, grinding work sorting the certificates and it had to be done precisely because some investors did not want them any more. The Indonesian stock market index had fallen from a peak of 680 in April 1990 to 370 in December, so many were now worth less. The task ground on into months. Leeson and Pearson got into a rhythm in the tropical heat. They were driven each morning in an air-conditioned car from their hotel to the two banks. They had been told of the high number of muggings in Jakarta, particularly of foreigners, and were warned not even to hang an arm from the window of the car as thieves had been known to cut off a finger for a ring. After a few weeks they were bored by being holed up and wandered out in the evenings to local bars, escaping unharmed. These excursions extended further after six months, when a twenty-year-old clerk called Lisa Sims was sent out from London to help them.

Lisa Sims had been recruited only two weeks before. Guy liked her open, friendly manner, and thought she would keep the customers happy. After two weeks he had asked if she would go to Jakarta to join Leeson and Pearson. Lisa said that she had to ask her parents first. She was one of three daughters of a printer called Alec Sims and his wife Patsy who lived in a neatly kept house in a Kent village. They had brought Lisa up as a confident but dutiful daughter and she had grown into a pretty, blonde-haired young woman, known as a good orgnanizer at her school in Swanley, Kent, which she left with eight O levels and two A levels. She had worked in a clearing bank for two years before joining Baring Securities. In Jakarta she soon took charge of outings, hiring cars at the weekend and organizing picnics in the volcanic interior of Java, the island where Jakarta is situated. She struck up a friendship with Leeson, and by the end of the year they were a couple.

By then the piles of paper had shrunk. The firm's auditors had talked of making a provision in its accounts against unsettled trades. But although there were $100 million of share certificates to be allocated, just a small proportion belonged to Baring Securities and Martin and Andrews calculated the risk to Baring Securities at $2 million. In the end Leeson and the others did a good job, and there was no loss recorded in the accounts. Indeed, Baring Securities ended up making a profit from the débâcle, because Leeson's team sorted out certificates held by Hongkong Bank for other banks, and was paid for its efforts. By the time he returned to London in March 1991 his reputation at Barings was high.

His reward for his Indonesian success was to join the Business Development Group as one of Martin's henchmen. That meant he was among the élite of the back office, being sent out to countries where the firm was considering setting up operations to scout out the territory. He travelled to Frankfurt, Manila and Hong Kong, often with a henchman called Tony Dickel, who was Baring Securities' development officer. But in September 1991 Leeson returned to futures and options settlement. This time his task was not simply to settle trades; it was to sort out a mess. Once more it centred around the Kevin Peat System. It was different from the other problems he had helped to clear up because there was a suspicion that it involved more than simple incompetence. It blew up over a small fund management company in London called PCFC Asset Management. PCFC was not one of Baring Securities' large and reliable customers. It was a bucket shop retail broker which advertised for business in newspapers, promising savers a higher return on their cash than they could get by depositing it in a building society or in bonds and shares. It failed to tell them how it would do that. In fact, PCFC was putting its cash into Japanese futures and options, bought and sold by Baring Securities. PCFC was taking risks about which it had failed to warn its customers, and was breaching the rules of Fimbra, the City body that regulated all fund management firms. In October it was suspended by Fimbra, by when it owed Barings about £300,000 in margin calls on Nikkei futures and options, bought over the previous nine months.

This should not have happened because all margin calls should have been collected from PCFC. Martin sued PCFC for £500,000 for good measure, and sent in Leeson to find out what had gone wrong. He discovered matters had not improved in futures and options settlements since his departure eighteen months before. By then the settlement department had abandoned Rolfe & Nolan for a different system called First Futures, whose maker had promised that it would be able to deal with Japanese margin payments. But First Futures arrived six months late, with a tendency to freeze, and was still not up to how Barings wanted to handle the peculiarities of Japanese margins. The London department had to keep using the Kevin Peat System. Each morning it would be faxed copies of the Tokyo and Osaka traders' 'blotters', the pads on which all trades were recorded. They would type these into First Futures and the Kevin Peat System. But the trades were all noted in Japanese, which led to mistakes. A First Futures statement might lack a reference to an option on which the Kevin Peat System had called for margin. The reverse could also occur, and had done in spring 1991 with PCFC. Its trades had been entered correctly on First Futures, but not on the Kevin Peat System. Although it was owed margin by PCFC, it mistakenly paid out Y30 million, rather than collecting the money. By the time Leeson arrived there was an impasse between Guy and Martin over the cause of the mess. Guy argued that Tim Ledger, then the head of futures and options settlement, and those under him, had been working fourteen hours a day, and had simply made a mistake. Martin was inclined to believe there was something more to it.

It was a delicate problem, which Leeson handled. He won the confidence of a twenty-one-year-old clerk called Gerry Lelliott, who had worked on PCFC and could explain the errors. Lelliott was impressed by Leeson and the way he moved with ease among the higher ranks of the firm but still had time for juniors like Lelliott. They had a drink together a few times, and Leeson regaled him with stories about hell-raising exploits. Leeson had once drunk a pint of someone's urine for a £10 bet, he said. Although he gave the impression he was on Lelliott's side, he was actually on the point of ruining his career. He now had in his hands not only Lelliott and Ledger's fate, but that of Guy. Martin had thought there was something suspicious going on. Now Leeson proved himself to be reliable by drawing the same conclusion. One evening Leeson went to Guy to warn him trouble was brewing. He was about to make accusations against several of the settlements people in his report to Martin but he emphasized that he would protect Guy. 'I've found out some things I am not going to mention,' he said. 'If I do, you will get screwed.' Guy said he had nothing to hide over PCFC, and Leeson should tell the truth. Leeson produced a report which suggested there had been collusion between the back office and PCFC to suppress margin calls. Martin called Ledger, Lelliott and another clerk in, and asked them to resign. Lelliott protested his innocence. He was shocked at Leeson's action in first befriending him to obtain useful information, and then throwing him to the wolves.

There were other problems with futures and options settlement. Tim Easun, one of Martin's henchmen, launched an investigation after the firm's auditors found flaws during the year-end audit. He was helped by Leeson. The auditors discovered that the settlement desk had not collected margin from some of the customers, which left Baring Securities having to pay margin on their behalf. This was a waste since the firm made most of its money in futures and options from customer margin. Easun wrote a memo to Martin to explain it. 'The non-segregated client bank account has been continually overdrawn over the last few months,' he wrote. 'Either margin calls have not been made, or collateral balances are not being utilized correctly, situations which should not occur in an efficiently run operation.'[3]

When Ledger departed, Leeson was appointed head of futures and options settlement and uncovered a good deal of sloppiness in how Baring Securities handled margin calls, particularly on Japanese exchanges. The Osaka exchange allowed collateral to be deposited in cash or Japanese government bonds (JGBs). It was more efficient for Barings to use JGBs because it left more cash spare to be deposited at its bank. Leeson found that it was not always done. 'In a worrying number of cases recently, we have been depositing large sums of cash to cover our margin requirement . . . as neither exchange pays any interest on cash deposited . . . this occurs at considerable opportunity cost to the firm,' he wrote in a memo.[4] Leeson gained what was virtually unique expertise in Japanese margin payments as he solved such problems.

It was a temporary job, for Leeson had won his spurs as a henchman and was due to be rewarded in the customary fashion with an overseas post. There had been talk of Australia, but this had receded. Another chance would turn up. He set about recruiting new staff in futures and options settlement. It was natural to turn to Morgan Stanley, and Leeson brought in an old workmate called Carl Gandy. The department was further reinforced with the hiring of Tony Railton, a foreign exchange settlements clerk at Morgan Stanley, whom Gandy knew.

As he worked Leeson was looking for opportunities and one came early in 1992. Among his sorties with Tony Dickel had been a trip to Singapore, where they had examined the possibility of upgrading Baring Securities' membership to full clearing status. This would allow it to broke and settle its own trades rather than going through Chase Manhattan. Trading on the Singapore exchange was only developing slowly. The value of Nikkei futures trades on Osaka was sixty-four times that on Simex during 1991. But Baring Securities already had its office in Ocean Towers and it made sense to become a full member of the exchange. By early 1992 the calls from Baring Securities in Tokyo for a full broking presence on Simex were getting louder. Killian's futures and options sales team wanted someone efficient to take care of their orders. In particular, they wanted somebody who could speak English properly; they did not want to have to keep spelling out what they wanted to a Singaporean trader. Communicating orders was fraught enough in the same language.

Killian had dealt with Leeson as head of futures and options settlement, and respected him. He was one of the only clerks who pleased Killian and Bruce Benson, an American who was Killian's deputy in the Tokyo office and who was often enraged by the discrepancies between the Kevin Peat System and First Futures. Benson reminded Vanessa Gibson of the tennis player John McEnroe. He was demanding, and could complain as loudly as McEnroe about the injustices of dealing with an inefficient back office. The tension was raised by time zones. By the time a US customer noticed a discrepancy, London settlement staff would have gone home. The customer would have to wait until the end of his working day before ringing Killian or Benson in Tokyo. Benson then had eight hours to boil up with rage before letting off steam at the settlements staff in London when they turned up for the next day's work. But Leeson was an exception to run-of-the-mill settlements staff, as far as Killian and Benson were concerned. Leeson was accurate, helpful and friendly. 'We need ten more Nick Leesons!' Killian wrote in exasperation in one memo to London. The omens were favourable for Leeson, and he clinched it by telling Dickel that he wanted to be considered for Singapore. On 19 March 1992 he was told by Dickel that he had been chosen to go to Singapore to prepare the ground for Baring Futures to be upgraded to full membership of Simex. That would mean setting up a back office for local futures and options trading – a task for which he was well qualified – and managing the traders Killian was going to recruit.

This was just the break Leeson had been seeking. To start with it would be a back office job, but there was every chance of it developing into something more interesting. Leeson had harboured an ambition to be a trader for a long time. At Baring Securities he had carried on dabbling in option trading for his own account, just as at Morgan Stanley. The atmosphere at Baring Securities positively encouraged it. Everybody knew that Heath, Fraser and Kelly were big personal account punters. Killian had pressed for his staff in Tokyo to be allowed to sell combinations of options known as bull and bear spreads on their personal accounts. It broke Baring Securities' basic rule that its staff should not take on the risk of selling options, and Martin refused to sanction the idea.[5] Yet a culture of personal account trading suffused Baring Securities. Why shouldn't a back office clerk have a go as well? He was not exactly the biggest gambler in town. In the last quarter of 1989 he had paid £8.81 in commission on contracts bought through

Baring Securities for his personal account.[6] This paled in comparison with the £2,098 paid by Primhak in the Tokyo office, but it was a start. Leeson persuaded Baring Securities to apply for him to be licensed as a trader. It was just a precaution in case a job as a trader came up. There was not an obvious opening at the time. This was as well, because the Securities and Futures Authority, which regulated all City broking firms, checked through county court records whenever it received an application for a licence to practise in the City.

The SFA caught Leeson dissembling again. On 10 March the SFA wrote to Johnson, Baring Securities' company secretary, to say that Leeson had lied on his application form. He had denied any outstanding debts, but court records showed an outstanding judgment against him for an unpaid debt of £639.[7] It was an overdraft, and National Westminster Bank had obtained a court order against him while he was in Indonesia. This could probably have been overcome if Baring Securities had been determined, but it was irrelevant by the time the letter came. Leeson was about to be sent to Singapore instead. It did not cause any undue alarm. Indeed, it was hardly noticed. There was no reply until the SFA wrote again in August asking if the firm wanted to go ahead with the application. Only then did Valerie Thomas, the head of compliance, write back to say it did not want to proceed.[8] Nine days after the first letter came Leeson was told he was off to Singapore. The appointment led to a typical argument between London and Singapore. Martin sent a fax to Killian and Simon Jones, saying that Leeson would report to both Jones and Gordon Bowser, who had taken over from Leeson as head of futures and options settlement in London. Jones erupted at this crass example of London interference. Bax wrote to Fraser to complain that 'once again we are in danger of setting up a structure which will subsequently prove disastrous, and with which we will succeed in losing either a lot of money or client goodwill, or probably both'. He insisted Leeson should report solely to Jones if Singapore was involved at all.[9]

Leeson was blissfully ignorant of these upsets and squabbles. On 21 March he married Lisa Sims at the eleventh-century church of St Edmund the King in West Kingsdown, near her parents' home. The manner in which they became engaged had been typical of their relationship. The previous October they had gone to Paris to watch England beat France in the quarter-final of the Rugby World Cup.

While they were on the train, fortified by a few drinks, Leeson had proposed. Leeson had grown close to Alec and Patsy Sims since returning from Indonesia. As his father drifted increasingly into his own world, the Sims had become a surrogate family. The wedding day was a symbol of that change. It was a bright and windy day with gusts so strong that women had to clutch on to their hats, and cigarette smoke swirled around outside the church. Everything had been arranged by Lisa and Patsy, and was a notch above Haines Way, Watford. Leeson and his best man, a friend from Parmiter's called Lawrence Tupkin, were in morning suits. Lisa arrived in a Rolls-Royce, dressed in full bridal array. All the hymns were traditionally English, including Blake's 'Jerusalem'. The reception was at the nearby Brands Hatch Thistle Hotel. Harry Leeson seemed an isolated figure, drinking and smoking in shirtsleeves at the long table where the bridal couple and their family were placed. Alec Sims told the guests that they had only just found out that Nick and Lisa were off to Singapore. They would be going straight there from their honeymoon and would be staying two years. They had promised to return often.

Tupkin delivered a suitably uproarious best man's speech. 'He's a bit of a jetsetter,' he said of Leeson. He gave an insight into the stag night. 'Last weekend was his last performance before getting married. He was tied up naked again, in the middle of a mini-roundabout, outside Brighton pier.' Then he gave Leeson a razor. 'For the most well-shaven man,' he said, to raucous laughter from Leeson's Parmiter's friends. Nick and Lisa took to the dance floor, the bridegroom shuffling round in embarrassed fashion before being put out of his misery by others joining in. Lisa was captured on video putting out her tongue at the cameraman, looking nothing like a demure bride. The couple were whisked away to their honeymoon in Venice: three days at the Cipriani Hotel. On 23 March, their last day before catching the flight to Singapore, the Japanese government unveiled a welcoming present. Stockbrokers in Japan had complained to the Ministry of Finance that investors had started to buy futures and options rather than the underlying shares because the broking commissions were lower. The government tried to close the gap that day by doubling fixed commissions on futures and options. This meant that it became cheaper to buy Nikkei futures and options on Simex rather than Osaka. At the same time Simex was taking a further step towards attracting investors away from Osaka. Earlier that month it had unveiled options based on the Nikkei 225, which could be traded on the floor just like futures. As the Leesons took off Simex was preparing itself for a rush of new business driven offshore from Osaka.

Landing at Singapore's Changi airport western visitors see two things. One is the neatness of the grass strips beside the runway. It might almost be a military airport for the precision and strictness of the way it is tended. The second is the Changi prison museum, where the 1940s huts and buildings of the camp in which Christopher Heath's mother was imprisoned during the war remain under palm trees. It lends the island an air of existing in a time capsule, as if the British still ruled. Even closer acquaintance with its countless technological and commercial achievements since independence does not dispel that aura of artifice. It remains unnervingly neat and well organized, like one big theme park that is scrubbed clean every night. Singapore is one of the three most densely populated territories in the world with Macau and Hong Kong, but there is none of Hong Kong's overt squalor and overcrowding. All slums have been razed to make way for neat housing and shopping malls, leaving only a small Chinatown for the tourists. The last place of unwholesome night-life, Bugis Street, where transvestite prostitutes used to gather, was demolished in 1988 to make way for the Mass Rapid Transit System. The MRT is all that Singapore's underground railway might be. Its marble halls gleam. Passengers boarding trains line up by doors that slide back only when a train is sitting behind them. There is no possibility of suicide, or of causing disruption to the smooth flow of Singapore's ever-present infrastructure. Everything works smoothly to carry passengers under the city to their jobs or to shop on Orchard Road.

Everywhere in Singapore there were signs of its nineteenth-century roots as a British entrepôt – a port where merchant ships set down goods to be transported to their final destination. The merchant banking feats of Baring Brothers in Asia were helped by the diplomatic triumph of Sir Thomas Raffles in setting up a British trading post in the Malacca Straits in 1819. Raffles had paid only three visits to the island before his death in 1826 but his name had been preserved visibly in the Raffles Hotel, founded in 1867 and reconstructed in 1991 into a tourist mecca, complete with a shopping arcade and a bar where visitors drink Singapore Gin Slings. It was close to the other symbol of British rule, the Singapore Cricket Club, and all around the two buildings were reminders that Singapore had transformed itself from the quaint Garden City it was even in 1975, when Geoffrey Barnett opened up an office of Baring Sanwa Multibank. The towers of the financial district sprouted at the southern tip of the island, looking out on cargo ships in the harbour. It was not simply Singapore's infrastructure that had been tightly controlled by Lee Kuan Yew's government until he stepped down in 1990; management of the economy was also firmly in its grip. The economy had grown at an average rate of 9.5 per cent during the 1970s, but the government decided in 1979 that this rate could not be sustained if the country remained dependent on low-wage industries such as shipbuilding. It introduced a 'wage correction' policy which forced firms to pay higher wages that could only be supported in higher-productivity industries.

One of those industries was financial services, and Singapore tried to build on the gains it had made in the 1970s through the Asian dollar market. It had managed to attract many overseas banks to the island. Banks such as Standard Chartered used it as a hub from which to manage their operations in Thailand and Malaysia. It worked to become the financial equivalent of the Asia trading post it had been in the past, which meant encouraging international aspects of financial services. It became a big centre for offshore insurance, and as foreign exchange trading became a global twenty-four-hour activity, Singapore competed with Tokyo to be the leading centre in the Asian time zone. It was not ashamed to copy innovations in New York or London. In 1987 it created a Sesdaq stock market for smaller companies, based on the Nasdaq market in the US. All this made it natural to launch the Singapore International Monetary Exchange in 1984. Financial futures were already an important part of financial markets in New York and London, and Singapore wanted to become the Asian centre. Simex was the first financial futures market in post-war Asia. It began modestly as an offshoot of the Chicago Mercantile Exchange. This was a huge and liquid market, and Singapore gained the CME's agreement to piggy-back on it through an arrangement known as a 'mutual offset link'. This meant that a contract bought on one exchange could be closed on another. A customer could trade from the Singapore morning to the Chicago evening, a useful innovation as markets started to run across time zones.

Simex started with one futures contract linked to Eurodollar bonds and another based on the exchange rate between the US dollar and the German mark. It came into its own two years later when it managed to exploit the Japanese Ministry of Finance's conservatism about derivatives by launching a Nikkei 225 contract. It was the first Nikkei future to be sold on a futures exchange and was well timed. Warrants provided one way of taking a leveraged bet on the Nikkei and Simex futures became another. Futures also provided a means for the cautious to hedge themselves against corrections in the Japanese market. The Simex initiative forced the Japanese authorities to relent and allow the development of a financial futures market in the home islands. Osaka, which was the second-biggest Japanese stock market, and chafed at its subordination to Tokyo, seized the initiative. In 1988 it began trading its own Nikkei 225 contract, followed by Nikkei options the following year. Business on the Osaka exchange exploded at the expense of Simex because Japanese pension funds preferred to deal on a familiar market. However, just as Osaka was crushing Simex's trade in the Nikkei 225 and other Japanese financial contracts, the Japanese authorities intervened again. During the collapse of the bull market in 1990 the government tried in vain to support the Nikkei by intervening in the stock market in the same way as it often tried to drive down the value of the yen in the foreign exchange market. It did not want to end up owning millions of unwanted shares, so it intervened by buying Nikkei 225 futures instead.

The Japanese government started a series of what were called price-keeping operations, which involved buying Nikkei futures on the Osaka exchange as the market fell. This failed to achieve its true purpose, because the weight of selling in the Nikkei was too great, but it had an unintended effect. Option prices were out of line because Japanese investors undervalued them, an opportunity that was being exploited by Su Khoo. The government created a similar effect for futures. Because it bought futures in the hope of affecting the stock market, it was in effect overpricing them. The price of Nikkei futures would rise above fair value each time it intervened. This presented a target as wide as a barn door to the US banks with the capability to arbitrage futures and cash markets. Throughout 1990 investment banks, including Salomon Brothers and Morgan Stanley, shot at it mercilessly. They sold futures and bought shares each time the government intervened. In a sense they were effecting the will of the government by bridging the gap between futures and cash markets, but by doing so, they made several hundred million dollars. To some government officials it amounted to exploitation by foreign speculators that should be halted as rapidly as possible. The only way to do that was to make it harder to buy futures. Quite apart from this problem the government also started to blame the volatility in the Japanese market on the rise of futures and options trading. These factors conspired to make the government impose controls on the Osaka market in the hope of preventing newfangled and unhelpful speculation.

The rise in broking commissions on futures and options that occurred as the Leesons flew to Singapore was only the latest of the government's measures to control Osaka. During 1991, under pressure from the government, the Osaka exchange raised commissions three times, and put up the initial margin that had to be deposited from 9 per cent to 15 per cent. When that failed to dampen activity, initial margins were raised again to 20 per cent. Trading hours were curtailed, and rules were introduced to make the arbitrage traders produce daily reports on their share trading. All this was meat and drink to Simex, which already thrived on tiny advantages over Osaka. Osaka had rules limiting market movements to a maximum of less than 0.2 per cent every five minutes. If the market dropped 5 per cent, which was common in the turbulence of the crash, traders had to wait three hours for the futures market to catch up. Furthermore, Osaka did not pay interest on margin accounts while Simex did. It helped to breathe new life into Simex during 1992. By the time Leeson arrived in Singapore, Simex trading in Japanese contracts was about to grow once more. Killian had seen it coming for a while, but the firm had been unprepared. When an investor phoned through an order for Simex, Killian or Benson had to keep the buyer holding while they rang Chase Manhattan Futures in Singapore. A couple were starting to become tetchy about it, saying they did not want to be kept waiting on a line to Tokyo. They wanted to go through to someone at Simex who knew exactly what was going on.

Leeson's first task was to set up a back office for Baring Futures. The shell company had existed since 1986. It applied for a licence to be a full clearing member of Simex, while Leeson worked on the back office. He recruited two women to help him, called Norhaslinda (or 'Linda') Hassan and Riselle Sng. They were not required to show initiative. Leeson was in charge. He found some settlements software called Contac that could be bought off the shelf in Singapore which could calculate margin calls and account information to be sent to London overnight. For once London would not have to rely on the Kevin Peat System to calculate margin. The next step was to ensure Baring Futures could trade. Killian had already recruited a young trader called Eric Chang, whom he knew from his days at Chase Manhattan. Leeson was to be its floor manager. This required him to take an examination to gain a licence, which he duly achieved on 26 June.[10] When Leeson took his place on the Simex trading floor, he saw everything to which he aspired. Since the mid-1980s, when many stock exchanges had replaced floor trading by broking over phones and on screens, futures exchanges had been the last bastion of physical trading. Futures markets combined the most modern and ancient types of trading. In offices in Tokyo and London traders sat by screens that showed minute price digressions, calculated with arcane option pricing models. But to buy the options or futures they needed they had to pick up the phone to a raucous futures trading floor where traders scrambled and shouted to execute orders over an uproar of clamouring voices.

Open outcry markets like Simex still existed in the late twentieth century because they provided a faster and smoother trading method than a network of screens. But as in a casino, the chaos of the pit provided cover for those who wanted to manipulate prices and break rules. There was a long history of abuses in the Chicago markets, the most common being bucketing, a variation of the traditional broking abuse of front-running. Because few customer orders were big enough to move a futures market, the trader could not front-run a customer by buying futures himself before revealing the customer's order. Bucketing was a more effective method of cheating. On Simex it might work in this way. An investor would put in an order to buy twenty Nikkei futures at the best price available in the market. When the call came, the Nikkei might be trading at 18,000, with each point change affecting the value of a contract by Y500. Instead of buying immediately at 18,000, the broker could signal to a friend to buy twenty Nikkei futures himself. If the index then rose by 10 points, the friend could sell his contracts for a Y100,000 profit. The broker could buy twenty contracts for the customer at the higher price, explaining that the market moved before he could execute the order. If the index fell, he could buy the contracts from the friend to protect him from a loss, and sell them to the customer, saying that he had done the deal before the market moved. The key was that he would be protected by the opacity of the trading pit. Nobody from outside the market could tell exactly what price he should have got.

Abuses like bucketing were rife in Chicago in the nineteenth century, where futures markets had a Wild West reputation. In 1867 a deputy sheriff even went on to the floor of the Chicago Board of Trade to arrest Benjamin 'Old Hutch' Hutchinson, a highly successful grain trader, for manipulating prices. The grain futures market was repeatedly cornered in the late nineteenth century, and Midwest farmers complained that the Board of Trade was a 'robber's roost'. Nor was malpractice stamped out in the twentieth century. Five Federal Bureau of Investigation agents who infiltrated the floors of the Chicago Mercantile Exchange and the Board of Trade in 1989 uncovered widespread law-breaking, including bucketing, and 'kerb trading', which was illegal trading after the market closed. A common violation was the prearranging of trades: a trader would agree on price ahead of time with a confederate, and close a deal before any competitors in the pit could jump in with counter-offers. The FBI found that the problem was rooted in dual trading: allowing a trader to act for a client or his own personal account. It was legal in itself, but it provided traders with an opportunity to defraud customers. Singapore had tried to crack down on similar offences by passing the 1986 Futures Trading Act, which set fines of up to S$100,000 or a jail sentence of up to seven years for bucketing. But, as in all exchanges, there was some gap between the written rules and accepted practice. The attention of the Simex authorities was divided between keeping the market clean and enticing as much trade as possible away from Osaka.

Above all Simex was not a clinical place where prices and trades were fixed visibly on screens. It was a complex ecosystem in which every organism had its place. The different creatures were marked out by their coloured jackets. In yellow were assistants who reconciled trades on the floor, the task Leeson had tried so hard to get at LTOM with Morgan Stanley three years before. In blue were officials of

Simex: dark blue for senior officials and a lighter shade for their juniors. Traders were traditionally in red but larger firms often sported bright plumages: Goldman Sachs was in turquoise; Barclays de Zoete Wedd in red and white stripes with the Barclays eagle overlaid; the French futures broking firm Fimat had an orange strip on the back, like a chic construction worker's jacket. Many of the red jackets were worn by traders called 'locals', small firms or individuals who traded for their own account. They did not have a flow of customer orders to help them. Instead, they made their money by being useful to the larger players. They would help out a big trader by taking a slice of a large position that he wanted to unload, and selling it on at a fractionally higher price. Locals came in various shapes and sizes, from the Singaporean couple called 'the husband and wife', who had met in the Nikkei pit, to entrepreneurs like Teo Kok Eng, who was the leading local. The big players would patronize the small locals, letting them grab a few crumbs when they were useful, ignoring them at other times on the trading floor. The biggest locals such as Teo were respected because of their influence on the floor.

The trading floor was marked out into areas, like enclaves on a medieval map. Every firm would have a booth or row of booths where its phone brokers would sit. These brokers were often women, whose job was simply to relay orders taken on the phone to traders a few yards away in the trading pits. They sat in front of a bank of telephones with speed dial buttons in front of them on a panel. Sometimes the women were Japanese, to make communications easier with sales staff or customers in Tokyo. They were there for the same reason Killian had asked for an English-speaker to run Baring Futures. It made things easier for Baring Securities' customers, who were often American or English. They sat, several to a booth, talking sporadically into the phone. The physical action took place in the pits, the octagonal amphitheatres with stages sunk into the floor, with steps rising in a ring above them. The pits displayed the hierarchy of traders. Locals stood a few steps down in the pit, while the traders of the large broking firms stood further up, sometimes lounging against a rail that partially encircled the top. There was one pit for each contract traded on Simex. The most intense action took place in futures pits, including the Nikkei pit. For several minutes at a time nothing would happen on the trading floor. Everyone would stand around on the rubber floor strewn with torn-up trading tickets. The Chinese traders would joke with each other, one man making as if to strangle another. The women phone brokers would gossip at the booths and some Chinese phone brokers might take a nap at the desk.

Then an order would come to a phone broker. She would turn to her firm's floor manager, who stood nearby and was in charge of managing the flow of trading. The floor manager would turn towards the pit and shout the order. At the same time he would signal it, using the system of hand gestures called 'open outcry' that was first developed in Chicago to avoid errors arising from traders failing to hear correctly. 'Bid a hundred at twenty-five! A hundred at twenty-five!' he would shout. As he did, he made two signals. He put fingers against his cheek to represent the number of contracts that he wanted to buy, and then made a second signal in front of him to represent the price. Each 5-point change in the Nikkei was called 'a tick' and the number of ticks was shown by the number of fingers held in the air. If the Nikkei had been in the range of 18,400 to 18,500, he would hold up five fingers to show the order was at 18,425. Five fingers held out three times would have meant 18,475. He showed whether he was buying or selling by the direction in which he moved his hand: if it was drawn towards him, he was buying; if it was pushed away, he was selling. As the pit trader signalled that order, others around him would start shouting to attract attention. They would signal a number in fingers, pushing their hands away to show they were selling. Their chance of selling – or 'filling' the order – was higher if the order was large, if they could shout loudly, and if they had a strong physical presence. This was the free market, red in tooth and claw, where trading often involved brute force.

The buyer would point at several other traders in turn until he had his hundred contracts: buy, buy, buy. If he could not get his hundred contracts at 18,425, he might just buy as many as he could. Or the floor trader might have signalled that he had discretion to go up a tick, by flicking an ear lobe once. Then the trader would start bidding again at 18,430 until the order was filled. As the traders did their deals they had to scribble the details on a pad of trading slips they carried. They were the only written record of what had happened, but micro-phones hanging from the ceiling of the exchange and video cameras attached to the walls and columns also recorded the shouts and signals.

If the buyer's and seller's trading cards did not match, the exchange could go back over the tapes to check what had happened. Blue-jacketed officials watched over the proceedings. One stood by a computer terminal at the side of the pit, watching all the bids and offers and entering the prices. These were displayed on large screens hung on the walls of the two-storey exchange. The screen by the Nikkei pit showed the bids, offers and trading price for the last transaction in each of the five quarterly contracts being traded at any one time. NKZ2 showed the price for the contract expiring in December 1992; NKH3 showed the price of the March 1993 contract. The Simex officials also enforced discipline, like school masters. No swearing was allowed, and the dress code was the same as at the Chicago Mercantile Exchange: under the brightly coloured jacket, traders had to wear ties, and denim trousers were banned, along with sports training shoes.

Beside the Nikkei futures pit was the Nikkei options pit. This was a quieter, less frenetic place than the futures pit. It naturally had a more elevated tone because options were more complicated to price than futures, and they were bought and sold mostly by large banks and more sophisticated investors. The futures pit was crowded with Singaporean locals, but there was less of a crush in the options pit and westerners predominated. They stood in a circle, and even when they were trading the pace appeared more relaxed. The options traders looked like a group of deaf-and-dumb friends having a casual chat. An added level of sophistication had developed in the options pit. Everything was mechanistic in the futures pit. The orders seemed complicated to an outsider because of the hand signals but they were actually simple. It was just a matter of buy or sell, a price and a quantity. But the options traders had gone a stage further. As well as selling a simple put or call option, an options trader could signal that he wanted to sell combinations, such as straddles and strangles. If he wanted to sell a straddle on the Nikkei, he would hold three middle fingers of one hand against the palm and let the thumb and little finger point outwards. Then he would swivel his hand from side to side. The most obvious gesture of all was for a strangle: it was a hand around the throat. This not only made the options pit more complex, it also meant that it was opaque. Somebody selling an option would have little idea what price could be obtained for it until a trader actually went to the pit and tried.

A hierarchy did not just exist physically on the trading floor, it also divided the customers who traded through Simex. Many types of customer might place an order with a phone broker. Some were simply investors with no connection to the broking firm, the largest of which were institutional funds, such as Fidelity or a Japanese pension fund. These funds would tend to invest mainly in shares and bonds, not futures and options. However, they would use derivatives markets to hedge themselves, or for limited short-term trading. If an investor thought Japanese technology companies were doing well but did not think much of the prospects of the Japanese market as a whole, it could buy shares in the companies it liked, and simultaneously sell Nikkei futures as a hedge against the whole market falling and dragging the technology companies down with it. Or a pension fund might try to cash in its future gains from a rise in the market by selling call options. It might hold a lot of shares that were staying the same value because the market was featureless and dull. In order to get some cash immediately, it could sell what were called 'covered call' options. It would get some premium immediately, but would owe money if the market rose. The bill would be covered by the rise in value of the shares it owned. The main thing about pension funds and other large institutional investors was that they were in it for the long haul. They invested mainly in shares because they tended to outstrip inflation in the long term. Derivatives were simply a means of protecting themselves or giving themselves a short-term hike.

Quite different were the hedge funds, such as the Quantum Fund. Hedge funds were lost amid the mass on stock markets, but came into their own on futures markets. Hedge funds first came into being in the 1960s in the US as vehicles for wealthy people – overwhelmingly millionaires – to achieve high returns on their cash. They could not obtain this through mutual funds, because regulators had restricted the way that mutual funds invested to ensure that ordinary people did not lose their savings. For example, mutual fund managers could hold a share but not sell it short. Hedge funds were formed as a means of evading such restrictions and giving rich investors more leeway. A hedge fund would often have fewer than a hundred investors – or partners – which meant that it did not have to register with the SEC. It would be registered offshore and its manager would work from an office in the Bahamas or Bermuda. He could trade from there either on screens or by picking up the phone to the trading floor of a futures market. Hedge funds were prominent players on futures markets because futures and options enabled them to take a bet on a market simply, and to leverage their bets. If the initial margin requirement was only 10 per cent, they could take a bet ten times the size with the same amount of cash. It was more risky, but hedge funds had to take risks to get their returns. The biggest funds – Quantum, Tiger and Steinhardt – had achieved annual returns of over 30 per cent by taking large, calculated gambles. Many of them were executed in the foreign exchange market or futures and options exchanges.

Customers often played one broker off against another. That was easy with Japanese futures and options because there were two exchanges. Customers also had the advantage of being protected from bearing the costs of errors. Many errors were made on the trading floor. There were misunderstandings among traders over the price they agreed, or even which was buying and which selling. Sometimes they would have to split the difference in a disagreement. Sometimes an error could be sorted out by looking at the video recording. But that meant one trader had to sell contracts he thought he owned, or buy others he did not want. The chain of communication was so stretched that a mistake could occur before an order even reached the pit. A floor trader might not understand a phone broker, or a pit trader might think a floor manager wanted him to buy when he was being asked to sell. Whatever the error, exchanges like Simex required a trader to make good his own error. If a customer ordered twenty contracts and the floor trader sold twenty by mistake instead of buying them, he none the less had to deliver twenty contracts. The most irritating thing was that the trader could never gain by a mistake. If the market price had fallen by the time he finally bought the twenty contracts, the gain had to be given to the customer, but if it had risen, he had to take the loss himself and give the customer the contracts at the original price. That meant that the trader had to mark down his own profits, or those of his firm, to cover. Sometimes traders felt as if futures exchanges such as Simex were trying to prevent them making an honest living.

Yet that was not how Leeson felt when he finally arrived as a floor trader on Simex. He could at long last wear the dark blue and yellow jacket of Baring Futures. Pinned to his lapel was his trading badge with three letters to identify him. Traders could choose the letters, and the newly married Leeson had selected LJS for Lisa Jane Sims. Leeson and Chang started on 1 July with Leeson sitting in a seat in the three-person booth of Baring Futures. At first they made a few mistakes as their signals were unfamiliar and Leeson was still finding his feet as a floor manager. But those in Tokyo noticed an immediate difference. Chase Manhattan had offered a decent service, but Baring Securities had been only one client of many. With Leeson it was different. When Gueler or Khoo rang up they had a familiar voice to talk them through what was going on in the market. For Killian and Benson it was a huge help to have someone who could talk to customers directly. They also had a reliable chap to take a visiting fund manager out for a drink or dinner and show him around Simex. It was the sort of attention on which Heath had built his equity broking business, but it had been sadly lacking in futures and options sales outside Tokyo. Killian found that he could always rely on Leeson to do the honours even if it required him to work late into the evening to settle trades. Leeson soon became all things to all men, from settlements manager to floor trader to entertainment director for visiting customers. As ever, he appeared to take easily in his stride everything he was required to do.

CHAPTER 8

Leeson's air of calm was deceptive. Being a futures and options trader was much harder to master than he could have imagined. In his other jobs he had dealt with problems that could be analysed calmly but on a futures exchange things changed constantly. The screens by his head flickered with new prices every time a new order went into the pits. Any mistakes were punished instantly with losses. For the first time he was on the side of the boundary that mattered most to everyone from Heath down. Sorting out back office failures was a painful necessity; making money was entirely different. That was what everybody cared about. If Leeson could not make it there, he would have failed in the big league. But there were myriad complications. It was not only that signals might get mixed up; selling was more tricky than it appeared. Orders did not come in a steady, well-paced flow. As the market moved, there would be an uncomfortable rush of orders and he would have to signal several orders for Nikkei futures at once. Chang would return with a mass of contracts, and Leeson had to share them out among his various customers. He was keen to please all of them in his crucial first few weeks. It was vital for Leeson's future that he should get them good prices because they had a choice of whether to trade on Simex or Osaka, and would switch their business if he was ineffective. Leeson could not go back to his customers to say that it had been impossible to obtain for them the prices he had promised, or to execute the whole of their orders. If mistakes were made, or Simex prices were unstable, he had to take the burden.

To outsiders he appeared to be taking to it remarkably quickly. It was not just his demeanour and accent that were a pleasant change to the house traders and Killian's customers, it was the briskness with which Leeson could fill orders. He would talk callers through the state of the market and offer a keen price for them to trade on Simex. Those who offered him discretion did not feel he was taking advantage. Indeed, he was almost always able to squeeze a good price for them. In Tokyo Benson was extremely impressed by Leeson's smooth execution of orders. From the Simex floor the strain was more visible. The action was becoming ever louder and more frenetic. Leeson's former employer, Morgan Stanley, was diverting a lot of business to Simex. Indeed, Morgan Stanley had been so active in poaching from other brokers that Simex had imposed a ban on any member firm's staff leaving without three months' notice. From the start Baring Futures was short of staff. The phones rang constantly and there were too few hands to answer them. A trainee called David Roberts, the son of a friend of Andrew Fraser's, was assigned to help Leeson out. He became known as 'Dog' because he had been unable to find his way into Bax's house, where he was staying, after returning from a lively night out. He was forced to shelter in a kennel in the garden with Bax's dog. Even with this additional help Leeson was having to struggle to keep up with the unceasing flow of orders. It made it far harder to provide the sort of service that would give Baring Futures a good start. Leeson was soon under a lot of strain.

Pressures like this were common for brokers and particularly for Baring Securities. The firm had often entered unfamiliar markets just as there was a rush of orders. That would lead to mistakes as its traders bought or sold shares or bonds. It was easy to get confused and end up with a few spare. On a futures exchange a pit trader might not count properly and trade 110 contracts instead of the hundred he intended. Baring Securities dealt with left-over contracts by putting them in what was called a suspense account. This was a house account in which it held all contracts it could not allocate to customers or to its own traders. It might be able to sell them to a customer the next day, or place them somehow. Otherwise it would have to sell them again, bearing any loss from the bid–offer spread. If it did not sell immediately, it risked the contracts falling in value due to a move in the market. This was tantamount to trading in a house account. Futures and options salesmen were not supposed to do that, but rules were sometimes stretched and the practice was quite widespread. Killian had suspense accounts and would sometimes hold on to spare contracts for a day or two in the hope they would rise in value. If he had spare

JGB futures, he would ask a bond analyst whether they were likely to rise. 'Come on up, baby, come on up,' Killian and a fellow salesman would say, watching the screens to see if they were making money. It was a means of getting out of an error without having to take a loss. If it did not work and the market moved the wrong way, Killian would have to sell the contracts in the suspense account and count the loss against his sales commission.

Suspense accounts were also used to hold unallocated contracts. The contracts could stay in a suspense account for a couple of days until their destination was known. This might occur when a fund manager rang to order some futures. The fund manager might be buying *en bloc* for several different investment trusts without knowing exactly how the contracts would be allocated. That was decided after the trade was done. All the contracts would be placed in a suspense account until the fund manager decided how to divide them up between different accounts. This could be taken a stage further. Brokers often had to deal with a rush of individual orders. It was simpler to place a combined order through the pit than try to deal with them separately. This meant the contracts had to be held for an hour or two in a suspense account before being allocated to the correct accounts. This was done by a method known as a cross-trade. Because Simex was a public exchange all trades took place on the floor. If a broker wanted to move contracts between one account and another, two traders from the firm had to go to the pit. One of them would signal a cross-trade by holding his hands crossed in front of him as if he was wearing a pair of handcuffs. Then he had to repeat a bid or offer three times before the other trader accepted. This allowed contracts to pass between two accounts. There were strict rules to limit cross-trades on most exchanges because they were private trades. However, Simex's rules on cross-trades were less strict than in Chicago, and many firms used cross-trades to switch their positions around.

The final use for suspense accounts was to absorb losses on other trades. One difficulty with trading on Simex was that it was a small exchange. If a fund manager placed a big order, he could easily move the price in the pit. A broker could quote the current price when the customer phoned, but then find that he had to pay more because the price moved as he executed the order. If the broker wanted to give a good price to attract business, he might knock off a little to compensate. This could be done either by using a cross-trade or by adjusting prices in the accounts. If it was done through a cross-trade, the two traders would move the contracts into the customer's account at a slightly lower price than had been paid. This could not be done too drastically. Simex rules generally forbade cross-trades at prices that were a great deal above or below the current market level. However, there was some leeway in the bid–offer spread for changing prices slightly. The alternative was just to place the contracts in the customer account at a slightly lower price and mark a compensating loss into a suspense account. It was done at the booth by an assistant who entered an adjustment as a trade was made. This was common at Baring Securities if a salesman could not get the price he had promised to a customer. The firm had twenty-five suspense accounts on its general ledger – its central balance sheet. Killian would often take a loss into suspense accounts to improve prices to customers slightly. It gave him an edge over other brokers and ensured that his customers would keep coming back to him rather than taking orders elsewhere.

Although the strains were obvious on the Simex floor, their effect only surfaced when trading finished and the second half of Leeson's working day started. He would take the lift down from the fourth floor of the Overseas Union Bank building, past the Delifrance café in the entrance hall and across the road. It was a relief to get off the floor. It was hot and noisy, and although Baring Futures had a prime booth next to the air-conditioning, the trading jackets were stifling. Most firms had jackets with aerated vents, but those of Baring Futures were made of solid material. Leeson would walk through a plaza opposite to Ocean Towers. Leaving the lift at the twenty-fourth floor he walked along the corridor to the Baring Futures office to settle the day's trades. He had to deal with thirty-seven accounts, including a suspense account opened on the first day. Simex accounts were designated with a five-digit number and it was numbered 99905. Trading was so heavy that it strained the Simex settlement system. When the Baring Futures positions had been entered on Contac, they were transmitted to Simex to be checked against other firms' returns, but the Simex system crashed constantly, leaving delays of three or four hours in which Leeson would not know if trades agreed. Many errors involved locals, and it was hard to settle them quickly because locals often employed low-paid settlements clerks, who went home as soon as they had made a stab at settling the day's trades, leaving problems for the next day. Even in the first two days Leeson was up until late in the evening trying to reconcile trades he had done with Simex records.

If there was any discrepancy Baring Futures had to make up the difference. As trading started the next morning Sng might call him to say the Baring Futures and Simex records of the previous day disagreed by forty contracts.[1] Leeson had to buy more contracts to cover this gap. If the market had moved, and he had to pay more, the price discrepancy would be marked into account 99905. It was known as an error account, which was the same thing as a suspense account. At the end of every day Contac would send details of the 99905 account to London along with the thirty-six others. It had been set up to send four pieces of information on each account: details of activity that day, closing prices on the exchange, positions in the account and the margin to be paid to Simex. On Friday 3 July 1992 Bowser rang from London to say he did not want to be sent all details of account 99905 because it had caused reconciliation problems. All the small errors were straining First Futures. Leeson agreed to set up another account to hold all minor errors, and send only the margin bill to London. He asked Sng what her lucky number was. She replied that eight was lucky in Chinese: the word 'bat' meant both 'eight' and 'prosperity'. It took only one or two keystrokes to set up a new error account numbered 88888. Leeson phoned the consultant who had installed Contac to ask him to adjust the software. Instead of getting all details of Account 88888, London would only be sent the margin call. This suited Leeson well enough because it meant no one could watch over his shoulder to see his fumbles as he tried to master trading.

The five eights account quickly became Leeson's means of compensating for the stresses and strains of Simex. It gave him the buffer he needed. As July went by he used it more and more regularly. More than 200 contracts passed through it each day in the last week. His first month seemed to go smoothly from the outside, but the bill came on the final day, when Leeson had to produce monthly accounts. The 31st of July fell on a Friday. By then the five eights account contained a loss of Y11 million (£49,200). Leeson had a choice of writing this amount off openly or trying to conceal it. It was a large sum to attribute to errors. There was a danger that if he declared it, he would show London he was not running a very tight ship. Because Leeson was in charge of the back office, he did not have to do so. He could adjust the accounts to hide the loss. His opportunity lay in the surplus cash given to Baring Securities by its customers to cover margin calls. The firm netted customer accounts to reduce the amount of initial margin it placed with Simex and the surplus was deposited at Citibank in Singapore. Although Leeson had no power to take money from the Citibank accounts, he could switch it around between accounts. It was simple to shuffle Y11 million from the main customer account into a sub-account for five eights. Leeson had changed the designation of the five eights account half-way through July. Simex had now registered it as a customer account, rather than a house error account. After a few days Leeson switched the Y11 million back into the main Citibank account again.

Leeson was now a fully fledged trader. He had applied to Simex for a licence to trade in the pit. Unlike the SFA Simex did not carry out independent checks in Britain, and on 12 August Leeson duly gained his licence. He needed some calm in the market to get on top of things and gradually correct the deficit he had concealed in five eights. He was not to get it. The Nikkei had been falling in fits and starts for eighteen months by July 1992, dropping more than 60 per cent from its peak in December 1989. On 18 August it scraped the bottom at 14,309. Japan was now in recession: industrial production had dropped to 6.2 per cent below that in July 1991. Japanese banks were bloated with bad loans and were heavily reliant on their share portfolios for capital, but as the Nikkei fell the value of these portfolios sank. It raised a huge spectre, because if people panicked and withdrew their deposits from banks, there would be a run on the banking system. That day the government announced measures to prop up banks, and said it would unveil an economic stimulus package by the end of the month. The Nikkei surged, pushing up to 15,268 by Thursday 20. More orders flooded into Simex as investors tried to catch a resurgence in the market. The surge made it much harder to fix errors if Leeson was left short of the market. The Nikkei was rising so fast that it was a great deal more expensive to buy long futures to replace a gap left from the previous day. By the time Sng rang to say there had been an error, the market would already be well above the level at which Leeson had been buying the previous day.

A change of 5 points in the Nikkei was known as a tick, and a tick was worth Y2,500 (£11) per contract. If the Nikkei was 20 points above the level where a mistake was made, this was a loss of four ticks. On a twenty-contract error, four ticks could cost Y200,000 (£900). But on that Thursday, the Nikkei had risen 617 points, or 123 ticks. A move of this size made a mistake thirty times more expensive. Instead of Y200,000 it cost Y6.2 million (£27,700). This was far too large a discrepancy to show to London. Bowser had by now recanted and asked for all the errors to be placed in account 99905 after all. The software had been amended to cope. But Leeson kept the five eights account for the mistakes that were too big to disclose. He also found other ways to conceal them. Sometimes he phoned up the Tokyo traders and asked them to take contracts from him. Khoo helped Leeson out a couple of times, thinking that it was for customers. One day he rang Ben Hoffman, a volatility trader who worked with Khoo, and said he had bought ten futures contracts by mistake and needed to put them somewhere because he was not allowed to hold contracts overnight. Leeson was suitably grateful when Hoffman agreed to take them. The traders were now willing to go a little out of their way to help Leeson. They owed him favours because he was providing such a good service on Simex. They trusted him to fill orders at a good price. That meant they would give him a little more discretion. Rather than insisting on an exact price, they might leave him to find the best one he could. They were rarely disappointed.

In the midst of the turmoil an event occurred that Leeson was later to classify as the start of his hidden trading in five eights.[2] On Friday 21 August the Nikkei rose by nearly 1,000 points on expectations for the forthcoming economic recovery package. It was a roller-coaster of a day on the Simex floor. Some 25,000 Nikkei futures were traded that day, well above the average in July. There was a cheer of relief as the bell rang for the end of the trading day. That week Baring Futures had been so busy that things had threatened to get out of control. Leeson had taken on a young clerk called Mitsuko from a firm of local accountants. She was employed to sit next to him, answer the phone if there was nobody else to do it, pass on orders to Leeson and phone back customers to confirm trades. That morning she took an order for twenty long futures for Fuji Bank but she misunderstood, thinking it was an order to sell. The order was passed through to the

Nikkei pit along with others, and was executed at the market price. By the time Simex closed the Nikkei was 200 points up from the level at which the firm had sold twenty futures. Leeson discovered this at about 8.00 p.m. that evening, as he sorted through the day's trading in Ocean Towers. Because it had sold instead of bought, it was out by forty contracts. Since the market had moved by forty ticks, it would cost an extra Y4 million (£18,000) to rectify. However, it was Mitsuko's error rather than Leeson's. He decided to ask Jones, who was working late, what to do. Jones told him to consult Baylis, and Leeson left Ocean Towers with the problem hanging over him.

In his time at Baring Securities Leeson had a pristine record. He was fearful to spoil it now by putting on record to Baylis, Heath's right-hand man, the difficulty he was having controlling Baring Futures. It would cast a pall on all he had achieved so far. In his own mind he started to blame Jones for the mess. If only he had been given enough backing, this would never have happened. He was supposed never to hold contracts overnight, and now he would be forty contracts short for the whole weekend. He worked himself up into a rage as he walked to the Hard Rock Café, one of the bars favoured by expatriates in Singapore for an evening out, where he had promised to meet a group of people from Baring Futures for a drink. As in other branches round the world, its walls were hung with framed rock memorabilia and there was an illuminated sign in the entrance showing guitars flying into a yellow sun. The dining area of the café was downstairs, and was air-conditioned to absorb the sweat and heat of a lively Friday night. By the time Leeson arrived the Baring Futures group was entrenched. As he walked in to the café he saw Mitsuko, who already knew of the error because Leeson had been trying to check it that afternoon. She was in tears at her mistake, and Leeson reassured her she would not be held to blame. As he swigged at a beer in the hot and crowded club, he resigned himself to putting yet another loss in five eights, rather than owning up to the mess growing around him every day at Baring Futures. The fact that it had been Mitsuko's error allowed him to place the blame for his problems on other people.

Next Monday morning Leeson faced an immediate dilemma over how to solve the difficulty of the forty short position Baring Futures now held. He could write to Baylis, as Jones had suggested. In practice he would not have been likely to get a prompt reply, since the Baring Securities directors had started to spend a lot of time agonizing over whether to break away from the Brothers. But Leeson had ruled it out anyway. He was going to see the thing through himself. If Leeson did not have the approval of Baylis, he could not put the futures in 99905, which meant that he had to use the five eights account to solve the problem. Leeson decided it was the only thing he could do. He told Sng to alter Barings' records, so the contracts were sold by five eights instead of the Fuji account. He then asked her to sell twenty more from five eights to Fuji's account at the original price. Although this was a forgery, it had the same effect as a cross-trade that transferred the loss of £18,000 and a short position of forty futures into five eights. A forty short position was now written into the five eights account, and Leeson had a further choice. He could either buy forty long contracts to match, hedging the short position, or leave it as it was. The Mitsuko error had crystallized in Leeson's mind a feeling that it was going to be impossible to hide the deficit indefinitely by using surplus cash in the Citibank account. The losses were already growing uncomfortably big. The alternative was to reduce his losses by trading. He could try to leave the open contracts in five eights and hope the market went his way.

Leeson had no authority to do so, but neither did he have authority to use five eights as he had done for two months. There was no way back unless the losses were eliminated. Leeson decided the only way of doing this was to trade. The £18,000 Mitsuko loss could be reduced if the short position stayed open a few days and the Nikkei dropped. He kept the forty contracts for three days, hoping the market would drop below Friday's level. He had some luck on Tuesday, but on Wednesday it rose further to 16,542. He was now sitting on a loss of £50,000. Leeson cut the position, but did not halt his trading. He now switched to being long of the Nikkei. By the following Monday he held 189 long futures in five eights. He had more success with this, as the market rose to 18,061. It was not enough. The chaos of August had led to a loss of Y49 million (£220,000), nearly five times the loss of July. Once more Leeson shuffled the Citibank accounts to hide the loss. Now things were out of hand. But Leeson did not have time to halt. Baring Futures was growing as more orders came into Simex. In August he hired another trader to work with Chang, called

George Seow, a solidly built young man who had worked as a sailor, and as a deck-hand on an oil rig. Seow had an aggressive streak, and claimed once to have taken revenge for being fined for being late back on board ship by tipping noxious chemicals into the harbour. He also had a loud voice and could easily shout over the crowd to fill an order. Despite all of Leeson's private worries, Baring Futures was a force to be reckoned with on Simex.

As George Seow was hired, Simex was heading towards the expiry of the September Nikkei futures contract on the tenth. It was to be the first time Leeson experienced an expiry as a trader because they only occurred quarterly, and Baring Futures had started trading three weeks after the previous one on 10 June. The run-up to expiry was a jittery period, because time was running out for investors who held futures that were on the wrong side of the Nikkei cash market. The Nikkei futures index was normally slightly above the stock market index, reflecting the additional cost of holding shares. But futures and cash indices would converge towards expiry, finally meeting in the last minutes, which were known as 'witching hour'. Ripples could even force the markets out of alignment, so that the cash market went above the futures market, which was known as 'backwardation'. As witching hour came near the large players in the Nikkei market, including hedge funds and big investment banks, sometimes tried to ramp the share market to increase the value of their long futures holdings. Trading would be very intense in the last days before expiry, not only because of attempts to ramp the market, but because traders that held large futures positions did not want them all to expire. Instead they would roll the positions over from September into December by selling out of September futures and buying a similar number of December contracts. This would cost money because December futures still had a premium over shares and would trade at a higher price than the September ones.

This made the first ten days of September a very busy time for traders, and gave all the brokers on the Simex floor a chance to demonstrate their skill in rolling over futures contracts. Despite the problems of the five eights account Leeson was determined to excel in this test. In order to roll over September futures in Osaka a trader had to do the two sides of the deal – the September sale and the December buy – separately. That meant taking a risk on the market moving between the execution of the two sides. It could work in the trader's favour. If the market fell after he had sold the September, it would narrow the price gap between the first deal and the second. Equally, he would lose if the market rose. A less risky trading method had developed on Simex where the two sides of the transaction could be done in a single deal, which was called 'a roll'. A trader could walk into the Nikkei futures pit and buy a roll at a single price. As the early days of September passed traders could often be seen at the Nikkei pit making the sign for a roll, which was a thumb and forefinger pinched together repeatedly. The price of a roll was set by the gap between the price of September and December futures. When the September contract was at 18,000 and the December one at 18,095, a trader could sell a roll between the two for ninety and buy one for a hundred. In other words, rolling over a long September contract into December cost a hundred points, or Y50,000. It was an expensive operation for customers, and any trader who could offer a better price for rolling over September to December could attract a lot of business.

Leeson rapidly started to achieve far better prices than the market for rolls. In the run-up to expiry he was given a big order for rolls by Banque Paribas, a French bank which was among Baring Securities' largest customers. He was also given a lot of orders by the Tokyo traders. Khoo wanted rolls to keep her option volatility book hedged, while Gueler was starting to arbitrage the Nikkei cash and futures markets and had to maintain his positions. First for Paribas and then for the Tokyo traders, Leeson consistently beat the market by up to 20 points, which was four ticks per contract. This meant that a trader rolling over a hundred contracts would gain Y1 million (£4,500) by doing so through Leeson instead of another broker. Paribas was very pleased with the results, and started to direct most of its orders for rolls to Baring Futures. Leeson's keen execution of rolls also came in very useful in Tokyo. Although Khoo had produced large profits for Baring Securities in 1991, competition from US banks was now eroding the profits of volatility trading. The arbitrage traders made their profits from wafer-thin gaps between cash and futures markets, so rolls at four ticks better than the market price could make a big difference to their profits. Although Leeson had been seen as a good executor of orders before then, the September rolls made him stand out. 'Amazing job, Nick,' Ming San Lee, a trader who worked with Gueler in

Tokyo, would say as Leeson produced yet another roll at a better than market price. Leeson had found the perfect means to impress those around him once more.

Nor did Leeson merely wait for orders to come through. He would phone Tokyo to offer his latest rolls at a bargain price, like a broker with a line of cheap stock to sell. There started to be some competition to gain the best rolls. The Tokyo traders would allocate them between different traders, and customers who were buying futures through the arbitrage book. Often a roll went to the person who demanded it most forcefully. That could be a trader who was not doing well and found these rolls useful to smooth over problems. The traders knew Leeson must have a means of getting such good prices, and some of them assumed it was by taking risks. He could do that by constructing his own rolls rather than going to the Nikkei futures pit to buy them. The Nikkei was rising sharply towards the 10 September expiry, which gave Leeson a chance to buy the two sides at different prices. He could first buy the December futures, and then wait before selling September futures. As the market rose the gap between the two contracts would narrow, allowing him to offer rolls at a better price. This was known as 'lifting a leg' or 'legging', because it involved keeping one side – or leg – of a matched contract open. It appeared to some traders that Leeson must be legging to be offering such prices. Magides rang Leeson from Hong Kong to warn him against taking chances to please customers. 'It's not worth putting your balls on the line,' he said. Magides realized that if the market moved unexpectedly against Leeson while he was legging rolls, the price gap would widen rather than narrow and he would be in trouble.

What Magides did not know was that Leeson had a solution at hand for any rolls that went wrong. He could write them off as another 'error' and put them in the five eights account. Because of the errors and problems of reconciliation, Baring Futures might find itself with a hundred short September futures, which it had bought at 17,800, when the December contract was trading at 17,900. If the market dipped below this, bringing the December contract down to 17,870, Leeson had the ingredients for a long roll at 70 points, which he could sell easily to the Tokyo traders. But if the market moved up he could not do it, and the hundred short futures would end up in the five eights account. In his own mind Leeson saw the good rolls as genuine, a mark of his trading prowess. The bad trades were something else entirely: just mistakes made by his floor traders. As he gained more approval from Tokyo he did not acknowledge the inextricable link between the two. All the good trades would go to those who depended on him to boost their profits; all the bad ones were stuck into the five eights account. Leeson was starting to siphon money from a hidden account in Baring Securities' balance sheet into the unknowing hands of its traders and customers. And as he did so he inflated his own reputation. Leeson had to carry out about 10,000 rolls each quarter. Most of these went to Baring Securities' customers, although some were for house traders. By executing the rolls at a price of four ticks better than the market, Leeson was in effect giving away Y100 million (£450,000) from the five eights account to those who he wanted to impress. It was hardly surprising that he was becoming popular.

This subsidy to Baring Securities' traders and customers took a heavy toll on the five eights account in the first ten days of September. But an even heavier burden was imposed by Leeson's attempt to get all the cash back by gambling on the market. He bought more long futures for five eights in the early part of September, hoping for a further rise in the market. His bet failed. Some US banks had been trying to ramp the Nikkei in the run-up to the 10 September expiry. But after the spike at the witching hour, the index fell back again, reaching 17,400 at the end of the month. As it fell Leeson started to lose greater amounts than he had contemplated. Heavy volatility meant that mistakes were costly. As the losses grew his grip on the five eights account loosened, and the traders started to realize that they could off-load mistakes easily. Leeson was not a tough manager. He might let off steam at whoever had made an error, but he would take the responsibility for sorting it out. That inevitably meant storing it in the five eights account, which he controlled. He had not lost his earlier ability to straddle the worlds of prefect and football-playing lad. The impact on five eights was disastrous. Within two months Leeson's use of it had ballooned from its early days. Just three months after he had started trading, the losses in the five eights account had risen from Y11 million to Y599 million (£2.7 million). Luckily for him the Citibank account held a great deal of spare cash. Once again he shuffled it by instructing Sng to debit Y670 million (£3 million) from the main

Citibank account and credit the sum to the five eights sub-account.

September was not an ordinary month. It was the end of Baring Securities' financial year, which meant that Leeson had to fool not only financial controllers in London, but the Singapore accounting firm that inspected Baring Futures' books, Deloitte & Touche. He did that by forging a document. Leeson wrote to Bowser in London asking for confirmation of the balances of accounts. Bowser replied on 2 October and Leeson used the letter to mock up an authorization of the balance of the five eights account. He changed the date of the letter to 7 October, and attached it to a statement of the five eights balance. It seemed to do the trick; Leeson did not get any questions from Deloitte & Touche. By now he was at the heart of an almost surreal web of deception. Leeson had told himself in the past few weeks that he could resolve his problems and take up the life of an honest trader. But he could not hope for such an outcome any more. He was deceiving an array of people in different ways, from traders in Tokyo to an accounting firm in Singapore. Even if he could wipe the slate clean, it would not stop him needing the five eights account. Only with its support could he supply fills and rolls at the prices that brought him admiration and attention. Only with it as a dustbin could he conceal the state of Baring Futures from those who expected so much of him. Among them was his wife of six months, who was so confident that he would succeed that she did not ask questions. Leeson had not confided his difficulties to her and could not face the thought of telling her how much of a mess he was in.

With all this weighing him down Leeson faced another difficulty. He could not simply keep altering the accounts at the end of the month because all the losses reappeared a couple of days later. The growing hole in the balance sheet was bound to be spotted eventually unless it could be filled. Leeson's efforts to do so by trading had been disastrous. He needed a way to borrow money. No bank would lend it since he could not justify a loan, but as he sat at the trading booth he could see an easy way to borrow money a few yards away. No one would even ask him why he wanted it. The solution lay in the option trading pit, where the circle of option traders stood around in gentle, sophisticated conversation. In the option pit Leeson could get all the money he wanted. He just had to stroll over and make a few gestures. The easiest way to raise a lot of money rapidly was to sell a straddle on the Nikkei, gesturing with three of his fingers held against his palm, and the thumb and little finger twisting from side to side. It looked like a plane entering turbulence, which was a suitable gesture for what Leeson was about to do. A straddle was a pair of options that would lose value if a market fell or rose. A straddle was similar to a strangle, the combination of options bought by the KIO in 1989, but even more risky to sell. The only way that the straddle seller gained was if a market remained stable. If this happened both options would expire worthless and he would keep all his premium. But this was unlikely, particularly if the options expired in six or nine months' time, because the market was almost bound to have moved by then.

Virtually any movement in the market would cost him money. He would lose more and more rapidly as the market moved, and lose most of all if the market bounced around. It was a huge gamble, but Leeson felt he had no choice. It was the only sure way to borrow money. In October he started to sell options. When a trader like Khoo sold a straddle, she would buy futures as well to offset her risks. She would buy long futures if the market rose and short futures if it fell. These futures would pay the bill if the market moved. It neutralized the delta risk, and meant she was only betting on volatility, not on a movement up or down in the market. Professional options traders would adjust their holdings of futures constantly to keep their positions hedged. It was why Khoo kept calling Leeson to buy futures although she was an options trader. This was known as 'dynamic hedging' because the positions kept changing. Leeson could not have done this even if he had wanted to. Dynamic hedging was complex and required an understanding of calculus, the core of the Mathematics A level that he failed at Parmiter's. But the last thing Leeson wanted was to hedge his straddles. He was in too deep trouble to trade a subtle strategy of volatility. He had to take a bet. If the market stayed level, he would keep the premium and fill the hole in the five eights account. If it rose or fell, he would lose. His straddles were highly unstable and put Baring Futures at risk. Leeson knew he had embarked on a dangerous course but he was beyond caring. He needed to raise a lot of money as rapidly as possible.

During October Leeson sold options worth Y828 million (£3.7 million) in the trading pit. He sold them at around the market price, which was 17,600. They passed through the gesticulating hands of the options traders out to the hedge funds and large investment banks behind them. Leeson was offering a very good price for volatility, and there were plenty of takers. He now needed the market to stay still for the options to retain their value. Some days Leeson could be seen on Simex, sitting hunched forward with his elbows on the desk and head in his hands, staring at the screens showing options and futures prices. He gazed at them intensely, as if calculating the most complex strategies. Traders from other firms started to feel intimidated by this picture of concentration, as if Baring Futures' chief trader knew something they did not. The image of superior intellect suited Leeson. He felt insecure about his education when he talked to options traders. As ever he was not above gilding the lily a little and told Dog Roberts he had taken a degree at the Sorbonne, the University of Paris. However, Leeson's image was an illusion. He had placed himself in a frightening predicament by selling options. It was enough to make anybody stare at screens. The least event in Japan, whether it sent the market up or down, was bad for Leeson. An announcement flashed up on the large screens above the Simex trading floor could spell doom for him if it rocked the market. Every bit of volatility ate away at his options premium, and a big drop in the Nikkei could blow an irreparable hole in the Baring Securities balance sheet.

Five months after his arrival on Simex he finally had some luck. The Nikkei kept juddering downwards in the second half of October, reaching 16,770 at the end of the month. Leeson simply doubled his bets on the market rising, and hoped. His perseverance paid off. The repeated interventions of the Japanese government prodded it back to life in November, and the index rose steadily back to 17,680 by the end of the month. At last Leeson had had a good month. The options were back in the range where he had sold them and his long futures position had paid off handsomely. The market had rebounded enough to gain him Y470 million from his futures, and Y35 million from his options. He could inject Y505 million (£2.3 million) back into the five eights account and close out his options. His crude option trading had worked and helped to staunch the flow out of the five eights account. There was still a heavy call for money. The expiry of the December contract meant that Leeson once again had to take risks to offer rolls for Tokyo traders and customers. The 'errors' this generated would be piled into the five eights account. He also had to deal with genuine errors being made by the Baring Futures traders. Seow's marriage was breaking up, and he was drinking heavily and becoming more slapdash. He was an aggressive trader, who would dominate the pit as he filled orders, but lacked much subtlety. Leeson found himself in the position of father-figure to Seow, not only absorbing his mistakes in the five eights account, but even letting him stay with him and Lisa at Christmas, because he had separated from his wife.[3]

The year-end deficit on the five eights account was Y395 million (£1.8 million), which Leeson hid once again by shuffling figures in the internal records. Despite the small distortions his concealment was creating on Baring Securities' balance sheet nobody in London had spotted the five eights account. The best chance to do so came on 11 December when details of margin calls on Baring Futures' accounts were printed out in London. Tony Railton saw the long list of margin calls for the accounts printed on a sheet of A4 paper. 'Can you reconcile this?' he scribbled on a note to Bowser, but the work was not done amid the rush to push out Baring Securities' first December financial year-end accounts.

In the early part of 1993 Leeson struggled on with the five eights account. He took to concealing it in different ways each month. In January he sold options; in February he shuffled the accounts. As he blundered on Leeson hardly realized, or cared about, the management crisis in London. His world was reduced to the Nikkei futures and options pits and the screens above them bearing snippets of information from Japan. But if Leeson was oblivious to the outside world, the opposite did not apply. Leeson had gone a little too far in his efforts to please the Tokyo traders. The rolls and fills he provided with the assistance of the five eights account were so good that his reputation was growing. Hoffman had taken over from Khoo as chief volatility trader in Tokyo, and had come to trust Leeson so much that he not only carried out most of his hedging on Simex, but allowed Leeson to do the hedging for him.

If Hoffman had bought some put options and wanted to hedge them, he would call up Leeson and let him know what was required. The phone line to Singapore might go dead in the frenzy of trading, but he could always be confident Leeson would return with well-priced fills. Eventually Hoffman decided it was only fair to give Leeson credit for what he was doing, since it was contributing so much to the profitability of the volatility book. While talking to Leeson one day he suggested that they should set up a separate profit and loss account to display his contribution. At first Leeson rejected the notion. It was attractive because it was a professional compliment. The Tokyo traders wanted to treat him as one of their own, rather than just somebody who dumbly executed the commands of others. Yet he knew it would be dangerous. If he was seen as a trader there was a much greater chance that someone would examine his books closely, and discover what was really happening. Leeson argued against Hoffman's suggestion, saying it would create regulatory problems. 'It's too much trouble,' Leeson said. Not long afterwards, temptation overcame him and he asked Hoffman to keep a separate spreadsheet of how much he contributed to the volatility and arbitrage books. Recognition did not come only in this form. By the March 1993 witching hour word had spread of Leeson's powers. Killian's salesmen started to charge a fee to customers who wanted Leeson's rolls. Fuji Bank, Chemical and Dean Witter were all keen to buy, and Leeson's prices were so good that they were charged a tick per roll.

As Leeson's star started rising Baring Securities was thrown into turmoil on the other side of the world. Four days after the witching hour on 10 March Baring and Tuckey expelled Heath and the other directors from the helm of Baring Securities in London. Both Baylis and Gibson, who were in charge of derivatives, were removed and Peter Norris took over temporary control of derivatives trading. Norris had little idea how the profitability of Japanese derivatives trading was achieved. The back office had not got much closer. The hole in Baring Securities' balance sheet was finally discovered in April by Tony Hawes. Hawes had been working for a month on solo consol-idation, which meant breaking down the London balance sheet and allocating the figures among three companies. It was not easy. After a few weeks Hawes had strolled into the office of Philip Vracas, Baring Securities' treasurer, to gripe at the quality of the balance sheet. He was unhappy that when he questioned an item on the balance sheet, he was often surprised by the answer. 'Nothing in this place is quite what it seems,' he said. Hawes found a willing listener in Vracas, who was unhappy with balance sheet data himself. In a memorandum to Broadhurst at the end of March Vracas called the accounts of the companies through which Baring Securities borrowed money 'a disgrace'. The firm had until then relied on a cursory balance sheet drawn up once a month from returns made by the firm's different entities around the world. Hawes had to do something better than that. He made a stab at dividing the assets and liabilities into the three companies.

Hawes allocated futures and options sales to the main Baring Securities company. Among the liabilities of the operation was cash deposited with it by customers. The assets balancing this liability were the payments sent to Baring Futures in Singapore and Baring Securities in Osaka to cover margin calls. When he added up the figures, a £10 million gap popped up between the liabilities and the assets. The firm seemed to have paid out £10 million in margin calls for customers more than it had received. This was a puzzle. Hawes put a line in the accounts to balance it, and resolved to find an explanation for the missing £10 million. He presented the results to a committee overseeing solo consolidation on 14 April. 'I do not understand that, Tony. Do you?' Broadhurst asked when they got to the £10 million. Hawes said he was not sure, although it might be a delay between Barings paying margin for customers and obtaining cash from them. Lynn Henderson, who was Broadhurst's deputy, was asked to look into it. After a few weeks, Henderson came up with several reasons for a timing gap between payments. It looked convincing enough but unfortunately it was wrong. Everyone had discounted the simplest explanation for a hole appearing in a balance sheet: fraud. At about the same time Hawes was appointed treasurer of Baring Securities, taking the place of Vracas, who was asked to leave by Norris and Broadhurst after a disagreement over the appropriate way of hedging the balance sheet. Broadhurst was also irritated by the way Vracas had criticized the holding company accounts. The appointment appeared to complete Hawes's rehabilitation at Barings.

The failure of the London managers to grasp what the £10 million represented almost did not matter. At the end of April Leeson struck another clement patch in the markets. In May and June the Nikkei stayed stable at around 20,000, and the straddles started to make money. He also had more luck with futures. During May and June he made Y112 million (£670,000) from futures and options in the five eights account. It meant he could close out his options, leaving himself with a profit in the five eights account. He had finally managed to retrieve all the money he had lost. It was an enormous relief. Leeson had nearly been destroyed, but he had rescued himself.

One Friday night in July Leeson and Lisa had a barbecue at home with friends. He finally confessed to his wife that he had been through a few problems at work and told her that at one point he had been £1 million down. She urged him not to take any similar risks again.[4] In the next few days Leeson transferred the remaining profit in the five eights account over to Tokyo, and was at last back to square one. It was not to last. He could not kick the habit of using five eights without having to disclose an uncomfortable truth to those around him. He was not an extraordinary trader; he could not conjure up amazing rolls without the five eights account to take losses. Without the account, he was just another order filler on Simex. There would be no more praise and recognition from Tokyo, and he would not be a father-figure to his traders any longer. Leeson had won popularity and respect easily for the first twenty-five years of his life. Now he could only do it through deceit. He soon started again.

He slipped into performing his feats systematically. So far he had produced results by taking risks and putting any gambles that went wrong into five eights. But it was time-consuming and messy. He was already subsidizing the accounts of Tokyo traders and customers from five eights. That could be done more simply. He could adjust the price of an actual trade, and switch a loss into the five eights account. This gave him a streamlined process for manufacturing sub-sidies. Traders at Baring Futures were soon using five eights to book trades at better prices into other accounts. They would record an actual price for a trade in one column of the daily records, and place beside it the price adjustment in the 'remarks' column of the records.[5] In August and September Y507 million (£3.1 million) of subsidies were funded from five eights, and Leeson again wrote options to cover the hole. His life was once more weighed down by the strain of concealment. But in September a piece of compensation arrived. Danny Argyropoulous was a twenty-three-year-old trader who had been sent to Singapore by his broking firm, First Continental Trading. First Continental had 120 traders on exchanges around the globe and was one of Killian's best customers. It was even allowed to rent space at Baring Securities in Tokyo, sitting near Killian's sales force. First Continental sent Argyropoulous, whom it regarded as one of its best traders, to trade JGBs, which was the newest Simex contract.

Argyropoulous had been born in Cyprus and brought up in London. When he left school he worked as a cycle courier in London, delivering packages to City offices. He had seen Liffe traders in pubs near the exchange, and liked the look of their jackets. Argyropoulous hung out in a pub nearby, asking if there were any jobs going. He was taken on by First Continental and quickly caught the hang of trading. Soon he had enough money to indulge his passion for sports cars. He owned a rare model of Lotus Esprit and a red Ferrari, on which he put the number plate DAN 1S. When Argyropoulous arrived at Simex, he and Leeson were practically the only British traders, and they soon struck up a friendship. First Continental cleared trades through Baring Futures so the two worked together. Argyropoulous would always share a coffee with Leeson at Delifrance before a day's trading, or a drink at one of the bars that had started to open along the restored waterfront of Boat Quay, although he was a teetotaller. He did not have a car in Singapore because he had written off two in Britain and his annual insurance premium had risen to £5,800. Instead he rode a mountain bike, and Leeson would drive him in to Simex each morning. Argyropoulous's long hair was tied in a ponytail and he wore rings in both ears. He had a trading badge with the initials VIZ, after the British comic for adults. He was full of energy and walked with a strut. Leeson could relax and mess around happily with him. He used to call Argyropoulous 'Bubble' after the cockney rhyming slang 'bubble and squeak', which meant 'Greek'.

Leeson was now growing into a powerful figure on Simex and was one reason why Simex was gaining ground on Osaka. The fills and rolls Leeson could provide were pulling business into Singapore. Baring Futures was well respected by the Simex authorities and its president Ang Swee Tien. Leeson was also growing physically. He had been living on his nerves for so long that he had begun drinking heavily to calm himself. He was also eating handfuls of sweets during the trading day. As a result he was starting to fill out noticeably. The recognition was not confined to Simex. Killian was so impressed that to give Leeson added authority he rewarded him with the grander title of general manager of Baring Futures at the end of June. Leeson was even coming to the attention of James Bax. In November Simex held its annual dinner, to celebrate its success. It was intended to provide a night of fun. Bax attended, sitting at the Baring Futures table along with Leeson, and even took part in the high jinks. The highlight of the night was a competition for broking firms to go up on stage to make fools of themselves. Baring Futures was drawn, and chose to mime to a recording of Joan Jett and the Black Hearts singing *We Love Rock and Roll*. Bax played air guitar on a broomstick and Leeson was the band's drummer, using a pair of chopsticks and a bucket. This was useful for Leeson. He had always tried to impress his managers, but he now needed protection from London. The more valuable he was to Bax and Jones, the more they might shelter him.

Not every night out was as innocent. Leeson had joined the Singapore Cricket Club to use its bar and play snooker. In October they were visited by one of Lisa's relatives and a friend. Leeson took them to the cricket club to play snooker one Saturday evening. By the time they decided to play, they had already been drinking, and Leeson refused to show his membership card when asked by a club scorer. The man called a member of the club's billiards committee, a Singaporean called Ananda Kunar. Kunar did not have any more luck. When he confronted Leeson and his friends, one of the three called him a 'fucking black bastard'. The evening ended even more nastily when Leeson's party confronted Kunar as he was getting into a taxi on the way home, and threw several punches at him. Leeson was hauled before the disciplinary committee, and suspended for a year for failing to control his guests. He later wrote to Kunar to apologize, saying that he was 'highly embarrassed' by the incident. This kind of drinking and fighting on a Saturday night would hardly have been noticed around Watford: it was the sort of thing Leeson had always done to let off steam from the pressures of the office. But it was very unwise in Singapore. The police enforced the laws strictly, and even expatriates could face the cane for vandalism. Singapore was not only a strict place, it was small. Every time Leeson drank a bit too much and did something outrageous, everybody knew about it on the Simex trading floor. He had always revelled in his ability to separate a rowdy private life from a strict work one. For the first time he was finding that to be impossible.

The pressure on him soon escalated sharply. By autumn the losses in five eights had accumulated once more. In the three months since his failed attempt to stop he had buried losses of £5.5 million. He wrote his usual options to fill the hole over the summer, selling straddles at around the market price of 20,000. It went disastrously wrong in November. Support for the Nikkei had weakened since the sharp rise of the previous year that had brought so many problems for the five eights account, and things had changed in Japan. The country had been ruled for thirty-eight years by the Liberal Democratic Party, although it had lost the July 1989 Upper House elections. By July 1993 several bribery and tax evasion scandals had undermined the LDP leadership so severely that it lost a general election. The new government of the Japan New Party felt less obligation to support the market. It stopped the price keeping operations that had distorted futures and options markets. The mood was worsened by big banks selling off securities holdings to bolster their weak profits. Despite the failure of many companies to repay loans Japan had so far avoided a big bankruptcy. It changed on 1 November, when Muramoto Corporation went into liquidation with debts of Y600 billion (£3.6 billion). Muramoto had been the archetypal product of the 1980s bubble. It had developed golf courses and sold memberships at inflated prices to Primhak and others. It augured badly for the Nikkei. Sixty directors of Japanese broking firms went on pilgrimage to the sanctuary of the Shinto sun goddess to seek redemption for the Nikkei.

Their trip was not successful. The Nikkei plunged from 19,700 at the end of October to 16,400 a month later. It fell well below the point at which the premium for the straddles covered the losses to which Leeson was exposed. Baring Futures had to pay a huge amount of margin to the investors to whom he had sold straddles. Some of them exercised the options and removed the cash. Leeson could not let it carry on. The hole in the balance sheet was threatening to grow to an unmanageable size. He returned to the pit to close out the straddles he had sold when the Nikkei had been at 20,000, and to sell others based on a lower Nikkei level, or 'strike price'. He had to pay a lot more for each straddle than he had received for it, because the Nikkei was well below the original strike price. He bought and sold options in large quantities. He had about 8,000 straddles bought over the previous three months. He bought those that had not been exercised back, and sold 12,000 others at a lower strike price. It was very expensive. The cost of reclaiming the straddles was Y2.9 billion (£17.4

million), and the total loss to be concealed in November was Y3.6 billion (£21.6 million). By selling straddles he contained the loss in the Citibank accounts, but he was still left with the hole in the Baring Securities balance sheet. This was growing rapidly because of the huge margin calls made against the old straddles. Leeson urgently needed to find a way of generating surplus cash to pay these illegitimate margin calls. If he could not do so the cash calls made daily by the five eights account would soon reach a level where they stuck out awkwardly.

He came up with an ingenious solution befitting his expertise as a clerk. He invented a business that appeared to consume cash. This was 'switching'. The opportunity to move orders between Simex and Osaka had struck the Tokyo traders before. Because Simex prices often moved faster than Osaka ones, it seemed possible for a trader to arbitrage the two. In the spring of the previous year, Gueler had been seeking new ways to make money. The cash–futures arbitrage book had been doing badly, and he was looking out for an alternative. For a couple of weeks he had tried arbitraging Nikkei futures between Osaka and Simex and made consistent profits of a few thousand pounds a day. Then Gueler was caught one morning with one leg of a deal, because he could not buy matching futures on the other exchange. He spent a worried lunch-time fearing the market would move against him. He was hardly able to eat his usual food in the doom and gloom room. In fact, the market went his way. But he was caught again several days later, and he decided switching was not worth it. The profits were too small for the risks. This was the correct decision for a trader, but Leeson had another reason to try switching. The firm had always made money by netting customers' positions, leaving it with spare cash. Leeson had already used cash from netting positions at Citibank to conceal the five eights account. Switching gave him a further opportunity to generate cash by netting off contracts. This was due to a Simex rule that was intended to attract business from arbitrage traders away from Japan to Singapore.

If a trader had matching contracts in Tokyo or Osaka, Simex allowed him to net them off before paying margin. Nobody in London knew of this rule and Leeson had concealed it from Gueler in Tokyo. It gave Leeson an opportunity. He could build up 'switching' positions on Simex and Osaka, and then demand a large amount of cash from London to pay initial margin on the futures. However, the netting rule would allow him to use some of it for five eights margin calls instead. But Leeson could not run a fake operation without it making profits. To gain cash for margin calls, he had to generate profits. It was a potentially dangerous step for he would be drawing attention to himself. Leeson had started doing so in a small way during the autumn. The November crisis meant he had to abandon restraint. As Leeson stepped up switching positions to cover margin calls for the five eights account, he started to create much larger profits. All of the switching was counted within the volatility book, which had been run from Osaka by Brindle after Hoffman had left that autumn. Leeson sharply increased the subsidies he was putting into the volatility book. He did so by adjusting prices to place Y750 million (£4.5 million) of subsidies into Baring Securities Japan, taking the losses into the five eights account.[6] Gueler was impressed by the rise in profits from Singapore, which could be seen clearly on the spreadsheet that Hoffman had prepared. It appeared that Leeson could exploit the differences between the two exchanges sufficiently to make exceptional profits when the market was volatile.

Even given the volatility, it was still difficult to understand how Leeson was making so much money in a type of trading that Gueler had himself abandoned before. At the start of December Gueler went to Baker's off-site meeting in Bruges. While he was there he called Tokyo, and heard things were going very well. The twists and turns in the Nikkei were boosting profits from volatility trading, and Leeson's switching had really come into its own. Gueler was pleased, and tried to explain switching to some of Baker's traders during one session. But he could hardly make sense of it himself, and he tailed off incoherently. Baker had to change the subject quickly to avoid an awkward silence. The truth was that Leeson was creating the profits almost casually as a distraction from the main task in hand, which was to stem what were actually losses from the growing volatility of the Nikkei. His writing of straddles had worked well enough for most of 1993 because of stability, but he was now being thrown around by Nikkei volatility. To fill up the November hole he had sold 12,000 straddles at a strike price of about 16,500. He had gained Y3.6 billion (£21.5 million) in cash, but had increased his gamble on the Nikkei remaining stable at that level. If the index dropped to 15,000 or rose above 18,000, he faced big losses. Almost as soon as Leeson had committed himself to the Nikkei remaining at 16,500, it rebounded from the fall of November. One month volatility doubled from 10 per cent in November to 20 per cent in December, and the Nikkei briefly touched 18,000. His November straddles were already in a fragile state.

Leeson ended the year with a loss of Y4.5 billion (£28 million) in five eights. He needed the Nikkei to fall sharply to regain control. Instead, the index spiked upwards to 19,000 as optimism grew in Japan over the state of the economy. Leeson was in even deeper trouble than in November. Once again he had to buy back his straddles, and sell new ones at the higher strike price. He had now abandoned the pretence of taking a view on the market. He was simply borrowing money. This meant that he usually waited until the end of the month to sell his options. Only then would he know how large was the hole he had to plug in the five eights account. It followed that he had to gamble on the Nikkei staying at whatever level it reached at the end of the month. January 1994 was a bad month for this tactic. The index rose throughout the month, but the last day of the month fell on a Monday. That weekend the Japanese government finally gained agreement from the LDP for a reform of the electoral system. This cleared the way for a fresh package of economic measures, the fourth in two years, intended to boost the economy. The market was so excited at the prospect that the Nikkei jumped 1,470 points on Monday. The November straddles in five eights suffered the worst fall in value Leeson had experienced in his eighteen months as a trader. It left a Y5 billion (£32 million) hole in the account at the month-end. Each time he bought back straddles he was losing money and increasing the hole to be covered by selling fresh ones. He now had to shuffle the Citibank accounts to hide Y1 billion (£6.5 million) of losses, and sell Y3.9 billion (£25 million) of straddles.

By January 1994 there were plenty of takers for Leeson's straddles. The volatility of the Tokyo market had worried many big investors, who wanted to protect themselves against the violent swings. The best way to do so was to buy straddles. Leeson could raise plenty of money by selling straddles and thereby taking over the risk. He could raise the most by selling straddles far out into the future. The farther out he went, the greater the risk he absorbed. Leeson abandoned caution, and sold straddles that would last for more than a year. He sold 1,300 straddles at strike prices of 20,000 and 20,500 that only expired in March 1995. He gained Y2.3 billion (£15 million) in premium for these. Because they lasted so long they were quite a good deal in the short term. The Nikkei would have to fall 3,500 points to 17,000 before all the option premium was eaten up. However, Leeson was an amateur in the world of options. He lacked an option pricing model on a computer that would show him the correct price for volatility. By borrowing blindly and in desperation Leeson was underpricing volatility. By January 1994 hedge funds and investment banks were trawling the world, seeking mispriced volatility. This was an adults' game and somebody like Leeson was way out of his depth. Every time he walked to the options pit to sell straddles he was shouting his ignorance of the market. The options traders assumed he was selling on behalf of a rather ill-informed or naïve customer, and piled in to take advantage of whoever it was.

This disaster of the end of January befell Leeson only a week after he returned from the off-site meeting at the Hong Kong Hilton where he first met Ron Baker. As he inflated profits to distract attention from his hidden losses, he had gone a step too far. He had not only gained respect from the Tokyo traders, but had caught the attention of their new boss. Leeson was subdued as Baker talked about going back to London to discuss his switching book. He knew that if it was examined too closely the edifice would crumble. But there was no way back now. As the losses in the five eights account increased, he was under greater pressure to create profits. Despite his predicament there was a large part of Leeson that could not help responding to the attention. He had always coveted the approval of his bosses, and he was edging into being seen as a fully fledged trader. It meant not only a larger year-end bonus, but the admiration of many at Barings. In mid-February Leeson was paid a bonus of £135,000. It was well below the £230,000 Baker had suggested. Killian was supposed to be contributing £115,000 to match Baker's contribution, but had just allowed Baker to meet most of the bill for a reduced amount. It still took Leeson into a wholly different bracket from a settlements clerk such as Bowser. Half of him was frightened at the huge losses that were now concealed in five eights, but the other half thrived on this attention and back-slapping. People now praised him as never before. He was not simply an efficient clerk. By squandering millions of pounds, he had turned himself into a star.

CHAPTER 9

In the New Year, Leeson paid a visit to the Raffles Hotel. He had been invited to meet for the first time one of the high rollers of the options pit, Philippe Bonnefoy. In his early thirties, smartly dressed and quiet, Bonnefoy was an archetypal hedge fund trader. He handled billions of dollars, invested in many markets, and he did not need to shout to get attention. Bonnefoy worked with an Austrian financier called Wolfgang Flottl. They had been together at Kidder Peabody in New York but had left when Flottl decided to set up a hedge fund in 1987 called Ross Capital. Flottl got some money from family connections and raised more from investors.[1] Ross Capital started with $500 million. It invested money in the US take-over boom of the late 1980s, including the $20 billion take-over of RJR Nabisco in 1989. After that, it had made profits from bond arbitrage. At first its trading was unsuccessful, and it looked as though most of the fund would be wiped out. But Flottl stuck with it, to the admiration of colleagues with weaker nerves. Ross Capital grew to over $3 billion in value. Ross invested some cash through an arm called European Bank and Trust, which was managed by Bonnefoy. Bonnefoy had come to Singapore to find brokers to take orders on Simex. He was considering betting on a rise in the Nikkei. It would be a big bet, for Bonnefoy's always were. He knew Heather Nicol, who was working in New York. He rang her to ask what Barings could tell him about the Japanese market, and she advised him to get in touch with Mary Walz.

Bonnefoy visited Tokyo to talk to some of Baring Securities' analysts about Japan. Then he rang Walz. Bonnefoy was going to Singapore for a day, and she arranged for him to meet Leeson. On 3 February Bonnefoy toured the Simex floor, meeting Ang Swee Tien. In the afternoon he met brokers in a suite at the Raffles. This was how he liked to arrange his trips. He was busy. The brokers needed him more than he needed them. The brokers would troop in one after another, one each half-hour. One of them was Leeson. Bonnefoy was not particularly struck by the young man. He made the usual broker pitch about how much business he did. 'If I need something, I'll be in touch,' Bonnefoy said, showing him out again. On 16 February Bonnefoy put his first trade through Leeson. He bought some call options, which gave him the right to buy futures at a profit if the market rose. It was a small order. Bonnefoy was farming out orders to several brokers to test them. It was easy enough for Leeson to get him the best price. He had the five eights account to take any losses. Shortly after that Leeson went away on holiday. He rang Brindle in Osaka to ask him to help if Bonnefoy rang while he was away. He got on well with Brindle, a twenty-six-year-old from Bolton, who had studied Japanese and economics at university and had helped Leeson when he was starting to sell options and wanted advice from an expert on option trading. Brindle supported Bolton Wanderers while Leeson supported Manchester City and they talked about the English football league over the line between their desks most days.

Leeson told Brindle that he had a highly confidential customer called Philippe. Brindle did not catch the second name clearly. It sounded French, something like Beaulieu or Banlieu. Brindle never got a call from Bonnefoy, but tucked the information away in his head. In mid-March Bonnefoy started making large orders for Nikkei call options, at a strike price of 20,000. Leeson was used to dealing in this size for the five eights account, but this was larger than any order he had taken for a customer. What was more, this was his own customer, not somebody referred through by Killian. Leeson was making a large amount of commission on Bonnefoy's trading. It would further raise his standing at Barings. Bonnefoy was tough, though. He would always push Leeson for a hard price. It did not matter, for Leeson had the five eights account. By chance Bonnefoy met Nicol at a cocktail party in London that spring, and told her he was giving a lot of business to Barings. 'I hope you are getting some credit for this,' he said. Indirectly Bonnefoy was gaining from Leeson's own options sales. Call options had fallen in price because the market had stabilized. Leeson had contributed to this by selling straddles. He had created a slight mispricing of Japanese equity options on Simex. Bonnefoy was not the only one to gain. Soros's Quantum Fund was also buying Japanese call options in the hope that the Japanese market was about to rise. Hedge funds tended to hunt together. Like sharks, hedge funds could sniff in the water the slightest trace of blood from a potential victim.

By the spring of 1994 Baring Futures was bleeding freely. Leeson started to ring the Tokyo office, offering to sell straddles to whoever wanted them. He was using the same tactic as he had done for some time with rolls. The straddles were clearly mispriced. If implied volatility in the market was 14 per cent, he could always offer options one or two points cheaper. It meant that anybody buying options from him did not have to pay as much in premium as the standard price in the options pit. As 1994 went by traders such as Brindle had bought so much volatility that they did not want more, so Leeson would sell to Killian's customers through the sales desk. A saleswoman called Wendy Carpenter worked out that a hedge fund must be buying through Leeson, and rang him to ensure that she did not tread on his toes. Leeson distracted her by suggesting that Killian knew all about it. 'Don't worry about it. Mike has got it covered,' he said. Even now Leeson was still offering exceptional prices for rolls. The largest buyer through Barings in the run-up to the March witching hour became Ross Capital. It bought 500 rolls through the Tokyo sales desk, and followed up with larger orders. In the end Ross bought 5,000 rolls for March, half the 10,000 rolls that Leeson sold. He was now offering rolls each at about Y10,000 (£65) cheaper than the market price, although customers had no means of knowing how he did it. In effect Leeson handed Ross and others a total of £650,000 from the five eights account in March, without any of them realizing.

As Leeson rode high on his connection with Bonnefoy, Baker was trying to come to grips with the arm of Baring Securities he had inherited. Equity derivatives trading had been named 'structured products', and was one of three divisions under Baker. Baker had bigger ambitions than trading on exchanges like Simex. He wanted to replicate his debt trading success. That meant using swaps and over-the-counter derivatives to create new instruments and sell them to customers. He had decided that Walz should run this from Hong Kong so in February she went to Hong Kong to rebuild operations there. She wanted to hire new people to cover equity markets in Thailand and Malaysia, but she also had to sort out the business that already existed. It required some diplomacy, for Gueler was in charge of trading in Japan, and Walz was not expert in exchange-traded futures and options. She started by reviewing with Gueler the trading done in Japan. On 27 February she and Gueler wrote a memo to Baker to explain what was done by everybody, including an explanation of Leeson's switching. Since Gueler had been deceived by Leeson, he gave Walz the standard explanation: that Barings was exploiting the orders of its customers to profit from the differences between Simex and Osaka. They reported this tactfully, referring to Baring Futures' 'pole position in the information flow'. It was making money because 'we see huge client orders (ours and others), we know well the locals and their trading habits, and we have an intelligent link into Osaka. We know all the bids and offers,' they wrote.[2]

This sort of thing was music to the ears of Baker, who would ceaselessly preach the gospel of being at the heart of markets. His debt trading arm was based on knowing that a German bank would value a piece of debt more highly than a Japanese pension fund, if it was repackaged correctly. Leeson seemed to be able to exploit a similar anomaly between Osaka and Singapore. But that renewed the question of who should be Leeson's boss. If there was an opportunity, Baker wanted to control and run it properly. He did not want to depend on one of Killian's people doing some trading on the side, out of reach. The question became urgent when Norris asked for details of how much money was being made by Leeson. Baker and Walz's proposals for trading limits in equity derivatives were presented to Baring Securities' risk committee on 16 March. The committee – Norris, Katz, Broadhurst and Hawes – met each week to review trading. It agreed the trading limits, but Norris added that switching profits had to be quantified. Later that Wednesday he sent an electronic mail message to Walz, asking her to split out Leeson's profits.[3] The exercise was a surprise. Gueler had not told Walz how much Leeson's switching seemed to be contributing. The profits were still being allocated to the volatility trading book, now being run out of Osaka by Brindle. Leeson's contribution was recorded on the spreadsheet set up by Hoffman, although not in the formal accounts. But when Walz asked for details, she found that the spreadsheet showed Leeson was contributing 60 per cent of the Osaka volatility book profits.

Walz was irritated at this discovery. She felt she had been kept in the dark up to then, and she was irked at being caught in the middle. 'I don't really know what game is being played here, and I don't really care,' she wrote in a memo to Baker on 30 March. 'The profit and loss profile of the group is radically different if Nick is "segregated", which may be what people are trying to do. Alternatively, he seems like a great trader, and he should have a more formal link with our group. You and Peter [Norris] work this out. All I care about is that whatever you guys do, it's a) not underhanded or demotivating to all the guys in Japan and b) that no one in our group has to waste any more time . . . Nick doesn't particularly want the profit and loss segregated, although he thinks it's in his interest to do so.'[4] This incident was not the only instance in which Walz had felt shut out of what others knew. She was having some difficulty imposing her authority. As a young woman, she was not naturally viewed by traditionalists at Baring Securities as carrying much weight. She was seen as someone who had to be tolerated as Baker's lieutenant, but if a difficulty had to be sorted out, their first inclination was to ring Baker rather than her. Walz was naturally plain-spoken and her efforts to assert herself did not always go down well at either Bishopsgate or America Square. Some of those there – women as well as men – thought she was over-aggressive. Like Vanessa Gibson, Walz was finding that women who asserted their authority at Barings tended to provoke resentment among their colleagues.

Walz's discovery discomfited Baker, who started to press Norris for more authority over Leeson. 'My most profitable trader doesn't work for me,' he complained. It made him re-address the question of Killian and futures and options sales. He had not been interested in it before, but he had found out just how important Leeson was now. Baker had to get a grip on Leeson. The simplest way of doing so would be to take over futures and options sales. Baker's change of heart coincided with a strong signal that Killian would not resist such a move. It would have been hard enough for Killian to oversee Leeson while he was in Japan; it became even more so in March when he decided to leave there for good and move to Portland, Oregon, to be closer to his customers in Chicago. Baker mooted to Norris the idea of taking on futures and options sales after all. He said that, at the least, he had to gain some control over Leeson. Although Leeson seemed to be making a lot of money through switching, he had no limits on the number of contracts he could buy or sell. It was hardly a professional way of managing a trader. Norris was content for Baker to extend his grip over the futures and options side and over Leeson. He agreed that Baker could allocate a trading limit to Leeson. Although he had been trading publicly for over six months, it was the first time it had been sanctioned from London. The limit was not in Nikkei futures, but JGB futures traded on the Tokyo International Financial Futures Exchange (Tiffe).

The JGB limit made sense to Gueler and Baker since the government bond futures market was bigger than the Nikkei futures market, and was then more volatile. Since Leeson's switching appeared to work best in high volatility, it seemed a good way of developing the business. JGBs were also an ideal chance for Leeson to manufacture profits on the scale now required. There were only two firms trading in JGB futures on Simex, and the exchange was keen to take business from Tokyo. It allowed more leeway for cross-trades in JGBs than other contracts. This helped him to manipulate profits. He had a good reason to make JGB trading a success, and he did not hold back. On the first day of his JGB switching Leeson crossed $1 million into the Japanese volatility book. Fuchs was so excited that he danced a little jig on the Tokyo trading floor. It seemed as if there was no limit to the seam of free cash struck by Leeson. There was something particularly impressive about Leeson's apparent mastery of JGBs, for investment banks had suffered huge losses in bond trading in February and March after the US Federal Reserve had raised short-term interest rates. This tightening of monetary policy ended the steady rise in bond prices that gave banks such a bumper year in 1993. Some investment banks had been caught badly. Goldman Sachs and Salomon Brothers suffered a heavy downturn in profits, but Barings seemed to sail serenely onwards. Japan was back in profit, and investment banking made an operating profit of £52 million in the first quarter.[5] Virtually all the bank group's £9.8 million profit came from structured products.

The reality was appallingly at odds with the illusion. In May the five eights account lost Y7.4 billion (£47 million), the largest amount

247

in its twenty-three-month existence. In a single month Leeson lost the equivalent of the entire first quarter operating profit. He was also losing his best customer. In May Bonnefoy began to sell off the options he had bought. Flottl was reacting to up to $1.7 billion being taken out of Ross Capital by the Bank for Labour & Business in Vienna (Bawag).[6] The bank's chairman was Flottl's father, Walter, and it had been one of the original investors in Ross Capital. When details of the link emerged in the Austrian press funds were pulled out from Ross Capital. Bonnefoy sold some of his options at a loss. He made his final trade through Leeson on 27 June. Brindle became intrigued by the investor who had bought and sold so many options so rapidly and started trying to find out his identity. Brindle had a Bloomberg terminal on his desk that could be used for communicating with other traders over a secure electronic mail system. He searched its directory for a Philippe. Instead of Bonnefoy, Brindle located a trader called Philippe who worked for Tiger, a hedge fund run from Bermuda. He assumed that it was Tiger for whom Leeson had been trading. But Brindle was not quite sure. After a time he and Gueler started to refer to the mysterious Philippe as Customer X. Leeson was not willing to let Bonnefoy go so easily. His secret trading was reaching a scale where his margin calls required as many excuses as possible. Leeson carried on talking as if Philippe was buying as heavily as ever.

In the middle of May Baker flew to Singapore to visit Leeson on his home territory for the first time. Leeson appeared to be on top of the world as he showed Baker around Simex. As they left the floor Leeson said casually: 'Let's go and see the president of Simex.' They went to Ang's office and just walked in without an appointment. Ang stopped what he was doing to welcome the two men warmly. Leeson did not need to tell Baker how valuable Baring Futures had become to the exchange: he could see it in the way he was treated. They went out for dinner that evening on a boat that took them to a restaurant at a fishing village. Leeson explained his trading. It sounded to Baker as if he had cornered Simex in a remarkable way. Customers wanted to deal on Simex because the margin calls and charges were lower. But Osaka was a bigger and more liquid market, where you could often get a better price for a large order because the market did not move as much. Baring Futures would fill the customer's order from a Simex house account, and then match its short with an equal and opposite long in Osaka. The customer got the lower costs of trading on Simex, while Baring Futures gained a better price on Osaka. It would pass on some of the price improvement to the customer, for which it was now being rewarded with a tick commission. It kept the rest itself. Leeson took hardly any risk because he now had large customers such as Refco, Dean Witter and the US trading firm Cargill. He could use the orders from these customers to crush any other trader who tried to stand against him.

This explanation was largely nonsense. In fact, there were only small profits at best to be made from a switching book between Simex and Osaka. By then other investment banks, including Goldman Sachs, had tried to imitate what they thought Leeson was doing, but they had no success. The price difference between Osaka and Simex was too fleeting and uncertain. Yet Baker was convinced. This was partly because Leeson was an exceptionally fluent liar. He had by then spent nearly two years fooling people and his patter had improved with practice. It also helped that Baker instinctively liked the sort of trading Leeson appeared to be doing. It involved using information about customer orders to inform your own trading. The risks were low because you were protected by customers, and profits could be high. But the biggest thing in Leeson's favour was the fact that Baker was not well versed in exchange-traded derivatives. He understood the sort of deals he had done at Bankers Trust well, but this was a different world. Leeson could talk confidently about margin calls, spreads, ticks and fills without much fear of challenge. He had found a perfect environment in which to commit a fraud: one in which few outsiders knew enough to grasp that something was wrong. There was nobody to check with because Leeson controlled the back office as well as trading. Switching sounded to Baker like an opportunity that Leeson was exploiting well. He decided that Leeson needed to be nurtured and encouraged to take it further.

The meeting only added to Baker's conviction that he had to take over futures and options sales. He was already picking up 40 per cent of its costs as compensation for his traders being able to buy and sell through Simex and Osaka without paying commission. Apart from this, as Leeson's profits increased, Killian was arguing from Portland that Leeson's switching earnings should be split with the sales team. Killian reasoned that if Leeson did not have a flow of customer orders, he would be unable to take matching positions in Osaka and these trading profits would dry up. Baker was irritated at what he saw as an attempt to muscle in, and exploded with rage when Killian sent him a memo arguing that 50 per cent of Leeson's earnings from trading should be allocated to Killian's team because they depended on customers. Baker showed it to Norris indignantly. Opposite Killian's claim he had scrawled: 'This is a greedy bastards' club.' He already had other worries about Leeson. He realized that US investment banks might be trying to lure Leeson away, given his dominance of Simex. Leeson had started to become well known. Reporters writing about Japanese futures would ring him up to ask him about Baring Futures' positions, or seek his views on the market. Leeson could not resist the chance of fame. *Futures and Options World*, the derivatives trade magazine, published a June supplement devoted to Simex. Leeson posed grinning in his blue and yellow trading jacket, and talked of opportunities in JGB trading for Simex.

Baker wanted to ensure that profits would not collapse if Leeson left Barings. He encouraged Leeson to hire another trader who could take over on the switching book when he was away. He did not want Seow filling in on what was now the most profitable trading book in Barings. Leeson promptly hired a British trader whom he and Argyropoulous knew. He was called Rob Leaning and he worked for a UK futures broker called Tullet & Tokyo. Leaning, the son of a newspaper printer, had left school at sixteen to join the Stock Exchange as a messenger. In 1990 he had been made redundant, and had spent a couple of months running a stall at Exmouth Market in Clerkenwell. He toured local council estates asking for anything tenants did not want, which he would sell. He had joined Tullet & Tokyo on Liffe, coming to Singapore to try to earn enough to become a local. He had worked on Simex since 1993 trading Eurobond futures. Leaning had fallen in with the two other British traders over football and they used to go out to local bars which had satellite television to watch matches. Argyropoulous and Leeson had nicknamed Leaning 'Chesney' over his resemblance to Chesney Hawkes, the British pop singer. He had long hair, which he tied in a ponytail, like Argyropoulous. Leeson had to fill in the form for Leaning's new trading badge as a Simex trader. He asked him what letters he wanted. 'I don't know. Something to do with West Ham, or cunt,' said Leaning.

'Right, cunt it is,' said Leeson, filling in Leaning's application with the letters CNT. It became the butt of endless jokes.

Baring Futures was now the dominant broker on Simex, and Leeson was king of the exchange. He had set out as just another order filler, but within two years he had bought himself enormous power, using Barings' money. His flow of orders from customers might be largely fictional, but it looked good to the outside world. Leeson had taken to guzzling huge amounts of sweets on the trading floor during the day and had become so much fatter that Leaning and Argyropoulous called him 'Fat Boy'. But Leeson did not need to buy his sweets. Rather like in a prison where cigarettes and sweets are currency, the Simex locals would go out and buy Leeson $100 of sweets or chocolate as a gift. He did not always repay the gifts courteously. He had started quietly and shyly, but he had come to behave as if he believed his own press. Before he had always scrupulously separated his quiet, controlled persona at work from the rampages of his weekend existence. Now they blurred. Leeson was so powerful that he could behave as he wanted at Simex. He would swagger on to the trading floor, threatening to cut out any local who had displeased him. If anybody incurred his wrath Leeson would buy a cream puff cake from Delifrance and slap it into the miscreant's face on the Simex floor. Sometimes he would walk up to someone who had offended him, insult him and simply walk away laughing. Leeson seemed to have gone beyond the point of worry about the five eights account. He had survived so long that he behaved as if he was invincible.

Leeson was not always nasty. He could also behave like a benevolent godfather, helping out locals who were in trouble. Sometimes he seemed just to give away small amounts of money to locals. Gueler was puzzled and asked him about it one day. 'You have to give some stuff to the locals sometimes. If you are ever in trouble, they'll help,' Leeson explained. Compared with the losses he had accumulated, the odd helping hand made little difference. One local who was new to Simex held some loss-making futures at the end of one of his first days of trading. Leeson took them from him when he realized that the man was in trouble. Sometimes in the pit Leeson hardly seemed to care what price he got. The locals thought he had a big customer who was not fussy about price. Leeson's closest trading link was with Argyropoulous, a talented trader who did best by making the odd intervention. Argyropoulous did not spend much time in the pits. Instead, he sat with his feet propped on a desk, playing Nintendo. When Leeson was about to trade JGBs he would call over to Argyropoulous. Because there were so few JGB traders Leeson often placed a lot of trades through him. Some of the other brokers were jealous of the links between First Continental and Baring Futures, and one rang up Baring Securities in Tokyo to complain that Leeson was unfairly close to Argyropoulous. It was only natural that Leeson's closeness to Argyropoulous provoked such complaints. Anybody who could get close to Leeson was able to gain from the money that he was throwing around.

Excepting the problems of the five eights account Leeson's life was now the most pleasant it had been since his arrival. He had his group of courtiers on the exchange and friends outside. He played centre half once a month for the Baring Securities football team, although his weight meant he was now a lot less fit. After work the traders would go for a drink at a bar on Boat Quay, such as Harry's Bar or the Off Quay. Leeson also spent a lot of evenings with Lisa and friends such as Argyropoulous on Emerald Hill, a more sophisticated street of bars and restaurants off Orchard Road. His success on the trading floor boded well enough for him to loosen the spending reins a bit. He and Lisa had ploughed his £135,000 bonus for 1993 into a flat in Blackheath, south London, but they could live comfortably. Leeson would buy bottles of his favourite wine, Chateau Trottevielle 1990, at Number 5, a wine bar on Emerald Hill. The wine was on the premium list but at S$131 was relatively inexpensive. At the weekends there would be a barbecue or picnic. By the standards of the Tokyo office in the late 1980s it was all rather tame. But Leeson's coarser streak was to get him in trouble once more. The problem arose one night on Boat Quay after Leeson was invited out for a drink by a sales representative called Aloysious Chhze, employed by the news service Reuters. Chhze had started to call him regularly about Simex, and the two had arranged to have a drink. Leeson started out with Argyropoulous, but the serious drinking began at the Off Quay bar after Argyropoulous had left.

By late evening the group was getting riotously drunk when they saw some women looking through the door, trying to make up their minds whether to come in. Leeson and Chhze decided to give them a treat in true Watford style. They turned their backs to them, bent over and bared their bottoms. Things quickly degenerated when the women came in after a few minutes with some men, and a row broke out in Chinese. Eventually Leeson stepped into the middle of the group and proffered his mobile phone to one of the women, daring her to call the police. When she did the police arrived rapidly and arrested Leeson and Chhze. They spent a night in the cells before being bailed by Teo Kok Eng, the biggest local on Simex, whose brother Teo Fai worked for Leeson. TKE – as he was known – also suggested a lawyer, which allowed Leeson to keep the incident secret from Barings. The tactic did not work well. After a few weeks the charge had been increased to indecent exposure, which could be punished by a jail term. Leeson decided to confess and told Jones. He also phoned Baker: 'I've done something stupid. I've let myself down, and I've got into trouble. I need some help.' Baker went to Norris to tell him what the firm's star trader in Singapore had got up to in the evening. Norris was irritated at the juvenile nature of the offence. Was Leeson really the right man to represent Barings on Simex? It was a far cry from the days when Geoffrey Barnett was Baring Brothers' man there in 1975. However, Norris felt he had no choice but to accept it as a *fait accompli*. Leeson was now virtually indispensable on Simex.

Baker used the opportunity to ram home again his claim on Leeson. He pointed out that Barings could not have coped with trading on Simex if Leeson had been jailed. 'You come to me when there is trouble. At least give me control,' he said. Barings rapidly provided its own lawyer, who argued successfully against a jail sentence. Leeson paid a S$200 fine. He had got off lightly, but he had been convicted of a criminal offence in Singapore, and Norris felt he had to inform the executive committee of the Barings board, which met at 8.30 a.m. every Wednesday morning at 8 Bishopsgate, chaired by Peter Baring. It was the first time Leeson had come to the attention of this august body by name. After the official business was out of the way Norris confessed there was another thing to report. 'It is slightly embarrassing, but one of our traders got drunk the other night and pulled a moon,' he said.

There was a startled silence.

'What did you say?' Peter Baring inquired.

Others in the room could not contain themselves any longer and started laughing. Then Norris admitted that it was serious because Leeson had been charged and fined.

'Well, maybe we should sack him. What does he do?' said Bolsover.

Norris said that sacking him would be awkward because he contributed a lot to profits in Singapore.

Bolsover was not satisfied. 'Whoever he is, he is an ambassador for Barings, and if he did that in Singapore, how bright can he be?' he said.

The discussion petered out with no decision being taken. Leeson had survived scrutiny at the hands of Peter Baring.

He was about to survive more serious scrutiny. In June two internal auditors were asked to fly out to Singapore to investigate Baring Futures. The internal audit department carried out checks on different operations in turn, questioning whether they were being run properly and safely. The need for an audit of Leeson was made more urgent by the fact that he was making so much. Leeson had reported an estimated profit of $30 million in the first seven months. There were other concerns in London. One of them was over the unreconciled loans to customers item in the balance sheet. This had now risen from about £10 million the previous spring to £75 million at the end of March.[7] Sacranie had become concerned about it, and had sent a colleague to ask Hawes if something was wrong. Hawes was himself worried that it had not been sorted out properly although he believed it was more a matter for financial controls than treasury. By now Leeson was sending a fax every afternoon to London requesting millions of dollars for margin payments for house and customer accounts. The cash was pouring into five eights, but Leeson had told Brenda Granger, an American who had taken over from Bowser as head of futures and options settlement, that it was to meet extra margin calls that Simex made in the middle of the day. The money had become known as 'top-up' funds. But Leeson hardly bothered to hide the artifice, giving Granger only a vague break-down of how much of the top-up went into house accounts and how much into customer accounts. He sometimes failed to provide even a rough estimate for the split.

The audit was led by James Baker, a thirty-year-old internal auditor, who was briefed by Hawes and Sacranie before his departure. Hawes told him about the top-up problem, stressing that he would at least like to know exactly how the payments were split.[8] Baker and his colleague, Ian Manson, spent almost a month in Singapore looking at Baring Futures. Baker and Leeson talked for hours about how Leeson made a profit from switching. Leeson spoke rapidly about crossing a leg here and giving up a tick there. Baker would ask him to go over it again, struggling to grasp enough to write an explanation in plain English. He unwittingly became Leeson's ghost-writer in a work of fiction. Their biggest tussles were over why Leeson did not reconcile Baring Futures and Simex accounts to show exactly where margin calls were going. 'My people are too busy. Every item is reconciled separately anyway,' Leeson said. Baker kept being out-argued by Leeson. 'Imagine that you had made a very big loss you wanted to hide. Couldn't you do that in the balance sheet?' Baker asked. No, Leeson insisted, it would be caught in London when all the accounts were reconciled. They also talked over the weakness of having the same man in charge of the back office and trading. Baker thought it would be better to have somebody else in charge, but Leeson said he liked doing it, because it kept him in control. 'If I didn't have to do the reconciliation, I could pack up at two p.m. and go and play golf. But I want to see everything done right. I'm the one who faces the flak from customers in the morning,' Leeson said, fighting his corner obstinately.

He won his argument. James Baker's twenty-four-page report opened with the warning of 'a significant general risk that the controls could be overridden by the general manager', but it was infused by the growing feeling at Barings that Leeson should be kept happy. The firm appeared to have stumbled upon a most extraordinary bubble of profit. Leeson had produced this cash, and it would be damaging if he left. The report said Leeson should retain a management role, but should no longer be directly in charge of back office tasks such as reviewing bank accounts and margin payments. The 'management response' from Leeson and Jones in the report promised to transfer all reconciliations to the Baring Securities accounts department on the twenty-fourth floor. Baker's report also recommended that a risk and compliance officer should oversee Baring Futures' trading. This was a more potent threat, since Leeson could hardly keep his subterfuge going if somebody was constantly looking over his shoulder. However,

Leeson had on his side Jones's antipathy to any interference from London. This suggestion had been headed off before the report was even completed. Bowser had moved to Hong Kong to be risk controller of Walz's fledgling operation there, and Jones insisted that a quarterly visit from Bowser would be enough. The net effect was that Leeson and Jones – for different reasons – managed to fend off all the most dangerous aspects of internal audit. Leeson could carry on being fêted as the king of Simex, and Jones could keep a grip over every aspect of trading and sales in Singapore without London interfering.

Despite this Leeson's defences against London were getting strained. He now depended heavily on Jones to block any London-inspired effort to poke behind the scenes, but it was becoming clear that Jones was not going to be there indefinitely. Norris and Broadhurst had him firmly in their sights, and he would be sacked when they could find a reason. Jones's relationship with Broadhurst had broken down in July over a financial controllers' conference that Broadhurst organized in London, which Jones had refused to let staff from Singapore and Jakarta attend on the grounds that they were too busy. Broadhurst gained the upper hand by getting Norris to speak to Bax, who overruled Jones. Jones was offended that Broadhurst had gone behind his back, and from then on the phone was answered frostily if Broadhurst rang. Norris had made his dissatisfaction with Jones clear by writing him a letter at the end of 1993, warning him to cooperate more with London. But Jones could not easily be dismissed. He appeared to be efficient, if troublesome. He seemed to have settlement in Asia under firm control, which was more than could be said for Latin America. Norris was biding his time. This made relations between them even more uneasy. Jones knew his days were numbered, and had responded by trying to gain Singaporean citizenship rapidly before he was forced out. His marriage had now broken up and he had limited rights to see his children. He divided up his annual holiday so that he could take every Wednesday afternoon off to go swimming with his children.

For Norris, Jones was only one problem. The integration of Baring Brothers and Baring Securities started in May, although the transfer to America Square had been halted. Barings had now opted to go instead to a building in London Wall, next to the offices of Flemings, its old rival. This delayed things, and created an administrative burden that took up most of Barnett's time. One obvious flaw in the new investment bank was the lack of anyone overseeing all the risks it took to make money, from lending to trading. Norris decided to set up a new department to do this, called group treasury and risk. It would report daily to a body called the asset and liability committee (Alco) that would be in charge of sanctioning trading. Norris thought that Maclean would be a good head of risk. He could be relied upon to sift through any risks cautiously. Norris did not think he would be too much missed as head of the bank group, which had made small profits before Baker came. But although Norris was designated as chief executive, he lacked authority to move Maclean. That would have to be done by Tuckey. Norris wrote a memo urging Tuckey to 'devote our most senior and experienced resources' to risk management.[9] He was out of luck. Tuckey rejected the idea and picked Hopkins for the job instead. Norris was not pleased. He regarded Hopkins as awkward to deal with and uncooperative. He disliked the way that Hopkins fiddled with his belt buckle in meetings. It was not an auspicious start for risk control in the investment bank.

All these back office hassles could not take away from the fact that equity derivatives trading appeared to be making ever more money. It was hard not to get carried away by the success. By August Leeson and the Tokyo traders appeared to have made £25.5 million profit, already well in excess of the £17.5 million that had been budgeted for the whole year. Baker's fortunes were in the ascendant, and he was becoming a little cocky. Baker was visiting Tokyo in early August when the management committee was starting to discuss plans for 1995. Most heads of departments had submitted formal plans, some up to fifteen pages long; nothing seemed to have come from Baker. He joined the meeting by phone from Tokyo, and was asked where his contribution was. 'I thought I sent something over,' said Baker. After a search, a hand-written sheet of paper was unearthed, containing an estimate that financial products would make a profit of £100 million in 1995. Fraser was irritated that this was all Baker could come up with, given that his trading was now so vital to Barings' profits. Baker was not abashed, and started talking about what he had done since arriving at Baring Brothers. 'When I came, I said I would make £6 million, and it was £11 million in practice. If my target is £100 million for 1995, I'm sure I can make £150 million,' he said. Baker still appeared to be Barings' best hope of mastering trading. The bond operation had just had another disaster, when a trader called Hugh Evans bought some bonds in Confederation Life, a Canadian insurance firm, just days before it abruptly collapsed. The bond arm lost £5.5 million, and Evans resigned.

If Baker was ebullient, Leeson was again facing problems in five eights. The Japanese market was once more veering downwards after a rally in June, when it reached 21,500. Leeson had sold Y8.1 billion (£52 million) of straddles at the peak of the market, which were losing money as the index fell below 20,000. Leeson briefly tried holding the Nikkei up by buying futures. It was a hopeless task. His straddles stretched for a year into the future. For him to keep the option premium, Nikkei volatility had to fall to an incredibly low level. It had to be below 10 per cent not just for a month, but for a whole year. Any analyst of modern Japan knew this was a fantasy. Baring Securities would never have existed if the Nikkei had been stable to that degree. Leeson tried to spook the market into a rally just before the witching hour of 9 September. He failed. The Nikkei drifted down during the rest of September, closing at 19,560 on the last day of the month. His futures gamble was the most costly failure to date. He had thrown away Y11.1 billion (£71 million) in his futile effort to support the market. The margin calls to London had surged as Leeson had bought futures. However, he was now used to hiding his tracks by making bigger profits. Structured products produced income of £7.6 million during September. By the end of that month Leeson had to hide a larger-than-ever hole in the five eights account. He started to sell straddles in huge quantities. In the last week of September he sold more than 8,700 straddles to the eager market. He raised Y8.9 billion (£57 million) in cash to stave off discovery once again.

The Nikkei options market was starting to buzz with rumours about what Baring Futures was doing. It was never completely possible to tell whether a broker like Barings was dealing for a customer or itself, but in this case it seemed plain that it had to be a customer. This was an enormous position, with a very large potential loss if volatility rose. It was far bigger than was usual for the Baring Securities volatility book. The less others suspected that Barings was taking all this risk itself, in the form of the five eights 'customer', the better it suited Leeson, so he started spreading rumours about his customer. Whenever a reporter rang to talk about the straddles he made vague comments about his customer. He had already gone further with Baker. In late August Baker had passed through Singapore, returning from a holiday in Australia. He went for a drink with Leeson in the Shangri-La Hotel on Orange Grove, set in its own gardens off Orchard Road. Leeson hinted that Bonnefoy was still trading through him, and that he was the mysterious customer. Leeson did not give Baker the customer's name, but he regurgitated the elaborate ritual of his first meeting with Bonnefoy in the Raffles Hotel. 'Whenever he comes, we meet secretly in a hotel,' Leeson said. He did not give Baker any more details. He was not under any obligation to do so. Futures and options sales was not officially part of Baker's empire. Baker was now becoming frustrated with the lack of clarity over who managed Leeson. His star trader did not have to let him know what was going on.

Leeson's power was growing not only within Barings. He was also flavour of the month at Simex over his role in JGB trading. Ang Swee Tien had faced many frustrations in trying to get JGB trading going before Leeson had taken an interest. It was close to the heart of the Japanese authorities, and they did not want trading to slip away from the Tokyo futures exchange. Pressure was exerted on the Japanese brokers on Simex not to participate in JGB trading there. One day Nomura Securities traded a little in the JGB pit, but it stopped abruptly the next day after a call from the management in Tokyo. Leeson's trading had been a godsend.

On Saturday 24 September Simex celebrated its tenth anniversary. Killian flew in for the occasion, after being invited personally by Ang. Baring Futures was presented with an award for volume at the anniversary dinner at the Westin Stamford Hotel, which was accepted by Bax. Simex made its own video to celebrate the occasion, in which were included interviews with two traders, Teo Kok Eng and Nick Leeson. The government conferred its ultimate mark of respect on Simex with the attendance of Lee Kuan Yew himself at the anniversary dinner, after which he made a speech praising its achievements. Lee described how average daily trading volume had risen 40 per cent since the previous year to 100,000 contracts, making it one of the world's top twenty futures exchanges. It had added a reputation for innovation to Singapore's existing place as a safe haven for funds. 'Singapore has the attributes to be the Chicago and the Zurich of East Asia,' Lee said proudly.

It was a rather stuffy dinner with a Chinese orchestra playing, and everybody had to behave since Lee was there. Afterwards the group had more fun. Leeson had taken to his role as the leading trader on Simex. He had bought a case of Dom Perignon champagne at Studebakers, a bar on Boat Quay, so that they could celebrate in style. Chang carried the case around during dinner, leaving Leeson free to lead the crowd. He was drinking heavily almost each night they went out. The Baring Futures traders would agree among themselves at the start of a night out who should drive him home later. Leeson was not above making up even wilder nights. One morning he was in late at Simex, and Gueler and Fuchs quizzed him about where he had been. Leeson once again started to embroider his story about Bonnefoy, claiming that Philippe and he had been out the previous night. They had started off drinking champagne, then had decided to go to a 'hostess bar' called Arabesque. It was part of the murkier night-life of Singapore, where young Singapore hostesses would join western tourists at their tables, and cajole them to buy champagne and other drinks at inflated prices. Leeson said the night had ended back at Philippe's hotel with two hostesses. He did not go into details, but the Tokyo traders could imagine. Talk about getting to know a customer well! Once again Leeson had proved himself capable of spinning a good yarn. It distracted attention from the fact that Barings' capital was now pouring freely down a drain.

The flow of margin funds out of London was now so heavy that Hawes was worried at how little was known about where it was going. Leeson or Linda Hassan were still faxing through the daily requests for top-up funds. The requests had now reached an absurd level compared with the original £10 million gap that had bothered Broadhurst. By the end of September the top-up funds amounted to £144 million.[10] This was still not being split up into house trading and customer margin funds. The profits from switching gave Leeson a ready excuse for demanding so much cash, since no one had grasped that all contracts on Osaka could be netted off against those on Simex. Leeson himself could hardly believe that he had sustained the illusion this long. It required one set of people in Barings to believe that he wanted cash for house trading, while another group thought that a mysterious customer was doing the trading. But Hawes did not have the authority to put his foot down and insist that Baring Futures stopped trading until the mess could be sorted out. It would have been against all Baring Securities' traditions to do it. Hawes also suffered from his own history. He was conscious of being seen as a failed trader who had been moved to the back office. In an odd way Leeson had greater authority than he did, since he had moved in the other direction. Baker certainly had more clout, since his financial products group was making so much money. Hawes did not feel strong enough to raise his head above the parapet and insist that everything stopped. What if he was wrong? Baker would be merciless.

So Hawes simply struggled on trying to improve matters gradually. He arranged a meeting with Leeson in Singapore on 6 October to talk over the funding problem. Given the size of Leeson's fraud it would have been highly risky to meet on the fourteenth floor, to which Baring Futures had moved. Leeson neatly got round this problem by not turning up. He was in London the previous weekend, and he phoned up Hawes to say he had to stay for a funeral. Hawes was left to see Linda Hassan, who was pregnant and replied to any testing question: 'You'll have to ask Nick about that.' Hawes finally caught up with him the following Monday in America Square and asked him once again to explain the Simex margining system. It was embarrassing to have to ask. It made Hawes feel stupid. Leeson was magnanimous as he went through it for a third time. He did not have any of the papers in front of him, so they had to talk it over generally. Leeson appeared eager to help as best he could, although he made it clear that it was a little tiresome to bother over these technical details. Hawes said he wanted to have a better breakdown of how much top-up margin was going to customers and how much to the house. Leeson promised to do what he could, and within a couple of weeks a more precise breakdown started to be faxed through to London each morning. Hawes was encouraged by that, but he still thought it was unsatisfactory for him to depend so much on Leeson. Backed by Hopkins, he started pressing to have a regional treasurer for Asia based in the Hong Kong office, who might be able to sort out the problem once and for all.[11]

Hopkins also had worries about Leeson, having started work at America Square in his new role as head of treasury and risk. He was concerned that Leeson might be making his money by breaking his trading limits. He looked at the trading data sent to London, which seemed to show that Leeson had made one trade four times over his limit. But the figures were ambiguous. Hopkins asked about it, and Walz told him that a number of smaller trades had been added together. His inquiries were soon halted by an odd piece of news: Leeson had gone on strike. Baker called Hopkins to say that Leeson was so upset at the questions that he had refused to trade any more that day. 'Could you call him up and calm him down?' Baker asked.

Hopkins rang Singapore, and got through to Leeson. 'I hear you're not trading,' he said.

'Oh, there is nothing happening anyway,' replied Leeson.

Hopkins told him not to worry. It was only a routine inquiry. They would sort it out soon by installing software to monitor the time at which every trade was made.

Hopkins did not regard the problem of Leeson's trading as exceptional. He had been unimpressed at what he had found at Baring Securities since his appointment in August. Soon afterwards he had become embroiled in a dispute with Katz over Barings' policy of accounting for all its trading assets in dollars. He argued that this put it at risk from currency movements. He had also had an uncomfortable run-in with Broadhurst. Hopkins did not think much of the information he was getting from Broadhurst's financial controls department. He needed reliable information about trading revenues in order to calculate risks. Hopkins asked Broadhurst out to lunch at a nearby Italian restaurant. As soon as they started eating Hopkins told him that he wanted to take shared control of revenue reporting. Because of the history of sour relations between the two men Broadhurst was not inclined to be flexible. He refused point blank. He was irritated, and had stopped eating after the first mouthful. 'Then you leave me with no choice,' Hopkins said. He told Broadhurst that he would appoint his own staff to gather information. Broadhurst lost his temper. 'Ian, you can fuck off,' he said. Broadhurst rushed round to see Norris after the lunch, still angry. 'Just keep that man away from me,' he said. Norris took Broadhurst's side instinctively, believing that Hopkins was empire-building.

The isolation of Hopkins created a serious flaw in the management structure of the investment bank. Although there was a head of treasury and risk, Norris was not inclined to take anything he said seriously. He thought he could restructure the back office of Baring Securities with the help of trusted younger men such as Gamby and Broadhurst. Hopkins had little hope of getting another of his wishes implemented. This was to have a forum where those in charge of controls and back office functions could discuss problems. He tried to get Norris to accept it by writing him a memo arguing that the systems and control culture were 'distinctly flaky', and suggesting setting up an audit sub-committee. He arrived with the memo in a sealed envelope at Norris's office at 6.00 p.m. on 28 November.

The idea of having to attend a further committee did not appeal much to Norris. 'Not another one,' he said, with a groan. He read the note briskly. It did not appear to say much, and he thought Hopkins was just playing office politics. He quickly dismissed the idea.

The other person getting worried about Leeson in October was Gueler. Since the previous year Gueler had believed that Leeson's switching profits depended on volatility. He had started to make big profits the previous November when volatility rose. One month volatility had now fallen back to 11 per cent, and it followed that Leeson's switching should be less profitable. The reverse was true that autumn: after the £7.6 million of September, equity derivatives made £4.7 million in October. There had to be another reason for these profits. Gueler and Fuchs began to suspect that Leeson was ripping off Customer X. Since such a big share of Leeson's trading now came from a single customer, it followed that most of his profits had to come from that customer as well. When Leeson had attempted to support the market in September he had explained it to Tokyo as Philippe's ploy. It was Philippe who was trying to hold the Nikkei steady so that his straddles would keep their value. But September's profits meant Leeson must have made a huge amount from buying futures for Philippe. Gueler thought it must mean the customer was blind to the prices Leeson was offering because he was desperate to support the Nikkei. He did not care much about a tick here or there in Leeson's prices. In fact, Gueler had stumbled on something close to the truth. Leeson was indeed squeezing his customer to create profit. Indeed, the customer was near to collapse because Leeson was exploiting him so badly. However, the customer was not Philippe at all but five eights. Barings itself was the victim of what Gueler thought was a scam on a customer.

Gueler started to agitate about this at the end of October. He worried that he was once again in charge of a trader who was doing something wrong, just as he had been in Hong Kong in 1993. Gueler was still officially responsible for Leeson's trading in Singapore and he did not want to catch the flak if Leeson was caught exploiting customers. So he phoned Walz to say he believed something was wrong. The internal audit report might have cleared Leeson of front-running, but he was not so sure. 'I think they should have a good hard look at what is happening in Singapore before it ends in tears,' he said. This warning fell on deaf ears. Gueler had a reputation for being jumpy, and Baker thought he was now overstrained. He told Gueler to concentrate on Japan, and Walz would take over Singapore. It was a relief to Gueler, once Baker confirmed that it would not affect his bonus. Yet despite Gueler's doubts over how Leeson was making profits, he thought he was talented. Fuchs went even further, referring to Leeson as the Michael Jordan of Barings, after the Chicago Bulls basketball star.

However the money was being made, there was a lot of it. In the past year, as the profits flooded in, the derivatives trading desk had been transformed from the cautious, introspective place of three years before, when Khoo led the way to the doom and gloom room for lunch every day. Gueler and the others had learned how to enjoy themselves, and even thrown their weight around a little. Leeson's profits had helped transform their nook of the trading floor into the most dynamic part of the whole operation.

They soon had a chance to show this. Ron Baker had organized a series of off-site meetings to round off an epic year for his group. Equity derivatives had made a profit of £40 million by November, compared to an expected £8.5 million. By the year-end Leeson had created £28 million of revenue through switching and £7.5 million more in his subsidy to volatility trading. Five eights had started as a means of ensuring Leeson kept his job for the first few awkward weeks in 1992. Two and a half years later it was a mainstay of the entire structured products group. Although Gueler's traders produced legitimate profits without his help, Leeson outshone them. On Friday 11 November Leeson flew with Leaning and Teo Fai to Japan to join the Tokyo traders at an offsite in Atami, a traditional Japanese resort to the south-west of Tokyo. The venue had been arranged by Gueler, who was a devotee of traditional Japanese customs. Now the Techno-peasants had arrived he was determined to do things in style. They travelled down on the Bullet Train from Tokyo, drinking on the way. Gueler had arranged for them to stay at a traditional inn divided into dormitories. Gueler had not seen Leeson in the flesh for some time, and did not expect him to have changed. As he emerged from the sauna at the inn, he could just make out a fat man in the bath. When he got closer, he realized it was Leeson. It soon emerged that few others shared Gueler's enthusiasm for Japanese cuisine. Leaning and Baker shunned the raw fish menu in favour of a visit to McDonald's, returning with Big Macs and a big cardboard cut-out of Michael Jordan.

Things degenerated further the next night. Gueler had organized a traditional Japanese dinner, complete with geishas. Despite the western connotations of the word, these were the genuine article: women who were trained from an early age in classical Japanese music and dance. The traders sat at two long tables to be served sushi and a large abalone, the giant shellfish which is a prized delicacy in Japan. Half-way through the evening, two geishas appeared, accompanied by an old woman who played the mandolin. It was high Japanese art but it did not impress Baker and Leaning. Gueler was sitting at the other table in deep conversation with some of the traders, when he noticed Baker and Leaning were displaying their disapproval by throwing sushi at the mandolin player. Gueler was mortified. In Japan the elderly are to be respected, and this was an act of flagrant disrespect. He stood up to divert Baker. 'Throw it at me! Throw it at me!' he shouted, in an effort to save the old lady. A few pieces were flung his way, but Baker still threw some more at the geishas. It was not atypical of Baker. He sometimes referred to his Asian visits as 'rock tours' and he enjoyed getting rowdy. On an evening out in Tokyo, he had acquired a golf putter and prodded a taxi driver in the neck with it on the journey back to his hotel. When Baker arrived he tried the same trick with the receptionist who was finding his key. The man got annoyed at being treated this way, took a large samurai sword off the wall, and thrust it at Baker. He had to make a break for the lift with his putter to avoid being badly wounded.

In between enjoying themselves the traders had a lot to discuss. A single topic dominated: whether Mr X was a fool or a genius. The answer seemed obvious enough to cool heads: he was a fool. Philippe, if Leeson's hints as to his identity were correct, was taking a huge bet on low volatility in the Nikkei 225. He had not only sold Y8.9 billion of straddles in September but had intervened massively in the market in a failed attempt to prop up the index that month. He appeared to have given away millions to Barings. It could be nothing compared with the losses he must have sustained. One man was attempting to corner one of the largest stock markets in the world single-handedly, trying to keep the Nikkei within a narrow trading range by buying futures and options. But this was madness. The Japanese government had tried a similar trick periodically since 1989 without success. Why should he do it? History was full of examples of failed attempts to corner markets. In theory the idea could work. Anyone could go into a market and buy relentlessly until he forced all the sellers into retreat. They would start to follow him, and buy at higher and higher prices. At that point he would make a large profit because he held all the stock, and could sell out at the peak. But, in practice, most attempts to corner markets ended in failure. Francis Baring's attempt to corner the cochineal market with Hope and Co. of Amsterdam in 1787 and 1788 had been an extravagant failure. The Hunt family's attempt to corner the world silver market in 1979 by buying $10 billion of silver with Arab partners also collapsed in ignominy.[12]

Customer X was now trying to corner Nikkei volatility. Anybody with an option pricing model, or even a bit of common sense, could see he must fail. Analysts at broking firms had started to put out research notes advising fund managers and investors to go long volatility in the Nikkei. 'Just how low is Nikkei 225 volatility, and where is volatility headed? The first answer is "very low", and the second answer is "up",' said a Salomon Brothers research note.[13] J. P. Morgan had issued a research note on 1 November saying that 'current low levels of volatility are unsustainable'.[14] Apart from anything else Mr X was trying to corner volatility in the wrong direction. Driving up volatility was one thing, since it could rise to extremely high levels, but Nikkei volatility could only go down so far. It was not possible for it to drop to zero, with the index closing day after day at exactly the same level. Anybody with deep enough pockets could simply sweat it out. Eventually the scheme would collapse just as surely as the cochineal market fiasco of 1788. That was what all the US investment banks were telling customers as November went by and volatility continued to fall. This had happened before in the Nikkei market. It would fall into a trading range and hover there over a few months, often propped up artificially by the government. This never lasted. Eventually investors' perceptions of Japan would shift or the government would stop intervening. When that happened the market would break out again and volatility would shoot up. Now was the right time to buy volatility and wait for something to happen.

Yet, however compelling the logic, investment banks could not find many takers as November wore on. J. P. Morgan's research failed to entice any of its big customers to buy volatility. Doubts were creeping in among even the most sanguine analysts. Perhaps Mr X was not a fool at all but a genius. This drive to corner volatility appeared to be working. Volatility had dropped to 10 per cent and it was still falling. The squeeze was starting to hurt. Every force seemed to be ranged against volatility. All option traders who were long volatility were dynamically hedging their positions. If the index rose they would all try to lock in profits by selling futures. If it fell they would all buy futures. This forced the market into a narrower range. It should have been balanced out by Mr X dynamically hedging his short straddles. But the five eights account was not hedged. Leeson needed every last piece of profit to fill the hole in five eights. Japanese companies had also started to flood the market with convertible bonds again, the first instrument ever traded by Baring Securities. It was equivalent to selling options, because the investors were buying an option on a rise in the company's share price. Volatility was forced down further, and traders started to cut positions. 'This is the cleverest man in the world,' one Goldman Sachs volatility trader said admiringly, as the market buckled under Leeson's options selling. Leeson's Mr X was a genius. He had devised an ingenious way of manipulating one of the world's largest markets.

One of the traders suffering from Leeson's crushing of the market through five eights was Brindle, who had adopted the view of the sophisticated trader and placed Baring Securities' volatility book in Osaka long volatility. Brindle would talk to Leeson most days, trying to pick up what was going on. Of all the traders in Asia Brindle was closest to Customer X. That access was envied by others. Gueler had been taken out to lunch one day by a trader from a rival firm, who tried to discover Mr X's identity. 'I could tell you, but I would have to kill you afterwards,' Gueler joked. As volatility fell in November Brindle lost money nearly every day. He was under pressure from Baker. 'If we know who is selling, what is Adrian doing buying?' Baker would ask. Brindle was about $1 million down when he spoke to Leeson one day in November. Leeson said his customer was doing so well from falling volatility that he was thinking of selling more straddles. 'I think he might be looking to sell more by the year-end,' Leeson said. It was too much for Brindle. He was not going to sit and watch volatility fall further. Brindle cut his options, crystallizing his $1 million loss. Leeson had won a victory for five eights at the price of Brindle's defeat. It was a sober reminder that Leeson was now making most of the team's money. Low volatility meant a fall in profits from Gueler and Fuchs's cash–futures arbitrage book. Leeson looked like the cat that ate the cream as he flew into Osaka on Saturday 19 November. It was Adrian Brindle's wedding, and he and Lisa had been invited to celebrate by the groom whom he had just deceived.

The round of travelling continued the following Monday when Leeson arrived in Hong Kong to meet Baker and Killian. They were meeting to plan the new order of things. From January Baker would gain full control over futures and options sales. Norris had decided that Killian's team would now become a leg of Baker's empire, rather than a rival. Baker relished the moment. He had never thought much of Killian, and he now had a chance to show it. Killian's year-end bonus in 1993 had been over £500,000. Baker was not going to let him go back to Portland with so much this time. He decided Killian should get only £250,000 for 1994.

In contrast, Leeson was flourishing. Baker was appointing him to be regional manager for the financial products group in Singapore. Leeson and Lisa booked into the Mandarin Hotel in Hong Kong. It was under a year since Baker had met him in Hong Kong, but during that time his fortunes seemed to have risen. Killian could not hold back his true feelings about the way in which Leeson had moved adroitly under Baker's wing. When Baker went to the toilet during one discussion Killian challenged Leeson about presenting himself as a house trader.

'I don't want to be caught in the middle of this,' Leeson said nervously.

'You're the reason why we got into trouble in the first place,' Killian replied bitterly. 'You have walked the line. You're trying to be in both camps.'

It was too late. Baker was going to reward Leeson handsomely. He told him he would be getting £350,000 in February, nearly three times his bonus the year before. Leeson protested, as was the form, saying he deserved more.[15] It did not worry Baker, who expected to improve the offer.

Even as he argued the illusion was fading. His brief moment of glory cornering the Nikkei was coming to an end. On Tuesday the Nikkei tumbled through 19,000, putting Leeson's September straddles near to the point where the premium was eaten up. He and Lisa flew back to Singapore for the last two days of the week. The five eights account was once again accumulating losses. By the end of the month the account was Y8.7 billion (£56 million) in the red. On Thursday and Friday he sold 8,500 straddles at a strike price of 18,500. It was no longer any good. He had cornered the market too successfully. Volatility had fallen to the point where the value of options was reduced. At the start of the year, when the Nikkei was extremely volatile, he had sold straddles for Y1.7 million (£10,900) each. Now he was raising only Y668,000 (£4,300) per straddle. It was not enough. He had pushed the market as far as it could go. Leeson was no expert on options but he knew how bad things were. He had rolled over his losses almost every quarter since October 1992 by buying back and selling options. Every time he did it he stored up a larger bill in the future. He had to pay the bid–offer spread every time he bought back the options he had sold. Even if the Nikkei was at exactly the same level, he lost 10 per cent each time, like a tourist swapping foreign currency several times. Apart from this, the straddles he had sold were badly mispriced. He had undervalued volatility, because he had not cared. He had just been borrowing money. But there was always going to be a reckoning, and now it had come. Five eights faced an avalanche of losses.

As the losses mounted Leeson was becoming cavalier in the way he created matching profits. Late on the Friday before Brindle's wedding a bank had bought JGB futures from Baring Futures. They had to be sold from the switching book and hedged on Liffe because the Tokyo exchange was closed. But the contract was not hedged properly because Leeson was away in Atami and then Hong Kong. The error was only picked up the day Leeson returned to Singapore, by which time Baring Futures had lost $1 million. It was an error that worried Gueler. It was the last thing Leeson needed, just as his losses in five eights were reaching ungovernable proportions. He compensated by creating profits. Gueler was told later in the day that Leeson had been so angry that he had gone out and earned $2 million for the switching book. It was quite a trader who could make money just like that. However, Leeson's rapid response could not assuage anxieties. Hopkins reported the mistake to the management committee, noting that 'reporting procedures need to be tightened considerably'.

Norris was in Tokyo on the Friday having a breakfast meeting with Gueler. They discussed the error and what it demonstrated about the firm. 'We've got a first-rate front office and a second-rate back office,' Gueler said.

'I know that,' Norris replied glumly. 'But I don't know how to push it any harder without it falling apart.' Despite Hopkins's warnings about mistakes, Norris did not think he was coming to grips with the task. He wanted somebody who would get out there and shake things up himself.

The Atami and Hong Kong meetings were simply preliminaries for the financial products group's main year-end off-site meeting to be held in New York. The offsites had been nicknamed 'jamborees' by one of the Tokyo traders, and the name stuck. This was to be the grand finale of the year for Baker, and all 120 people now working for the financial products group were to be flown in to New York for a three-day meeting. News got around Tokyo that the event would cost $300,000. It irritated Gueler's traders because they felt they would be footing the bill from their 1994 earnings. Gueler wrote a memo to Baker saying it should just be for senior traders, but the protest was quashed. Walz told him that if he was going to be the regional manager for Japan he would have to toe the line. News that the whole team was to fly from Singapore to New York pleased Leeson's traders. Leeson was tickled by the fact that they were asked to travel on different planes so that a crash would not wipe out the entire group that was making so much money. 'We're that good,' he said proudly to Argyropoulous. Argyropoulous spent the first days of December pretending to be a secret service agent. 'Mr Leeson, please come this way,' he would say, coming up behind Leeson on the Simex floor. On Saturday 3 December Leeson flew to London. It was a week before the New York offsite, but Lisa's grandfather had died and he was to join her at the funeral. He was on the same flight as Argyropoulous, who had upgraded Leeson's ticket to first class because he wanted company on the flight.

Baker had been rather dismayed that Leeson was having to take a week away from the Simex floor for Lisa's grandfather's funeral. Leeson was now earning huge amounts each month, and Leaning and the others could not reproduce it when he was away. Baker did not want his star trader ambling around in the home counties for a week doing nothing. He arranged an alternative. Baker told Leeson he should go into 8 Bishopsgate at midnight each night the following week, and spend the night trading from the fifteenth floor. He could see the screens giving Osaka and Tokyo prices from Walz's desk, and instruct the Simex traders by phone. It was the first time Leeson had worked in 8 Bishopsgate, in the inner sanctum of the Brothers. By that time it seemed pointless. The deception would soon be over, and Leeson would be finished. The Sims drove him into London from West Kingsdown on Sunday night and went to see the Christmas lights.[16] Leeson went to Walz's desk and called Singapore. He raised Y1 billion (£6.4 million) for five eights by selling straddles, repeating it the following night. On Wednesday morning he went to America Square to meet Baker and Norris. His promotion to regional head of financial products for Singapore would accord him equal status with Gueler in Tokyo. Norris exchanged a few pleasantries with the firm's current star trader. He might have had a few doubts about employing a trader who dropped his trousers in a bar, but you had to be pragmatic. If Baring Securities threw out all its employees who lived a wild life, there would be a lot fewer on the trading floor.

On Thursday the Leesons flew to New York. Leeson was still in first class thanks to Argyropoulous. It annoyed Norris when he arrived in New York that evening and saw the travel arrangements. The new head of financial products in Singapore had not only brought his wife, but seemed to be travelling first class on the firm. Norris had imposed a business-class-only flying policy, and was annoyed that it was being flouted. He made a mental note to follow it up. The Leesons were staying with most of the others at the fifty-storey Sheraton New York

Hotel, off Times Square. Everything was to be paid for by Barings, down to a $100 cash allowance handed out to everyone on arrival. All the flights carrying staff to New York were to be met, with the exception of Killian's. He was as elusive as ever. 'Killian arriving today. Flight information unknown,' said the conference briefing pack.[17] Baker's victory had reduced Killian's status, and he was a reluctant guest at the feast. On Friday Leeson's new role as Singapore regional manager was confirmed by his inclusion in the nineteen-person management committee, which met at the Sheraton to discuss the business. They met again that night for an élite dinner at the Hudson River Club, with views over New York harbour and the Statue of Liberty. The heads of the financial products group congratulated themselves quietly over seared filet mignon of yellowfin tuna, washed down with Alexander Valley 1991 Chardonnay Reserve. Leeson sat opposite Maclean. He struck the head of the banking group as a pleasant but rather retiring young man.

It was a different story later that night when some of those at the conference went for a few drinks on the Upper West Side. They went to the Surf Bar, where spirits are served in small plastic model sharks. After a few drinks things became a little too lively. Miho Takeuchi, who was an assistant in Tokyo, shouted '*Sekuhara!*', a Japanese word for sexual harassment. She complained she had been touched by one of the Tokyo derivatives salesmen. With a few drinks inside him Leeson was assertive. 'Either he gets fired, or I leave!' he shouted, pointing at the miscreant. Gueler calmed things down, and the salesman returned to the hotel to be ticked off by Baker. The evening was only starting. Leeson and a futures and options salesman from Hong Kong stayed up drinking to 4.00 a.m., while Lisa slept at the hotel. Leeson had plenty of reason to avoid reality through alcohol once more. It had been a disastrous day for the five eights account. The Nikkei had toppled through 19,000 again, on the day of the December witching hour. While Leeson had sat around the baize table that morning with the rest of the management committee, thousands of put options had expired on Simex, giving the five eights account a large bill. He lost Y4.1 billion (£26 million) in a single day. By now Leeson was averting his mind from events. He could no longer sell options, and it was near the year-end. Baring Futures would be audited soon by Coopers & Lybrand, the accounting firm that examined the

London books. There was hardly any hope that Coopers would miss the deepening hole in the balance sheet.

Leeson had hardly sobered up by the next morning, the centrepiece of the New York offsite: a day of talks and discussion on the financial products group. The staff were seated in rows, with an aisle down the middle, in the Versailles Terrace of the Sheraton, adjoining the hotel's main ballroom. The most senior executives, led by Norris, Maclean and Baker, sat on a podium at the front of the room. The session started at 9.00 a.m. with a talk by Norris on Baring Investment Bank, the partially realized entity of which he was chief executive. Norris had reason to be well satisfied with the year in spite of various tribulations. It looked as though Barings would virtually match its bonanza profits of the previous year. The financial products group could take a great deal of credit for that. Norris showed a slide breaking down contributions from different areas: financial products had contributed 23 per cent of pre-tax profits in the first nine months of 1994; the rest of the bank group had only added a further 2 per cent. Norris showed his management matrix, combining control by regional managers such as Leeson, and product managers such as Walz. 'Where are we going?' asked one slide. It answered that Barings did not want to compete 'head-to-head with the bulge bracket', the term denoting Wall Street firms such as Goldman Sachs. Instead it would focus on emerging markets. Financial products would be in the lead of a 'second-phase expansion' into emerging markets. Baring Securities had led the way with equity broking around the world. Now Baker's team would push in with derivatives.[18]

By the 10.30 a.m. break, Leeson could face no more, and went to the bar. He started drinking Bloody Marys with a trader called Stuart Burden and was still there by the end of lunch, when Walz was due to speak. Carpenter was in the bar, and Leeson begged her to share another drink with him: 'Come on, just one more.' But Carpenter insisted on going back up, so he had to follow. After Walz's speech, Benson enacted a pantomime with some helpers to show how the futures and options sales business worked. He said that he was Mr Big of the Big Insurance Company and wanted to hedge a portfolio. His order was passed to the pit, and a trader made all the open outcry signals. The audience laughed and applauded appreciatively. Many of them had never been on the floor of a futures exchange and seen the rough end of the business. Leeson watched the show from the back with Seow, Chang and Leaning. Then he left to drink some more. He missed Baker's round-up at 5.00 p.m. Baker was not content to bask in past glories; he had a message to deliver. They were not there just to enjoy themselves. Baker wanted a cohesive group that worked together, exchanging information from all corners of the globe. If you listened to customers and traders in each market and could bridge all the gaps among them, there were huge profits to be made. Baker thought there could be opportunities all over the world like the Simex–Osaka arbitrage. He was already pondering moving Leeson to Brazil to trade futures there. With a well-organized business the possibilities were limitless.

Baker stood at the front of the room, gazing intensely at the troops arranged before him. 'Being good is not enough! Being talented is not enough! Everyone must be connected to our strategy, or we will find you, and weed you out, and get rid of you, and replace you with people who are!' he said. He reached out with his hand as he spoke, imitating the action of digging out a weed. 'Information arbitrage is our business,' Baker went on. 'If you don't know what an information curve is, then find out! Position yourself in an information curve! Dominate the curve! We want to capture information from local markets, and transfer it to money centres such as London and New York. That is value added! That facilitates information arbitrage!'

Norris was taken aback by the intensity of the speech. It was an amazing end to the New York jamboree. Even if some of Baker's troops were not sure what he was talking about, the message was delivered with a force that transfixed them. Norris described to Tuckey later how amazing Baker's show at the New York weekend had been. He was able to generate *esprit de corps* among his group in a way few others in Baring Brothers could emulate. The staff finally drifted out of the room to prepare for a final dinner celebrating their achievements. Leeson carried on drinking. He was no longer able to sit and talk coherently about what he was doing, when he had been painted as Baker's model for how their group was going to conquer the world.

The final dinner was held at Grand Central Station in mid-town Manhattan. The conference organizers had arranged for food and drink to be brought in from a nearby hotel. Two balconies above the station concourse were roped off, and a two-piece band was playing. The

274

financial products staff had to walk through commuters and vagrants at the station's entrance on Vanderbilt Avenue, riding escalators to the balconies where champagne was being served. There was a small Christmas tree in one corner and the station's columns were decorated with wreaths. There was only one topic of conversation: the extraordinary speech by Baker. People kept mulling it over. 'Am I connected? God, I hope I am,' the Tokyo traders joked. Baker was in his element, although he was unhappy that Leeson had not shown up. He was beginning to find Leeson a little too much to handle. Walz was overstretched, and Baker wanted to find someone to oversee exchange-traded derivatives who would not be prone to dropping his trousers or annoying the chief executive by travelling first class. But he was not too concerned for the moment. Of all the financial products group Leeson had found the information curve most deftly and was exploiting it best. Baker had not grasped the truth. The information curve Leeson dominated was not in Asian financial markets, it was inside Barings. For two years Leeson had existed between traders and salesmen, between Tokyo and Singapore, between front and back office, between Baring Securities and the Brothers. Now he had brought them all to the point of collapse.

CHAPTER 10

As Christmas approached Diarmaid Kelly became more and more intrigued by Customer X. Whoever he was, he was costing Kelly money. The sluggishness of the Nikkei since the autumn had reduced profits from broking in Japan, which was where Kelly's heart lay. It had been how he had begun with Heath fifteen years before. As volatility fell, broking slipped into loss. Nobody wanted to buy shares in a flat market. In the last four months of the year Japanese broking lost £5.9 million. It was hardly a disaster since the rest of Barings was making so much money, but it was galling to watch this damage being inflicted by one of Barings' customers. Kelly wanted to know more about Customer X and what he was doing. It was a delicate task, because nobody buying futures and options through Barings would want details of what he was doing leaked to the firm's stockbrokers. But as deputy chairman Kelly could pull a bit of rank. He asked Norris to find out more. It irked Norris to be used as a go-between, but he dutifully ordered Walz to dig up something on Customer X. Walz already knew more about Philippe than others, since she had partly introduced him. A little grudgingly she tackled the task. She rang Leeson to check again what Philippe was up to. Leeson reeled off his usual vague story about Philippe and his strategy of being aggressively short volatility. He dissuaded Walz from checking things further by pointing out that Philippe did not clear his trades through Barings, but Fimat. This meant that Barings was not at any risk from European Bank and Trust defaulting on any money it owed.

The conversation worked a treat. Walz wrote back to Norris on 19 December, rebuffing Kelly's effort to wheedle information out of Singapore. She pointed out that Leeson did not seem to know about the connection between Philippe and Ross Capital 'even if there is one'.[1] Since Philippe did not clear trades through Baring Futures she had not tried to dig out more. 'I have not asked Nick to get balance sheet information from him,' she wrote, adding that since Barings was not clearing, he would probably refuse it. 'I expect that, given the nature of the account, he would have the attitude of "I will show you my financials when you show me some credit" and I would have some sympathy with that.' Finally Walz turned to the phenomenon that was enthralling the Tokyo traders: Mr X's sale of options was so large that everyone wanted to know what was going on. 'Periodically, we do get calls in Tokyo from people wanting to know what we are up to, but this seems an age-old problem,' she wrote. 'This activity may therefore be frustrating for our equity sales desk . . . but I think it is a bad idea to alleviate the frustration by giving the market inform-ation about our "customer" that they should not have. This can only hurt our books, the customer, and our credibility on Simex.' Having beaten back yet another vague effort to discover what was going on Leeson went into the market again, selling straddles worth Y2.3 billion (£15.5 million) in the run-up to Christmas. Goldman Sachs was one of the heaviest buyers and it was joined by other investment banks, including CSFP, SBC and Paribas.

Leeson flew out of Singapore to London three days before Christmas. He had avoided as much as possible thinking about the five eights losses, knowing he was on the brink of disaster. On the last day before he left Argyropoulous had rigged up the Baring Futures booth with Christmas lights and they had worn Father Christmas hats. It did not amuse Simex officials, who deemed it 'an inappropriate expression of religious devotion'. Back in London, saved from the daily reminders of his fate, Leeson could relax further. He met Dog Roberts in a bar two days before Christmas, and after a few rounds had loosened up sufficiently to boast a bit of his adventures as a trader in Singapore. 'I did one trade that could have sunk Barings,' Leeson said, but Roberts took it as mere bragging. After Christmas Day with the Sims the Leesons flew to Ireland with Mark Green, an FCT trader whom Argyropoulous had introduced to them. They stayed at Bailick Cottage, a hotel in County Cork, where Leeson loosened up even further. He and Green went on drinking binges around the local town, and Leeson got so drunk one night that he locked Lisa out of the room. The staff had to bang on the door for forty minutes before it was opened. Between drinking sessions Leeson managed to run up a £65 phone bill to Singapore. Some of this was spent fixing an accounting problem. Leeson had overlooked the year-end, which fell on 30 December. Hassan rang to ask what she should do about the loss in the five eights account for December, which was now Y7.8 billion (£50 million) because he had stopped selling straddles.

The figure did not tell the whole story. Leeson had actually borrowed £150 million more by selling options. He had received this money in premium, but could expect a bill for at least that amount in the next few months. The more volatile the market, the higher this bill would be. How could he have thrown away £200 million in two and a half years? In fact, it had not been hard. He squandered £23 million by subsidizing customers and Barings' traders in Japan between July 1992 and November 1993. His subsidies to traders and fictional 'switching' profits during 1994 added up to £36 million, which included about £7.5 million of the revenue from the volatility book. He also contributed a share of Gueler's cash–futures arbitrage revenue of £5.5 million. These subsidies came partly from price adjustments. Adjustments boosted Barings' accounts by Y1.3 billion (£8 million) in 1993 and a further Y1.6 billion (£10 million) in 1994. Leeson also inflated the profits of house trading and customers by giving them rolls at exceptional prices. Gueler's book gained at least Y40 million (£250,000) a year from roll subsidies. He gave far more away in subsidies to customers. The losses were increased still further by selling options. Although it was a simple way for Leeson to get cash, it was extremely expensive. The straddles he sold for £23 million in November 1993 lost £75 million over the following few months. He also lost money heavily by selling and buying back straddles. The bid–offer spread on straddles could rise to 10 per cent in illiquid markets. The very act of selling and buying back constantly for more than two years cost him about Y5 billion (£30 million).

Leeson had found it easy enough to spend the money to puff up his reputation. It was harder to conceal the damage. He had to think a bit to devise a way to get his clerk, Linda Hassan, to cover the deficit in a manner that would hold until he returned to Singapore. It was no use simply shuffling money in the accounts for the usual couple of days. These were year-end accounts that would be audited by Coopers & Lybrand. The solution he devised on the telephone

278

from Ireland was bizarre. He made up a non-existent trade that a customer was supposed to have carried out through Baring Futures, buying 2,000 put options on the Nikkei. This brought the balance back to zero by making it appear that the money was owed to Baring Futures by Simex. That begged the question of who had done the trade, but Leeson ignored it. He had lived on his wits for long enough now to take his deceptions one at a time. He was not even certain that he would return to Singapore. It appeared a long way away from Ireland, and Leeson made a half-hearted effort to convince his wife they should stay in Britain instead.[2] But he had done too good a job of appearing a successful trader. She had been in Hong Kong, and had heard the bonus he might get by simply staying with Barings until the end of February. By 7 January they were back in Singapore. The fourteenth-floor Baring Futures office was its usual calm self when Leeson arrived back. The lack of any alarm was a hopeful sign; Leeson thought the auditors might have examined the accounts already and missed his deception. But the comfort was short-lived; he discovered they had not yet come.

There were other worries for Leeson to deal with. While he was away Simex officials had quizzed the Baring Futures settlements staff about the amount of margin payment in an account they used to tot up positions held for customers. It held Y24 billion in margin rather than Y34 billion. This was $100 million less than the amount required by the Simex margining system. The settlements clerk said she had to refer to Leeson before she could explain it. On 11 January Simex wrote to Simon Jones asking about the discrepancy, and complaining that no one could answer questions when Leeson was away. The letter ended with a reference to the five eights account, saying that Barings appeared to be financing margin payments on what was a customer account, and it pointed out that this was against Simex rules. This missive did not impress Jones, especially when he spotted that it had converted Y10 billion wrongly into $10 million. He circled the error, and sent it down to Leeson. Once again Leeson had a chance to untangle the discrepancies thrown up by his own deception. Hawes was still trying to pin down the same point. Despite Hopkins's backing for his effort to appoint a treasurer to cover Asia, nothing had happened. It left Hawes to keep trying to untangle the unreconciled 'loans to customers' item in the balance sheet. This had fallen slightly from

£143 million in September to £120 million at the end of the year, but it was still a far larger amount than he felt comfortable with. Apart from anything else it made it hard to calculate the true cost of funding futures and options trading, for which Walz had been pressing.

Hawes's doubts about Leeson's requests for funds were shared by Granger, who regarded it as her job to keep Leeson's operation supplied with enough cash to keep running. But she and Tony Railton had grown more and more sceptical about funding the requests Leeson was sending through daily, which only very roughly broke down the amount into house and customer accounts. In fact, Leeson was drawing figures from the air, one day telling Hassan to allocate it 50/50, and the next 60/40. Virtually all of the money was flowing into margin payments for five eights, which was indeed being financed by Barings although it was supposed to be a customer account. On 28 December Railton had sent an electronic message to Granger casting doubts on Leeson's daily requests for dollars. 'The best case scenario is that Nick is calling for the right US dollars, but is changing the wrong figures on his breakdown sheet, worst case is that it's plain rubbish,' he wrote. Hawes made another stab at resolving the problem on 11 January by trying to persuade Bax to get a local manager to carry out something called the 'Singapore Project'. He gave Bax details of what he wanted, including an 'identification of the causes of the very large and consistent requirements for funding from London' and a 'confirmation that house margin is provided in the correct fashion'. Hawes added that he suspected 'London is providing margin against Tokyo positions'.[3] It was a brave try, but it fell again at the fence of Jones. Bax simply passed it to Jones, who drew up some replies with Leeson, thus blocking Hawes once more.

On Friday 13 January the worries started closing in once more. Leeson was called by Pang Mui Mui, an accountant with Coopers & Lybrand, who was looking over the Baring Futures books. She told him she could not trace the documentation for the £50 million 'receivable' that Leeson had inserted in the accounts from Ireland. A receivable was an accounting term for a debt owed to a firm in accounts. This news was hardly surprising since Leeson had not made up a cover story for the £50 million receivable. He had simply hoped it would not be noticed, given his success in getting away with crude deception.

But alarm bells had now rung. He blustered to Pang that the gap was probably just a computer error.[4] This put her off for a few days, but he would have to come up with something better if she returned to the subject. He hoped that she would not. In the meanwhile, he carried on trading with the five eights account. He had some success that Friday, which turned out to be very lucky despite the omens. The expiry of January options on the Nikkei fell on that day, and at the witching hour the Nikkei was only just below the 19,500 strike price on some straddles he had sold the previous September. He had hit it on the money. These options expired worthless, and he could keep all the premium. Leeson also had 5,000 futures riding on the market, and these gained on the day. By the close of Friday 13 he had made a genuine gain of $5 million for five eights. This was more like it. Leeson could go home for the weekend with some cause for relief and optimism that he could solve his problems.

At the weekend – extended for a day by a public holiday – things looked containable. He only had a few futures in the five eights account. The overwhelming risk was from the straddles he had sold during the previous two and a half years. Those in the account had mostly been sold in the previous months as the market fell to between 19,000 and 20,000. There were 65,000 options in the account, which meant the five eights account held a risk equivalent to owning £1.8 billion of shares.[5] The strike price of these options averaged at 19,200, which meant they were at their most valuable when the Nikkei index was at 19,200. The previous Friday it had been more or less there, closing at 19,240. Five eights contained what was, by Leeson's new standards, a small profit of £20 million on options, but this profit was highly vulnerable to moves in the Nikkei. Leeson had solved this problem up until now by selling new options if the market moved away from the strike price he needed. He could no longer do this because he had forced down volatility to the point where the price of straddles had fallen. This meant that his fate was well and truly pinned to the Nikkei remaining at 19,200. He therefore had to throw everything into the effort to keep the market there. If it moved, Leeson would have to try to push it back. He knew that it would need a lot of ammunition; it would be one man against the rest. He had prepared by telling his staff on 10 January to start netting off all the futures positions in the five eights account against the switching account. This was against Simex regulations, but would reduce the margin it owed to Simex.

Leeson's last illusion of prosperity was shattered rudely on Tuesday morning. He was used to watching the market being manipulated in a few yards of space on the Simex floor, but his fate was now taken in hand in an elemental way. At 5.46 a.m. on 17 January 1995, an earthquake measuring 7.2 on the Richter scale erupted under the island of Awajishima, sixty miles off the port of Kobe. A shock wave ripped through Kobe and the region round Osaka, destroying 25,000 buildings and killing more than 3,000 people. It was the worst earth- quake in Japan since the Great Kanto earthquake, which had killed 140,000 people in Tokyo and Yokohama in 1923.[6] Leeson was woken by Argyropoulous with the news. The earthquake even shook build- ings in Osaka, eighteen miles from Kobe, but the impact on the Osaka Securities Exchange was economic rather than physical. Kobe was at the heart of the central industrial zone of Japan and production was disrupted. Economists forecast Japan could lose half a percentage point of economic growth that year. There was a wave of selling on the Japanese stock market and the Nikkei tumbled as soon as Simex opened. The index did not fall too far. The market was uncertain whether the Japanese government's rescue package would inject cash into the economy and increase growth. But Leeson had no choice about how to react. He had to do something to push the market back towards 19,200, and to recoup any loss he made on the way down. He waited a day and then, as the market continued falling away from 19,000, he stepped over to the futures pit and started buying heavily.

Leeson reacted to the market fall in exactly the opposite way to a sophisticated options trader. Instead of buying short futures to cap his loss, he bought long futures. Before the earthquake he had gained as the market fell because it was just above the ideal level of 19,200. He had cashed in further by holding 4,000 futures contracts that were short of the Nikkei. This meant that he gained Y10 million for each fall of 5 points in the index. As soon as the earthquake pushed the index down through 19,200, Leeson did the opposite. On Thursday 19 he bought 6,000 long futures for the five eights account. This closed his short position and created a long one of 2,000 contracts. A further fall now meant he would lose both on options and the futures.

But he did not stop there. Japanese government bond futures were moving in the opposite direction to Nikkei futures because investors were switching out of equities into bonds. This meant JGB futures prices were inversely correlated to Nikkei futures. Leeson now switched over his JGB position as well. Having had a long position in JGBs, he switched it into a short position of 5,000 contracts on 19 January. This meant everything was pointing in the same direction. All of the options and futures in the five eights account lost money as the Nikkei fell. In effect, he was doubling his bets. He did not want to follow professional traders by locking in profits and capping losses. The only way to escape now was by betting on the Nikkei returning to 19,200. If he lost, his career was over. It made no difference to him how much cash he threw away in the process.

On Friday Leeson went further. He bought 8,000 more Nikkei contracts to put the five eights account 10,000 contracts long. He had now convinced himself that he could push the market back up to above 19,000, after its momentary weakness following the Kobe earthquake. The two years of deception and loss had left him with no sense of proportion. All that mattered was to save himself somehow. On the following Monday the market opened 30 points up and drifted upwards for an hour. Then, just as his futures bets of the previous week appeared to be paying off, it crashed with frightening speed. All the market's old volatility had been revived by the earthquake. The Nikkei whipped down by 1,175 points during the day, wiping £34 million off the value of the futures contracts he had bought in the previous week and causing a loss of £69 million on the options. He was now more than £100 million adrift of the fragile point of stability he had reached ten days before. Yet Leeson was not too desperate to stop feeding profits into Barings through the switching book. Even as he was losing £34 million, he transferred profits of £680,000 into the switching account. Leeson was not the only trader in trouble. Fuchs had taken a short option position on the Nikkei to balance a fall in revenue from arbitrage as volatility fell. It was sensible, but Fuchs got caught by the market's fall, which was so rapid that he could not get himself out. 'Cover that fucking position,' Gueler shouted at Fuchs as the market went into freefall. They ended the day having lost £951,000 on the option position, their biggest-ever loss in a single day.

Compared with the £100 million Leeson had thrown away it was nothing. But nobody knew about Leeson's loss, while Fuchs's loss was public knowledge. It was still weighing on Gueler's mind when he heard a cheerful greeting from Leeson over the line from Singapore the following morning. 'Hey, this is great. I just made $1 million at the open,' Leeson said. He said he had executed one leg of a trade for a customer, and the market had moved in his favour before he could cover it in Osaka. 'There's no way that I can give this to a customer. It's too good,' he said cheerfully. By the end of the day Leeson had reported his largest-ever single day's profit from the switching book, of £3.3 million. By now Gueler was becoming tired of Leeson's unstoppable success. He and Fuchs could not work miracles as Leeson appeared to. Their arbitrage book had its ups and downs, as the previous day had shown. Brindle was also feeling burned by his experiment with going long volatility against Leeson's customer in December, and had allowed another long volatility position to expire before the earthquake. Gueler's goodwill had been stretched by Leeson's apparent ability to make profits at will. He enjoyed the days when Leeson was away, and he and Fuchs could show they could make arbitrage profits without him. Nobody could accuse them of needing Leeson then. What was more, Leeson's switching book was eating up the funds they needed for arbitrage. The more cash was sent by London settlements and treasury to Singapore to cover Leeson's margin, the less was available for Gueler's trading.

Leeson's bout of buying futures to retrieve the money lost as the market fell not only alienated Gueler, it also set off alarms in London. The Simex margining system had slowly caught up with the growth in futures in the five eights account following the Kobe earthquake. Leeson's faxes to London calling for margin suddenly escalated to the point of stretching Barings' bank facilities. The fax sent to London at the end of trading on Tuesday demanded so much cash that Barings could hardly cope. Granger sent a message by computer to Hawes: 'Awaiting breakdown from my buddy Nick . . . (once they creatively allocate the numbers),' she wrote.

Being questioned from London did not put Leeson off trying to support the market. On Wednesday 25 January he launched an explosive burst of buying for the five eights account. The Nikkei had just steadied on Tuesday, bouncing back from its awful Monday low to close 276 points up, pushing it back through 18,000 to 18,060. Leeson could feel the market drifting in his direction. He decided to push it further by again doubling his bet. He had sold 10,000 futures as the market plummeted on Monday, but he now stepped into the Nikkei pit again. As trading opened on Wednesday the line from Simex to Tokyo was quiet. Then Gueler was called by an equity salesman in Singapore. 'What the hell is going on? Baring Futures is buying heavily,' he said.

Gueler rang Leeson to quiz him on what was behind such an extraordinary buying spree.

Leeson pretended it was for Customer X. 'I don't know what's happening. The guy is crazy. He is buying futures like there's no tomorrow,' he said.

'This is the weirdest thing I have ever seen. The guy must be insane,' Gueler said.

Fuchs was aching to get more information on what was going on. By pretending to the Tokyo traders that he was largely in the market for Philippe, Leeson had a perfect excuse for not telling them any more. They were starting to get frustrated at being the last to know what was happening. Other banks would ring up to confirm gossip about Simex. Gueler and Fuchs found themselves in the embarrassing position of not knowing. One day Paribas rang the desk to say Baring Futures had just crossed an order for 6,000 contracts on the Simex floor.

'Come on, guys. You must know,' one of the salesmen said. But they could not find out what was going on.

'Nick's just bought 1,000 futures,' one of Leeson's assistants would say from Singapore.

'Why didn't you tell us?' Fuchs would complain.

It would make arbitrage trading easier if they knew what orders Leeson was putting into the market. Gueler reasoned that it would not be front-running for them to know as the orders went into the pit. It would allow them a fractional head-start, without the risk of it being improper use of inside information. But Leeson was now having to trade so heavily for five eights that he did not want to be watched over. 'I'm not allowed to tell you until after the orders are through,' he would insist.

Gueler had to restrain Fuchs. 'Don't push it too far. We're not supposed to know,' he said. They had to resign themselves to knowing not much more than any other trader in the Tokyo market about what Leeson and Customer X were doing.

That had not prevented others from trying to find out more. One of the futures and options salesmen in Hong Kong, called Giles Scott, reasoned that if Customer X was buying so heavily through Leeson, he might be interested in the Hong Kong market. So many of his customers were now chatting about Customer X's trading that he was intrigued. He rang Leeson on the Simex trading floor. Although he was British, Scott often affected a laid-back, mid-Atlantic drawl. 'Is that Big Balls Nick?' he asked. 'Some of my clients have been commenting on the size of your gonads.'

Leeson laughed amiably.

'Listen, you've got to tell me who this customer is,' Scott said.

'I'm not supposed to say,' Leeson replied. He started talking obliquely about Philippe. He only met Mr X in hotels, and when he rang the call would be passed through several exchanges.

Scott pressed him to discover if the customer wanted to buy futures and options on the Hang Seng index. 'You've got to get him to give me a call. It's a must,' Scott insisted.

'I'll try, but don't hold your breath,' Leeson replied.

This false trail gave Leeson an ideal cover as he started to build up futures in the five eights account. He also made sure he could report large switching profits. That Wednesday Leeson bought 10,000 futures for the switching account, losing Y140 million (£1 million) on futures trading during the day. But he transferred this loss and some extra by crossing the futures into five eights. By the end of the day he had reported £857,000 profits on Nikkei trading and a further £657,000 on JGB arbitrage. To London it appeared he was taking full advantage of the switching opportunity afforded by Customer X's relentless buying.

Leeson's buying on Wednesday only made the cash drain on London worse. At 4.00 p.m., Hawes went to the asset and liability committee (Alco) meeting to break the news. Leeson had demanded so much cash that it would have gone over Barings' limit with Citibank in Singapore had it not been for an error in booking another trade. It was strong stuff for the Alco, which had only been meeting since November. While Hopkins was in charge of monitoring risk daily, the committee was supposed to set overall policy for trading. It was chaired by Maclean, and it met every afternoon in America Square in a glass-fronted room by the trading floor. The Alco had seven other members: Norris, Baker, Barnett, Broadhurst, Hawes, Hopkins and Katz. In practice attendance was patchy. It was an uneasy combination given the past rivalries and present tensions. Baker was impatient at sitting around with the others, and Norris liked to get through things as rapidly as possible. 'Looks fine to me,' Norris would say briskly if there seemed any threat of delay. He liked meetings to be over in twenty minutes at the maximum. He had plenty of other things to be getting on with. In contrast Hopkins liked to think things over at length, preferably sleeping on any big financial decision. Having mustered his intellectual ammunition Hopkins tended to pick on those whom he did not respect. Walz would sometimes turn up at the Alco in place of Baker, and did not always appear to be fully on top of her brief. He would ask her questions that seemed designed to show he had a better grasp of derivatives.

Hopkins would also get irritated at the lack of any obvious contribution from Barnett. 'What do you think of that, Geoffrey?' Hopkins would ask, as Barnett sat silently. The atmosphere at the Alco rapidly became unpleasant. At one of the early meetings there was a stand-up row between Baker and Katz. That afternoon the meeting was peaceful, since only Katz and Broadhurst were there to hear Hawes's concerns. Hawes went through his difficulties in getting information out of Leeson, and outlined the problems they were now facing in funding his trading. Broadhurst thought it was a bit academic to sit there simply discussing it among the three of them. If anything was to be done Norris would have to listen. He did not believe Hawes would have the nerve to confront Norris himself, so he ascended the spiral staircase in the middle of the trading floor to the fifth-floor office Norris shared with Sacranie and Greer. Norris had not come to the Alco meeting because he was caught up with something else. Broadhurst told him he should listen to what Hawes had to say. Norris absorbed the news, and realized Leeson had to be prevented from overstretching the banking lines. The best person to ensure that was done was Baker, who was in New York, having flown there after a visit to Latin America. Norris decided to use his train journey home that evening usefully by calling Baker from his commuter train. He told Baker that

Leeson's trading had to be cut. Baker got the message, although he did not like having to reduce trading because Hawes could not fund it.

Baker's frustration with Hawes had increased in the previous two months and he was now getting to boiling point. Baker had taken to referring to him as 'Forrest Gump'. In addition, Baker did not want to upset Leeson because he had heard rumours, which Leeson had encouraged, that Morgan Stanley was interested in hiring him. He had been talking to Norris about the size of Leeson's bonus. Norris was not keen on paying more than £200,000. 'Anything more is just going to be spent on beer. This guy's not ready to be treated like a mature professional. It will corrupt him to give him ammunition,' Norris said. He recalled Leeson's trouser-dropping antics and the first-class air ticket. Fraser shared Norris's reservations about paying upwards of £350,000 to Leeson. 'Must we pay this dreadful little man so much money?' he had asked. Baker thought they were being absurd. 'You are just being prurient,' he told Norris. He wanted to ensure Leeson's loyalty by paying him £550,000. Notwithstanding this, he set about finding Leeson to get his trading down. It was not an easy matter. It was by now getting hard to track down Leeson outside office hours. Hawes had been trying to get more information from Leeson, but by the time he arrived at his desk in the morning it was already late afternoon in Singapore. He would ring on Leeson's mobile number. 'I'm by the swimming pool,' Leeson would tell him cheerfully, avoiding detailed discussion of his margin calls. By the time Baker had a chance to deal with the problem, it was late at night in Manhattan and he was in his room at the Regency Hotel.

Barings' management was now stretched across time zones. Baker was five hours behind London and thirteen hours behind Singapore and Tokyo. Baker called Gueler to try to find out what was going on in Asia.

'We must reduce these positions. I want those contracts down,' he said. Gueler replied that Leeson had already reduced his positions. The two men were speaking at cross-purposes. Gueler had already spoken to Leeson after hearing that Hawes needed the JGB positions reduced. Leeson had told him that it had been done already, not admitting that his Nikkei trading had ballooned. Then Baker rang Leeson to reiterate the message. Once more Leeson talked about reducing JGB trading.

Baker went to sleep in his New York hotel, satisfied that the message had got through. He was still oblivious the next morning to what was really happening on Simex.

By 7.30 a.m., he was in Baring Securities' New York office dealing with something else Norris had asked about. Baker rang London and got through to Sacranie. The call was recorded, as were all calls at Barings. It helped to sort out any disagreements between traders and customers, and to keep traders in line. It was now 12.30 p.m. in London and Norris was preparing for a management committee meeting that afternoon at 3.15 p.m. Norris had also asked Baker to find out for him how Fuchs and Gueler had lost £950,000. Fraser had been pressing for an explanation. Baker described this to Sacranie first. Then he went on to try to explain how Leeson had apparently made a profit of $5.5 million on Simex during the previous day. 'We made a lot of money on cash–futures [arbitrage], and Nick had an amazing day on Simex,' he said enthusiastically. 'The thing is, that you try to describe how that money was made. There's a mesh of volumes in the market . . . which was sort of a perfect trading environment for Nick to work in.'

'Huge liquidity and gaps,' Sacranie prompted.

'Yes. The trading size was huge. For example, at the opening bell, Daiwa would have bought 50,000 Simex contracts, and Merrill Lynch would have followed with a similar order. In addition, Baring Singapore *was* the market. I mean, he just had a corner there. So everybody wants Nick to do their business,' said Baker keenly.

'Right.'

'So he was able to fill orders in Simex by buying futures in a stock that never reached market twenty to thirty ticks lower,' Baker went on.

'Amazing.'

'In terms of the size of the orders, and in terms of the opportunities you were seeing, it was just one of those, you know, sort of great days, and he's just absolutely the centre, in the vortex of the information curve there,' said Baker, warming to his favourite theme.

'Phenomenal,' said Sacranie. But he knew that large profits could signal risks. 'Are you comfortable that he didn't take any specific or directional risk during that day?' he asked.

'I trust the guy a fair bit. It's really hard for me to say. I think he – I think he just sees opportunities that are phenomenal, and he just takes them.'[7]

Then Baker called Gueler at home. It was just before midnight in Tokyo and Gueler was about to go to sleep. 'Can you hold on one second?' he asked.

'You're just putting your coke spread away, Fernando?' Baker asked jokily.

'What?' replied a surprised Gueler, who had never taken cocaine.

Baker asked him about trading in Singapore and Tokyo that day: 'What's your total P&L [profit and loss] today?'

'Total P&L, over three and a half million dollars.'

'And how much of that did Nick make?'

It was a delicate question for Gueler, who was sick of being the poor cousin of Leeson. 'Nick was about two point seven, two point eight, if that. Without Nick today in Tokyo, we made $250,000,' he said proudly.

'That's fantastic, Fernando.'

'Yeah, and yesterday in Tokyo we made about a million,' Gueler went on enthusiastically.[8]

Baker called Sacranie back to give him some more details. 'We made three and a half million out there. Two and a half million on Simex and about $300,000 in Tokyo,' he said.

'This is just one man?' Sacranie asked, incredulously.

'Not really. I think that's another simplification. I think if you take away what he's made, we had a pretty good month in Tokyo. But he's . . . They're not bad . . . The books in total made about $15 million month-to-date, of which he would have made about $12 million or $13 million.'

'Brilliant,' said Sacranie and turned to the vexed question of Leeson's bonus: 'Ron, do you think in the light of his current performance, his expectation has gone further up?'

'I think 450 [thousand] is the minimum. I think 450 to 500 . . . I think Nick lost £20,000 because of his behaviour, and he understood that . . . But he is close to Morgan Stanley. I get a lot of Morgan Stanley off him. I think we can't underestimate the fact that someone's going to come along at some point,' Baker replied.[9]

After speaking to Fraser to reassure him about the hedging loss in

Tokyo, Baker finally got through to Norris to discuss the problems Hawes was having in funding Leeson's trading.

'I'm not happy about the strain they're putting on our funding position ... A 2 per cent move in the market on the Simex end would blow straight through available funding, and safety,' Norris said.

Baker thought Leeson ought not to be constrained in this way. 'I think it would be a mistake for us to not be able to tolerate a 5 per cent move.'

Baker and Norris talked over the fact that Leeson now apparently had 15,000 futures contracts matched between Osaka and Simex. 'Nick, I would guess, in order to be sensible, should come down from 15,000 to seven and a half,' Norris said. 'What I'd like to see [is] a couple of days with those positions half where they are now, and maybe we can work out what we need to do about this.'[10]

With matters seemingly in hand, Norris went to the management committee meeting, which he chaired at 8 Bishopsgate in Tuckey's absence. Norris told the others about the loss on the hedging position on Monday. He also disclosed Leeson's $9 million earnings for the week. Kelly was still a sceptic about Simex. 'You do not make $9 million in a week with no risk,' he said firmly. But Norris stuck to the explanation for Leeson's ability to generate profits on Simex, which had been refined over and over again in discussions among managers since the August audit report. It appeared that the crisis was abating and they would be able to untangle things the following day. Norris had decided the best way to sort things out was to discuss it at length at Thursday's Alco meeting, with Baker calling in from New York.

By later that evening Leeson was once more spoiling Norris's neatly laid plan. Having put 10,000 long futures into five eights on Wednesday, he doubled his bet again, amassing 27,200 long futures in five eights. It was such a large position that the rumours about what Barings was doing became deafening in Tokyo and other Asian markets. Leeson made a loss of £17 million on the Nikkei futures for the day, but reported healthy profits by crossing trades into five eights. He now had 8,100 short JGB futures in the five eights account. His reported profits totalled £807,000 for the day. However, Leeson had gone a step too far. He had relied on distracting London with profits, but Norris and Baker now wanted him to cut back his Nikkei trading, no matter how much money he could conjure up for them.

On Thursday morning, 26 January, in New York Baker was greeted by a crisis. Leeson's overnight call for funding had escalated further, and the Osaka Securities Exchange figures showed he had increased the number of Nikkei futures Baring Futures held. Norris wondered if Baker was deliberately defying him in order to force Hawes to allocate more funding to his operations. 'Do you think these guys are just pushing the envelope?' he asked Sacranie. By late morning Walz was facing hard questions about what was going on from Hawes and Norris. She was worn out by the time Baker called from New York. 'What's happened today? You've got the Forrest Gump all over you,' said Baker.

'I do. I really do. A lot of children under my roof,' Walz agreed wearily.

They shared some gripes about Hawes. 'He freaks people out,' said Baker.

'He doesn't give comfort.'

'No.'

'When I left the office, we were talking about his concern over the JGB position and how it's gotten so big . . . and I said "Look, we'll do whatever we need to do."'

They talked about how Broadhurst and Hawes were worried about Leeson's funding. 'We have to watch it, but it doesn't help to have a bumbling dickhead running around giving us . . . signals about what might be going to happen,' said Baker.

'That's absolutely right. But what happened today is that Nick doubled the size of the Simex position.'

'It's bad.'

'It's very bad,' Walz agreed grimly and added, 'I really don't know how it happened. Nick and I had spoken about how he was going to be cool . . . and then there was a flurry of activity on Wednesday.'

She described being told off by Norris. 'I talked to Hawes again. I told him to get absolutely clear what he needed . . . And Tony, like a bumbling idiot, probably focused in on the JGB thing. I don't really know . . . So Norris called me today and he said "Frankly, Mary, I'm not amused."'

Then Walz pondered whether Leeson had broken his trading limit of 200 Nikkei futures.

'What I don't want to do is give an ambiguous signal to Nick here about the business. It just pisses me off. There ought to be rules, and we need to know what they are, but we cannot tell the guy: "Cut your position,"' Baker said.

'He is in an unfortunate position, though, because he is settlement, he is cash management and he is the trader, and there's a problem, because there's nobody else to call but him about it.'

'Yeah.'

'So you know, I've tried to be pretty cool about it, but I did say one thing to him. I said: "Look, the flurry of this activity, Nick, if it turns out, you know, something goes awry and we've got more than our 200 deltas, I'd rather know that now than later."'

'Yeah.'

'He said: "I know what you're saying, Mary." Today I'll know about the deltas, period.' Then Walz explained the excuse Leeson had used not to reduce contracts on Osaka. 'I had a pretty clear conversation with him, though, about what he should be trying to do tomorrow, and it's difficult, because the flow has been away from Osaka, with the market in Singapore. And if a customer comes in, and he wants to buy a lot, he's going to have to give him bad execution, or he's going to have to use somebody else's line in Osaka, and he said he couldn't do that.' Almost in passing Walz put her finger on the truth underlying all the confusion. 'And this is the other thing that I said to Nick, that the rumour about us is that we are the customer . . . Hawes said that was what he heard people in the market saying, so I told Nick.'[11]

Then Baker rang through to Norris to apologize for Leeson's fresh trading. 'You know, I'm sorry about this mix-up . . . It really isn't my fault because I told him to cut the position back . . . He told me that he'd already done it, but what he and I did not say to each other was that he was clearly talking about JGB contracts,' Baker said.

By now Norris had relaxed because the funding no longer appeared to be such a problem. Barings had got some cash back from the exchanges in margin, and Hawes was less worried. 'I mean, we're comfortable up to a 5 per cent market move,' Norris said.

'I apologize to you once again,' Baker said humbly.

'That's OK. Bye-bye.'[12]

Baker called Walz back to reassure her that the atmosphere was cooling down. 'I talked to Norris, and Norris has calmed down as well . . . We can't have Norris running about worrying about nuts and bolts, and internal treasury problems,' he told her.

'He insists on having an amateur treasury operation.'

'It just drives me nutsy, because at the end of the day . . . the management committee of the bank has to stop thinking about funding the Simex position,' Baker said, in frustration. Finally, he railed again about Hawes's inability to clarify funding. 'We want to back this guy, we just want to know what the hilt is. So why can't the dick tell us what the fucking hilt is?'

'I can check it out with him. I can tell you what the fucking hilt is . . .' Walz replied.

'So it turned out pretty okay, and I will give it one more try . . . but it looks like it's not a big deal any more,' Baker said with relief.[13]

The last ordeal was now due in half an hour. It was the Alco meeting, which Norris had arranged to thrash out concerns about the Simex operation. It would not be attended in the usual desultory manner. Norris had imposed a three-line whip to ensure the thing was sorted out, and he could turn his mind to something else. He had drawn up a list of possible risks with what Leeson was doing, which he had faxed to Baker in New York. Since everybody had been deceived into believing that switching was the way Leeson was making money, Norris had listed anything that could disrupt it. Maclean's chief worry was that Barings might meet a huge order on Simex, and then be unable to match it on Osaka because of a catastrophic failure such as the exchange suddenly closing. Given the fact that a large earthquake had just struck the region, this was not beyond the bounds of possibility. Norris had also listed the 'PR risk' of Barings' trading being misinterpreted. More and more calls were coming into the Tokyo office about the futures held in Osaka, which had been dubbed 'the Barings overhang'. It was not the sort of thing that made Peter Baring and Tuckey comfortable. The committee assembled around an oval table in its usual room off the trading floor. There was a microphone in the middle of the table so that Baker could hear the others and contribute himself. This time there was full attendance from all of the Alco members as well as Walz. The agenda showed that structured products had made

£11.9 million so far in January, of which Leeson had made £6 million in Nikkei switching and £4.7 million in JGBs.

'I'll lead off,' said Norris, taking the lead as confidently as ever. 'Just some basic points . . . There's a very unusual business opportunity here at the moment, and I think we should want to back that, or take advantage to what the hilt is . . .'

Norris had been told by Walz that Barings now had 32,000 short Nikkei futures on Simex, which was 29 per cent of the total outstanding contracts on the exchange. This was supposed to be matched by 16,000 long futures on Osaka, where each futures contract was double the size. 'Thirty two against sixteen, which is two and a half billion on the line,' Norris said briskly. 'How much of that is client, and how much of that is house. Do you know?'

Baker replied from New York that all 8,000 contracts of two days before had belonged to Barings.

'How much margin do we have posted?' asked Norris.

'About £300 million,' replied Baker.

Norris pointed out that Osaka would require £500 million more in funding.

'So are you saying that all the businesses combined are using a billion pounds?' Baker asked.

'I think that's what I'm saying. I'm not saying it with a huge amount of confidence . . .' Norris replied.

They turned to the risk of not having enough money to meet margin calls, and Broadhurst raised the possibility of one of the exchanges forcing Barings to sell off positions.

'I can't see that they can possibly close us down, since it's what you're talking about, Geoff, but I do think we'd lose enormous credibility with Simex, and with the customers, and with the people on the floor, if that happened. So the business would definitely suffer,' said Baker.

'As would our bankers,' added Broadhurst.

'Why shouldn't we pick some really wacky number out of the air, like half a billion dollars, and say that's what we should try to make available as a worst-case scenario . . . I don't have a real feeling myself for what the limits are,' Baker said.

'There's a possible solution for that, but first of all, are we only to use Citibank?' Maclean asked.

'You know, I think it clearly makes a lot of sense for us to have stand-by facilities with a number of people in Singapore, if that's possible,' Baker replied.

'Very expensive, Ron,' someone interjected.

'We are making a lot of money, aren't we? I don't know what they cost but [if we] sleep better at night and it's going to . . . free the business up . . . I think the cost will be worthwhile,' Baker countered.[14]

The conversation drifted on, with Baker only able to hear snatches of it because the microphone on the table in America Square was not picking much up. After forty-five minutes they decided that the funding was solid enough to allow Leeson to hold what futures he had. 'Nick Leeson is to be advised that: 1. There should be no increase in the Nikkei position beyond this level; 2. If the market rises then he should look for opportunities to cut the position,' the minutes read.[15] Baker and Walz left the meeting to try to sort out how much funding Leeson should be allowed for JGB trading.

At 2.35 p.m. in New York (7.35 p.m. in London) Baker rang Walz again to check how things had gone. By this time Walz was feeling messed around by those at America Square. 'I have to tell you, I'm really paranoid. I really do hate the lack of information on the whole thing. It's weird. [We are] discussing all these issues when we have no information about what funding actually goes there,' Walz complained.

'The treasurer of the bank should respond to the business need. The treasurer has no idea how to do that,' Baker said firmly.

'You're a bit harsh on that,' Walz said, pointing out that the cash management was handled by the settlements department as much as Hawes. 'Anyway,' she added, 'all the stuff we said about tomorrow's trade I've already agreed, but I'm going to get on the phone and just do it one more time, and make sure Fernando understands.'

'From their perspective, what happened was understandable. I can't criticize him, because Hawes came on, and had a conversation about JGBs,' said Baker, in Gueler's defence.

Walz told Baker that Leeson was going to answer Hawes's list of questions in his Singapore Project memo of 11 January. 'So Nick is going to write a response to all these points, and that will be here Monday, and I'd like to see it.'

Baker once more started venting his frustrations with Hawes: 'You know, there will be worse jobs than being the treasurer of the bank. If you were given that job, you would have that thing fixed up. It would take you six months, and you'd have none of this crap, and then you'd want another job.'

'Anyway, so . . .'

'I'm critical of those guys, and I'll go on being critical of them.'

'All these scraps of paper on my desk,' Walz sighed wearily.

'What's George [Maclean] say? I would think it puts George completely around the twist,' Baker asked.

'Not really, because George likes to pick up a problem and chew it around. He [does not] function like a machine. A machine does not have problems to chew on.'

'So you will talk to Nick?' Baker asked.

'Yes, I will talk to him tonight at 11.00 p.m.'

Walz had discussed with Leeson reducing some of the Nikkei position by crossing it with Morgan Stanley.

'Don't tell him he has to cross his position, for Christ's sake,' Baker warned.

'He can cross five or six thousand contracts with Morgan Stanley in the morning, and I think that's what he's going to try.' Walz mused a little about whether Leeson was becoming too clever for his own good. 'It does make me wonder how much . . . I'm sure he knows what his position is, and you do have to be a little bit careful, you never know, he can't get too big for himself.'

'Absolutely. That's why I think he should know where his tolerances are,' Baker said.

Walz mentioned Bill Sproule, a trader whom Baker was thinking of hiring from Bankers Trust to take charge of exchange-traded futures and options. Walz was keen for him to arrive so that she could concentrate on her operation in Hong Kong. 'To me, when you get somebody like Bill, it's an enormous thing, you know. It's on the ground,' she said.[16]

At 7.27 a.m. on 27 January Walz called Gueler in Tokyo. She was still trying to pin down Leeson's trading. It was the end of the trading day, and Fuchs and Gueler were trying to get away for the weekend. 'Do you know if we reduced our Nikkei position?' Walz asked Fuchs.

'I don't think we did,' Fuchs replied.

'Gee. Do you know if we increased it?'

'We didn't increase it either . . .'

Then Gueler came on line saying that the market had not moved up enough for Leeson to be able to cut the Nikkei position. It had risen 30 points to close at 18,104. He was unhappy at being used as a middle man between Walz and Leeson, but he talked it through with her.

'I heard from Nick at lunch,' he said.

'OK,' Walz said.

'This is only talking to Nick, but if the market were to go up, then we would be in an unwind position. But we weren't able to decrease anything today.'

'OK.'

'He talked to Morgan Stanley about reducing, and they want to do some. I think it's a matter of timing. I think they want to cross them at a higher level as well. Depends on what Nick says, but we didn't increase anything.'

'OK,' Walz repeated, thankful for small mercies. Then she asked for a breakdown of all Barings' trading on Simex and Osaka, and Gueler read out numbers for the two exchanges. Gueler assumed Leeson's positions were matched between exchanges. In fact, they constituted a single long position worth £2.5 billion. Gueler pointed out that Leeson's 16,000 contracts on Osaka made up 14 per cent of the entire market.

'This is probably one of the biggest positions we have ever had in Osaka?' Walz asked.

'Yes,' Gueler confirmed.

'Like by a factor of . . . ?'

'We have blown the last position by like, something in the order of 50 per cent.'

They started discussing Leeson's excuses for not reducing his position.

'What you are telling me in telling me that we didn't do anything today is that it is actually a pretty illiquid position, and there is some sensitivity in how we get out of it?' Walz asked.

'We can get out of it without losing money, but we have an impact on the market,' Gueler replied.

'That is inconsistent, 'cause if it was that easy I would have felt we would reduce some of it today, just to prove that we could . . .'

'Yeah, but I think, in Nick's words, he said that the market was pretty . . . what is the word that he used . . . that the market being pretty soft . . . then we kind of would have an adverse effect on the market,' Gueler said uncertainly.

'Yes, but could we have done a thousand lots, or something, just to prove that we could do it, couldn't we?' Walz pressed him.

'I think that we moved a couple of hundred lots, and I am not sure if he did . . .'

'We were free and easy, and we should have done it just to get people off our backs, right?'

'If it were free and easy, he would definitely have done it.'

'So therefore I must understand that it is probably not free and easy,' said Walz sharply.

'It's not free,' Gueler insisted stubbornly.

'And therefore, I must understand that to be perhaps more significant than I thought, because it's not something that's easy and liquid and simple.'

Gueler still dragged his feet. 'Yes, but I thought the situation was like, if you could unwind it great, but it wasn't that desperate that we have to unwind it like asap.'

This was too much for Walz after days of struggling to bring down Leeson's trading. 'True, but it doesn't take a brain surgeon to understand that there are about five or six people sitting around interested in this position, and how it works and needing some colour on it . . .' she said in exasperation. 'If people in the market see that we have this giant position that doesn't move, and somebody felt like fucking us around, and moved the market up so that we have a huge margin call . . . Wouldn't that be fun!' she exclaimed, with heavy sarcasm.[17]

As this conversation took place Leeson was busy embellishing another part of his increasingly complex fraud. Pang had not been put off by his bluster about a computer error and still wanted to know more about the £50 million receivable Leeson had put into the 1994 accounts. Coopers & Lybrand had told Rachel Yong, the financial controller for Baring Securities in Singapore, that it would not clear the accounts if this was not resolved. That afternoon Leeson met the auditors to explain. It had been a month since he had first covered the £50 million hole, but time had not helped a great deal. There was no obvious reason for Simex to owe Baring Futures £50 million.

Leeson quickly changed his story, saying that the £50 million was owed by a US broker called Spear, Leeds & Kellogg, which had bought an over-the-counter option from the firm, and still owed the money.[18] By describing it as an over-the-counter option Leeson made sure that Coopers could not simply check with Simex. The story also had a veneer of truth, as SLK occasionally bought futures and options through Barings. But it was rather flimsy, since not only had this trade not taken place, but he had no authority to sell over-the-counter options. The auditors promptly sent what was called a 'status report' on the progress of the audit to Coopers in London, repeating the story of the SLK receivable. It virtually brought to an end a successful week of deception for Leeson in which he had lost Y7.4 billion (£49 million) of Barings' money while reporting amazing profits from a bogus trading activity and fooling nearly all of Barings' most senior executives in London.

There was one last task. Walz caught up with him that evening to ask what was stopping him reducing his trading. Leeson spun a story about it being hard because the two exchanges would react differently to a large selling order. Afterwards Walz spoke again to Baker.

'What did Nick say?' he asked her.

'It's pretty tough, actually, to get through the paranoia thing for him . . . it's like "If I had to go out and over a couple of days get rid of all the positions, and I did it, and the market was crashing, that would be the worse-case scenario,"' Walz reported.

Leeson had estimated Barings could lose $1 million by selling rapidly, and repeated his explanation that it would make the Simex market fall faster than Osaka.

'The market in Singapore is one that almost always over-reacts, which is what it's done all the way along, which is why he makes the money . . .' Walz explained.

Baker and Walz worried away at details of Leeson's explanation, becoming ever more confused. 'I think we kind of go along a stumbling path, where we look at one thing at a time, and I think the dynamics are more complicated than that,' Walz said.

They tried to work out a way that Leeson could sell the positions, but got nowhere.

'All this work just drives me nutty. I just want to retire,' Baker complained.

'In all of this, I think I want to just understand this a bit more with Nick . . .'

'Is he still around?'

'Yes.'

'Call him back.'

After an hour, Baker rang Walz again to see if the deadlock had eased. 'How did things go with Nick?' he asked.

'I called him, and he didn't call me back, so I don't know,' Walz replied.[19]

Leeson had gone home for the weekend, evading the interrogators around him.

The following Monday, 30 January, was the eve of the Chinese New Year. Ceremonial paper dragons paraded through the Simex pits for good luck. Ang Swee Tien and other notables watched the display benignly from the fourth-floor balcony. As they looked down, Leeson crossed 3,000 Nikkei contracts under their noses. By this time Leeson's constant use of cross-trades had annoyed other brokers and he had provoked complaints from several investment banks. One trader complained once to the Simex authorities when he saw Leeson and Argyropoulous standing at a pit with a local broker. He thought they were fixing a trade. But while Simex suspended the local for three months, nothing was done to Leeson. In January other brokers on the floor could see huge trades being crossed by Leeson at the highest or lowest prices of the day. One thought that Leeson was laundering money, which explained why he did not seem to care about prices. A few days later Simex put out a circular to all brokers, reminding them of rules on cross-trades. By the time Leeson crossed his 3,000 contracts the day had gone well. The market had risen 650 points on the day, from 18,100 to 18,750. It seemed to be lifting clear of the 18,000 danger zone. The five eights account gained Y8.65 billion (£58 million), and Leeson closed 6,570 of the Nikkei futures to leave himself with 20,600. It appeared he might have got away with his defiance of London the previous week. The relief was short-lived. When Leeson returned to Ocean Towers that afternoon another letter was waiting from Simex.

This time Simex had complained to Simon Jones about margin payments. It had done a spot check on Barings' positions on 30 December. The letter said Barings had held a short position of 13,039 Nikkei futures for customers that day, and there had been a danger that its margin deposit was insufficient to take the risk. It was only a routine check, but any questions about funding were unwelcome. Jones had also broken with custom and sent a copy to London. Worse was also coming from London. Later that day Broadhurst talked to an accountant called Duncan Fitzgerald, who was managing the Baring Securities audit for Coopers & Lybrand. He showed Broadhurst part of the Singapore status report on Leeson's explanation for the £50 million gap in the balance sheet. Broadhurst's reaction was exasperation. Every year he faced difficulties when some trainee accountant misinterpreted something in the balance sheet. This could not be correct. 'God, we've got another bumbling idiot out in Singapore,' he said. However, he was worried by the note. He had heard nothing about £50 million being missing. Broadhurst went to Norris's office to talk to him, but found only Sacranie. The two had a brief conversation, then Broadhurst spoke to Gamby and Hawes. Neither could make sense of it. That evening Hawes sent an electronic message to Jones and Leeson. 'To us here, this looks a very muddled and strange comment,' he wrote,[20] asking for an explanation. Leeson received it the following morning. He left a message on Hawes's voice mail saying he would get back to him as quickly as possible about the £50 million.[21]

Leeson had one thing protecting him from this renewed assault: Broadhurst and Jones were not talking to each other. After the row the previous July relations between them had deteriorated so far that Bax had advised Broadhurst to pass messages through him. 'I think we should put in place a plan to replace Simon,' Broadhurst had said. Bax's defence of Jones was getting weaker and he had not put up much of a fight. 'You might be right,' he had replied. For now Broadhurst was reliant on others to tackle Jones. He went to see Norris who was not especially struck by Broadhurst's visit. There was always a lot of traffic through his room and he was used to trying to sort out people's problems, ranging from professional to personal. He sometimes joked with Sacranie that he was the office psychiatrist. 'I get in every morning, and put on a white coat,' he said. He pointed at the blue sofa opposite his desk. 'I even have a couch!' Norris found the tale of the missing £50 million so confused that he told Broadhurst not to raise it at the Alco meeting that day. Somebody had to find out what had happened before they started jumping up and down.

In any case Norris had plenty of other things to resolve. The one occupying most time was inevitably the question of how much everyone was going to be paid in bonuses. He had tried to impose what he regarded as a more rational method of calculating bonuses in the autumn. The result had been a long wrangle over who contributed what. The brokers, led by Fraser and Kelly, had argued fiercely that they were being forced to subsidize corporate financiers.

An even worse headache was Mexico. The problems of 1993 in Latin America had not been fully resolved despite Gamby's effort to sort out the mess left by settlements staff resigning from New York. Now the difficulty had resurfaced in a different form in Mexico. Baring Securities had once again got into an emerging market early, and had obtained a seat on the Mexican stock exchange to deal directly in Mexican shares. It had involved a considerable outlay: $5 million to buy membership of the exchange and a further $3 million in capital. But it had as usual entered with more enthusiasm than prudence, taking up its seat just before a full-blown financial crisis struck Mexico in December 1994. On 19 December Mexico had devalued the peso and triggered a wave of selling by overseas investors who doubted whether it could meet interest payments on government debt. By mid-January the peso had dropped by 40 per cent, and the US government led an $18 billion refinancing package. The strain was too great for Baring Securities. It used local settlements software, adapted to foreign currency transactions with a spreadsheet that had been devised by its back office staff. Like the Kevin Peat System, it was not up to the task. The volume of trading was so great that the system packed up. Baring Securities was unable to settle transactions and it suspended its stock exchange membership. This was a radical step by comparison with its past efforts to struggle on while fixing the problem but Norris had stepped in and insisted on it. The head of the local office was summoned back to London, while they all pondered what to do next.

Norris could not believe the Singapore problem would prove as serious as Mexico. He told Broadhurst he would have a word with Bax. By this time Leeson was in the middle of devising an excuse at Ocean Towers that he hoped would pass muster. He decided to amend his story once again, changing the deal from an over-the-counter options sale, which was clearly causing a fuss in London. Instead, he wrote a note to Jones saying it was a trade between SLK and Banque

Nationale de Paris, a customer of Baring Futures. BNP had profited by £50 million, and Baring Futures had paid the cash to the French bank, but his staff had failed to collect the money from SLK. Leeson said he had not sought approval because none of Barings' cash should have been at risk. 'As the trade was to have no impact, referral was not made, so blame me!' Leeson wrote cheerfully. He said that the cash would soon come in from SLK. 'There are obviously a lot of errors that I can be hung on, to which I take full responsibility,' Leeson wrote at the end. Jones was shocked at the note, and scribbled some queries on it. It was clear that Leeson had been pushing boundaries in a way he had not realized. At 7.30 a.m. the next day, Wednesday 1 February, Jones met Leeson and quizzed him over it. Leeson promised to get written confirmation, and assured Jones the cash was on its way from SLK. However, Jones was still uneasy at the affair. Even if everything Leeson said was true, Baring Futures had still been out of pocket by £50 million for nearly two months before the auditors had spotted it. Jones went to see Bax to pass on his worries about Leeson.

The following day Jones and Leeson met the Coopers auditors, who insisted that they needed proofs of the transaction. Despite having told Jones the previous morning that the deal had been between SLK and BNP Leeson stuck with the version he had already told Coopers. Jones did not contradict him. He then returned to the fourteenth floor of Ocean Towers and provided the necessary proofs by forging them. He typed a note from Baker confirming that he knew of an over-the-counter deal with SLK and then forged Baker's signature on it. Then Leeson took a letter signed by Richard Hogan, the managing director of SLK, cut out Hogan's signature and stuck it on two forged letters. One was dated 1 October 1994 and was an order for the option Leeson had invented; the other was dated the previous day and was a confirmation of payment from SLK. Finally he told a clerk to switch the cash from one Baring Futures account at Citibank to another and get a statement before restoring it to its original place again. Leeson gave all the proofs except one to the auditors that evening. The payment confirmation letter was supposed to go directly from SLK to the auditors. At 7.16 a.m. the next day, he faxed through the two pages himself from his apartment. The top of both these sheets, which were supposed to have been sent from SLK in New York, bore a line imprinted by his fax machine. 'From Nick & Lisa,' they read.[22] Leeson did not remember how his fax machine was set up. It was a rather large flaw, but it did not matter. Later that day Coopers cleared the 1994 accounts.

By Friday various explanations had filtered through to London, creating as much confusion among the London managers as over exactly how Leeson made his exceptional profits. Gamby still thought he had done an unauthorized trade but he warned Railton and Granger not to probe Leeson about it, telling them the matter was being handled 'at the highest levels'. Railton was due to fly to Singapore to look at the funding problems. 'I don't want any mention of this to Nick Leeson,' Gamby advised him. Broadhurst was calming down, however. Fitzgerald had told him the missing £50 million had been paid by SLK, and the alarm he felt on Monday receded. Broadhurst's mood improved further when a fax arrived from Bax in Singapore. 'As you know, recent incidents have highlighted the current operational weaknesses of our Simex business, and an urgent need for a new approach,' it started.[23] Broadhurst was in Norris's room, and they read it together. In the last paragraph Bax suggested that a deputy should be appointed under Jones. 'Halleluiah!' said Norris, and Broadhurst threw both his arms in the air. Broadhurst himself had been suggesting appointing a deputy to Jones as a means of breaking through the impenetrable barrier. It would be a Trojan horse, as far as Norris and Broadhurst were concerned. Once there was a deputy on the ground in Singapore whom they would control, it was only a short step to getting rid of Jones altogether. Broadhurst felt like breaking open some champagne. It appeared the affair had at least broken the deadlock over Jones and at last they had the bane of his life on the run.

To improve matters further Hawes and Railton were flying out the next day to Singapore. Railton was to fill in for the pregnant Hassan, while Hawes would sort out the margin problems. If it went well the whole thing could soon be sorted out. It was urgent. Leeson's trading had led to a sharp increase in his demands for margin cash. The hole in the balance sheet for 'loans to customers' had risen from £10 million to £150 million. Granger was unhappy at Leeson's inadequate explanations for where the money was going. She thought she was being asked to fund house trading and Leeson had encouraged that belief, telling her he had no other funding. 'Brenda, London is the cash cow. You are funding Singapore,' he told her.[24] Leeson was now very scared. Railton would be working each day at Ocean Towers, and could find the five eights account at any time. The afternoons were less of a worry because Leeson could take charge, but each morning he would be stuck on the trading floor while Railton poked around. Hawes presented less threat since Leeson had already bamboozled him for months, but there were bound to be awkward moments. The strain was becoming too intense to be hidden completely. Leeson had been gorging food and drink for the past year, but now he could hardly hold them down. He was vomiting constantly in the toilets by the Simex floor. When they called Gueler and Fuchs would be told that Leeson was sick. It was also making him paranoid. Leeson had started to think that somebody was bugging his phones and had stopped using some of them for fear of giving away his next move in the market.

That Monday, 6 February, as Hawes and Railton were starting work in Singapore, a further problem over funding cropped up in London. Barings had spent the previous two years pressing the Bank of England to allow it favourable treatment for its trading on Osaka and Simex. Because its arbitrage and volatility books consumed so much cash, there had been a danger that it would exceed the limit laid down in the 1987 Banking Act. This specified that no bank could lend a sum equivalent to more than 25 per cent of its capital to a single borrower. The point of the rule was to stop a bank recklessly lending so much that it would collapse if one borrower defaulted. This had hardly mattered until solo consolidation of Baring Securities took place in 1993. Now that Baring Brothers' capital flowed straight into its broking arm it had to observe that rule for any trading activity of Baring Securities. Maclean had realized early on that there could be a problem, and Barnett had written to the Bank of England in January 1993 to point this out. In his letter he had posed an interesting argument, arguing that by posting margin money with a futures exchange such as Osaka, Barings was not lending to one borrower. The clearing house in Osaka had thirty-nine members, so Barings thought the margin payment was in effect split thirty-nine ways. This would mean that Barings would never come anywhere near breaching the 25 per cent limit. The Bank was used to banks indulging in this sort of hair-splitting, and Christopher Thompson, the supervisor who handled Barings, passed the letter on to its Policy Unit for them to hand down a pronouncement.

There the matter had rested while months stretched into a year. The 1987 act was tightened slightly by a European Union directive which was enforced in October 1993, but still no reply came. As Leeson's trading escalated, so did the amount of cash deposited with exchanges. In September 1994 Maclean realized it had breached the £117 million limit implied by the 25 per cent rule. He spoke to Thompson, who said that he knew the Bank owed Barings a response but 'the matter was buried reasonably deep in his in-tray', according to Maclean's note of the conversation.[25] Thompson said he did not mind Barings exceeding the 25 per cent limit occasionally until it was sorted out. In fact, Thompson did not know half of what was occurring. Because the unreconciled gap represented by Leeson's margin calls for the five eights account had been put down in the balance sheets as 'loans to customers', Barings was not reporting these sums to the Bank. Had they been included Barings would have been well over double the limit. However, the uncertainty had drifted on until Barings finally received a reply. On 6 February Maclean told the bank's management committee, chaired by Andrew Tuckey, that the Bank would not allow it an escape clause. This meant that Barings would have either to limit its derivatives trading sharply, or find another means of breaking up the exposure. Maclean told the committee that all might be saved. Barings might evade the 25 per cent rule by putting the money through Sanwa and other banks. It would place a filter between London and Asia, reducing the direct exposure.

It was not an immediate problem although it would have to be dealt with promptly. The more pressing issue was resolving the ambivalence over Leeson's funding requests. Hawes started his week by talking over his worries with Bax, who told him that Leeson was under a lot of pressure. 'Why don't you deal with it?' Bax asked. Hawes was tired of asking Leeson about funding and not being able to pin him down fully. So he sat down methodically to write down all the questions that had occurred to him over the funding. It came to twenty. He faxed a copy over to Hopkins, who had returned from holiday, having missed the previous week's debate about the unreconciled £50 million. Hopkins in turn sent a copy to Baker to look at. Baker had only been told by Norris the previous day of the

£50 million trade, and he thought Hawes was going to pin the blame for his own mismanagement on Leeson. When he saw this long list of questions Baker exploded. On Wednesday he went over to America Square for the daily Alco meeting, and walked into Norris's office brandishing the list. He had written by the side of some questions swear-words about Hawes, such as 'bastard' and 'fucking idiot'. Baker was irate. 'What I've written is so disgusting that I've had to snowpaint some of it out,' he said. Norris found it vexing that Baker was behaving like this. It was the second time he had gone beyond the limits of what Norris considered acceptable behaviour. Directness was one thing, but Norris found Baker's behaviour a lot more crude than he had believed him capable of up to now.

They stood in front of the windows in his office looking out over the City roofscape. Norris tried hard not to raise his voice. 'You're dealing with these people entirely the wrong way,' he said. 'There is no point in complaining about the questions. You should come up with answers.' There was hardly any time to discuss it before they had to walk down a floor to the Alco meeting. Having got what appeared to be confirmation that the £50 million had been repaid, Norris was now ready to place the incident formally on record. Confusion still reigned though. Norris explained it as an 'operational error' in not collecting money on a trade brokered between SLK and BNP, which was not the same version of the story as in the Coopers audit report. He did not mention the question of whether Leeson had been authorized to carry out this trade. Hopkins was scornful that Baring Futures had failed to collect money owed for so long. He had been on holiday for the previous two weeks, and he was amazed at the mess that seemed to have been drifting on while he was away. It was confirmation of exactly the sort of thing he had been complaining about for several months. 'Will we get interest on this?' Hopkins asked. Norris said he was unsure. The confrontation was awkward for others to watch. Norris had already signalled that he wanted to push Hopkins aside. They had gone to lunch before Hopkins's holiday. 'What are your life plans?' Norris had asked. Hopkins had thought little of it. 'Happy where I am,' he said. When he told his wife, she thought the question sounded worryingly calculated.

Tony Railton had now been at work for several days trying to reconcile some of the funding requests. He had hopes of coming to work in Singapore. He liked the atmosphere and the friendliness of the people in the streets. So he did not want to offend Leeson because he realized his future in Singapore rested on him. Meanwhile, Leeson was doing his best to keep Railton distracted and away from Ocean Towers as much as possible. He arranged tennis matches for him in the mornings while Leeson was at Simex. In the afternoons he could control what Railton saw. It was easy for Leeson to pull rank on Railton, since he had headed futures and options settlement before Railton arrived. His other advantage was that the clerks were very loyal. One of them, Pamela Chiu, was working with Leeson on the Simex floor. She asked the women in Ocean Towers if Railton was teaching them new things. 'Not really. He's spying on us,' one replied. They had been careful to refer everything back to Leeson.

Pamela did not like Leeson being under suspicion and warned him about it on the Simex trading floor. 'Be careful of Tony, Nick.'

Leeson reassured her. 'Oh he's fine. He's fine. Nothing to worry about,' he said breezily. 'I've done nothing wrong.'

Hawes too was still working away in Singapore to try to get some answers out of Leeson but he was having a great deal of difficulty pinning him down. The back office staff did not know what to make of Hawes. 'I think Baring Futures is in big trouble,' he said one day on the fourteenth floor of Ocean Towers, but his remark was accompanied with a smile. They thought he was joking.[26]

On Thursday 9 February Hawes went with Jones to see a Simex official to talk about the funding problems. She mentioned in passing that Barings was long of the Nikkei. 'No we are not. We are short,' said Hawes. He had swallowed Leeson's story that his long futures position on Osaka was matched. 'Okay, we will check,' the Simex official said. Hawes had a final meeting with Leeson and Jones on that day. They met in Jones's office. Leeson told him Simex had checked. He was correct: Barings was short. Hawes showed him a chart he had drawn with all the questions he wanted Railton to answer. Leeson looked at it and made a couple of polite comments. The subject switched to the SLK trade. Leeson repeated the version he had given in his note to Jones. 'I've been careless, and it won't happen again. I'm sorry,' he said. He was acting like a schoolboy hauled up in front of the headmaster. But Hawes was not satisfied. 'I would like to see the dealing tickets,' he said. Leeson left the room, promising to go and search for them. Hawes and Jones waited for twenty minutes but there was no sign of Leeson. Hawes suggested that they go and look themselves but Jones dissuaded him. 'The auditors are still there,' he said. After a while Hawes gave up. That afternoon, Bax called Norris to ask whether he could keep the SLK problem out of the management letter, a document attached to the annual audit. He feared that the authorities might crack down if they saw it. 'You know what it's like here,' he said. Broadhurst was in Norris's room as he was speaking to Bax and Norris asked him to pass on this request to Coopers.

On Saturday 11 February Norris flew from London to Asia, his first tour for several months. He was to visit Hong Kong, Kuala Lumpur, Bangkok and Singapore to carry out an odd assortment of tasks. He was seeing new managers in Kuala Lumpur and Bangkok, and Barings was considering joining both local stock exchanges. In Hong Kong his task was more delicate. A Baring Brothers executive whom he knew well was having an affair, and as ever Norris had been dragged in to solve the problem. The wife had asked Norris to intervene. Singapore was the most important stop on the trip. Barings was again in the middle of untangling problems in Australia. It had a joint venture merchant bank there called Baring Brothers Burrows & Co. but was winding this up. It wanted stronger links with McIntosh Securities, a broking firm in which it had a 20 per cent stake. This was to be discussed at a summit in Singapore that Friday.

While Norris was out in Malaysia on Monday 13 February the management committee in London was hearing a report from Ian Hopkins on the SLK affair. Hopkins noted that the firm had yet to claim interest from SLK and that the episode had 'brought to a head the need to build a proper operational infrastructure in the Singapore futures operation, and particularly the need to devolve settlement responsibility from Nick Leeson'. Tuckey, who chaired the meeting, did not devote much discussion to this point. Hopkins was surprised that nobody appeared upset at such a large sum going missing for a month, but the others seemed perfectly content that it had now been dealt with.

This lack of concern about a mistake being made in Singapore was characteristic of meetings of the management committee and executive committee that headed Barings Investment Bank. On paper the management structure created by Norris and Tuckey looked as effective as that of any of its rival investment banks. But in practice Barings' directors would hardly question the day-to-day running of operations within the bank. The tradition of Barings was one of partnership. Despite the fact that it was now wholly owned by the Foundation, the directors referred to themselves as 'partners' of Barings. The ethos was that different 'partners' would report what was going on in their part of the bank, and how things were going. It would have been regarded as indelicate for one to start quizzing another aggressively about his part of the business. If there was ever an awkward confrontation, it would not take place in a forum like a committee. It would have been a departure from tradition for anyone to start demanding explanations about the missing £50 million. It did not happen. No one seeing the formal management structure of Barings could guess that the charts counted for little. In practice the management and executive committees carried out only gentle overseeing of the managers below them. The story of the missing £50 million filtered to the top of Barings' management structure only to be noted in passing, and then ignored.

On Tuesday the Tokyo traders went for a night out with the futures and options sales desk, and debt traders. Now that they were all part of the same group under Baker, Gueler wanted to find a way of cementing some friendships. Spirits were high. The year had started very well, and the new group was making a lot of money. The profits flowing from Leeson had been extraordinary and he had taken care to subsidize the other books generously. By now the financial products group had shed some of its old inhibitions from the days of the doom and gloom room. Some traders were now happy to show they could be just as exuberant as any of Baring Securities' equity brokers during the 1980s bubble. They were living through their own bubble of profits, this time created by a single man rather than a government. This was just as intoxicating. Many had come as analysts and researchers. Like the foreign language teachers who were first recruited by Heath in the 1980s, they had arrived with a technical skill, rather than an aptitude for trading. It had now become more of a buzz to make money than devise spreadsheets. Despite the new mood Gueler remained a stickler for a good deal. He dug out what he regarded as the perfect venue: a bar in Tokyo called the Sapporo Beer Hall. The party could be entertained for $30 a head, with beer for everyone.

They started playing drinking games at the start of the evening. Then one of the traders threw some meat at others sitting at a different table. Soon a full-scale food fight developed and they only narrowly escaped being ejected.

By this time in Singapore Railton was growing seriously worried at what he was discovering. His first task had been to track the margin payments that he and Granger had made to Singapore to cover Leeson's daily requests. By Wednesday 15 February Railton could not get the figures to reconcile and realized that his worst fear of December was true. The breakdown of figures between customer and house accounts was meaningless. Nisa Kader, one of the settlement clerks, was simply changing figures in accordance with Leeson's instructions to make up the total. Railton did not suspect Leeson of a deliberate fraud; he simply thought he had been covering up chaos in the back office. Leeson, meanwhile, had been frantically trying to cover his tracks. He had encouraged Railton to start by reconciling his JGB trading, with which he had lost about Y12 billion (£81 million) in five eights during the previous six weeks. On Wednesday, as Norris arrived in Singapore, Leeson altered the accounts by making a fictitious purchase of 7,000 contracts 745 points below the market price. This created a gain of £170 million in the accounts, which he reversed the following day, allowing him to show the requisite profit. Leeson was now hanging on by his fingertips as Railton unscrambled the mess. Railton's worst problem was that, when he reconciled margin payments with all the known trading, he came out Y14 billion (£95 million short). This gap was caused by the five eights account, which Railton had not counted. He reported his problem to Granger and Gamby in London. He thought he must have missed something that Leeson would be able to explain.[27]

Leeson was hard to pin down. He was not simply trying to avoid Railton, although that was part of the reason. He was also battling desperately to keep the Nikkei above 18,000. That Wednesday it toppled below the danger point, closing at 17,991. Leeson was now buying frantically, throwing Barings' cash away. He ordered Seow into the Nikkei pit to buy each time the market moved below 18,000 and was himself doubling up in the JGB pit. He had gone beyond restraint. Five eights now held more than 50,000 Nikkei futures and 27,000 JGB futures. The Nikkei strained to fall into a lower range.

The only thing stopping it was Leeson. He was slowly being dragged towards the edge of a precipice no matter how hard he pulled in the other direction. On Thursday it dropped 210 points to 17,781. Nothing that Leeson could do would stop it. He was over the edge and falling. When he came off the trading floor at 2.15 p.m., Leeson knew in his heart there was no hope left. He had two hours to prepare himself, for at 4.30 p.m. he was due to meet the bank's chief executive. Norris spent the day looking around Baring Securities in Singapore before his talks with McIntosh the next day. He had breakfast with Bax and they lunched together on Boat Quay. They discussed Norris's visit to Kuala Lumpur and Bangkok, both of which came under Bax, and Norris sounded him out about what he wanted to do next. Loretta, Bax's wife, wanted to return to London by 1997 and Norris thought Bax could be the right man to take over equity broking at Barings in London from Fraser in due course.

His last meeting of the day was with Leeson. As Leeson came up to the twenty-fourth floor he had to go into the men's toilets to be sick because he was so gripped by nerves. He need not have worried. Norris did not have any inclination to quiz him, particularly when he saw Leeson sweating slightly, though in an open-necked shirt. Norris did not mention the SLK deal. He wanted to get this meeting over as fast as possible. The two men talked a little about the market, and Leeson stammered an explanation of his switching book and the ticks and turns he could give to customers. It was largely incomprehensible to Norris. He had never been a trader himself, and the floor of a futures exchange was an alien world. In any case Norris was as impatient as ever. He was hardly taking in what Leeson said. He did not raise the story of the missing £50 million, or even question Leeson over the strain he had been imposing on the funding from London. It was his last chance to save his bank, but he did not pause long enough to see what a mess the young man sitting in front of him was in. Norris soon ushered Leeson out, and turned his mind to other things. That evening they both attended a dinner at the local Polo Club, but they did not talk again. Although Norris's cursory inspection of Leeson had failed to alert him, directors in London were still concerned about the trading. At midnight Singapore time, the Alco again discussed Leeson's trading in London. It decided to set overall limits on switching and to instruct Leeson that he should not increase his trading.

The following morning Diarmaid Kelly heard a rumour that Barings was in trouble. It was the second one of the week. On Wednesday a director of Schroders had phoned Peers in London. He told Peers of a rumour that a US bank had terminated positions with Barings after discovering its mystery customer had defaulted on 20,000 Nikkei futures. This time, the rumour came from Hong Kong. A fund manager at Jardine Fleming had rung the Hong Kong office to pass on rumours that it was in trouble, and some fund managers might not deal through it any more. Kelly had been warning fruitlessly for over two months about the Customer X rumours. Now he had had enough. At 8.27 a.m. he decided to ring Ron Baker directly to find out exactly what was going on. In Bishopsgate Baker was taken aback to be rung by Kelly. As far as he was concerned any information he gave Kelly about Barings' switching would go straight into the market. He played a very straight bat.

'You couldn't just run me through where we are on these Japanese futures?' Kelly inquired silkily.

'Er, in what respect?' Baker asked guardedly.

'I'm just trying to work out what our positions are at the moment, either for ourselves or on behalf of clients. You know, whether most of them are matched, or if they are open positions, or whatever,' pressed Kelly.

'Well, we have no delta position . . . let me come back to you with what our open contracts are,' said Baker, fencing.

'Um, okay, it's very difficult to get a straight answer out of the Tokyo office. I don't think they know.'

'Yeah, I mean I hear you, but I wouldn't want it to go to a customer.'

Kelly moved smoothly up a gear. 'No, we're not going to tell a client, Ron. We're slightly in the dark here, trying to cope with other brokers telling the clients that we are bust,' he said pointedly.

Baker started to explain what he thought was the illusion of the Osaka long futures. 'On that list, we'll come out with quite a massive exposure on Osaka . . . and if you just look at that in isolation, which people would be entitled to in Japan, it would appear as if we had an extremely large position.'

Kelly pointed out he had been told that Barings held 20,000 long futures for three customers. 'I'm just trying to work out what our position is, because no one here knows. I'm not worried about the risk of it, because I'm satisfied that you all know what's going on, but I have no idea how to explain to someone what the position is.'

Baker attempted to fend him off. 'You see, the thing is, that's very useful information to a client that's going to try and work out which way round we are, and squeeze us.'

Kelly let his irritation show a little. 'We're not going to tell them what position we're in, Ron. It would be nice just to explain internally to people here that we are not going under, and certainly explain to clients, who are I suspect soon going to stop dealing with us because of the competition telling them we are a risk. I mean, there's some quite big firms telling them . . . "Don't deal with Barings."'

'Oh, these are our competitors now. Would we say the same thing about them?'

'Good God, no!'

'Why?'

'We would never ever say about a competitor that a client shouldn't deal with them . . . We might say his research is crap. That's different. We'd never suggest a client couldn't deal with them on fair value. Awful thing to do, even when it's the case.'

'I'm not sure that giving up information is a way of solving that, Diarmaid.'

'No, we are not giving out information. *I just want to know!*' Kelly said sharply.

Baker promised to get back to him.

Baker rang back half an hour later to confirm that Barings was long 20,076 futures in Osaka.

'So we're long 20,076, and we're short of the same amount in Simex, is that right?' Kelly asked.

'Yes, I'll come round to you later and sit down for twenty minutes with Mary Walz. We'll just go through everything bit by bit, so it's really very clear what's happening,' Baker replied.

'That would be kind, because . . . we can't explain these things at all, or decide what to say, if we don't fully know what it is.'

'Let's say I try and get around about 11.30.'

'Fantastic, Ron. I'll see you later.'[28]

Seven minutes later, at 9.03 a.m., Kelly was back on the line. 'Ron, sorry it's Diarmaid again, because we're under pressure, certainly in

Hong Kong, to have something to say to people before Jardine Fleming sort of stop dealing with us. Apparently, it's gone out on the Morgan Stanley, Goldman Sachs morning wire to be careful about using Barings as a counter-party.' This time, Kelly was not going to be diplomatic in not pressing for information. 'Am I right in thinking that we have three big clients, and these positions tend to arise when one of these big three, which are what? The Bermuda hedge fund, and who are the other two?' asked Kelly.

'I really don't want to go into . . . we can't tell JF who our customers are,' Baker insisted.

'I am not going to tell JF.'

'I don't want to tell the Hong Kong sales force.'

'I am not going to tell the Hong Kong sales force.'

'I'm not sure it's correct to say we have three big customers,' Baker tried to stall.

'Ron, look, it's *me* talking to you,' said Kelly in desperation. 'I haven't decided what we will say to clients . . . Forget about the customers, forget about Flemings, forget about Morgan Stanley. I'm just asking you as a member of Baring Investment Bank Management Committee, *who the customers are that we are dealing with*.'

'There's a list of them, Diarmaid.'

'Well, who are the big ones, just so I know?' Kelly pleaded.

'The hedge fund in Bermuda, Tiger and Refco,' Baker conceded.

'So apart from this slightly strange guy, these are all big players in the futures world.'

'Yeah.'

'So that's the anodyne answer to that: big and known futures players.'

'Yeah.'

'So what happens is these guys come on and give an order in Simex, which they prefer to deal in because it's more efficient blah de blah, correct?' Kelly asked.

'Yeah.'

'So Simex doesn't have the volume, so we do it in Osaka, and then sell them a Simex contract exactly matching the one that was bought in Osaka?'

'Exactly.'

They discussed the risks, touching on the question of the exposure to the Osaka exchange. 'For Bank of England purpose, what we're trying to do is have someone like Sanwa Bank stand between us and the [Osaka exchange],' Baker explained.

'There is a European Union regulation, isn't there?' Kelly asked.

'It's more Bank of England. It's been there for a while . . . the Bank of England get a bit niggly, but we are trying to pay a bit of money away to Sanwa Bank. We've got to pay them to take the Osaka exchange rather than us. They must think we're idiots.'

Kelly turned to the question of what Customer X was doing. 'Do we happen to know out of interest why these guys are playing?' he asked.

Baker explained that he thought the hedge funds were trying to go short volatility. 'By keeping Nikkei trading in a tight range, volatility has fallen and they have made a bit of money out of that.'

'At the moment, it's manifesting itself by going long of the futures, stop the market falling by implication.'

'Yep, yep.'

Kelly started to question Baker about the way Barings paid margin, pressing to find out if there was any risk from a hedge fund collapsing. 'We put up margin on behalf of customers to Simex?' he asked.

'Yep.'

'We collect it?'

'Yep, so we're holding it in advance,' said Baker, wrongly.

'Yeah sure, but our risk could be a cock-up in settlement. That would be a funding thing.'

'We will always hold margin on behalf of a customer before we posted it.'

'OK.'

'But we are a bank with a billion US dollars of capital. We have substantial funding lines and credit lines in Singapore,' Baker went on.

'Absolutely. The only risk is a funding risk, whereby for some reason or another because of some cock-up in settlements . . . we haven't called the margin off the clients,' said Kelly, putting his finger on exactly the reason why Barings was about to collapse.

'Simex comes to us for the margin.'

Kelly ran through a version of the story for external consumption. 'OK, so I wouldn't be out of order if we told clients that the position

317

they see in Osaka represents a facilitation for agency trades that we're doing in Simex,' he said.

'Yeah, you wouldn't be out of order.'

'Therefore, there is an equal and opposite matching position in Simex, which they can't see . . . therefore I can say we do have a risk to the Osaka stock exchange.'

'Yep.'

'Which you don't mind revealing.'

'Yep.'

'And also that Simex is the counter-party, and not the client.'

'The reason is, we are the major agency broker in Simex . . . if Morgan Stanley and others were in Simex and doing as much business as we are, then they would have similar profiles, but they can't get in there, and they'd love to be in there,' Baker elaborated.

'Right, now could you get your guy in Hong Kong to stomp on to the floor, and gather some of the more senior people around him and explain just that, so that when their clients ring up they can rebut it?' Kelly asked, reassured at last.[29]

It was one of Baker's final tasks before going on holiday. He flew off to Verbier the following morning in a party including his daughter and two friends from Australia. But Baker was not contented. He had spent several weeks trying to get Leeson to reduce his trading on Simex and Osaka, but it seemed only to have grown. Baker was now getting angry. It appeared that Leeson was deliberately defying him.

As the positions had grown that week, Gueler had been bemused and rang up Leeson to ask what was going on. 'What are you doing? I can't believe you did that,' Gueler said. Later on Friday 17 February Walz and Baker became irritated when they saw the Osaka figures for the day. They showed Leeson had put Barings' positions up by 2,000 contracts and had not telephoned them to explain it. Baker was in a foul mood. On Saturday he tried to ring Gueler from Verbier because Leeson was avoiding his call. On Sunday night at 8.00 p.m. he talked to Walz to see if she had reached Leeson. She had not, so Baker rang Leeson himself as soon as he got off the phone. It was 4.00 a.m. in Singapore, but he did not care about waking Leeson up. He left a message on the answering machine. Leeson called him back two hours later. Baker did not mince his words: there was no excuse for Leeson not reducing positions. 'If you lose $1 million getting them down, it's money well spent. I want them at 10,000 by the time I'm back. Do you understand?'

'I understand completely,' replied Leeson.

'If those positions are not reduced, I'm going to come down there personally, and sort you out.'

'I hear you,' Leeson said.

An hour later Leeson picked up Argyropoulous at his apartment. He had also been driving Railton into Ocean Towers from his hotel so that he could keep an eye on him. 'Baker just called, and ripped me a new arsehole,' he said ruefully. He appeared ready to obey, but in practice he could not do so without removing the last prop from the Nikkei. Too many investors were now hedging themselves against the Nikkei dropping by buying short futures. It meant more attention than ever was focused on the Barings overhang. That morning an analyst at Goldman Sachs in Tokyo sent a research note to customers that discussed what Barings was doing. It was headlined 'Tug o' War' and talked about a tussle between Barings and investors selling futures through other investment banks. 'One broker (who shall be unnamed, but not unknown) has enormous open interest in March Osaka Nikkei 225 futures . . . Their position and net change of open interest seem to indicate a "line in the sand" at the 18,000 level. Their futures activity increases when the cash market approaches or breaches that level,' the analyst wrote. He warned Goldman Sachs's customers to prepare for a further fall in the Nikkei. 'Once the trend asserts itself, it is usually both persistent and forceful,' the note said.[30] If Leeson obeyed Baker this fall would come sooner. He could not afford just to let the index drop away from 18,000. Instead Leeson closed some Nikkei futures in Osaka to make it appear as if he was obeying, and added some more in Simex. His futures in five eights now comprised half of the entire March futures market.[31]

Leeson, the Nikkei and Barings were all near to collapse by Monday evening. Railton was trying to find Leeson to talk about the missing £95 million, but he did not return to the fourteenth floor of Ocean Towers, saying he was sick. At 4.48 p.m. in Tokyo Gueler called Walz to pass on the news that Leeson seemed to have reduced his trading positions at last. The Osaka figure had fallen by 1,900 futures. 'Mary, how's it going?' he asked.

'Good. How are you,' replied Walz.

'Not too bad. Nick reduced the position by 19,000.'

'Nineteen hundred, I think you mean.'

'Nineteen hundred, I meant.'

'Good.'

Gueler said he had been chatting to Wendy Carpenter, whom Baker wanted to replace Killian in Tokyo.

'He's outta here,' Walz said briskly when Gueler mentioned Killian.

'She said, "My long-term plans don't really include him." So I don't think he's going to be sticking around,' Gueler confirmed.

They went on to discuss the state of the market and Leeson's trading. 'Well, I think it's good to unwind this, because it's just getting detrimental now. All these rumours and things we have to deal with,' said Gueler, mentioning another analyst's note on Barings.

'That's interesting.'

'We're long 20,000.'

'How can we be long 20,000? We should be down.'

'That's open interest, that's open interest, ummm,' said Gueler, confused.

'We should be down below that.'

'Yeah, we should be down below that. We've reduced the position by a lot. How come . . . ?' Gueler trailed off before Walz realized he was looking at Friday's figure on Osaka. 'So now, we're down to 18,100,' Gueler said. He read out the names of the forces now massing against Leeson and Barings. 'The big open interest on the other side are Daiwa, Nomura, Morgan Stanley, and Goldman Sachs and Nikko.'

'Like how big? Who's got the biggest? Nomura?' Walz asked.

'No. Daiwa is 7,000. Nomura and Morgan Stanley are 6,000. Goldman and Nikko are about 3,300ish,' Gueler reported.

'Really? They have grown considerably because the only one who had a decent-size position of above 5,000 was Nomura I thought, so Daiwa's come out of the woodwork. What does that mean? Nothing, I guess.'

'Yeah. They all got short,' said Gueler, musing innocently on the menace at their door.

'Yeah. Pretty funny.'

They talked about the rumours that Barings was in trouble, and Gueler related how he had bought futures on Simex earlier in the day for the arbitrage book. 'So we were buying, buying, buying on Simex, and Nick calls up and says, "This is really visual, you guys, everyone in the market knows this."' He recounted how a trader called Chris Taylor had been joking that other firms thought Barings was being funded by Japanese gangsters who were laundering money. 'Chris Taylor says, "Ferd, forwarding to you a report from Goldman Sachs . . . Fernando Gueler seen arm-in-arm with a burly, curly-haired Japanese man [from the] Shinjuku district."'

Walz started laughing.

'It's getting ridiculous, but it's good, it's good. It's being reduced . . .' Gueler said.

They discussed how Baker had called up Leeson that morning. 'Apparently, Nick said, "Ron read me the Riot Act of 1792 or whatever,"' Gueler said.

'Yeah, well we talked about it on Friday, and it was of some concern that we increased it by 2,000 and didn't get a phone call in explanation of it.' Walz thought Leeson had been trying to be macho by keeping his position: 'It's much more manly to prove you can cut it down so you control it, rather than to just keep taking money, and stuffing it up.' She related her conversation with Baker. 'I counted the hours for him, and told him what time it was in Singapore relative to Switzerland or France, or wherever the hell he is . . . He must have just hung up and picked up the phone to Nick because he called him at about four in the morning,' she said, laughing.

'Oh, that's good . . . I'm really glad Ron did it. I'm on the phone with Nick. I said, "Nick, man, you know" . . . it's like the joke is to try and bring him down to it.'

'Yeah.'

'It's really difficult to dissuade Nick, when Nick goes, "Fuck, man," and you know today he has to sit down and forgo . . . I said, "Nick, man, I know just how you feel, OK? . . . I mean we're just at capacity, you know."'

'I'm not sure we're at capacity, so much as we're at credibility capacity. We need to prove that it's OK.'[32]

That afternoon the management committee had once again talked about Leeson and the rumours that Barings was in trouble. Norris emphasized that Leeson's positions were being reduced to prevent any further publicity. Fraser had moaned a little to Kelly about this *volte face*: 'It's just bloody typical. We go on about it for weeks, but it takes someone from Schroders to ring up for them to take it seriously.'

By now it was Tuesday morning in Singapore and within a few hours Leeson was on his way to Simex once again. He was gradually being put under pressure by Railton, who was still nervous of him but had insisted on a meeting that evening. The Nikkei was hovering just above 18,000, closing at 18,096. There was no doubt about the direction that it was heading. Leeson and Railton met late that afternoon in a conference room at Ocean Towers. Dusk was falling but Leeson did not switch on the lights. As they talked over the missing cash, it grew darker and darker in the room. Railton started to have difficulty making Leeson out. 'I am too tired to discuss it. Let's talk about something else,' Leeson said. They switched the subject to the pay Railton should expect if he moved to Singapore now that he and his wife, who was visiting, had decided they wanted to settle there. If Railton replaced Hassan that would be the end of Leeson, but he had no intention of being around that long. He had persuaded Lisa the previous weekend to leave Singapore as soon as he got his bonus. He was stringing things out, hour by hour.

On that Tuesday morning in London Walz asked Gueler on the phone about the rumour that Leeson was about to leave Barings. 'Are we going to lose Nick to Morgan Stanley? That's everybody's favourite rumour.'

'I heard all this stuff, and I don't know what's going on,' Gueler replied.

'You know, I'm sick of these scumbag bond guys. They are just like the tackiest, most rumour-driven people . . . It's unhealthy and it's stupid. I mean it all comes from rumours.' Walz believed the rumour was being spread around by Lee Knight, who traded bonds in the financial products group in Tokyo, and had the reputation of being a keen gossip.

'Believe me, I never heard anything from Lee.'

'It all comes from Lee. Lee must have told like ten people.'

'Ah-hah.'

'I don't know where he gets it, you know. Bond people are scumbags. We're going to turn this equity thing into the most hot-arse professional thing,' Walz said defiantly.[33]

On Wednesday morning Leeson returned to Simex. He had distracted Railton's inquiries for one day. He had almost started to relax.

But it could not last. The day he had feared for so long had arrived. He no longer had any hope and so all the tension was evaporating. He had lost. An eerie calm had broken out in the market as everybody waited for the plunge below 18,000. Nobody thought that Customer X could hold it back any longer. Leeson watched the market drifting up and down. He had virtually fixed in his mind that he had to leave when it broke 18,000 again. The five eights account contained so many Nikkei futures that each 10-point fall in the index cost Barings £1 million. Leeson had started the year with a loss of at least £200 million latent in five eights but he had thrown so much away in six weeks that it was now Y70 billion (£470 million) in loss. But the truce continued one more day. The Nikkei closed slightly up at 18,109. During Leeson's struggle the rest of the market had gained a grudging respect for Mr X. Whoever he was, he was brave. That morning Goldman Sachs had published another research note on the Barings overhang. 'The investor behind the large futures position is certainly very determined,' it said.[34] The market could talk about little else. At midday Leeson got a call from Darren McDermott, a reporter with the news service Associated Press. 'There is a lot of talk about your guy taking big positions,' McDermott said. Leeson was calm. 'Yes, we've been getting questions about this,' he said neutrally, and added that the futures were balanced: 'At the end of the day, we're even.'

That evening he met Railton again at Ocean Towers and finally allowed him to quiz him about the £95 million. Railton pointed out that Barings seemed to be missing Y140 billion. He expected Leeson to come up with an explanation but Leeson appeared unworried. 'Yes, I agree with you,' he said calmly,[35] adding that Railton would have to find some more information to sort it out. Then he went home, leaving the problem still preying on Railton's mind.

At the same time in London Norris was chatting on the phone with Baker in Verbier. Baker had taken another break from skiing to discuss the hiring of Bill Sproule, but Norris had some news for him. Baker was to join the management committee in place of Ian Hopkins, rather than simply reporting through George Maclean. Baker had long coveted a seat around the table with the others who ran Baring Investment Bank. Despite all the profits Baker had brought to Barings, somebody like Kelly could still pull rank by saying he was a member of the management committee. This would change now. Norris gave

Baker a little gossip, as if inducting him to a secret society: he would notice that Fraser and Tuckey did not get on. Fraser was a broker at heart and too outspoken for Tuckey's tastes; Tuckey preferred the discreet ways of Baring Brothers. If there was something tricky, Tuckey liked to solve it outside the meeting and then present it as a *fait accompli*. Baker would learn all this when he joined the élite ranks. Baker was pleased, although he was surprised to be put there in place of Hopkins. He wondered if Hopkins would suspect him of engineering it.

On the morning of Thursday 23 February Gueler was called by Leeson as he sat at his desk in Tokyo. Leeson seemed oddly calm. The tension of the Simex trading floor was absent from his voice. 'How's life?' he asked, seemingly happy to chat rather than trade. 'Well, you seem in an especially good mood today,' Gueler remarked. Leeson did not reply. The market was far more turbulent that Thursday. It opened slightly up, then started falling. The weight of selling that had been long expected finally came. The Nikkei dropped through 18,000. Leeson's losses were spiralling. In addition to his Nikkei losses, he was losing £8.5 million for each 10-point rise in JGBs. JGBs gained as rapidly as the Nikkei fell. Leeson hardly bothered to trade; there was little point. In mid-morning he gave a tour of the floor to a new local. Then he had to cope with Railton, who was again trying to get information out of him. Leeson evaded him by doing some trading in the JGB pit, rolling March futures over into June. It made no difference but it distracted him. Railton gave up after Leeson agreed to meet him at Ocean Towers in the afternoon. The index carried on falling, dropping 277 points to close at 17,830. By the time the bell rang the five eights account had lost £65 million on the Nikkei, £61 million on JGBs and £17 million on his options. In a single day £143 million of Barings' money had disappeared without trace. It was the end. Leeson knew his time as a trader was over. He could either wait for his pursuers to catch him, or run. Wearing his blue and yellow jacket he walked out of Simex for the last time.

Leeson was not the only one who had troubles. Argyropoulous was $130,000 down that day for FCT as a result of the JGB rally. He had been having a bad month, was $400,000 down and had been grumbling about it. The previous week he had told Leeson he was having a very bad day and had been taken aback when Leeson laughed. Leeson apologized. 'You know, I wouldn't usually laugh, but in comparison with the kind of day I've been having, it's a walk in the park,' he explained. Seow had an awkward problem. He had been caught swearing again in the pit, and had been banned for a month. He and Leaning were going for a drink that afternoon at a bar on Boat Quay called the Escape Club which had a pink neon sign and had been decorated like a beach bar. They asked Leeson along, and they went at about 3.00 p.m. There was a table in one corner under a fake palm tree, and Leaning, Seow and Leeson sat there while Leeson pondered silently what he had to do. The traders had already been planning a weekend away in Phuket, the beach resort in southern Thailand, where they would play golf. After an hour Leeson had not got much closer to a plan, and was due back in the office to see Railton. He returned to Ocean Towers to find that storm clouds were gathering. An assistant to Hawes had sent a fax through to Singapore questioning Leeson's call for $45 million in margin funds the previous day and why the figure was rising when Leeson was supposed to be reducing his positions. The fax said it was hard to understand this: 'There is something very odd here.'

The memorandum was addressed to Hawes, who was due to fly in that night from Tokyo following his talks with Sanwa. However, Jones had seen it and started to question Leeson about it when he arrived on the twenty-fourth floor of Ocean Towers. Leeson told Jones that he had to leave early that afternoon to look after Lisa, who had suffered a miscarriage. Jones, Railton and Leeson went down to the fourteenth-floor office together, but after a few minutes Leeson slipped away. It was to be the last time they saw him. Leeson could remain no longer. He had dragged things out for two and a half years, but he was finally about to be discovered. He went down to the underground car park and got into a blue Mercedes which he had borrowed from Teo Fai, who was in Hong Kong. Then he phoned Argyropoulous to arrange to meet him at the McDonald's close to his flat. They had a coffee, then sat around watching videos of football matches for a while. Leeson started to talk about his problems, saying he had lost money but he did not reveal the full extent of the disaster. 'Should I face the music or not?' he asked Argyropoulous. Eventually he came to a decision: 'Fuck it, I'm going away for a long weekend.'

Argyropoulous told him to remain professional. 'I've had a bad day too, but I am going in tomorrow,' he said. But he could not dissuade him. 'Don't tell Lisa about this,' Leeson said. He went home and persuaded Lisa that he had to get away immediately. They packed their bags and Argyropoulous drove them to the airport.

Lisa, who did not realize the gravity of what was happening, was cheerful on the drive to the airport, insisting that they stopped to return a video disc and pick up their deposit at a video store. She and Argyropoulous joked about Leeson being Reginald Perrin, the hero of a British comedy series, who abandons his job. They got to Changi airport at 7.00 p.m., agreeing to meet the others at Phuket that week-end. As they said goodbye Lisa took Argyropoulous aside to tell him she had left behind her birthday card for Leeson in the rush. It was his twenty-eighth birthday on Saturday and she asked Argyropoulous to bring another one to Phuket, and to remind a friend coming out from Britain to bring them a jar of powdered milk. Leeson asked him to take the Mercedes back to the Golden Shoe car park in Singapore and hand the keys to Teo Fai when he returned from Hong Kong.

The Leesons flew out to Kuala Lumpur and checked into the Regent Hotel at about 10.00 p.m. Leeson left an imprint of his company credit card to demonstrate his good standing. Even if the young couple before the desk clerks ran out without paying, it was reassuring that the name of Barings stood behind them. Leeson had booked tickets to Phuket the previous week, but they were from Singapore so they would have to find another way to get there. But that was a problem for another day. They went to sleep, Lisa still half-amused by what they had done. Leeson had not told her much beyond insisting that he was under strain and they must leave. He had done what he felt she would have wanted; bonuses would start being paid the following day.

By the time the Leesons arrived at the Regent Hotel Jones and Railton had been at work with Yong on the fourteenth floor of Ocean Towers for several hours, trying to discover the reason for the £95 million gap and Leeson's escalating margin calls. By 9.30 p.m., they had not managed to solve it and Jones and Yong went home. Railton rang Granger to pass on the news. He told her there were problems and they could not reach Leeson at home or on his mobile phone. But Jones was still confident that it could be cleared up the following day. As a token of their seriousness Jones was going to insist that Leeson came to the Baring Futures office first thing the next morning. No matter what Leeson said, he was not going back to the Simex floor until they resolved it. It was 2.00 p.m. in London, and Granger went in to see Gamby later that afternoon to tell him. Gamby was not happy. The idea that they could not track down Leeson disturbed him. The questions had been going on a long time without answers. For the first time Gamby put a sinister interpretation on everything they knew. Perhaps Leeson had realized the mess was out of control and had transferred some of Barings' money to his bank account. Gamby put on his coat and set off for America Square. He walked into Norris's office just before 4.00 p.m., as the Leesons slept in Kuala Lumpur. 'I could be about to make a big fool of myself here, but I think we've got a problem,' Gamby told Norris.

EPILOGUE

In spite of the fears of the bankers who had spent the weekend vainly trying to save Barings, the Nikkei did not fall catastrophically when the Tokyo Stock Exchange opened at midnight on Sunday, London time. On his Toshiba laptop, made by one of the Japanese companies whose rise had created Heath's fortune, Terry Burns watched the Nikkei dip sharply. Then the nerves of investors around the world held, and it bounced back to close 664 points down at 16,809. This was a fall of just 3.8 per cent, less than half the amount feared by the London bankers. As things had turned out, the Sultan of Brunei might have got a bargain by taking on the futures and options in the five eights account. The exaggerated fears could be excused. From the Bank of England, the collapse of Britain's oldest merchant bank had appeared to be a calamitous event; in the world's bond, share and derivatives markets, the loss of a bank with only £308 million in share capital caused only a few ripples. The loss of Baring Brothers & Co. in 1890, at the height of its powers, had been absorbed smoothly. How much more easily did Barings plc, a small bank with a great name, disappear into the vast pool of the world's capital markets a little over a century later. At a stroke all the equity that Lord Ashburton had handed over to the Baring Foundation passed instead to the investment banks that had bought the short side of the futures Leeson amassed in January and February. From them it passed on to a web of investors and hedge funds that had listened to all the rumours the directors of Barings had spent a month ignoring.

On Monday afternoon Peter Baring telephoned the *Financial Times* to say he would like to talk about what had happened. At 4.00 p.m., he met John Gapper and Richard Lambert, the *FT*'s editor, in his office next to Tuckey's. It was not a large room, plainly decorated with a few watercolours. Even at work Baring maintained a puritan discipline. He described calmly how Norris had broken the news to him on Friday, and the weekend efforts to rescue the bank. Baring still did not comprehend the full extent of Leeson's deception. 'Of course, what happened should not have happened. It would be idle to think otherwise but I think that it could only have happened quickly. If it had happened over a long period of time, I am confident that we would have caught it,' he claimed. His least cautious remark was when he let slip the Customer X rumour. 'Let us suppose that the putative associate approached our trader, and said: "You should build up a hidden long position at Barings such that when they find it, they can never remain solvent. I will build up an equal and opposite short position. When Barings duly fails we will have a wonderful chance of making a profit,"' Baring said.[1] He added that this appeared to be a sensible explanation. It was an unwise remark. Baring did not intend to offer it as an excuse, but it triggered a burst of public recrimination and he was immediately accused of trying to distract attention from the weaknesses of the bank's management. The Bank of England had not found any evidence of a single investor being on the other side of the futures and options trades during the weekend. Despite this, rumours persisted that Leeson had opened a secret bank account which held £20 million of Barings' money. Investigators tried to track down a story that Leeson had opened six more accounts in Germany in April 1994. They did not find any evidence that it was true, although the story later surfaced in both British and German newspapers.

While Peter Baring was elaborating the conspiracy theory the Leesons were sitting out the uproar in a beach resort on the north coast of Borneo. By coincidence they were not far from Brunei. The couple had tried to get to Phuket from Kuala Lumpur on Friday, but all flights were full. Instead they had flown to the resort of Kota Kinabalu in Malaysia. Leeson had been trying to avoid facing up to the extent of the havoc he had caused, but in Kota Kinabalu he discovered the truth. The Leesons tried to get a flight to London but could not find one, and instead settled on a Royal Brunei flight to Frankfurt on Wednesday morning. After stops in Brunei, Bangkok and Abu Dhabi, they arrived in Germany early on Friday morning, 3 March. Leeson was arrested and locked up in Höchst prison in Frankfurt. Lisa flew back to Britain on a private plane chartered by the *Daily Mirror*, and gave an interview protesting at stories portraying her husband as a high-living criminal. He still had not confessed what he had done, and she believed he was only a pawn, an illusion helped by the disclosures which had started to surface about the weaknesses in Barings' management. On Thursday the *Financial Times* contained details of the August internal audit report as well as the five eights account.

While the recriminations mounted Barings remained in administration, unable to trade or pay any of its debts. The company was being run by a team of administrators from Ernst and Young, which was trying to pick a buyer from among all the banks and investment banks that had expressed interest. It was hard work. In theory a London merchant bank was a plum acquisition. Barings could probably have gained £1 billion by putting itself up for auction a few weeks before, but it was harder now. Not only did it have a loss of £830 million from Leeson's trading, but it owed $100 million to the holders of bonds issued in 1986, when Sir John Baring established Barings plc, and $150 million to holders of bonds issued in the spring of 1994 which had helped to fill the 'black hole' at Baring Securities. Anybody wanting to buy Barings faced having to spend £600 million to pay off debts, before putting fresh capital into the business. This meant paying £1 billion for a bank that might still have hidden losses. Furthermore, most banks did not want to buy the whole thing. ABN Amro had now decided that it wanted the merchant bank and BAM, but did not want Baring Securities because it overlapped with Hoare Govett. The Dutch bank struck a deal with Smith Barney to make a joint bid, with Smith Barney taking Baring Securities. It was fine by the merchant bankers of 8 Bishopsgate, who wanted a divorce from Baring Securities and had tried to find a separate buyer for themselves. However, it did not suit the administrators, who wanted to keep the whole business together for the sake of neatness, and sell it to a single buyer.

They found one in International Nederlanden Group, the Dutch bank formed by a merger between the Dutch postal bank and the insurance company National Nederlanden. ING was the main rival to ABN in the Netherlands but lacked its larger rival's investment banking strength. The bank had about £1 billion in spare capital and had been looking for an acquisition. At the start of the week Robert Fleming had decided to tout for business among potential buyers of Barings. A team of corporate financiers led by Bernard Taylor, a merchant banker who had moved from Barings to Flemings in 1993, contacted ING and persuaded it to make a bid. Instead of taking on all the liabilities by making an offer for the whole company, it offered to buy Barings Brothers, Baring Securities and BAM separately. This had the effect of lopping the head off the company, leaving the bond-holders virtually unpaid. By putting in £660 million in cash, ING could pay Barings' immediate debts and have £200 million in new capital. The Baring Foundation received a nominal £1 for handing over ownership, compared with the £1 billion that it could have expected a week before, but it was ideal for the administrators because it meant Barings would avoid having to be liquidated. If that had occurred, not only would the bondholders have lost all their money but all the cash on deposit at Barings would have been at risk. This included money placed in the bank by Baring Asset Management on behalf of its customers and could have meant the Queen losing money, a possibility about which some newspapers had speculated eagerly.

Within ten days of the collapse the fourth-floor trading room at America Square was once more back in action. Apart from its futures and options operations Barings had resumed business as before. ING had not dismissed anyone although Norris and Baker had stepped down from day-to-day management. The Dutch bank was in an awk-ward position because the government had set up an inquiry by the Board of Banking Supervision into the collapse. There was talk of it being completed within six weeks, and ING did not want to pre-empt this by dismissing anyone prematurely. It created an uneasy mood at Barings, since Aad Jacobs, the chairman of ING, had said that it appeared as though somebody in the bank had been helping Leeson. 'It is almost impossible that you can lose that kind of money . . . without the help of someone in the bank,' he said.[2] Similar thoughts emerged elsewhere. Andrew Baylis appeared on a BBC *Panorama* programme to say that 'the most senior people' at Barings must have known that cash was transferred to pay the margin calls. Baylis said it could not have happened when he had been there because it would have been picked up by what he called Richard Johnston's 'risk control unit'. He was talking before it emerged that Leeson had opened the five eights account, and been trading heavily through it, while Baylis was in charge of derivatives at Baring Securities.[3] Christopher Sharples, the chairman of the Securities and Futures Authority, said he believed it was 'extremely likely' that some of Barings' senior managers would lose their licence to practise in the City as investment bankers.

On 3 April Peter Baring and Andrew Tuckey resigned. Baring had offered his resignation just after the purchase by ING, but had been persuaded to stay on for the handover. Baring departed altogether, but Tuckey stayed on in a diminished role. In common with the other senior executives he had not taken his bonus for 1994, but he now reached an agreement with ING that he would be paid a fee of £100,000 a year as a 'consultant' to the corporate finance operation. ING wanted to retain his touch as an adviser to companies such as Lloyds Bank. On 1 May ING finally acted against the others it regarded as responsible for the collapse. It told twenty-one managers that it wanted their resignations. Those who refused were dismissed. In London it got rid of Norris, Baker, Barnett, Broadhurst, Gamby, Granger, Hawes, Hopkins, Maclean and Walz, as well as Helen Smith, the head of market risk under Hopkins. Some of them, such as Norris, who had always regarded himself as culpable in the collapse, left without any protest. Others, such as Maclean, were in any case close to retirement and went without too much fuss. Hopkins, who believed he had been prevented by Norris from tightening controls, was one who did not accept the verdict and insisted on being dismissed. In Singapore Bax, Jones and Wong left. In Tokyo Gueler and William Daniel, the office manager, resigned. Five Japanese managers left: Motoharu Hanawa, treasurer; Hideo Kaneko, head of settlements; Vincent Sue, risk manager; Satoshi Yamada, head of futures and options settlements; and Teruo Yashima, financial controller in the Osaka branch.

The effects of the collapse were not confined to Barings itself. The event was a profound shock for the merchant banks and brokers of the City of London. There had already been tremors in the autumn from Warburg's problems. This made depositors less willing to put their cash in merchant banks, when they could put it with clearing banks with vastly more capital for only a shade less interest. The Barings collapse concentrated minds powerfully. The Bank of England spent several days trying to reassure any depositors who pulled money out of merchant banks, and helped to calm nerves. But after the example of Barings, Schroders and others had to ring-fence cash held by their fund management arms to ensure that only a small proportion was held in the sister merchant bank. Beyond the problems of deposits the merchant banks faced the wider question of whether they could survive in the modern world. Not only did their capital base seem too small to cope with accidents, but it became clear their management could easily be overstretched. In a world where barriers had broken and global investment had come back, small merchant banks appeared to be sailing on too rough a sea. Barings had not faced any larger risks in the 1990s than in the 1890s, but technology and communications had changed since then, and merchant banks were no longer fitted for the task. The realization had come home strongly to David Scholey as he sat in the Bank of England on the weekend of the collapse, and he had started to steer Warburg rapidly towards safety in the arms of a larger bank with far deeper pockets.

On 9 May Scholey reached agreement with Swiss Bank Corporation to take over Warburg, creating an investment banking arm of Swiss Bank called SBC Warburg. Swiss Bank had a large balance sheet and expertise in derivatives. It had bought a Chicago futures and options partnership called O'Connor Associates in 1991, and moulded equity and bond trading around futures and options. Even more than the collapse of Barings, the take-over of Warburg signalled an end to the ambitions of British merchant banks to rival US investment banks. The US ratings agency Moody's Investor Services analysed their weaknesses in May: 'Although the London merchant banks once possessed unrivalled financial power, at its peak during the late nineteenth and early twentieth century . . . [they have] been undermined by lack of capital, weak franchises outside the UK, burdensome cost structures, and volatile profitability resulting from a greater degree of proprietory trading in the 1990s.' It told global investors that the industry was 'ripe for consolidation and acquisition'. This rapidly proved correct. On 6 June Kleinwort Benson agreed a £1 billion take-over by Dresdner Bank, the German bank. Take-overs were not confined to merchant banks. Smith New Court, the broking firm formed from Smith Brothers, the old jobber, during the Big Bang, was bought by Merrill Lynch for £526 million in July. It left only Schroders and Rothschilds as large independent merchant banks. Sir Evelyn de

Rothschild declared his intention for Rothschilds to stay that way, and Win Bischoff confirmed the same objective as he took over as chairman of Schroders.

In June Christopher Heath announced his return to investment banking. Since his ejection from Baring Securities, he had harboured ambitions to start again but it had taken longer than he had hoped to gain the backing of investors. He finally managed to get $50 million in start-up capital from investors including National Finance, a Thai bank, the life insurance company Equitable Life, and Caledonia Investments, the investment vehicle of the Cayser family. Heath's firm was to be called Caspian and would have offices in London and New York, concentrating on emerging markets in Latin America and Asia. This time he hired Andersen Consulting to build a single information technology network that would link all Caspian's offices. Heath snared an unexpected recruit as chairman. Rupert Pennant-Rea, who had resigned from the Bank in March after details of an extra-marital affair were published in the *Sunday Mirror*, agreed to become Caspian's non-executive chairman. Caspian's first hirings included Jeff Wecker, a Goldman Sachs derivatives trader who had arbitraged Japanese warrants against the Japanese stock market at the turn of the decade. Richard Greer left Barings to join Heath, while Jim Reed returned to the fold from Nomura. Heath also took back office staff from America Square and Neil Andrews rejoined him as the head of settlements. After two years away from the City, Heath was reforming his old family and getting back to the life on which he thrived.

By July Leeson was becoming frustrated. Singapore had filed a dozen charges against him, accusing him of 'cheating' Simex by not depositing the correct sums in margin and of fraud in concealing the £50 million hole in the year-end balance sheet. Meanwhile, the Serious Fraud Office had made a rapid inquiry into how Barings had collapsed, and found no evidence of wrong-doing by anybody in London. This meant there was not going to be any British challenge to Singapore's claim for Leeson's extradition. After his arrest Leeson had hired a solicitor called Stephen Pollard, from the London firm of Kingsley Napley. Now Pollard decided it was time to use their most powerful weapon: Lisa Leeson. He called a press conference, at which she appeared with Alec and Patsy Sims. At the press conference Pollard claimed that the trial should be held in London rather than Singapore, arguing that a Singapore trial would not cover the most important matters, including 'information, daily and monthly, communicated by Leeson to his superiors'. The strong implication was that somebody else was in league with Leeson, although the solicitor avoided saying so explicitly. Pollard knew his client was not actually going to suggest any such thing when it came to court. However, the substance was irrelevant to the main impact of the occasion, which was the sight of Lisa Leeson tearfully reading out an appeal from her husband not to allow him to be 'thrown to the wolves' in Singapore.[4] 'Leeson is happy for you to insert the name of your publication in the letter,' Pollard added helpfully at the end of the press conference.

Attention was focused even more sharply on the failure to control Leeson when the Board of Banking Supervision issued its 337-page report on 19 July. The board said there had been 'a failure of controls of management and other internal controls of the most basic kind' at Barings. The bank had had a lax control culture in which senior managers were not clear about their responsibilities. It blamed Barings for not recognizing that the freak profits from apparently riskless arbitrage could not be real, but this was the only failure for which Peter Baring and Andrew Tuckey were blamed by name. The larger share of the blame was allocated to the managers most directly involved, particularly Norris and Baker. Baker told investigators candidly: 'There is no doubt in my mind that my lack of experience in the area was a contributing factor to what happened.' Jones was criticized harshly. The report described his failure to separate Baring Futures' back office from trading, as he had indicated he would do in the August audit report, as 'reprehensible'. The report also criticized Coopers & Lybrand for failing to pick up Leeson's forgeries and fraud. Although the report noted that Barings shared out a higher proportion of operating profits than other investment banks, it did not accuse senior managers of having been careless because of greed. It concluded that other banks needed to learn lessons from the collapse. Banks now relied more on trading for profits, and 'rapid product innovation and sophisticated technology' had to be understood well by managers, who should visit their overseas operations regularly.

The Bank of England itself escaped relatively lightly. There had already been complaints that the Bank had avoided a rigorous inquiry into its own failure by having the collapse investigated by the Board of Banking Supervision, of which both George and Quinn were members. George argued that the inquiry would be fair because he and Quinn would not take part in drawing up the conclusions about the Bank. The most prominent damage suffered by the Bank was the resignation of Christopher Thompson, who had been in charge of supervising Barings and had allowed Maclean to advance more than 25 per cent of its capital to cover futures and options trading on the Osaka and Simex exchanges. He resigned just before the report was published, but he was the only Bank supervisor to do so. Quinn chose to sit out the storm, just as he had done two years before when the BCCI report was published. The report recommended that the Bank should toughen up its supervision, and suggested seventeen improvements.

This was not enough for the House of Commons Treasury and Civil Service select committee, which questioned George and Quinn fiercely three days after the publication of the report. The Labour MP Brian Sedgemore called for the resignation of Quinn. After two hours of questioning George finally snapped. He accused them of conducting a 'witch-hunt' against the Bank each time a bank got into difficulties. 'Actually getting able people to do the job is becoming damned difficult. How on earth do you think we get people . . . when you go through this kind of procedure every time there is a problem?' he asked.[5]

The collapse raised wider questions about supervision of banks and investment banks than whether the Bank of England carried out its duties properly. Barings was an institution that had been relatively easy to supervise in the first few years after the Bank was given formal supervisory powers in 1979. It had only a minor banking business, carrying out familiar transactions, such as acceptance credits, and underwriting share issues. That had changed with the growth of Baring Securities and the move into a more complex and international broking and trading operation. The Bank then had to share supervisory responsibilities with the Securities and Futures Authority in the UK and with other supervisors outside Britain. These included the Osaka and Simex exchanges, which were hardly on the best of terms since they were competing fiercely for business. The theory ran that all supervisors would cooperate to pass on information to one another around the world. In practice Simex had not told the Bank of England of any of its concerns, and certainly had not talked to Osaka. Simex itself made an effort to reform in the wake of the collapse, appointing a panel of experts to recommend changes. But the bigger question of how central banks and other supervisors could keep a proper eye on investment banks that sprawled over continents and financial activities remained. Banking and securities regulators had found it hard cooperating because they had different standards and methods, but the collapse gave a renewed impetus to discussions between banking, investment banking and insurance regulators.[6]

In September Leeson himself finally spoke directly about the collapse. He gave his version of events in an interview in Höchst prison with David Frost. He told a good story, albeit a partial one. He pointed out that the five eights account had originally been opened at the request of the London office. Leeson then told the story of Mitsuko's error and the evening in the Hard Rock Café. He claimed that the five eights account had lain dormant until then. It was a lie, since he had been using it heavily for more than six weeks by the time Mitsuko's error occurred. Leeson then went on to claim that five eights had only been used during 1992 to conceal the errors of traders under him. He did not admit that most of these 'errors' had been failed efforts to make himself look good by taking trading risk and legging trades. His audience would hardly have accepted his own description of these failed trades as 'errors' if he had explained it honestly. However, he was accomplished at bending the truth subtly for his own ends and portrayed himself as a victim of circumstance who had tried to save traders working for him, and had not been stopped by his superiors. Frost accepted the account without much question despite the fact that Leeson offered no plausible explanation for what he had done. Leeson's version proved a public relations success. He convinced even Frost's co-presenter on BBC's *Breakfast With Frost* that he was hard done by. 'I was just looking at Nick Leeson thinking he looks really modest and unassuming . . . and a rather worried young man,' remarked Sarah Baxter as she chatted with Frost.[7]

Leeson's campaign to be tried in London received a boost from an unlikely quarter in October with the publication of the Singapore report into the collapse. It had been carried out by accountants from Price Waterhouse in Singapore, aided by Sundaresh Menon, a lawyer who took part in questioning witnesses in London. Unlike the Board of Banking Supervision, which accepted that everyone had been fooled by Leeson, the Singapore inspectors accused Norris and Bax of conspiring to cover up the losses made by Leeson in January and February. They suggested that Norris tried to hide the losses because it could have led to his dismissal. The inspectors had no direct evidence, but argued that Norris had dealt with the SLK discrepancy suspiciously, trying to play it down. They also criticized Norris for ignoring Hopkins: 'In our view, the collapse might have been averted if Mr Hopkins's concerns had been taken seriously, and acted upon promptly and effectively,' they said.[8] Following publication of the report, the Singapore Ministry of Finance suggested that charges could be brought against Barings' managers. The Commercial Affairs Department, the Singapore equivalent of the Serious Fraud Office, reinstated an investigation that had largely lapsed following the collapse. Despite the Singapore report, the Serious Fraud Office reiterated that it had found no evidence justifying a prosecution of Leeson in London. Leeson's last hope was a private prosecution brought against him by the bondholders, using evidence supplied by Leeson's solicitor. The bondholders went to court on 27 September, arguing for the trial to be held in London. However, the SFO rapidly moved in to quash the case.

With this slim hope gone Leeson abandoned his efforts to stay in Germany and accepted his extradition to Singapore. He made a formal apology to the Singapore courts for doubting the quality of justice that he would receive there, and was flown back, arriving at Changi on 23 November. He walked off the plane in a green sweatshirt, running shoes and a black baseball cap worn in street style back-to-front. He was photographed with a large grin on his face, hardly looking the part of the penitent arriving to face justice. He was remanded for a week in Changi while his lawyers talked to prosecutors about a deal. Within a week Leeson had agreed to plead guilty to two sample charges with the others being dropped. Hopes rose that he could face as little as two years in prison. But this proved to be over-optimistic. On 2 December he appeared in court. His lawyer did not claim that anyone else had been involved, merely asking for clemency. However, Judge Richard Magnus, who said Leeson had 'spun a web of deceit', sentenced him to six and a half years in prison: six months for deceit of Coopers & Lybrand and six years for cheating

Simex. It was a strong signal to the other brokers on Simex to pay margin accurately. The sentence was backdated to 2 March 1995, which meant it was in effect five years and nine months. He was taken to Tanah Merah, a high-security block in Changi jail whose name means 'red earth'. Leeson's lawyers were disappointed at the verdict but opted not to appeal, given the risk under Singapore law of the sentence being increased.

In the immediate aftermath of the crash Leeson was dubbed by Eddie George a 'rogue trader', who had apparently brought down Barings unaided. It was an astonishing idea. Yet by the time Leeson went to jail, it was fast becoming the decade of the 'rogue trader' in financial markets. In June 1994 a trader called Joseph Jett was dismissed by Kidder Peabody, the US investment bank, for apparently conjuring up $350 million of fake profits by false accounting. Jett had been one of the US firm's leading traders. In October 1995 Toshihide Iguchi, a bond trader, was accused by his employer, Daiwa Bank, of concealing trading losses of $1.1 billion for eleven years. Finally, in June 1996, Yasuo Hamanaka, the head copper trader of Sumitomo Corporation, was accused by his employer of trying to manipulate the world copper market. Hamanaka struggled to support the world copper price in the first half of 1996, against the efforts of hedge funds such as Quantum, which were trying to drive it down. He finally lost his battle, and Sumitomo faced a loss of up to $4 billion. In none of these cases did a 'rogue trader' seem to have gained personally through the deceptions, except in inflated bonuses. They instead appeared to have drifted into deception in an effort to be seen as star traders. In each case the 'star trader' was quickly disowned when his effort collapsed. The institutions that had paid them large sums and praised them for their extraordinary feats in financial markets condemned them as 'rogue traders'.

Barings was not alone in placing huge power in the hands of a financial trader who exploited it. Many others ventured into financial trading in the 1990s as a means of compensating for falling earnings elsewhere. Those without adequate controls had to trust young men and women whom they paid highly to buy and sell financial contracts that were too complex for most managers to understand. It left them vulnerable to being deceived on a grand scale. Barings was particularly vulnerable. Baring Securities had always relied on one or two people to make most of its money: Sliwerski's warrant trading was followed by Khoo's options trading. It had kept chasing for the latest pot of gold in the world's markets, trying to outwit larger firms by fleetness of foot. This made Baring and Tuckey uneasy, and they tried to halt it by expelling Heath. Yet within a couple of years they had fallen into the same trap. They were so distant from day-to-day events that they did not observe the warning signs, and Norris was rushing along too fast to spot them. Baring Brothers prospered in the twentieth century as a cautious partnership that took no risk and did only things with which it was familiar. There were few controls; only a few were required. Yet by the time Leeson made his name on the trading floor of Simex, it was trying to run a global investment bank with the same technology, culture and people. Barings was painfully ill-equipped to prevent a rogue trader turning himself into a star at its expense.

A year after the crash the Securities and Futures Authority took action against nine of Barings' former managers. The SFA told Norris, Baker, Bax, Broadhurst, Gamby, Hawes, Hopkins, Maclean and Walz they had failed to show 'due skill, care and diligence' and were guilty of misconduct. They faced bans of up to three years from the City and costs of £10,000. Peter Baring and Tuckey did not face a similar fate. The SFA said that it had found 'no evidence indicating that responsibility for the insolvency of the group can be attributed to their actions', although it noted that Tuckey had undertaken not to seek a senior management job in the City for now and Peter Baring had retired. Norris accepted his ban without demur, and went to work for a friend's publishing company. He accepted he had been at fault. It was a different story for Hopkins and Baker. Both believed they had been unfairly treated. Although he did not dispute the SFA ban formally, Hopkins appealed to MPs sitting on the Treasury and Civil Service select committee. He said he had tried to act as a 'whistleblower' inside Barings but had been ignored by Norris. Baker went further. Along with Walz he launched a legal effort to persuade the SFA not to ban him. He also gave explosive evidence to the Treasury committee in June 1996, arguing that other Barings executives had 'knowingly or unknowingly' taken part in a conspiracy to conceal the fraud. He told MPs Bax must have known there was something wrong when Leeson forged Baker's signature to justify an unauthorized £50 million trade.

The Singapore authorities did not pursue the conspiracy theory raised in the inspectors' report. The Commercial Affairs Department announced in June that there was not enough evidence to start proceedings against Bax, Jones or Argyropoulous.

By the summer of 1996 only a few of those most intimately involved in the events leading up to the collapse still worked for Barings. Michael Baring emerged from the collapse most successfully, becoming head of equity broking and trading at ING Barings. Andrew Fraser left after Michael Baring's promotion. Diarmaid Kelly left the bank to set up a research company. Broadhurst and Gamby obtained senior jobs at a computer systems company near the City. Maclean retired and took up golf. Barnett looked for work in a voluntary organization. Hawes worked as a consultant. Jones remained in Singapore. Bax returned to Britain. Killian stayed working for ING Barings in the US. Heath, Greer and Reed all started again at Caspian, along with several others who had worked before for Baring Securities, including Neil Andrews. This time they worked from smart offices with sliding glass doors and polished floors. Caspian was Heath's second chance to make a fortune. By coincidence it was in almost exactly the same place. Caspian's office on Bishopsgate was within sight of the building where Heath had started selling Japanese shares with George Henderson & Co. It was boarded-up, and in the basement was a betting shop.

The Baring Foundation carried on in a diminished form. It had been due to receive £24 million as its share of Barings' £204 million operating profits for 1994; instead, it got £10 million, which Jacobs decided to pay as a goodwill gesture.[9] It was a one-off payment to enable it to honour the grants it had promised to charities already. Its stream of income from owning Barings abruptly halted and it was left with a portfolio of £45 million, from which it expected to generate £1.7 million in 1996. A year after the crash, it was preparing to restart its charitable grants, at 10 per cent of their former level. Many bondholders were also forced to live in reduced circumstances. Among them was Bernard Lax, who was seventy-nine years old at the time of the collapse. He had been born in Poland and fought in the Polish Free Forces in the last world war. After the war he started a small company trading army surplus. His success came when the French changed the shape of their ten-franc coins. He arranged to buy 8,000 tonnes of them for scrap metal with loans from a Swiss bank. It was enough to bring him a nest-egg of more than £250,000 when he retired in the mid-1980s. In 1994 his son Jacob invested £25,000 in Barings perpetual subordinated notes on the advice of a friend. They paid a fixed interest rate of 9.25 per cent, 2 percentage points above the rate then being offered by a building society. Bernard Lax thought that this sounded like a good deal. He consulted the manager of his local branch of Barclays Bank, who said there was no better name in which to invest than Barings. Lax followed his son by investing £200,000 of his life savings in the Barings bonds.

Lax did not pay much attention to the 'subordinated' part of the title. That meant he was second in line after the Foundation if Barings collapsed. This was the reason why Barings paid 9.25 per cent. He lived in Hampstead, but would often walk around Docklands to see the new retail developments springing up where his own firm had been. One day as he wandered in the City he found himself in Bishops-gate. He suddenly thought that, since he had so much invested in Barings, he might as well take a look at it. Lax walked into the lobby and chatted to the uniformed attendants at the front desk, who used to refer to members of the Baring family by their first names. Peter Baring would be called 'Mr Peter'. There was a large oil painting of the Great Fire of London on the far wall. It was all very impressive, not at all like a high-street bank. It seemed unquestionably solid.

When it collapsed he lost his £200,000. He and his wife sold their house in Hampstead and moved to a bungalow. They still had savings at Barclays, which gave them something to live off in a reduced way. Lax could no longer help his two daughters in Israel financially and had to sell his car. He and his wife both had problems with their health over the next year. He did not blame Jacob. 'It is like crossing when the traffic lights are green, but a drunken idiot runs into you,' he said. He kept the remainder of his cash in a Barclays deposit account that paid only a modest interest rate. Barclays kept sending him leaflets in the post, offering a better return for a little more risk. After the fall of Barings, he ignored them.

NOTES

PROLOGUE

1. Ziegler, Philip, *The Sixth Great Power: Barings 1762–1929*, Collins, 1988, p. 48
2. ibid., p. 269
3. Board of Banking Supervision, *Inquiry into the Circumstances of the Collapse of Barings*, HMSO, 1995, p. 97
4. Bax, James, Internal memorandum to Peter Norris and others, 3 February 1995
5. Board of Banking Supervision, op. cit., p. 37

CHAPTER 1

1. Baring Securities, Internal telephone records, 29 March 1995
2. Ziegler, Philip, *The Sixth Great Power: Barings 1762–1929*, Collins, 1988, p. 97
3. ibid., pp. 31–2
4. Baring Foundation, *Report on Activities 1994*, p. 3
5. Gresham Mercantile Ltd, Private memorandum to Barings plc, 27 February 1995
6. Barings plc, Presentation at the Bank of England, 26 February 1995

CHAPTER 2

1. Raw, Charles, and others, *Do You Sincerely Want to be Rich? Bernie Cornfeld and IOS*, André Deutsch, 1971
2. Lord Russell of Liverpool, *The Knights of Bushido: A Short History of Japanese War Crimes*, Chivers, 1985, pp. 167–8
3. Ito, Takatoshi, *The Japanese Economy*, MIT Press, 1992, p. 63
4. Beasley, W. G., *The Rise of Modern Japan*, Weidenfeld and Nicolson, 1990, pp. 243–9

CHAPTER 3

1. Orbell, John, *Baring Brothers & Co. Ltd. A History to 1939*, Baring Brothers & Co., 1985, p. 1
2. Kay, William (ed.), *Clay & Wheble's Modern Merchant Banking*, Woodhead-Faulkner, 1990, p. 13
3. Ziegler, Philip, *The Sixth Great Power: Barings 1762–1929*, Collins, 1988, p. 88
4. Orbell, op. cit., p. 83
5. Wilson, John F., *British Business History 1720–1994*, Manchester University Press, 1995, p. 203
6. Orbell, John, *Asset Management at Barings: A Note on the Origins* (unpublished), p. 4
7. Baring Far East Securities Ltd, Internal profit projections, 1984

CHAPTER 4

1. Bond Underwriters Association, Tokyo
2. Baring Securities, *Current and Future Capital Requirements*, November 1991, p. 4
3. Barings plc, Internal management accounts, January 1988
4. Henderson, Lynn, Internal memorandum to Rupert Lowe and others, 16 February 1990

CHAPTER 5

1. Baring Securities, Internal management accounts, 1991
2. Baring Securities, *Current and Future Capital Requirements*, November 1991
3. Dare, John, Private letter to Christopher Heath, 29 October 1991
4. Norris, Peter, Internal memorandum to Barings plc executive committee, 14 July 1992
5. Baring Securities, Internal management accounts, 1992
6. Sliwerski, Trevor, Internal memorandum to Richard Katz and Diarmaid Kelly, November 1992
7. Greer, Richard, Private letter to Christopher Heath, 19 October 1992

CHAPTER 6

1. Baker, Ron, Internal business plan for emerging market debt, 6 August 1993
2. Baring, Peter, Speech to Mexican Bolsa centenary conference, April 1994
3. Board of Banking Supervision, *Inquiry into the Circumstances of the Collapse of Barings*, HMSO, 1995, p. 199
4. Baring Securities, Internal management accounts, December 1993
5. Baring Brothers, Internal management accounts, December 1993
6. Baker, Ron, Private memorandum to Peter Norris, January 1994

CHAPTER 7

1. Leeson, Nick, with Whitley, Edward, *Rogue Trader*, Little, Brown and Company, 1996, p. 20
2. ibid., p. 22
3. Easun, Tim, Internal memorandum to Ian Martin, 26 September 1991
4. Leeson, Nick, Internal memorandum to Ian Martin and others, undated
5. Martin, Ian, Internal memorandum to Diarmaid Kelly and Roy Johnson, 30 January 1990
6. Baring Securities, Futures Department internal commission analysis, January 1990
7. Securities and Futures Authority, Letter to Baring Securities, 10 March 1992
8. Baring Securities, Letter to the SFA, 4 September 1992
9. Board of Banking Supervision, *Inquiry into the Circumstances of the Collapse of Barings*, HMSO, 1995, p. 3
10. Lim Choo San, Michael, and Tan Ng Kuang, Nicky, *Baring Futures (Singapore) Pte Ltd: Report of the Inspectors Appointed by the Minister for Finance*, Singapore Ministry of Finance, 1995, p. A ix

CHAPTER 8

1. Leeson, Nick, Interview for *Inside Story: £830m*, BBC, 1996
2. See Preface
3. Leeson, Nick, with Whitley, Edward, *Rogue Trader*, Little, Brown and Company, 1996, p. 55
4. ibid., p. 64
5. Lim Choo San, Michael, and Tan Ng Kuang, Nicky, *Baring Futures (Singapore) Pte Ltd: Report of the Inspectors Appointed by the Minister for Finance*, Singapore Ministry of Finance, 1995, p. 23
6. ibid., p. 175

CHAPTER 9

1. *Business Week*, 9 May 1994
2. Walz, Mary, and Gueler, Fernando, Internal memorandum to Ron Baker, 27 February 1994
3. Norris, Peter, Interoffice memorandum to Mary Walz, 16 March 1994
4. Walz, Mary, Internal memorandum to Ron Baker, 30 March 1994
5. Baring Securities, Internal management accounts, March 1994
6. *Business Week*, 9 May 1994
7. Board of Banking Supervision, *Inquiry into the Circumstances of the Collapse of Barings*, HMSO, 1995, p. 107
8. Lim Choo San, Michael, and Tan Ng Kuang, Nicky, *Baring Futures (Singapore) Pte Ltd: Report of the Inspectors Appointed by the Minister for Finance*, Singapore Ministry of Finance, 1995, p. 41

9. Norris, Peter, Internal memorandum to Andrew Tuckey, 7 June 1994
10. Board of Banking Supervision, op. cit., p. 107
11. Hawes, Tony, Memorandum to Baring Securities risk committee, 7 November 1994
12. Fay, Stephen, *The Great Silver Bubble*, Hodder and Stoughton, 1982
13. Salomon Brothers, *The 1995 Season for Japanese Equity Derivatives*, December 1994, p. 5
14. J. P. Morgan, *Hedged Positions on the Nikkei are Cheap*, 1 December 1994
15. Leeson, Nick, with Whitley, Edward, *Rogue Trader*, Little, Brown and Company, 1996, p. 133
16. ibid., p. 135
17. Talking Point Conference and Incentive Travel Organizers, *Baring Brothers & Co., New York*, December 1994
18. Norris, Peter, *Investment Banking Group and Financial Products Group*, December 1994

CHAPTER 10

1. Walz, Mary, Internal memorandum to Peter Norris and Sajeed Sacranie, December 1994
2. Leeson, Nick, with Whitley, Edward, *Rogue Trader*, Little, Brown and Company, 1996, p. 153
3. Hawes, Tony, Memorandum to James Bax and Ian Hopkins, 11 January 1995
4. Lim Choo San, Michael, and Tan Ng Kuang, Nicky, *Baring Futures (Singapore) Pte Ltd: Report of the Inspectors Appointed by the Minister for Finance*, Singapore Ministry of Finance, 1995, p. 118
5. Board of Banking Supervision, *Inquiry into the Circumstances of the Collapse of Barings*, HMSO, 1995, pp. 72–3
6. *Sunday Times*, 22 January 1995
7. ING Barings, Internal telephone transcript, New York, 27 April 1995
8. ibid.
9. ibid.
10. ibid.
11. ibid.
12. ibid.
13. ibid.
14. ibid.
15. Baring Investment Bank, Internal minutes of Alco meeting, 26 January 1995
16. ING Barings, Internal telephone transcript, New York, 27 April 1995
17. ING Barings, Internal telephone transcript, London, undated
18. Lim and Tan, op. cit., p. 118
19. ING Barings, Internal telephone transcript, New York, 27 April 1995
20. Lim and Tan, op. cit., p. 120
21. Leeson with Whitley, op. cit., p. 169

22. Singapore Criminal Court, *Public Prosecutor vs Nicholas William Leeson: Statement of Facts*, 1 December 1995
23. Bax, James, Internal memorandum to Peter Norris and others, 3 February 1995
24. Board of Banking Supervision, *Inquiry into the Circumstances of the Collapse of Barings*, HMSO, 1995, p. 101
25. ibid., p. 173
26. Chiu, Pamela, Interview for *Inside Story: £830m*, BBC, 1996
27. Board of Banking Supervision, op. cit., p. 10
28. ING Barings, Internal telephone transcript, undated
29. ibid.
30. Goldman Sachs, *Japanese Indices: Tug o' War*, 20 February 1995
31. Board of Banking Supervision, op. cit., p. 62
32. ING Barings, Internal telephone transcript, undated
33. ibid.
34. Goldman Sachs, *Japanese Arbitrage; It just keeps going, and going . . .* , 22 February 1995
35. Board of Banking Supervision, op. cit., pp. 10–11

EPILOGUE

1. *Financial Times*, 28 February 1995
2. *Financial Times*, 10 March 1995
3. BBC *Panorama*, 13 March 1995
4. *Financial Times*, 8 July 1995
5. *Financial Times*, 20 July 1995
6. Basle Committee on Banking Supervision, *The Supervision of Financial Conglomerates*, 24 July 1995
7. BBC *Breakfast With Frost*, 10 September 1995
8. Lim Choo San, Michael, and Tan Ng Kuang, Nicky, *Barings Futures (Singapore) Pte Ltd: Report of the Inspectors Appointed by the Minister for Finance*, Singapore Ministry of Finance, 1995, p. 80
9. *Financial Times*, 7 March 1995

INDEX

Visit Penguin on the Internet
and browse at your leisure

- preview sample extracts of our forthcoming books
- read about your favourite authors
- investigate over 10,000 titles
- enter one of our literary quizzes
- win some fantastic prizes in our competitions
- e-mail us with your comments and book reviews
- instantly order any Penguin book

and masses more!

'To be recommended without reservation ... a rich and rewarding on-line experience' – Internet Magazine

www.penguin.co.uk

READ MORE IN PENGUIN

In every corner of the world, on every subject under the sun, Penguin represents quality and variety – the very best in publishing today.

For complete information about books available from Penguin – including Puffins, Penguin Classics and Arkana – and how to order them, write to us at the appropriate address below. Please note that for copyright reasons the selection of books varies from country to country.

In the United Kingdom: Please write to *Dept. EP, Penguin Books Ltd, Bath Road, Harmondsworth, West Drayton, Middlesex UB7 ODA*

In the United States: Please write to *Consumer Sales, Penguin Putnam Inc., P.O. Box 12289 Dept. B, Newark, New Jersey 07101-5289*. VISA and MasterCard holders call 1-800-788-6262 to order Penguin titles

In Canada: Please write to *Penguin Books Canada Ltd, 10 Alcorn Avenue, Suite 300, Toronto, Ontario M4V 3B2*

In Australia: Please write to *Penguin Books Australia Ltd, P.O. Box 257, Ringwood, Victoria 3134*

In New Zealand: Please write to *Penguin Books (NZ) Ltd, Private Bag 102902, North Shore Mail Centre, Auckland 10*

In India: Please write to *Penguin Books India Pvt Ltd, 11 Community Centre, Panchsheel Park, New Delhi 110017*

In the Netherlands: Please write to *Penguin Books Netherlands bv, Postbus 3507, NL-1001 AH Amsterdam*

In Germany: Please write to *Penguin Books Deutschland GmbH, Metzlerstrasse 26, 60594 Frankfurt am Main*

In Spain: Please write to *Penguin Books S. A., Bravo Murillo 19, 1° B, 28015 Madrid*

In Italy: Please write to *Penguin Italia s.r.l., Via Benedetto Croce 2, 20094 Corsico, Milano*

In France: Please write to *Penguin France, Le Carré Wilson, 62 rue Benjamin Baillaud, 31500 Toulouse*

In Japan: Please write to *Penguin Books Japan Ltd, Kaneko Building, 2-3-25 Koraku, Bunkyo-Ku, Tokyo 112*

In South Africa: Please write to *Penguin Books South Africa (Pty) Ltd, Private Bag X14, Parkview, 2122 Johannesburg*